THERAPEUTIC RECREATION SERVICE:

principles and practices

RICHARD KRAUS, Ed.D.

Department of Recreation and Leisure Studies,
Temple University

2nd edition

Saunders College Publishing
Philadelphia

Saunders College Publishing
West Washington Square
Philadelphia, PA 19105

Library of Congress Cataloging in Publication Data

Kraus, Richard G.

Therapeutic recreation service.

Bibliography: p.
Includes index.

1. Recreational therapy.   2. Handicapped–Recreation.   3. Aged-
Recreation.   4. Recreation and juvenile delinquency.

I. Title.

RM 736.7.K7 1978   362.1   77-11340

ISBN 0–7216–5507–6

Therapeutic Recreation Service: Principles and Practices   ISBN   0-7216-5507-6

2   1 4 7   9 8 7

Preface

This is the second edition of a book designed as a text for college and university courses on the provision of recreation programs for the ill and disabled in both institutional and community settings. As in the first edition, its purpose is twofold: (a) to provide a theoretical rationale for the development of therapeutic recreation services for such groups as the physically disabled, mentally ill, mentally retarded, socially deviant and dependent aging and (b) to offer practical guidelines for the operation of such programs, including detailed examples of activities and leadership methods.

Over the past three decades, therapeutic recreation has become a rapidly growing and dynamic field. It has shifted its focus from the hospital setting to a broader concern with the disabled in both institutional and community programs. Today, recreation specialists work closely with medical, social service and other rehabilitation specialists in providing a total continuum of service. In order to provide a comprehensive picture of therapeutic recreation today, I have drawn up-to-date information from a variety of sources:

I. A considerable bulk of material regarding contemporary trends, concepts and professional development in therapeutic recreation service has been excerpted from such publications as journals, conference reports, research surveys and similar documents. In this regard, I wish to express my appreciation to a number of college and university educators who have written or carried out research in this field or who assisted me directly in gathering material. These include the following individuals: Elliott M. Avedon, Doris L. Berryman, Scout Lee Gunn, Gene A. Hayes, Fred W. Martin, Gerald S. O'Morrow, John A. Nesbitt, Carol A. Peterson, H. Douglas Sessoms and Thomas A. Stein. I am also grateful to William Theobald and William Knott, who were helpful in providing information on Canadian developments.

II. Hundreds of hospitals, training schools, municipal recreation departments and other agencies were asked to submit printed materials, such as program schedules, leadership manuals, annual reports and similar documents. Although it is not possible to list all such contributors, a number of the agencies that responded generously are as follows: Athens, Ohio, Mental Health Center; Blythedale Children's Hospital, Valhalla, New York; Brainerd, Minnesota, State Hospital; Chicago, Illinois, Park District; Chillicothe, Ohio, Correctional Institute; Coldwater, Michigan, State Home and Training School; Detroit, Michigan, Department of Parks and Recreation; Downey, Illinois, Veterans Administration Hospital; Dutchess County, New York, Psychiatric Day Care Center; Evansville, Indiana, Psychiatric Children's Center; Fairview Hospital and Training Center,

Salem, Oregon; Flint, Michigan, Department of Recreation and Parks; Illinois State Training School for Boys, at St. Charles; Illinois State Training School for Girls, at Geneva; John Umstead Hospital, Butner, North Carolina; Junction City, Ohio, Treatment Center; Karl Holton School for Boys, Stockton, California; Keystone Training and Rehabilitation Residence, Scranton, Pennsylvania; Lafayette Clinic, Detroit, Michigan; Lima, Ohio, State Hospital; Mansfield, Connecticut, State Training School and Hospital; Midwestern Regional Centre, Palmerston, Ontario; Mt. Sinai Hospital, New York, New York; Muscatatuck State Hospital and Training Center, Butlerville, Indiana; National Institutes of Health Hospital, Bethesda, Maryland; National Wheelchair Athletic Association, Woodside, New York; New Haven, Connecticut, Department of Parks and Recreation; New Lisbon State School, New Jersey; New York Association for the Blind, New York; Northern Minnesota Therapeutic Camp, Brainerd, Minnesota; O. H. Close School for Boys, Stockton, California; Ohio Reformatory for Women, Marysville, Ohio; Ontario School for the Blind, Brantford, Ontario, Canada; Parsons, Ohio, State Hospital and Training Center; Penetanguishene Mental Health Centre, Ontario, Canada; Pennsylvania State Department of Public Welfare; Plymouth State Home and Training School, Northville, Michigan; Porterville, California, State Hospital; Rainier State School, Buckley, Washington; Recreation Center for the Handicapped, San Francisco, California; Rockland County Mental Health Association, New York; San Antonio, Texas, State Hospital; San Bernardino, California, Y.W.C.A.; Souris Valley Hospital, Weyburn, Saskatchewan, Canada; Spring Grove State Hospital, Catonsville, Maryland; Springview Hospital, Springfield, Ohio; Toledo, Ohio, Mental Health Center; Traverse City State Hospital, Michigan; United Cerebral Palsy, New York, New York; Washington, D.C., Department of Recreation.

In particular, useful materials were received from such practitioners or state consultants as William P. Dayton, Office of Mental Health, State of Pennsylvania; Richard Endres, Brainerd State Hospital, Minnesota; Dorothy G. Mullen, then of the Office of Public Health, Connecticut; Barbara Mumford, Salem, Oregon; Janet Pomeroy, Director of the Recreation Center for the Handicapped, San Francisco, California; Richard Stracke, V.S. Hospital, Kansas City; and Byron Welker, Muscatatuck State Hospital and Training Center, Indiana. In addition, Terry W. Knight and James M. Montagnes of the Penetanguishene Mental Health Centre and Al Sinclair of the Midwestern Regional Centre sent useful materials on Canadian therapeutic recreation. Don Henkel and Yvonne Washington sent recent materials from the National Recreation and Park Association and National Therapeutic Recreation Society, as did Patricia J. Lawrence and Richard Patterson of the Therapeutic Recreation Section of the California Park and Recreation Society. Clark T. Thorstenson and M. Sydell Post sent information on the new Utah licensing law in therapeutic recreation.

III. As a third source of information, I relied heavily on my own direct experience in the field of therapeutic recreation. Although my chief professional role over the past 25 years has been that of university professor, I also served for 12 years as a part-time recreation leader in a large private psychiatric hospital. At other times, I was coordinator of senior citizens' events for a county recreation department, activities leader in a private nursing home and program specialist with retarded children and deaf teen-agers and adults. I have also conducted numerous workshops for professional organizations in this field and have carried out research related to recreation in psychiatric rehabilitation.

The first edition of this text was extremely well received by professors and students throughout the United States and Canada, although a number of reviewers commented that it needed fuller conceptual content. A strong effort has been made to provide such analysis in the present edition and I have also given heavy emphasis to the presentation of practical guidelines for program development. For example, detailed descriptions are given of such relatively new methods as *sensory training* and *remotivation,* as well as of *behavior modification, token economy* and similar techniques. The trend toward deinstitutionalizing the mentally ill is discussed in detail, as well as other contemporary efforts in the direction of *mainstreaming* the disabled. A much fuller treatment of *leisure counseling* is provided with a summary of *systems analysis* approaches to programming. As in the earlier edition, each major type of disability grouping is described in detail, and helpful guidelines are provided in major areas of activity. The Appendices provide useful bibliographies and lists of organizations, periodicals, films, national personnel standards and other materials, and suggested questions for class discussion, student assignments or examinations follow each chapter.

It is my hope that this textbook will continue to be of real value not only to those who are preparing to enter this career field but also to those currently employed in it. If this goal is achieved, major credit should go to those practitioners in the United States and Canada who had a vision of the potential value of recreative experience in meeting the needs of the disabled in our society and in promoting their total rehabilitation. As individuals, and as members of professional organizations past and present, their contribution has been immense. Thanks to their efforts the lives of millions of Americans and Canadians, young and old, have been enriched.

RICHARD KRAUS

Contents

CHAPTER 3

PROFESSIONAL DEVELOPMENT IN THERAPEUTIC RECREATION SERVICE.. 63

CHAPTER 4

PROGRAM PLANNING AND THERAPEUTIC TECHNIQUES 99

CHAPTER 5

RECREATION AND MENTAL ILLNESS............................ 123

CHAPTER 6

RECREATION FOR THE MENTALLY RETARDED AND LEARNING DISABLED.............................. 165

CHAPTER 7

RECREATION FOR THE PHYSICALLY DISABLED 199

chapter 1

Therapeutic Recreation Service: Past and Present

In a large state-sponsored school for retarded children and youth, extensive programs of sports, hobbies, social activities, art and music are provided. Elderly residents in a nursing home enjoy hobbies, discussion groups, entertainment, bingo, singing and crafts. In the psychiatric ward of a municipal hospital, patients are involved in a variety of individual and group activities, including creative dancing, cooking, games and outings. Orthopedically disabled children in a community attend a summer day camp with facilities specially designed for their use.

In thousands of similar settings around the United States and Canada today, groups of children, youth and adults with varied kinds of disability are being provided with specially planned and directed *therapeutic recreation service*. Over the past two decades, this field has become an important tool of rehabilitation and a key area of specialization within the broad field of professional recreation.

MEANING OF THERAPEUTIC RECREATION SERVICE

Exactly what does this term mean? How did it come into being? What are its goals? Who is served by it? Who provides it? What does it consist of? It is the purpose of this textbook to provide answers to these questions.

In a broad sense, recreation provides important therapeutic benefits for all human beings. It offers the opportunity for the physical activity, emotional release, social involvement and creative expression essential for healthy personal adjustment. This is particularly true with respect to mental health. Gray points out that tension, boredom, monotony and frustration in daily living contribute to emotional disorders for millions of individuals, who are troubled by feelings of insecurity, alienation and depression. For many, creative and satisfying leisure activities represent a vital tool for *building* sound mental health and *preventing* disability. Gray concludes,

> As therapists, recreation personnel have a role in curing the sick, but as devotees
> of the recreation movement, we all have a role in developing a society that will
> help keep people well.[1]

Thus, *all* recreation may be seen as therapeutic. However, in a more specific sense, the term *therapeutic recreation service* is used to describe those leisure-related programs and experiences that are provided for individuals who have special impairments. Such persons have intensified needs for constructive and enriching recreational outlets but are often unable to enjoy those outlets provided for the public at large. Specially designed programs must be developed, therefore, both to contribute to their recovery and rehabilitation and to make their lives as full and happy as possible.

Past Descriptive Terms

In the past, several other descriptive terms were applied to this field of service, including (a) *hospital recreation*; (b) *medical recreation*; and (c) *recreation for the ill and handicapped*. For a variety of reasons, these terms are no longer fully descriptive.

Hospital recreation implies that recipients of service are patients in a residential treatment center. However, therapeutic recreation programs are also provided in many community-based settings. The term *medical recreation* suggests that programs must be carried on under direct medical supervision. Obviously, many individuals with mental or social disabilities may require specially designed recreation programs; however, those need *not* be under medical direction. Similarly, the term *recreation for the ill and handicapped* is no longer used today because of its emphasis on the word "handicapped." Today it is believed that, although many individuals have disabilities, they need not be significantly handicapped. Indeed, it is the task of therapeutic recreation service, along with other rehabilitation services, to minimize the functional limitations of those it serves.

In some settings, the term *recreational therapy* has been used to describe this field of service. For example, in a manual describing programs offered by its Physical Medicine and Rehabilitation Service, the Veterans Administration states the following:

> Recreational therapy is a professional and integral part of Physical Medicine and
> Rehabilitation Service. . . . The role of recreation in patient treatment becomes
> greatly expanded in the rehabilitation of long-term, chronically ill, and psychiatric
> patients. Recreation helps the patient accept and utilize constructively a pro-
> longed period of hospitalization. Recreation activities develop interpersonal
> relationships, resocialization, relieve anxieties and tensions, and promote the
> patient's ability to more fully participate in society.[2]

---

[1] David E. Gray: "Exploring Inner Space," *Parks and Recreation*, December, 1972, p. 19.
[2] *Manual on Physical Medicine and Rehabilitation Service*. Washington, D.C., Veterans Administration, Manual M-2, July, 1966, pp. 4–6.

Although there has been considerable pressure to define the field as a specific therapy comparable to physical or occupational therapy, this position has been challenged by a number of authorities. Knudson writes,

> "Is *recreation* therapy?" *Since the word therapy has different meanings for different people, the answer requires a distinction. If therapy is defined as prescribed or medically guided participation of the team mobilized for a potential therapeutic attack on illness, then most assuredly recreation is frequently therapy. But recreation cannot be labeled as therapy in the sense of a precise cure for a specific ailment.*[3]

This point of view is generally accepted throughout the field, although some authorities have stressed that recreation's value lies in its ability to meet overall human needs, rather than its specific therapeutic benefits (see pp. 58–59). Most practitioners agree that it is essential not only to cure disease but also to prevent disability and help the patient realize his or her maximum potential as a human being. During the treatment process, recreation contributes to the patient's constructive outlook, strengthened self-concept, healthy socialization and overall recovery. Shivers, for example, points out that the term "therapeutic" connotes

> . . . *activities which appear to support the morale, physical reconditioning, and mental outlook of those who are undergoing medical treatment. The term is also used to identify those activities which provide psychological stimulation and physical involvement to those individuals for whom medical treatment is no longer necessary, for whom custodial care is pertinent, for those afflicted by permanent disability, and for those who are either home-bound, handicapped, or confined to institutions.*[4]

The emphasis on using recreation as a specific treatment modality was reflected in a statement of the Public Health Service: "Therapeutic recreation is the specific use of recreational activity in the care, treatment and rehabilitation of ill, handicapped and aged persons with a directed program."[5]

Some authorities have stressed the idea that therapeutic recreation is a *process*. A statement formulated at the Ninth Southern Regional Institute on Therapeutic Recreation at the University of North Carolina defined it as

> . . . *a process which utilizes recreation services for purposive intervention in some physical, emotional, and/or social behavior to bring about a desired change in that behavior and to promote the growth and development of the individual.*[6]

---

[3] A. B. C. Knudson: "Concepts of Recreation in Rehabilitation." In *The Doctors and Recreation in the Hospital Setting*. Bulletin No. 30. Raleigh, North Carolina, North Carolina Recreation Commission, 1962, p. 40.

[4] Jay S. Shivers: "One Concept of Therapeutic Recreation Service." *Therapeutic Recreation Journal*, 2nd Quarter, 1971, p. 51.

[5] *Health Resource Statistics—1968*. Washington, D.C., Public Health Service, 1968, p. 185.

[6] Statement formulated at Ninth Southern Region Institute of Therapeutic Recreation, University of North Carolina, 1969. *Cited in* Virginia Frye and Martha Peters: *Therapeutic Recreation: Its Theory, Philosophy, and Practice*. Harrisburg, Pennsylvania, Stackpole Books, 1972, p. 41.

Inherent in this view is the principle that the therapeutic recreation specialist does not simply lead therapeutic activities or provide a service that automatically achieves rehabilitative outcomes for participants. Instead, the leader seeks to help individuals discover their own potential and to assist them in achieving important recreative benefits for themselves. Peterson, for example, suggests that the essential purpose of a therapeutic recreation service system

> . . . is to provide opportunities for individuals with limitations to gain leisure skills and attitudes, and/or to exercise recreative abilities within a framework of preventative, sustaining, or remedial services in order to enable or encourage recreative experience.[7]

Summing up, then, therapeutic recreation service may be perceived as a form of professional service that provides recreational and related activities specially designed to meet the needs of individuals suffering from some significant degree of illness or disability. It seeks to help these participants help themselves through a process of referral, counseling, instruction or actual program development. It may be provided in an institutional setting, where its primary purpose is to contribute to the process of overall recovery and to facilitate successful return to the community. It may also be a continuing service intended to enrich the quality of the lives of those with permanent disability in institutional or community settings by providing important psychological, physical and social benefits.

As this text makes clear in later sections, therapeutic recreation may represent a carefully prescribed and structured activity within a formal institutional or agency framework, or it may represent a much more casual or informal program opportunity to which disabled persons living in the community come of their own volition for self-directed involvement. Similarly, it may be segregated, for disabled persons only, or it may provide the opportunity for "mainstreaming" the disabled by integrating them in social settings with the nondisabled.

GOALS OF THERAPEUTIC RECREATION SERVICE

The goals of therapeutic recreation vary widely, according to the setting in which programs are provided, those offering the service and the individuals or groups being served. This author has written the following elsewhere:

> Basically, the aim of therapeutic recreation, like that of rehabilitation, is to help the ill, disabled, aged, or retarded person help himself or herself to live the fullest physical, mental, social, psychological, and economic life possible within the limits of his or her illness or disability. It seeks to return a happier, more productive, and better adjusted human being to community living or, short of this, to help him live as fully as possible in some type of sheltered environment.[8]

[7] Carol A. Peterson: *In* Elliott M. Avedon: *Therapeutic Recreation Service: An Applied Behavioral Science Approach.* Englewood Cliffs, New Jersey, Prentice-Hall, Inc., 1974, p. 131.
[8] Richard Kraus: *Recreation Today: Program Planning and Leadership.* Santa Monica, California, Goodyear, 1977, p. 182.

O'Morrow has identified two key alternative approaches to developing therapeutic recreation service:

The clinical approach focuses on the use of recreation in the treatment of illness or disability. The nonclinical approach centers on the broader conception of recreation: the subjective enjoyment and enrichment of the patient's living experience.[9]

This distinction is somewhat arbitrary, since many agencies or therapeutic recreation specialists seek both to meet general human needs of the patient or client and to use recreation as a specific technique in dealing with physical, emotional or other forms of disability within the treatment process. Recreation has become recognized as a key aspect of healthy living in an era in which leisure has become increasingly available for the majority of the population. Luther Terry, formerly Surgeon General of the United States Public Health Service, has pointed out that the modern concept of health is concerned with the capacity of human beings for coping with or adapting effectively to all the physical, emotional, intellectual and social demands of their environment. Life, writes Terry, is a dynamic process involving a variety of stimulus-response relationships:

Meaningful activity is important to health throughout the life span. In order to mature—physically, intellectually, emotionally and socially—a child must be exposed to appropriate stimuli. And so too must the adult if he is to remain at his peak. Today, people are increasingly involved in leisure activity. . . . More and more people have time on their hands. Moreover, the injudicious use of leisure time is a characteristic feature of both maladjusted teen-agers and adults, and of retired, elderly persons. Too often, because of ignorance, indifference, or inertia, we are faced with the time-consuming and difficult task of reestablishing a human capacity which need never have been lost.[10]

Thus, the goal may be seen as a generalized one of helping the ill or disabled person deal more effectively with personal problems of leisure. On the other hand, recreation may be seen as a specific modality used to achieve certain direct aims of rehabilitation. For example, an excellent statement of purpose was developed by the Veterans Administration, and applies to many chronic disease or psychiatric hospital settings:

1. *To facilitate the patient's adjustment to hospital life and to make him more receptive to treatment.*
2. *To facilitate the patient's early physical, mental and social rehabilitation, recovery and discharge.*
3. *To assist in minimizing the risk of unnecessary readmission, by aiding in the patient's transition to his community, following discharge.*
4. *To improve his morale and sustain it at a high level.*
5. *To encourage the formation of habits and attitudes which will permit his confident participation in normal activities.*
6. *To compensate for his disabilities and limitations while inspiring him to fulfill his potentialities.*
7. *To channel his aggressive drives into appropriate outlets.*
8. *To encourage his desire to remove or overcome the physical or mental barriers that stand between him and a normal life.*

---

[9] Gerald S. O'Morrow: *Therapeutic Recreation: A Helping Profession.* Reston, Virginia, Reston, 1976, p. 123.

[10] Luther Terry: Preface to *Recreation in Treatment Centers.* September, 1965, p. 3.

9. *To stimulate new or dormant interests and talents, as well as to reestablish old ones.*[11]

Other Examples of Program Goals

When dealing with specific areas of illness or physical or mental disability, the goals of therapeutic recreation service may vary considerably.

For example, program activities for *psychiatric* patients are generally designed to bring them face to face with reality situations, help them gain self-confidence and improved self-concepts and promote socialization. Programs for *aged persons* in nursing homes may also seek to improve the individual's alertness and awareness of the environment, through such special techniques as sensory training or remotivation, as well as strengthen his or her morale by providing positive and enjoyable leisure outlets. In settings for the rehabilitation of those who have suffered severe *physical* trauma, such as a stroke resulting in paralysis or other serious loss of function, paraplegia or amputation, the emphasis is on helping the patient learn to live with his or her residual powers, gain new recreation skills and become able to travel and take part in community-based recreational events.

When there is no direct problem of illness requiring on-going medical care in an institutional setting and when the individual is able to live in the community itself, the goal of therapeutic recreation service may chiefly be to help him enjoy his leisure to the fullest and gain acceptance within community groups and programs. Avedon and Arje, for example, describe the purposes of sociorecreative programming for the *retarded* as

1. *Providing recreation education and information which will develop the individual's capacity for meeting his own leisure needs.*
2. *Using recreation to improve the general health, minimize atypical appearance, and modify behavior to help retardates become more socially acceptable in community settings.*
3. *Offering a variety of recreational and social experiences to help individuals learn and practice needed skills.*
4. *Counseling retarded youth and adults about recreational resources in the community and arranging opportunities for involvement.*
5. *Acting as a liaison between the community and the retarded individual and his family to assure acceptance of retarded persons in community programs and facilities.*
6. *Coordination of community wide efforts to meet the vocational, educational, social and recreational needs of the retarded.*[12]

ROLE OF THE THERAPEUTIC RECREATION SPECIALIST

Therapeutic recreation specialists are *not* concerned solely with providing activities for ill and disabled persons in institutional or community settings.

---

[11] C. C. Bream, Jr.: "Rehabilitative Recreation in V. A. Hospitals." *Recreation*, May, 1964, pp. 224–225.
[12] For a detailed statement, see: Elliott M. Avedon, and Frances B. Arje: *Socio-Recreation Programming for the Retarded, a Handbook for Sponsoring Groups.* New York, Teachers College, Columbia, Bureau of Publications, 1964, pp. 4–6.

Today they may also serve as counselors to patients or clients, as community educators and organizers, as researchers and consultants and in a variety of other roles. Nesbitt has described the extremely diversified tasks that a typical therapeutic recreation specialist might undertake:

> *Therapeutic recreation specialists perform many roles and functions in the course of a week, during a work day, within any given hour. They move quickly and easily from role to role. In a short period of time a therapeutic recreation specialist will set up a day room for the evening . . . arrange for a large group of patients to participate in a community recreation program . . . set up a special party for a small group of patients not yet ready to go into the community or act on their own . . . and sit down for one-to-one counseling with a patient having problems socializing with other people . . . . The therapeutic recreation specialist performs many roles—therapist, administrator, supervisor, leader and consultant among others. . . .*[13]

Therapeutic recreation includes a wide variety of social situations and deals with an extremely broad range of disabilities or levels of impairment. For example, specialists working primarily as program leaders may be employed in any of the following types of situations:

1. Community recreation situations (operated by either voluntary agencies or public recreation and park departments) in which mildly disabled individuals mingle and take part in activities with the nondisabled in a fully integrated way.
2. Community recreation programs in which disabled individuals with somewhat more severe levels of disability—such as an orthopedically disabled child with limited mobility—may take part in some activities that are integrated with the nondisabled and may also be involved in some activities or groups that are designed specifically *for* groups of disabled individuals.
3. Community recreation situations in which the only participation by physically or mentally disabled individuals is within specially organized, separate groups, and they do *not* mingle with other participants.
4. Institutional settings in which the recreation specialist may be responsible chiefly for providing mass activities with little direct therapeutic purpose—seen chiefly as leisure time programs—such as films, entertainment, informal sports or bingo.
5. Settings in which he or she may provide program activities and services that are designed to meet the needs of groups of patients, or of individuals, in terms of deliberately prescribed programs that consciously serve treatment goals.
6. Situations in which the recreation specialist may provide programs that operate on several levels: (a) prescribed individual or small-group activity of an instructional or carefully supervised nature; (b) large-group activity that patient groups are required to attend but in which their actual participation is more or less voluntary; (c) programs involving completely free choice, whether concerned with participation in mass events or small-group-oriented or individually oriented programs.

In addition to their involvement with groups of patients or clients, therapeutic recreation specialists must also relate meaningfully to other persons concerned with the needs of the disabled. In so doing, they act as organizers, advocates, consultants and team members, within the broad spectrum of rehabilitative and social services.

---

[13] John A. Nesbitt: "The Mission of Therapeutic Recreation Specialists: To Help and to Champion the Handicapped." *Therapeutic Recreation Journal*, 4th Quarter, 1970, pp. 2–4, 41–42.

Therapeutic Agent

When serving as a therapeutic agent, the recreation specialist is involved in a "helping" relationship. Collingwood describes this relationship as one

> ...in which a "helper" (counselor, teacher, parent, recreational therapist) attempts to better the "helpee's" (client, patient, student, child) lot in life and help him to live his life more effectively.[14]

Collingwood stresses the importance of such facilitative conditions as empathy, respect, genuineness, concreteness, immediacy and confrontation as key interpersonal elements in such helping relationships. After establishing a strong feeling of rapport and trust, the recreation specialist is more effective as a therapeutic agent. Systematic human relations training is often necessary to help recreation specialists serve more effectively in this critical role.

Community Organizer

On an entirely different level, the therapeutic recreation specialist may be employed by community agencies that do not provide direct service, to act in a promotional, advisory or organizational role, assisting and encouraging other groups to provide recreation for the disabled as part of a multiservice approach. In Canada, for example, a study of recreation programs for the disabled in the province of Alberta indicated the following ways in which specialists working for municipal recreation and park departments could assist voluntary agencies to provide such programs:

> Providing or adapting facilities for use by the disabled
>
> Helping set up community recreation programs in cooperation with institutional recreation authorities
>
> Assisting in the provision of transportation services
>
> Sponsoring leadership training seminars or workshops
>
> Helping to bring about a greater public awareness and appreciation of the recreation needs of the disabled
>
> Sponsoring demonstration projects.[15]

Consumer Advocate

Therapeutic recreation specialists have moved from a position of "institutional lethargy," ignoring the social and cultural injustices commonly perpetrated against the disabled in society, to the more aggressive position of consumer advocate. Hillman points out that it is critical today that therapeutic recreation specialists raise forceful voices in promoting public awareness of the needs of the disabled and in fighting for fuller funding and fairer treatment with respect to

---

[14] Thomas Collingwood: "The Recreation Leader as a Therapeutic Agent." *Therapeutic Recreation Journal*, 4th Quarter, 1972, p. 147.

[15] *A Report on the Survey of Recreation Services for the Disabled in Alberta.* Advisory Committee on Recreation for the Disabled, Edmonton, Alberta, Department of Recreation, Parks and Wildlife, 1975, p. 28.

leisure services.[16] However, the disabled must be given the opportunity to act as their own spokesmen and to define their own needs and goals. The therapeutic recreation specialist must therefore seek to help them to become more knowledgeable consumers of leisure services and to work effectively within the sociopolitical process.

Edginton and Compton point out that the consumer advocate role may involve acting in the following capacities: (a) initiator, planner, strategist or organizer; (b) investigator or ombudsman; (c) mediator, arbitrator or negotiator; (d) lobbyist; (e) counselor; (f) technician or resource specialist; (g) educator; and (h) critic, analyst or evaluator. They conclude that

> The development of stronger advocate and consumer roles within parks, recreation and leisure services for and with special populations is long overdue. Higher levels of advocacy and consumerism will yield more efficient, relevant and quantitative services to our special populations. In addition, it will encourage members of special populations to assume a more active role in determining the quantity and quality of services rendered by parks, recreation, and leisure service agencies, and serve to enhance the quality of life of each individual.[17]

Team Member

In addition to their relationships with patients or clients and with the public at large, therapeutic recreation specialists must also develop effective working relationships with individuals in a wide variety of other professional disciplines. The recreation worker must be able to relate closely to occupational therapists, physical therapists, doctors, vocational counselors, social service personnel, mental health aides and ward personnel, nurses and volunteers. In many medical settings, Shivers and Fait point out, recreationists have become accepted members of the rehabilitation team through their skilled involvement with patients and are accorded significant status:

> The recreationist functions at the same level and with the status of an occupational therapist, physical therapist, vocational guidance counselor, or psychologist.[18]

Although in some hospital situations therapeutic recreation specialists are regarded in a narrow and superficial light, in many others they have full access to all medical files and case histories and play an important role in case presentation and analysis. Within community settings as well, therapeutic recreation specialists are likely to have close contact with the parents or relatives of disabled individuals, with administrators and supervisors of community recreation programs and with social workers, vocational counselors and school teachers.

Their roles, then, are complex and challenging. In some cases, the task may be frustrating and difficult because clients or patients, overwhelmed by the

---

[16] William A. Hillman, Jr., in *Therapeutic Recreation Journal*, 2nd Quarter, 1972, p. 50.

[17] Christopher Edginton and David Compton: "Consumerism and Advocacy: A Conceptual Framework for Therapeutic Recreation." *Therapeutic Recreation Journal*, 1st Quarter, 1972, p. 31.

[18] Jay S. Shivers and Hollis F. Fait: *Therapeutic and Adapted Recreational Services.* Philadelphia, Lea and Febiger, 1975, p. 36.

difficulty of their life situation or the losses they have suffered, have become extremely passive or lack the confidence or desire for participation. Whatever the situation, though, the therapeutic recreation specialist must recognize that his or her contributions are critical in the lives of disabled persons.

THE SCOPE OF THERAPEUTIC RECREATION SERVICE

What specifically are the settings in which therapeutic recreation service is carried on? They fall under several major headings.

Hospitals of All Types

These include hospitals under varied sponsorship, such as Veterans Administration, military, public health, state, county, municipal, voluntary, sectarian and proprietary hospitals. They serve many types of patients: general, psychiatric, pediatric, chronic disease, geriatric and others. Some are long-term, while others involve short patient stays.

Nursing Homes

These generally are regarded as extended-care facilities for ill or disabled aged persons, although they may also include persons of middle age who have suffered from heart attacks or strokes who cannot live independently.

Schools or Residential Centers for Those With Specific Disability

There are thousands of such institutions throughout the country that house, either permanently or for a period of years, the physically disabled (blind, deaf, orthopedically or neurologically impaired) or the mentally retarded or emotionally disturbed. As in the case of hospitals, they operate under a wide variety of auspices: voluntary agency, sectarian, municipal, county or state-sponsored.

Special Schools or Treatment Centers for the Socially Deviant

These include adult penal institutions, such as prisons, jails or other detention centers, as well as work camps, reformatories and special schools for youth who have been committed by the courts for delinquent behavior. They may also include special schools or shelters for emotionally disturbed children and youth or those from broken families or families incapable of providing adequate care. In some cases, these include custodial treatment centers for alcoholics or drug addicts.

Homes for Aged Persons

There are increasing numbers of residential centers for aged persons who cannot live independently or with their families but do not require intensive nursing or medical care and can meet some of their own needs independently. These centers may include municipal, county or state homes for aged persons, residential centers sponsored by sectarian agencies or service organizations or even low-income housing projects with special units for the aged.

Centers for Physical Medicine and Rehabilitation

These are treatment centers for those who have suffered serious physical disability but are no longer under treatment for the acute phase of their illness or injury and are being given varied forms of physical, psychological, vocational and social rehabilitation to facilitate their return to their families and community life.

Programs Operated by Public Recreation and Park Departments

Such agencies have traditionally concentrated their efforts on serving the nondisabled population of all ages with recreational activities and facilities. However, in recent years many have initiated programs to serve the disabled— particularly the mentally retarded and physically handicapped.

Programs of Voluntary Agencies

A number of national organizations have been established to promote services for specific groups of handicapped children, youth or adults, such as the blind, deaf, cerebral palsied, physically handicapped or mentally retarded. Usually operating through county or local chapters, many of these organizations sponsor recreation programs specially designed to meet the needs of the disabled.

After-Care Centers and Sheltered Workshops

Particularly in the fields of mental illness, mental retardation and drug addiction, many organizations have established after-care centers, sheltered workshops, drop-in centers and similar facilities to provide multiservice programs to meet the needs of those who have been institutionalized and who need assistance adjusting to the demands of community life. Such programs frequently include recreational and social activities.

It is the function of all of these different types of agencies or institutions to provide therapeutic recreation service to meet the needs of the physically, mentally and socially disabled in our society.

NUMBERS AND TYPES OF DISABLED
PERSONS IN THE UNITED STATES

There have been numerous attempts to measure the number of disabled or handicapped persons in the United States. In 1968, the Social Security Administration reported that there were 18 million people between the ages of 18 and 64 with some work limitation as a result of health conditions. About the same time, the National Society for Crippled Children and Adults estimated that one out of seven persons in the United States had a permanent physical disability. The total number of persons who are chronically ill or disabled or who suffer from emotional problems that prevent their successful functioning was calculated in the early 1970s to be in excess of 40 million. However, this figure, which was produced by the 1970 census, is regarded as incomplete; for example, it does not include the disabled in institutions.

More recently, statistics compiled by the Bureau of Outdoor Recreation and the National Center for Health Statistics indicate that there are approximately 68 million persons in the United States with limiting or disabling conditions. This figure includes the following subcategories of disability:

11.7 million physically disabled (including half a million people in wheelchairs; three million who use crutches, canes, braces or walkers; plus mobility-impaired elderly, amputees and those people with illness such as chronic arthritis, severe cardiovascular disorders, and cerebral palsy)

12.5 million temporarily injured (broken limb, injury to back or spine, severe burns, etc.)

2.4 million deaf, and 11 million hearing impaired

1.3 million blind, and 8.2 million visually impaired

6.8 million mentally disabled (mentally retarded, severely emotionally disturbed, brain damaged, severely learning disabled)

1.7 million homebound (chronic health disorders, wasting diseases like multiple sclerosis)

2.1 million institutionalized (mentally disturbed, mentally retarded, terminal illness)

7.6 million suffering from heart conditions

18.3 million arthritics

14.5 with severe respiratory ailments, such as bronchial asthma[19]

It is extremely difficult to give a precise number of persons with disabling conditions, partly because the severity of impairment varies considerably within each condition and partly because many persons fall into more than one category. Different government or voluntary agencies tend to come up with widely varying statistics; for example, the number of persons with some type of cardiovascular or blood vessel disease has been reported to be as high as 25 million, in contrast to the figure of 7.6 million cited above.[20] In addition, although it was reported that 2.1 million persons were institutionalized in a given year, the Statistical

---

[19] Terri Schultz: "The Handicapped, A Minority Demanding Its Rights." *New York Times*, February 13, 1977, p. 8–E. *See also Trends for the Handicapped.* National Park Service and National Society for Park Resources, Washington, D.C., 1974, p. 4.

[20] Ronald C. Adams, Alfred N. Daniel and Lee Rullman: *Games, Sports and Exercises for the Physically Handicapped.* Philadelphia, Lea and Febiger, 1972, p. 18.

Abstracts of the United States indicate that there are over 5 million admissions to mental hospitals or outpatient psychiatric clinics in a given year, along with several hundred thousand persons cared for annually in institutions for the mentally retarded, or other related health facilities.[21]

In some categories of disability, only a percentage of the population is in need of specially designed recreation services; in others, all of the individuals suffering from a particular disability are limited to the degree that they cannot function independently.

In addition to the figures just cited, there are other major population categories that include persons who have serious impairments and might require specially planned and guided recreation programs. These include those suffering from alcoholism (estimated at 10 million), drug abusers (1.5 million) or individuals in correctional or penal institutions. In many cases, individuals suffer from multiple disability. For example, in a high percentage of cases in which there is a serious physical disability, the individual also has severe psychological problems stemming from or relating to the other disability.

Although a relatively high proportion of those with acute mental illness or social disability are institutionalized, many such persons live in the community. Similarly, the majority of persons with physical disabilities or mental retardation are not institutionalized. A study carried on by the Social Security Administration revealed that only about 7 per cent of all severely disabled persons in the United States were residents of long-term hospitals, special schools or homes. Thus, although therapeutic recreation service is found most frequently in institutional settings, over 90 per cent of the individuals who might require special leisure services do not live in such settings.

ACTIVITIES IN THERAPEUTIC RECREATION SERVICE

O'Morrow points out that when he first entered the field of therapeutic recreation in a state psychiatric institution he was reprimanded for suggesting a counseling service. His role, the superintendent made clear, "was to be in the institution, not out in the community surveying recreation resources and following up ex-patients as to what they were doing during their nonworking hours." The range of services he provided was limited to administration, activity programming, leadership and coordination of services with other professional disciplines.[22]

Today, this situation has changed markedly. Therapeutic recreation specialists in most settings are encouraged to assist in diagnosis and rehabilitation team planning. They are often expected to provide counseling, referral and other forms of personal assistance with respect to developing community programs and cooperative arrangements among public and private agencies. In many situations, the emphasis is not so much on *providing activities* as on developing a *social climate* or living situation in which the patient or disabled client can function with satisfaction and increasing social capability.

---

[21] *Statistical Abstracts of the United States.* Washington, D.C., U.S. Bureau of the Census, 1976, p. 86.
[22] O'Morrow, *op. cit.*, p. 124.

Milieu Therapy Approach

Pattison, for example, describes the "milieu therapy" approach found in many psychiatric treatment settings today in the following terms:

> *The thrust of milieu therapy is not to unlock specific psychodynamic conflicts but rather to provide integrating, guiding, rehabilitating social experiences. This begins with those socializing activities that the most regressed patients can participate in, then on to social activities requiring more ego control and personal-relatedness, and finally to reality-oriented social functions that are part and parcel of everyday living. Seen in this perspective, the adjunctive therapies are experiences in socialization and social interaction. The task of the adjunctive therapist is not that of individual therapist or extension thereof, but that of a social systems specialist.*[23]

Similarly, in many community-based treatment centers or halfway houses that serve discharged mental patients, those attending day clinics and others with psychiatric problems, recreation serves particularly as a means of helping individuals regain social competence and confidence. For example, in one halfway house

> *. . . the club provides opportunities for mental patients, discharged patients, and persons under psychiatric care to participate in social rehabilitation programs, recreation, and other activities. Through this means, they can make social contacts, reestablish social adequacy, reorient social status, regain lost skills, and restore lost self-confidence . . . to make the gradual readjustment back into the mainstream of community life. . . .*[24]

Other Therapeutic Modalities

Not infrequently, the therapeutic recreation specialist may be called upon to provide other forms of activity therapy. Typically, *A.D.L.* (activities of daily living) has become an important part of treatment programs, and patients may become involved in shopping, cooking their own meals, home maintenance activities, planning trips and outings and similar activities that help prepare them for the demands of independent, noninstitutional living. In nursing homes, where there may be many disoriented older patients, therapeutic recreation specialists are likely to be called upon to provide programs in *sensory training*, *remotivation* and *reality orientation* (see Chapter 9). In working with disturbed or dependent youth, alcoholics or drug abusers, *behavior modification* or *reality therapy* techniques may become an integral part of the activity program (see Chapter 10).

It would be a mistake, however, to assume that therapeutic recreation workers spend all their time counseling, making referrals, consulting with community groups, carrying out research and providing these related forms of treatment. In many situations, their primary responsibility continues to be that

---

[23] E. Mansell Pattison: "The Relationship of the Adjunctive and Therapeutic Recreation Services to Community Mental Health Programs." *Therapeutic Recreation Journal*, 1st Quarter, 1969, pp. 19–20.

[24] Jerry S. Hong, and Ralston S. Bauer: "Have You a Halfway House Program?" *Parks and Recreation*, November, 1966, p. 914.

of planning, organizing and carrying out a well-rounded program of recreational activities that would include the following major categories.

Social activities: parties, cards, discussion groups, bingo, clubs and informal game room or lounge programs.

Sports and active games: dual sports, such as golf, tennis, badminton, bowling, shuffleboard and horseshoes; team sports, such as basketball, volleyball and softball; and individual activities, such as skating, swimming and archery.

Entertainment: professional entertainment or programs presented by community theatre groups, bands, orchestras or dance clubs; watching television, listening to radio and listening to records; films; and patient talent shows.

Hobbies: various types of collections, such as stamps, coins or matchbooks; creative writing; ham radio; construction activities; bird-watching; and cooking.

Arts and crafts: drawing, painting and sculpture; ceramics, leathercraft, weaving, print-making, jewelry work and macramé.

Performing arts: dramatics, instrumental music (learning to play instruments or taking part in bands or orchestras), choral music, ballet and modern dance.

Service activities: in a large hospital situation, being on the staff of a hospital radio station or newspaper or assisting in the conduct of the recreation program.

Outdoor recreation: swimming and other water sports, picnicking, camping, nature study and group travel.

Motor activities: gymnastics, stunts and tumbling and other motor learning activities, particularly of a developmental nature, especially for the retarded or those with perceptual motor problems.

Special events: barbeques, carnivals, holiday celebrations, scavenger hunts, treasure hunts or progressive contests.

These and many other specialized activities may be found in therapeutic recreation programs. In hospitals with several hundred patients or more, the range of activities may be extremely diverse. By contrast, in nursing homes with only a small number of patients (many of whom may be in wheelchairs or confined to their beds), program activities are likely to be extremely limited.

HISTORY OF THERAPEUTIC RECREATION SERVICE

It is helpful in analyzing the present role of therapeutic recreation service to examine its historical background. Undoubtedly, prehistoric man discovered for himself, at an early point in his history, certain crude forms of treatment for his ills. Krusen writes that at some time prior to the Paleolithic Age, probably before the year 7000 B.C.,

> . . . the first primitive man who crawled into the sunshine to receive benefit of its warmth and vitalizing effect unwittingly started the practice of heliotherapy; the first man who bathed a wound in some woodland stream unknowingly instituted the practice of hydrotherapy; and the first man who rubbed a bruised muscle unconsciously introduced massage.[25]

---

[25] Frank H. Krusen: *Physical Medicine.* Philadelphia, W. B. Saunders Co., 1941, p. 9.

In most primitive societies, the approach to the treatment of illness was based on magical belief in the supernatural. Prehistoric man believed that everything in nature was alive with invisible forces and possessed supernatural powers. Disease was caused by evil spirits that entered the body, and many techniques were used to drive out these demons. Primitive man often sacrificed animals or human victims to heal the ill. He wore amulets to guard against evil spirits, and medicine men or witch doctors carried out detailed rituals intended to cure victims of disease.

Often, art, music, dancing, chanting and other expressive activities were used in this healing process. As an example, among the American Indian tribes of the Southwest, medicine men conduct an elaborate ceremony that goes on for days in a special medicine hut, involving chanting, the use of herbs, incense and the making of sand paintings with colored sand and crushed minerals—all as part of a highly secret process intended to cure the diseased.

In a sense, such elaborate rituals carried on by primitive and prehistoric man represented an early form of therapeutic recreation service. They demonstrate a fundamental truth—that many forms of illness are psychosomatic in nature rather than organic—and the fact that many forms of treatment that have no medical base can be highly effective in healing illness.

Therapeutic Recreation in Pre-Christian Societies

History has recorded a number of references to the early use of therapeutic recreation in ancient societies.

For example, in ancient China varied forms of medical gymnastics and massage were used as far back as 3000 B.C. These included free exercises that were combined with breathing, sitting, kneeling, lying and standing positions. They were based on the view that bodily inactivity led to disease and were intended to prolong human life. The Chinese healing arts often included such magical practices as making sacrificial offerings and frightening evil spirits by beating gongs and shooting off firecrackers. Avedon states that an ancient Chinese surgeon is reported to have used recreational activities for a variety of purposes. "In one instance he operated on a poisoned arrow wound in the arm of General Kuan Kung, while encouraging the General to use the unaffected hand in a table game."[26]

As early as 2000 B.C., Egyptian temples were established to treat the mentally ill by providing games and other pastimes. Priests were said to have been aware that healing was promoted by the beauty of the temple and its surrounding gardens and the songs and dances of temple maidens. One source reports that:

Patients . . .were required to walk in the beautiful gardens which surrounded the temples, or to row on the majestic Nile. . . . Dances, concerts, and comic representations were planned for them . . . .[27]

---

[26] K. C. Wong, et al.: *History of Chinese Medicine.* Tientsin, China, Tientsin Press, 1932, p. 37.
[27] W. A. F. Browne: *What Asylums Were, Are, and Ought to Be.* Edinburgh, A. and C. Black, 1837, pp. 141–142.

Similarly, in the Indian province of Kashmir during the second century B.C., a physician named Charaka is said to have advocated the use of toys and games to divert patients and promote their recovery. Dock and Stewart describe Indian "professional musicians and storytellers who cheered and diverted patients by singing and by reciting poetry."[28]

In ancient Greece, the use of recreation became a more highly recognized technique in the treatment of the ill. The Greeks named their health temples asclepions, after the highly revered god of healing, Asklepios. One of these temples was at Epidaurus and was similar to a fashionable modern health resort. The temple was an architectural masterpiece built on a high hill with an outstanding view. Under medical supervision, patients enjoyed scenic walks and exercise and massage in a gymnasium, diet, bathing in mineral waters, an outdoor theater and an extended program of treatment similar to that in a modern spa.

Hippocrates, known as "the father of medicine" in ancient Greece, was said to have written a number of treatises on the use of exercise to prevent disability and obesity, and other Greek writers, such as Aristotle and Plato, stressed the importance of exercise in maintaining sound health.

The Romans developed an elaborate system of therapeutic exercise under the leadership of the pioneer physician Galen, who lived in the second century A.D. He developed and classified exercises that improved muscle tone, such as digging, diving, carrying weights and rope-climbing, as well as others involving sparring, punching ball play and other movements. The Roman baths represented a remarkable advance in treatment approaches. The Baths of Caracalla in ancient Rome were tremendously expensive:

> . . . covering acres of land, they accommodated thousands of persons in the most grandiose manner. The spacious interior had high arched ceilings and was beautifully ornamented with marble and exquisite inlaid mosaics. There were auditoria, gymnasia, reading rooms, patios with cool foundations, soft music, and swimming pools to delight the patrons and provide diversional therapy.[29]

Therapeutic Recreation in the Middle Ages

Following the fall of the Roman Empire, the treatment of the mentally ill, mentally retarded, crippled or other disabled persons tended to be extremely cruel and punitive.

It was thought that persons who suffered from such disabilities had been cursed by the gods. The mentally ill in particular tended to be treated like animals, chained and manacled, beaten and tortured to drive out their madness or subjected to such devices as revolving beds or whirling cages to calm them.

In England, a typical example of institutional care for the mentally ill was found in Bedlam (the name is derived from Bethlem and was the popular name for the Hospital of St. Mary of Bethlehem in Lambeth, England), built originally as a priory and used to house the insane as early as 1402. As its name

[28] Lavinia L. Dock and Isabel M. Stewart: *A Short History of Nursing.* New York, G. P. Putnam and Sons, 1938, p. 26.
[29] Josephine A. Dolan: *The History of Nursing.* Philadelphia, W. B. Saunders Co., 1969, p. 59.

has come to suggest, it was a place of uproar and confusion, as well as cruel treatment. As late as 1815, the "lunatics" were placed on view before the public; the revenue from exhibiting the inmates on Sunday for one penny per visitor netted hundreds of pounds a year. Erikson writes,

> Like strange animals the mad . . . entertained, performing dance and acrobatics . . . in the popular mind, (they) were creatures apart. They lived outside of the human social order, and thus belonged truly to nature. A madhouse was like a zoo, and the antics of the inmates afforded the public a bizarre diversion.[30]

Most institutions during the Middle Ages and well into the Renaissance period served chiefly to confine the seriously ill or disabled and did little to uplift the spirits of patients. In a few hospitals, such as St. Catherine of Siena or St. John's Hospital in Bruges, beautiful frescoes or paintings were displayed to provide diversion and improve the morale of the plague sufferers or lepers who were receiving care. However, well into the 18th century, most hospitals were dark, dismal and lacking in rehabilitative services.

In terms of physical care, there was general disapproval of games and sports during the early Middle Ages; however, beginning in the 14th century, there was a renewed interest in the early Greek and Roman cultures, including their sports and exercises. Mercurialis wrote the first modern text on therapeutic exercise, *De Arte Gymnastica*, in 1569, outlining principles for the use of gymnastics from a medical perspective. A number of other authorities, including Hoffman, Tissot and Ling, over the next three centuries promoted varied forms of adapted sports, gymnastics, massage and therapeutic exercise, contributing ultimately to the development of both occupational therapy and physical therapy.[31]

Therapeutic Recreation in the 18th and 19th Centuries

Early in this period, most hospitals provided little real care; often they were little more than prisons. Dolan describes Newgate Prison of East Granby, Connecticut; this institution, with a pathetic history of torture, was the first colonial prison in Connecticut:

> Prisoners were not segregated according to sex, type of crime or mental condition; the mentally ill and mentally retarded shared quarters with the most vicious criminal. Screams were heard for quite a distance from the dungeons to which all inmates had to descend every night.[32]

Gradually, however, medical pioneers began to introduce new and innovative services. Dr. Benjamin Rush, a leading American physician who was on the staff of the Pennsylvania Hospital in Philadelphia in the 1780s and who was shocked by the lack of care or comfort for the "lunatics" in this setting,

---

[30] Joan M. Erikson: *Activity, Recovery and Growth: The Communal Role of Planned Activities.* New York, W. W. Norton, 1976, p. 7.
[31] *Adams, op. cit.,* p. 6.
[32] Dolan, *op. cit.,* p. 176.

fought for better hospital conditions and services. Dolan writes,

> *. . . he called attention to the need for diversional therapy for psychiatric patients;*
> *for suitable companions to listen sympathetically to patients . . . for a plan for*
> *recreation and amusement; for personnel to direct these activities; and, lastly, to*
> *separate the mentally ill from those who were convalescing. . . .*[33]

By the early 1800s, varied forms of therapeutic recreation had been introduced in a number of hospitals—particularly those serving psychiatric patients. In a description of the York Retreat, an English mental hospital in 1819, physicians were urged to involve patients in "regular employment" and "bodily exercise," and to interest them in activities that would confront them with reality and involve their emotions:

> *. . . every effort should be made to divert the mind of melancholiacs by bodily*
> *exercise, walks, conversations, reading, and other recreations. Those who*
> *manage the insane should sedulously endeavor to gain their confidence and*
> *esteem, to arrest their attention and fix it on objects opposed to their delu-*
> *sions. . . .*[34]

During the 1830s and 1840s, so-called "insane asylums" were established, and those considered mad were placed in these isolated, secure institutions where they were segregated from criminals, paupers and those with other forms of illness. For the first time, insanity was regarded as a form of illness rather than a divine curse or a crime, and medical practitioners sought to treat it rationally. As Chapter 5 will show in detail, the conviction grew that occupations of various kinds would be helpful in overcoming mental illness and restoring rational functioning. In many hospitals in America and abroad, such activities as checkers, chess, backgammon, bowling, swinging, gardening, reading and writing were provided. Mental patients were permitted to dance and engage in or listen to music, to take part in outdoor sports, to use "airing courts," rocking horses and a variety of other pastimes or forms of equipment.

One of the best examples of therapeutic recreation in a psychiatric setting was found in the Brattleboro, Vermont, Retreat, founded in 1836 as the Vermont Asylum for the Insane. An early description of this hospital made clear that "due provision has been made for the exercise, amusement, and employment of the patients." In addition to gardening and farming, there were many pastimes:

> *Battle-door, chess, draughts, and the like amusements will be afforded. The*
> *females will be employed in knitting, needlework, painting, etc. Carriages will be*
> *provided for the daily riding of the patients in suitable weather, and they will also*
> *take daily walks with nurses and attendants. A small and select library . . . and*
> *several periodicals will be furnished for the purpose. . . .*[35]

In addition to mental hospitals, other forms of treatment or custodial institutions gradually came into being in the United States during this period.

---

[33] *Ibid.*, p. 159.
[34] "Description of the York Retreat, 1819." Taken from *Biennial Report for 1950–52,* California State Department of Mental Hygiene.
[35] Ardis Stevens: "Recreation in Community Mental Health." *Therapeutic Recreation Journal,* 1st Quarter, 1971, p. 14.

Institutions were provided for the deaf in 1817, the blind in 1832, the mentally retarded in 1850, the crippled in 1867 and the epileptic in 1890. In addition, many destitute, widowed, orphaned and sometimes crippled, blind or retarded individuals continued to be sheltered in what were originally known as almshouses that came to be called poorhouses, or county farms; many such facilities exist even today, particularly in the American Midwest.

In many of these institutions, varied forms of diversional activity began to be provided. Particularly in mental hospitals, exercise was recommended for general health, occupational activities provided a regular daily routine and sense of accomplishment and the specific diagnosis of the patient's illness and therapeutic needs was used as the basis for planning recreational activities. As medical services improved for wounded servicemen in military hospitals, a strong impetus was given to recreation by the great nursing pioneer, Florence Nightingale. In her text on nursing, published in 1873, she urged that nurses should pay attention not only to the patient's body but also to his mind and morale. She urged that music and conversation be encouraged, that beautiful objects be placed in patient wards, that the family be encouraged to visit and that patients keep small pets. Florence Nightingale was the first to introduce innovations such as furnished classrooms and instruction for soldiers, reading rooms, day rooms and recreation huts that have become an accepted part of military life. Under her leadership, so-called bedside occupations were introduced in military hospitals to cheer up injured soldiers.

Gradually, new forms of occupational and physical therapy were refined. In the 1870s and 1880s, S. Weir Mitchell helped to develop new forms of sequential exercise and massage, which led to more complex systems of physical therapy. In the following decades, Dudley Sargent, an American physician and physical educator, created new forms of apparatus and gymnastic systems that were useful both in school and college programs and in working with the disabled in medical settings. In mental hospitals, there was increasingly less reliance on custodial seclusion, physical restraints and sedatives and a growing understanding that patients should be occupied—both with practical, work-connected tasks and with physical, mental and social activities that contribute to their recovery. By the early 1900s, a rationale had been well established for activity therapy programs, and many hospitals were making use of such modalities, although they were not recognized as areas of special professional expertise until the 1920s.

The United States in the 20th Century

Soon after the entrance of the United States into World War I, the Red Cross began to provide recreation programs in hospital wards and convalescent homes. Recreation leaders were employed in a growing number of military and veterans' hospitals during the 1920s. It became more widely recognized that recreation—among other innovative rehabilitative techniques—was of value in reducing the length of the patient's stay in the hospital and the extent and duration of his disability.

Gradually, federal laws, such as the Federal Vocational Rehabilitation Act of 1920, the Social Security Act of 1936 and the Barden–La Follette Act of

1942, provided for improved rehabilitation services for both children and adults in the United States.

Typically, during the 1920s public school systems began to offer special classes for disabled children, with special transportation. By 1929, there were a number of special public schools for the blind. In institutional settings during the 1920s and 1930s, the custodial approach to caring for disabled children shifted to a stronger emphasis on reeducation and reintegration of the disabled into community life.

Varied forms of rehabilitative services came into being. More and more, recreation emerged as one of these services. As a single example, at the Lincoln State School Colony in Illinois a recreation department was established in June, 1929, in order to ". . . conduct a program of activities, consistent with the interests and abilities of mentally handicapped children . . . to serve as a substitute for former repressive measures of control." More and more state and private institutions began to develop extensive recreation programs.

A number of national organizations took the lead in developing such services. For example, the Association for the Aid of Crippled Children began as early as 1900 to provide services for disabled children in their homes, in schools and in hospitals. It operated camps and summer programs for the disabled and brought occupational therapy and similar modalities into the homes of crippled children as a demonstration service and a means of parental education.

The growing recognition of the need for recreation for the disabled was demonstrated in the so-called Bill of Rights for the Handicapped that was drawn up at the White House Conference on Child Health and Protection in 1932. This statement called for

> . . . a life on which his handicap casts no shadow, but which is full day by day with those things which make it worth while, with comradeship, love, work, play, laughter and tears—a life in which those things bring continually increasing growth, richness, a release of energies and joy of achievement.[36]

During this period, public concern about the disabled continued to grow steadily. Programs of rehabilitation were greatly strengthened through Federal Social Security legislation along with workmen's compensation acts, public assistance laws and other government efforts to support health care on the local level. O'Morrow points out that recreation became an increasingly important part of this overall trend, particularly in military hospitals:

> During the 1920's and 1930's, individuals with varied backgrounds and representing various disciplines directed programs in hospitals, institutions, and special centers and schools. World War II found Red Cross personnel and volunteers providing recreation services. Also, military personnel with an education or interest in physical education or recreation were assigned to hospitals and reconditioning units.[37]

During the war itself, there was a marked acceleration in the hospital recreation movement. Red Cross recreation personnel increased to a total of

---

[36] *The Handicapped Child, Report of the White House Conference on Child Health and Protection.* New York, D. Appleton-Century, 1933, p. 3.
[37] O'Morrow, *op. cit.,* p. 102.

1809 at the end of World War II and, following the war, became a permanent part of peacetime Red Cross services to the armed forces. In 1945, the Veterans Administration founded a Hospital Social Services Division. This included Recreation Service along with Canteen, Library, Chaplaincy and Voluntary Services; recreation personnel were assigned to all hospitals.

Therapeutic activities were refined in many long-term rehabilitation centers and convalescent programs, with adapted sports and modified games for amputees, paraplegics and those with other major disabilities. Adams, Daniel and Rullman point out that in the United States and other countries that had suffered major casualties in World War II, there was a new determination to give veterans with service-connected disabilities the opportunity for full physical, social and economic rehabilitation. In a review of the development of wheelchair sports, they write,

> As part of the vast rehabilitation program, sports were suddenly seen by some as an important aid to rehabilitating the disabled veterans. The program of wheelchair sports began at various Veterans Administration Hospitals throughout the United States. . . . More and more disabled men joined into the new wheelchair sport until finally several complete teams were officially organized. Thus basketball became the first organized wheelchair sport in history. . . . As the interest in the sport grew, the range of disabilities of the participants also increased. Added to the list of war-injured were those paraplegic because of polio, amputees, and other orthopedically disabled individuals.[38]

A number of major federal agencies, chiefly within the Department of Health, Education and Welfare, initiated programs to provide enriched vocational, educational and recreational opportunities for children, youth and adults of all types—the mentally retarded, the physically disabled, the mentally ill, drug abusers, the aged and others. With the funding under major federal laws passed during the period from the 1950s through the 1970s, assistance has been given to professional training, research and direct community services in therapeutic recreation. In general, such aid has not been directed to supporting on-going programs but rather to short-term demonstration or special project grants designed to encourage stronger local efforts. However, particularly in the field of mental retardation and aging, substantial on-going assistance has been given to direct program service. Medicare, for example, has reimbursed thousands of expanded programs of activity therapy programs in nursing homes and related health care facilities.

As will be shown in later chapters, following World War II there was sharply increased recognition of therapeutic recreation service as an important rehabilitative discipline throughout the United States and Canada. Along with this came a marked expansion of recreation programs for the ill and disabled in both institutional and community settings.

Extent of Therapeutic Recreation Today

Although there has been no comprehensive survey of all forms of institutions or agencies providing services, several surveys *have* been carried out that give a picture of key aspects of the field in the United States and Canada.

---

[38] Adams, *op. cit.*, p. 8.

1959 REPORT ON RECREATION IN
HOSPITALS

At the request of the Council for the Advancement of Hospital Recreation, the National Recreation Association sponsored a national study on hospital recreation. This study gave a picture of the types of hospitals that provided recreation service, the number of personnel employed, the activities offered and similar information. Overall, it found that 42.4 per cent of the 3507 hospitals responding to the questionnaire had organized recreation programs.

Larger hospitals tended to have organized recreation programs, while smaller ones did not. Typically, 88.4 per cent of hospitals with 500 to 999 bed capacity offered recreation service, while only 48.7 per cent of hospitals with between 100 and 499 beds offered it. The study explained the pattern of varying recreation sponsorship among types of hospitals by pointing out that

> ... in these institutions, particularly in the state institutions devoted largely to mental illness and tuberculosis, the patients tend to stay for longer periods of time and, therefore, are in greater need of organized recreation activities. ... The low percentage of organized recreation programs in municipal, proprietary and miscellaneous hospitals is probably due, at least in part, to the fact that most of these hospitals treat acute conditions. Patients remain in these institutions for a relatively short period of time, and the need for organized recreation programs is therefore not as obvious as in the institutions where the length of stay is longer.[39]

Many hospitals provided swimming pools, gymnasiums, auditoriums, athletic fields and special recreation rooms, although wards, solariums and day rooms were also used heavily for recreation. The most popular activities were passive or mental activities, such as reading, radio, television-watching and movies (found in 86.4 per cent of the hospital); arts and crafts (72.5 per cent); social activities (61.0 per cent); musical activities (47.6 per cent); active games and sports (47.0 per cent); service activities (43.4 per cent); and nature and outing activities (33.2 per cent).

SURVEY OF COMMUNITY
RECREATION SPONSORSHIP

In 1964, the National Recreation Association and the National Association for Retarded Children assisted Marson in carrying out a survey of 2000 community recreation departments to determine what community services were being provided for the mentally or physically disabled.[40] The 427 responding agencies indicated that they provided either recreation facilities or programs for the disabled. However, only 202 departments responded to a follow-up survey that sought fuller information.

In 139 communities, the mentally retarded were served separately in such facilities as playgrounds, community recreation centers, parks, swimming

[39] John E. Silson, Elliott M. Cohen and Beatrice H. Hill: *Recreation in Hospitals: Report of a Study of Organized Recreation Programs in Hospitals and the Personnel Conducting Them.* New York, National Recreation Association, 1959, pp. 22–23.
[40] Ruth Marson: *In* Morton Thompson: "The Status of Recreation for the Handicapped, as Related to Community and Voluntary Agencies." *Therapeutic Recreation Journal,* Vol. III, No. 9, pp. 20–23.

pools and day camps. In 164 cases, the physically handicapped were served separately, in similar facilities.

The variety of programs offered was quite limited. Only about one-third of the responding groups provided transportation assistance to disabled participants, and many special programs were supported financially by fees or contributions from parents or interested community groups. Marson concluded that

> Despite the tremendous growth of recreation, new developments in medical science and increased leisure for Americans, there has been a great lag in developing recreation services for the handicapped by community recreation departments. We believe that the next few years will show a marked increase in this service by communities.[41]

PLAY IN PEDIATRIC HOSPITALS

In 1968, Williams carried out a survey to determine the status of therapeutic play activities in pediatric hospitals or children's units in general hospitals.[42] Her questionnaire covered such elements as the extent of programs, nature of personnel responsible for them, activities offered and techniques used. Of the 48 hospitals surveyed, 46 (96 per cent) replied. Of these, 30 hospitals (65 per cent) indicated that they offered some form of supervised play programs.

The findings indicated that therapeutic play in children's hospitals was generally quite limited and that there was a need to develop this field further and provide specialized training for workers in this field.

NATIONAL SURVEY OF SENIOR CENTERS

In 1969, the Institute for Interdisciplinary Studies of the American Rehabilitation Foundation published the report of a study of Senior Centers carried out by Anderson.[43] This survey was funded by the Administration on Aging, of the United States Department of Health, Education and Welfare. The final study report was based on findings from 1002 senior centers that responded to a long-form questionnaire covering such topics as the clientele served, types of programs and other services, budgets, facilities, staffing patterns, size of membership and relations with other community social or health agencies.

Anderson found that, despite the widespread attention recently given to the need for developing social and recreation programs for older Americans, these programs tended to be quite limited. First, it was apparent that even if the active membership of these centers averaged as high as 150 to 200 members each, it would mean that less than 1 per cent of the population in this age group throughout the country was actually served by senior centers. Fewer than half of the centers reported having full-time directors. Generally, their facilities were

---

[41] *Ibid.*, p. 23.

[42] Yvonne B. Williams: "Therapeutic Play Services in Children's General Hospitals in the United States." *Therapeutic Recreation Journal*, 2nd Quarter, 1970, pp. 17–21.

[43] Nancy N. Anderson: *Senior Centers: Information from a National Survey*. Minneapolis, Minnesota, Institute for Interdisciplinary Studies, American Rehabilitation Foundation, 1969.

inadequate, and they operated with annual budgets that averaged $27,000—certainly not enough to provide the varied services needed by citizens in many communities.

In Section 304 of the Older Americans Act, Congress gave its strong support to

> . . . the establishment of new or expansion of existing centers providing recreational and other leisure time activities, and information, health, welfare, counseling and referral services for older persons and assisting such persons in providing volunteer community or civic services. . . .[44]

The Anderson report makes clear the need to give stronger support to the development of multiservice senior centers throughout the country in order to meet these goals.

RECREATION SERVICE TO DISABLED CHILDREN

In 1971, Berryman, Logan and Lander of the New York University School of Education published a comprehensive report on recreation services provided to meet the needs of disabled children in a sampling of large metropolitan areas throughout the United States.[45] The findings were based on a three-year study financed by the Children's Bureau of the United States Department of Health, Education and Welfare. It explored several thousand potential sponsors of recreation services for disabled children and youth; a high percentage of these agencies were reported as providing such services.

This extensive study of potential resources for serving disabled children pointed out (a) the need to develop more programs integrating the disabled with the nondisabled, (b) the need to eliminate architectural barriers that keep the disabled from participating in community programs, and (c) the need for more specialized programs in hospitals and residential schools. Based on this Children's Bureau report, it is clear that many potential resources exist but program services need to be developed more fully.

RECREATION SERVING THE DISABLED IN MAJOR CITIES

In 1971, the Community Council of Greater New York carried out a study of administrative problems in recreation and parks, involving a sample of 80 cities with populations of 150,000 or more throughout the United States.[46] Forty-five cities (56.2 per cent of the sample) participated in the study. A high proportion of these cities provided one or more forms of recreation service for special populations suffering from physical, mental or social disability.

---

[44] See *Older Americans Act of 1965* (Public Law 89–73), Section 304.
[45] Doris L. Berryman, Annette Logan and Dorothy Lander: *Enhancement of Recreation Service to Disabled Children.* New York, New York University School of Education, Report of Children's Bureau Project, 1971.
[46] Richard Kraus: *Urban Parks and Recreation: Challenge of the 1970's.* New York, Community Council of Greater New York, 1972, pp. 28–29, 81–82.

The examples of such programs offered by large cities included day camps for the mentally retarded, busing programs for the blind and aged, resident summer camps for the physically disabled, a "meals on wheels" program for the home-bound, physical development and social activities programs for various disabled groups, after-care programs for discharged mental patients and many similar types of services.

THERAPEUTIC RECREATION IN CANADA

In 1974, Peter Witt reported on a study he had made of federal, provincial, local government and voluntary agency services for the disabled throughout Canada.[47] With the assistance of a grant from Recreation Canada, part of the Federal Department of National Health and Welfare, he examined in particular intergovernmental and interagency relationships and programs. In general, he found that interest in support for therapeutic recreation service had grown. The federal government, for example, had begun to spend millions of dollars through "local initiatives" programs to stimulate local services for the disabled. Provinces like Ontario and Alberta had employed full-time provincial consultants to promote and help coordinate recreation for special populations on the local level. On the national level, major voluntary health organizations, like the Canadian Association for the Mentally Retarded, the Canadian Rehabilitation Council for the Disabled and the Canadian Mental Health Association, had taken positive steps to promote fuller recreation services for the disabled throughout the nation.

However, in a detailed examination of special programs for the disabled on the municipal level (cities, towns, boroughs or other government authorities), Witt found that the picture was less favorable. Questionnaires were sent to 2382 local government agencies; 663 (28 per cent) replied. Witt summarized his findings on this level:

> A total of 145 out of 663 communities (21.9 per cent) indicated that they offered, co-sponsored, or provided facilities or money to serve one or more of six specific disability groups mentioned in the survey: the blind, the deaf, the mentally retarded, the physically handicapped, individuals with learning disabilities, and individuals with psychiatric problems.[48]

In another survey of institutions serving groups with similar types of disability, Witt found a somewhat more positive picture. Of 422 responding institutions, 235 (55 per cent) reported offering recreation services; 189 (45 per cent) reported that they did not. Finally, in a survey of voluntary community agencies throughout Canada, it was found that 102 of 196 responding agencies (52 per cent) provided some form of recreation service for the disabled. Witt came to the conclusion that there was a wide range of concern on all levels that needed to be transferred into more effective action and made a number of recommendations for improved coordination, communication and training to strengthen therapeutic recreation service in Canada.

---

[47] Peter A. Witt: *Status of Recreation Services for the Handicapped.* University of Ottawa and Recreation Canada, Department of National Health and Welfare, 1974.
[48] *Ibid.,* p. 65.

THE CURRENT STATUS OF RECREATION SERVICE

Based on the available evidence, it is apparent that although there has been a considerable growth in the provision of therapeutic recreation service for the disabled in both the United States and Canada, programs need to be much more fully developed if they are to meet total community needs. In 1970, David Park wrote,

> If the public recreation program is to provide adequate recreation programs and resources for the total population, we must realize that there are significant numbers in our communities who will require special programs and it is the communities' responsibility to provide special programs for these special groups.[49]

Similarly, John Nesbitt has pointed out that only a small percentage of the nation's estimated seven million disabled children are being served by camping programs and that most of the existing programs are provided for only a brief period of time during the summer.[50] A key problem in this area is the marked communication gap between therapeutic recreation specialists and community recreation and park administrators. For example, Richard Stracke reported in 1969 the findings of a survey of 500 community recreation administrators in 40 states.[51] His report showed that only 18 per cent of the administrators had frequently worked or cooperated with therapeutic recreation specialists in providing services for the disabled. Seventy-four per cent of them felt that therapeutic recreation should *not* be confined to hospitals or institutions, and 84 per cent felt that their communities had inadequate programs serving the disabled.

Overall, although a substantial proportion of municipal and county recreation and park departments now serve the disabled, it is clear that only a small proportion of those needing special services actually receive them.

PROMOTING THERAPEUTIC RECREATION SERVICE

What steps need to be taken to improve the provision of therapeutic recreation service in both institutional and community settings?

Arousing Public Concern

The great mass of people tend to be unaware of the needs of the disabled population until they are brought to their attention. In some cases during the past few years when budget cuts have resulted in inadequate programs in state

---

[49] David C. Park: "Therapeutic Recreation: A Community Responsibility." *Parks and Recreation*, July, 1970, p. 25.

[50] John A. Nesbitt, Curtis C. Hansen, Barbara J. Bates and Larry L. Neal: *Training Needs and Strategies in Camping for the Handicapped.* University of Oregon, Center of Leisure Studies, 1972, p. 29.

[51] Richard Stracke: "The Role of the Therapeutic Recreator in Relation to the Community Recreator." *Therapeutic Recreation Journal*, 1st Quarter, 1969, pp. 26–29.

institutions for the mentally retarded—with newspaper and television coverage of neglected children and adults in filthy, crowded wards—public concern has compelled immediate state action in restoring needed funds and hiring personnel for such institutions.

However, such efforts to arouse public concern and support must not be keyed only to crisis situations. There must be a fuller recognition of the needs of the mentally and physically disabled of all ages and in all settings. Every effort must be made to help those living in the community to lose their fear or resentment of the disabled and to accept them as human beings. In past centuries, the crippled and deformed or mentally ill were shut up in custodial institutions—away from the public eye or conscience. Today, however, we have accepted the principle of total rehabilitation and involvement in community life, when possible, for the disabled.

Developing More Effective Programs

There is a need for improved research and professional efforts to develop models of effective service, as well as the need to improve communication with related disciplines, such as medicine, social work or other rehabilitation fields.

Timothy Nugent points out the need for more therapeutic recreation professionals to become cooperatively involved in such large-scale programs as the National Wheelchair Games, which serve many thousands of disabled persons with track and field, archery, swimming, bowling and other forms of sports competition—all under the direction of laymen. More unified efforts with the general public and with other recreation and park professionals are vital to promoting the broad field of therapeutic recreation service, in Nugent's view.[52]

In many cases, professional organizations need to develop entirely new programs and services to meet emerging needs of the disabled. For example, the American Alliance for Health, Physical Education and Recreation, which has traditionally been concerned primarily with the needs of children and youth in schools and colleges, has moved vigorously into the field of serving the aged. In 1975, the Older Americans Act was amended to broaden the definition of social service to include "services designed to enable older persons to attain and maintain physical and mental well-being through programs of regular activity and exercise." Since then, the National Association for Human Development, in cooperation with the President's Council on Physical Fitness and Sport, under a grant from the Administration on Aging, has initiated a national program of exercise for people over the age of 60. AAHPER has made a strong effort to link exercise programs with nutritional services being provided at hundreds of agencies funded by Title VII of the Older Americans Act. In addition, AAHPER has encouraged research, demonstration programs and conferences in the area of geriatric fitness—an excellent example of organizations moving vigorously into new programs serving special populations.[53]

In many states and communities, new professional relationships have been developed to promote and improve therapeutic recreation services. In some cases, municipal departments in neighboring communities or counties have joined together to cosponsor programs for the disabled (see pp. 327–328). In

---

[52] Timothy J. Nugent: "Research and Demonstration Needs for the Physically Handicapped." *Journal of Health, Physical Education and Recreation*, May, 1969, pp. 47–48.
[53] See American Alliance for Physical Education and Recreation Newsletter, *Update*, March, 1977.

other cases, local government has funded voluntary agencies assuming special therapeutic recreation responsibilities on a contractual basis. Such efforts are essential to upgrade the overall level of recreation service for the disabled.

Improving Therapeutic Recreation Curricula

A closely related area of concern is the need to develop more sharply defined programs of professional education in therapeutic recreation service in colleges and universities throughout the United States and Canada. Although a number of colleges now offer majors in therapeutic recreation service, the content of such programs varies widely, as do the opportunities for meaningful clinical experience or field placement and the standards of training.

In the fields of occupational therapy or physical therapy, professional training is carried on in close cooperation with medical authorities or educators and with the certification of practitioners approved on a statewide level under standards approved by medical societies. Although the question of the degree of medical knowledge or orientation required by therapeutic recreation specialists is not fully resolved, it is clear that a more precise definition should be developed concerning the nature of required preparation for professionals in this field.

Closely attached to this area is the problem of upgrading Civil Service or other employment requirements in this field and the elimination of nonqualified personnel in professional recreation positions.

Developing Working Relationships Between Therapeutic and Community Recreation Personnel

In the past, when the bulk of therapeutic recreation was carried on in hospital settings, the need for improving the relationship between therapeutic recreation specialists and community recreation and park administrators was not as pressing as it is today. With the trends toward breaking up large state hospitals and other institutions and developing new, community-based, smaller facilities and providing a variety of rehabilitation services within communities themselves, the relationship becomes more crucial.

Throughout the country, strong efforts have been made in this direction. Many state recreation and park societies include branches or sections concerned with therapeutic recreation service. Presently, many municipal recreation and park departments not only provide services for the disabled, or cooperate with other agencies that do, but also have employed therapeutic recreation specialists to head up their own programs.

Expanding Government Support of Therapeutic Recreation Service

Inevitably, it is more difficult and expensive to serve the disabled child, youth or adult than it is to serve nondisabled persons. The requirements of expanded or specially trained staff, modified or special facilities and transportation arrangements mean that the cost of providing therapeutic recreation is higher than that of meeting the needs of nondisabled participants.

Since this is the case, both the federal government and the individual states have contributed significantly in promoting therapeutic recreation programs on the local level. Typically, states have established demonstration programs, formed task forces to develop statewide plans, supported research and provided financial aid to meet the needs of disabled persons.

In Canada, similar needs exist, and provincial governments have been active in assisting local municipal and voluntary agencies in upgrading therapeutic recreation services. In 1975, a study of therapeutic recreation in the Province of Alberta identified the following ways in which agencies felt that the provincial or national government could be helpful to them:

Provide lists and access to written materials on recreation in the agency setting

Sponsor leadership training seminars or workshops

Help develop University or Community College curricula

Aid in the provision of transportation services

Sponsor research or demonstration projects

Provide money for provision of facilities specifically for the disabled or for adapting existing facilities, or to support special programs or provide needed equipment[54]

The federal government in the United States has been active in providing financial support for therapeutic recreation service, particularly in areas relating to mental retardation, the physically handicapped and, more recently, aged persons. For example, William Hillman points out that the President's Panel on Mental Retardation issued a report in October, 1962 that expressed considerable support for the recreation and leisure needs of the retarded, along with other high priority topics such as education, vocational preparation and institutional care. Whereas, in the past, recreation had been viewed as a "fringe" benefit, now, through the experiences of special educators and vocational counselors,

. . . it was observed that failure to provide the retarded individual with adequate leisure skills often resulted in his failure to adjust in the community setting.[55]

As a consequence, subsequent federal legislation included numerous specific programs of financial support for recreation programs serving the retarded. The Division of Educational Services of the Bureau of Education for the Handicapped of the United States Office of Education provided substantial assistance to state-related schools to enhance services to the disabled. The Division of Mental Retardation, now part of the Rehabilitation Services Administration of the Department of Health, Education and Welfare, has supported numerous recreation programs, including daytime activity centers for mentally retarded adults.

The Division of Training Programs of the Bureau of Education for the Handicapped initiated a program, authorized by Public Law 90–170, for the training of physical educators and recreational personnel to work with mentally retarded and other disabled children. In November, 1976, the 94th Congress

---

[54] *Report on the Survey of Recreation Services for the Disabled in Alberta, op. cit.*, p. 46.
[55] William A. Hillman, Jr.: "Federal Support of Recreation Services Related to Mental Retardation." *Therapeutic Recreation Journal*, 3rd Quarter, 1969, pp. 6–12.

enacted Public Law 94–142, the Education for All Handicapped Children Act, that resulted in dramatically increased services to the disabled, including physical and occupational therapy and recreation, which were identified as important "related services" for the disabled.[56] This law, which came about as a consequence of pressure from parents' organizations and lawsuits seeking to force local educational agencies to provide a free and appropriate education for the disabled, will place much greater pressure on school boards, administrators and teachers to upgrade their services for impaired children and youth. These laws, coupled with changes in the Federal Register establishing "physical education and recreation as an integral part of programs for the education of handicapped children," make it clear that service for the disabled will continue to be sharply expanded in school-related programs.

Other federal support has been given to universities exploring the role of play in the lives of the disabled, demonstration programs, comprehensive state planning for the disabled, information centers on recreation for the disabled and a number of special college programs for training therapeutic recreation specialists (see Chapter 3). The Administration on Aging has given substantial support to university departments preparing administrative personnel for multiservice centers, consultants and researchers concerned with gerontology and geriatrics. In May, 1976, the Federal Department of Health, Education and Welfare issued guidelines primarily to govern programs administered under HEW, but also to guide other Federal departments and agencies, stating that otherwise qualified disabled individuals might not be excluded from participation in any programs or activities receiving federal financial assistance.[57] These detailed regulations, based on the Vocational Rehabilitation Act of 1973, made it clear that schools, colleges or other agencies receiving any form of federal assistance would have to offer fuller opportunities to the disabled. Numerous conferences have been held in the United States and Canada to promote the elimination of architectural barriers that prevent the use of recreation and park facilities by the disabled.

Obviously, it is not enough. As succeeding chapters will show, although there has been tremendous growth in this field, with many outstanding programs now in operation throughout the United States and Canada, great numbers of disabled individuals are still unserved. The entire field needs a sharper focus, a clearer identity, improved professional preparation, stronger processes of selection and, finally, a higher level of local, state and federal support. This can be accomplished only when the rationale for therapeutic recreation service is thoroughly developed and understood.

SUGGESTED TOPICS FOR CLASS DISCUSSION, EXAMINATIONS OR STUDENT PAPERS

1. Develop a meaningful definition of contemporary therapeutic recreation service, outlining its basic elements and goals.

---

[56] David J. Szymanski: "P.L. 94–142, The Education for All Handicapped Children Act." *Therapeutic Recreation Journal*, 1st Quarter, 1976, pp. 6–9.
[57] *Newsletter of The Committee on Recreation and Leisure.* Washington, D.C., the President's Commission on Employment of the Handicapped, July, 1976.

2. Describe three distinctly different settings for therapeutic recreation service showing how its objectives and program content vary according to the nature of the setting and the population group being served.

3. Propose several steps that need to be taken to strengthen therapeutic recreation service today, including such elements as public understanding and support of the field, the role of government and professional preparation.

4. Describe the expanding scope of therapeutic recreation service, including what you regard the most important trends of the past several years.

chapter **2**

The Rationale for Therapeutic Recreation Service

This chapter will present the underlying concepts, values and goals of therapeutic recreation service. It will also clarify the role of recreation within the total structure of rehabilitation service to the disabled today and outline a number of models and examples of sequential program development. It must be stressed that from the perspective of good health, recreation is *not* solely of value to the emotionally or physically disabled person. *All* individuals have important needs for release, self-expression and involvement that can be satisfied effectively through leisure involvement. A recently presented and widely accepted definition of recreation sees it as

> . . . an emotional condition within an individual human being that flows from a feeling of well-being and self-satisfaction. It is characterized by feelings of mastery, achievement, exhilaration, acceptance, success, personal worth, and pleasure. It reinforces a positive self-image. Recreation is a response to aesthetic experience, achievement of personal goals, or positive feedback from others. It is independent of activity, leisure, or social acceptance.[1]

Seen in this light, recreation is vital as a form of therapeutic experience for the entire population and a preventative of illness, even among so-called "normal" individuals, in that it helps to minimize emotional strains and to keep the individual functioning in a healthy way. The focus of this text, however, *is* on the use of recreation with persons suffering a significant degree of disability who therefore have acute unmet needs and special problems with respect to leisure. In the past, the people of United States have been so work-oriented in their prevailing philosophy of life that they have paid little attention to recreation and leisure needs as a society. Despite our respect for play as an important economic factor in modern society, we tend to be unaware of its serious social purpose and value.

---

[1] David E. Gray and Seymour Greben: "Future Perspectives." *Parks and Recreation*, July, 1974, p. 49.

Therefore, as we examine the rationale for therapeutic recreation service, it is important to ask what support there is for this field. Do medical practitioners understand and support recreation as part of the total treatment procedure or overall service for the disabled?

VIEWS OF MEDICAL PRACTITIONERS

The strongest support for recreation as a form of rehabilitative service has come from psychiatrists who have seen diversional activities as useful in arousing the interest and improving the morale of the mentally ill. Over the past several decades, leading psychiatrists have given eloquent support to this field.

Dr. Menninger, codirector of the Menninger Clinic in Topeka, Kansas, Chief of Army Neuropsychiatric Services during World War II and past President of the American Psychiatric Association, has vigorously supported the use of recreation. In a speech before the National Recreation Congress in 1948, he stated,

> It has been the privilege of many of us practicing medicine in psychiatry to have had some very rewarding experiences in the use of recreation as an adjunctive method of treatment. Along with direct psychological help, hydrotherapy, shock and insulin therapy, many of us have, for years, used various forms of education, recreation and occupation in the treatment of our patients. Within the American Psychiatric Association—a national organization of approximately 4,500 psychiatrists—we have a standing committee on leisure time activities (based on) the assumption that professional recreation experience can contribute to psychiatric practice, and psychiatrists can add to the knowledge of professional recreation workers.[2]

Menninger stressed the value of recreation, not only in the treatment program of mental patients but also in helping former patients to remain well. He outlined three key psychological needs that can be met for many individuals through recreation: (a) competitive games as an outlet for instinctive aggressive drives; (b) creative activities in art, music or literature as a release for erotic drives; and (c) entertainment activities as a means of providing relaxation and vicarious involvement.

He also pointed out that a conspicuous symptom of many persons who are mentally ill is their inability to feel comfortable with others or to identify with and belong to a social unit. The process of gradually helping a patient become resocialized is readily carried on within group recreational activities, such as parties, ball games, square dances or dramatic productions. Menninger wrote,

> Some very concrete evidence of the relation between avocations and mental health was revealed in a survey made at our clinic some years ago. A group of well-adjusted individuals was surveyed as to the type, number and duration of their hobbies. The findings we compared to those from a similar survey of a group of psychiatric patients. In the well-adjusted group, both the number and

---

[2] William C. Menninger: "Recreation and Mental Health." *Recreation*, November, 1948, p. 340.

the intensity of the pursuit of hobbies was far in excess of those of the patients. This cannot be interpreted to mean that, because the individual has a hobby, it necessarily keeps him well. It does mean, however, that a well-adjusted individual learns how to play and does include play as an important feature of his life, much more frequently than does the average maladjusted person.[3]

Another leading psychiatrist and former President of the American Psychiatric Association, Alexander Reid Martin, took a deep interest in the relationship between leisure behavior and mental health. He pointed out that many otherwise highly successful individuals are unable to deal effectively with leisure in their private lives. Often, they are compulsively driven by work. Martin wrote,

Psychiatry has an extensive and intensive interest in leisure because, in most instances of psychoses and neuroses, the earliest and most unamenable signs and symptoms are disturbances in natural recreative functioning. They include sleeplessness, inability to relax, so-called nervous and mental tension, fear of leisure, and the compulsive need to keep going. Furthermore, the first signs of recovery are shown in a return to natural recreative functioning. Improvement is never revealed as clearly in the patient's attitude toward work as it is in his attitude toward leisure and relaxation and in the free play of his body, mind, and feelings, that is, in the free play of his whole personality.[4]

Probably the most eloquent spokesman of the need for recreation in promoting mental health generally, as well as in the treatment of psychiatric patients, has been Paul Haun. His view of play was that it represented an essential aspect of healthy life and constituted a natural rhythmic alternative to work.

In making a "medical case" for recreation, Haun wrote,

It provides patients and appropriate staff members with many familiar social roles through which pleasant and accustomed expressive interaction can occur. It affords the patient a physiological escape from somatic pain and disruptive emotional experiences. It capitalizes upon and supports the non-pathological elements of his personality. It constitutes a path by which he may return from the malignant equilibrium of defensive withdrawal, first to the make-believe universe of the play world and then, after finding this tolerable, to the yet tighter existence of prosaic day-to-day existence. It offers a gratifyingly wide opportunity for instinctual discharge in socially acceptable channels without the need for complicated sublimations.[5]

A similar statement of support was made by Robert H. Felix, a leading psychiatrist for over 30 years and Director of the National Institute of Mental Health. He commented that the problem of filling leisure with satisfying activity is particularly acute in many mental hospitals simply because many patients have so much free time. Beyond this, however, Felix believed that recreation serves

[3] *Ibid.*, p. 343.
[4] Alexander Reid Martin: "Professional Attitudes and Practices." In *Recreation for the Mentally Ill.* Washington, D.C., Conference Report, American Association for Health, Physical Education and Recreation, 1958, p. 15.
[5] Paul Haun: *Recreation: A Medical Viewpoint.* New York, Teachers College, Columbia, Bureau of Publications, 1964, p. 52.

as a "great healing force" in providing a means by which leisure can be molded to promote physical and psychological well-being:

> *The greatest value of recreation is that it can be prescribed as a definitive thera-*
> *peutic treatment. Particularly in the field of psychiatry . . . recreation plays a*
> *positive role in the care and treatment of the mentally ill. Because the activities*
> *included in recreation programs usually require some degree of skill and con-*
> *centration, recreation allows the patient to lose himself in the activity at hand,*
> *giving his mind a rest from the mental and physical problems that beset him. It*
> *provides a controlled outlet for the release of tensions that otherwise might be*
> *directed inward or toward others. It offers a means whereby the patient can*
> *acquire and put into practice new knowledge about himself. And recreation*
> *helps morale by giving the individual a feeling of satisfaction and accomplishment*
> *at having mastered some small skill or compensated for a handicap.*[6]

Felix concluded that recreation contributes significantly to the "more rapid physical, mental and social rehabilitation of the patient," and thus has come to be recognized as a clinically oriented discipline, acknowledged by other branches of the medical and health professions.

Support by Other Medical Practitioners

It seems likely that psychiatrists have been particularly supportive of recreation as a valuable form of therapeutic experience because they were fully aware of the character of many mental hospitals. For almost a century, mental health care had been carried on in huge, impersonal, custodial institutions. Although treatment approaches varied from time to time, mental hospitals, like other large bureaucratic structures, tended to have an institutionalizing effect on both staff and patients. Patients in particular were robbed of their personal identities, treated in a dehumanized, mechanical way and totally regimented in their behavior. Recreation was recognized as a way of helping them become *people* again, reinforcing their sense of self, their pride in individual accomplishments and their effective relations with others.

However, psychiatrists were not the only physicians to give strong support to recreation. A leading heart research specialist, Dr. Joseph B. Wolffe, formerly President of the American College of Sports Medicine and Medical Director of the Valley Forge Medical Center and Heart Hospital, reported on the specific contribution of recreation in the treatment of patients suffering from acute thrombosis, congestive heart failure and allied illnesses:

> *A survey of 1,000 patients has shown that carefully selected recreation to suit the*
> *patient's problem and personality resulted in reduction both in drug requirements*
> *as well as length of hospital stay, when compared to the control group in the*
> *institution without the program.*[7]

It was found that a special activity program resulted in lessening drug requirements for various types of patients from 30 to 50 per cent and actually

---

[6] Robert H. Felix: Preface to *Recreation in Treatment Centers*, September, 1962, p. 3.
[7] Joseph B. Wolffe: *The Doctors and Recreation in the Medical Setting.* Raleigh, North Carolina, North Carolina Recreation Commission, 1962, p. 19.

shortened their hospital stay by approximately 15 per cent. As an example, Wolffe points out that in the treatment of neurocirculatory asthenia a reduction of 35 per cent in the need for sedatives and tranquilizers was noted as a consequence of a carefully planned patient recreation program.

The value of therapeutic recreation in the field of physical medicine and rehabilitation has been affirmed by Dr. Howard A. Rusk, Director of the Institute of Physical Medicine and Rehabilitation of the New York University-Bellevue Medical Center in New York City. An internationally known authority in the rehabilitation of the physically disabled, Rusk stressed the need for patients to become involved in their own rehabilitation and in the achievement of greater emotional, vocational and social self-sufficiency. He asked,

> *What good does it do for a chronically disabled person to learn to walk again if he is so withdrawn and fearful that he will not leave his home? For a handicapped child to realize his highest potential for physical functioning if his emotional and social growth is stunted in the process? For a post-psychiatric patient to be vocationally rehabilitated but unable to make further progress toward healthy social interaction with others?*[8]

Rusk pointed out that in rehabilitation centers disabled children spend a great deal of time following directions for ambulation and self-care exercises. Often, the recreation session gives them their only opportunity for independent action, with a minimum of adult direction, that will be helpful in achieving social and emotional maturity. Rusk was one of the first authorities to stress the need for providing recreation counseling that would help discharged patients achieve full social independence following their return to community life.

Summarizing these statements, it is apparent that leading practitioners recognize and support the need for recreation in hospital settings.

This recognition comes, in part, from an awareness of the value of recreation as an important element in the healthful living of *all* persons.

RECREATION'S CONTRIBUTION TO HEALTHFUL LIVING

Increasingly, we have come to recognize that all people need a degree of release, and the opportunity to fulfill certain fundamental drives, if they are to function effectively. The very concept of health implies far more than physical well-being alone. The Preamble to the Constitution of the World Health Organization states, "Health is a state of complete physical, mental and social well-being and not merely an absence of disease or infirmity."

Thus, to be healthy implies a harmonious interrelationship of all the elements of one's person—physical, social, emotional and intellectual. Among other elements, it implies the ability to work productively. However, work cannot be permitted to dominate our lives; instead, it must be balanced with recreation. Both work and recreation provide the opportunity for the exercise of one's powers, creative expression and accomplishment. Recreation's special contribution is the opportunity for refreshment of one's mind, body and spirit. Meyer points out

---

[8] Howard Rusk: "Therapeutic Recreation." *Hospital Management*, April 1960, pp. 35–36.

that recreation is the time during which we pause, change our pace and re-cover our energies in order to ease the strains and demands of a mechanized and competitive society. He writes,

> *The physiological concept of "stroke" and "glide" for the harmonious perfor-mance of any body organ applies equally to the total body operating as a syn-chronized machine in the execution of any task requiring the expenditure of energy. The "stroke" is the thrust, the "glide" the recovery. Our whole life is a continuous "stroke" and "glide" and psychologically the "stroke" is our work phase, our vocational pursuit, and the "glide" our recreation, our recovery. The harmonious relationship between work and recreation is essential for . . . good mental health.*[9]

This does not mean that recreation provides only relaxation. Particu-larly for those workers whose job is boring or monotonous or makes few physical demands, recreation may provide a challenge that is more demanding or exciting than work. For example, many individuals become far more involved and com-mitted in their play than in their jobs. Even the commitment of spectators in many forms of entertainment is often so great that it is not uncommon for sports fans to have cardiac seizures at major sports events.

Hans Selye, a physician who has done outstanding research and written extensively on the concept of stress, points out that it is a mistake to assume that rest and relaxation are necessarily desirable:

> *. . . simple rest is no cure-all. Activity and rest must be judiciously balanced, and* every person has his own characteristic requirements for rest and activity. *To lie motionless in bed all day is no relaxation for an active man. . . . Many a valuable man, who could still have given numerous years of useful work to society, has been made physically ill and prematurely senile by the enforcement of retirement at an age when his requirements and abilities for activity were still high. This psychosomatic disease is so common that it has been given a name:* retirement disease.[10]

Selye points out that one of the most fundamental laws regulating the activities of complex living beings is that no one part of the body must be dis-proportionately overworked for a long period. Stress serves as an equalizer of activities within the body; it helps to avoid one-sided exertion. It is necessary to achieve balance in the full range of activities if sound health is to be maintained.

Recreation can make an important contribution in helping individuals meet their total psychological and social needs. In a study of personality drives, Abraham Maslow suggested that human needs begin at a basic level related to maintaining existence or survival and that when these needs are satisfied, the individual moves on to progressively newer and higher levels of need. For example, the primary needs are for *physiological* well-being, based on maintaining adequate nutrition, freedom from the elements, avoidance of illness and similar threats to health. The second level of human need is based on the need for *safety*,

---

[9] Martin W. Meyer: "The Rationale of Recreation as Therapy." *Recreation in Treatment Centers*, September, 1962, p. 23.
[10] Hans Selye: *The Stress of Life*. New York, McGraw-Hill, 1956, p. 265.

Being in a wheelchair need not be a handicap! Participants release their arrows at an archery meet sponsored by the National Wheelchair Athletic Association, while another athlete competes in the shot-put, with a special guard to control the movement of her chair. Wheelchair basketball has also become extremely popular.

The intense urge to excel is shown in the faces of these severely disabled men and women competing in wheelchair racing, weight-lifting and other events sponsored by the National Wheelchair Athletic Association.

which Maslow characterizes as security, stability, freedom from fear or chaos—the need for structure, order and law. People normally prefer a safe, orderly, predictable and organized world.

Maslow points out that when both physical and safety needs are fairly well met, the individual will next require love and *affection*:

> He will hunger for (affectionate) relations with people in general . . . and will strive with great intensity to achieve this goal. He will feel sharply the pangs of loneliness, of ostracism, of rejection, of friendlessness, of rootlessness.[11]

On the next level, most people in society have a need or desire for a stable, firmly based and high evaluation of themselves, which Maslow refers to as *self-esteem*. This is closely related to the desire for strength, adequacy, a sense of mastery and competence, the capacity for independent action and recognition or appreciation from others. Following the satisfaction of the physical, safety, love and esteem needs, Maslow contends that there are significant needs for individual *self-actualization*, for satisfying the urge to *know and to understand* and, finally, *aesthetic needs*.

Within this context, it is easy to see how recreation provides a varied and rich opportunity to meet significant human psychological needs. Within our society, there are numerous examples of how such needs are not being met and how their deprivation causes serious effects on individual well-being.

The problem of human loneliness offers one such example. Even in a crowded society, many individuals lead lives of great loneliness. An Ohio State professor of psychiatry, John Whieldon, has found that loneliness is not so much an active phenomenon as a void—the incapacity to develop meaningful relations with others. He writes,

> One of the basic processes of childhood is to resolve one's loneliness. To do this, everyone must learn to make meaningful emotional contact with others.[12]

The lonely person, Whieldon believes, has never learned to do this or has lost the capacity for it. As a consequence, he falls back on a variety of defenses, such as sexual promiscuity, daydreaming, tantrums, narcissism, hyperactivity or the "last defense"—schizophrenia. Numerous studies have indicated the damaging effects of social isolation. The obvious value of recreational pursuits in overcoming the problem of loneliness and isolation is clear. Most leisure activities are carried on in group settings, and it is possible from earliest childhood to encourage participation in play groups, clubs, teams or musical or theater organizations that help youngsters develop the capacity for relating to others.

Tension, strain and boredom are also important characteristics of modern life. Recent research has indicated that about one person out of every four in the United States is using sedatives or tranquilizers. In some occupational groups or social classes today, the incidence of strain and tension is such that serious social and familial breakdown occurs at a high rate of frequency.

---

[11] Abraham Maslow: *Motivation and Personality*. New York, Harper and Row, 1970, pp. 35–50.
[12] John Whieldon: "A Study of Those 'Blues' That Start in Loneliness." *New York Post*, June 5, 1964, p. 77.

What this suggests is that many of our health-related problems in modern society stem from a sense of lack of involvement and physical release, from boredom and from the unfulfilled need for meaningful social contact. To illustrate, one might point to the extremely high incidence of such social diseases as addictive gambling, drug abuse and alcoholism. In a study of motivations for drinking, Riley, Marden and Lifshitz found that Americans drank for such reasons as the following: "to be sociable," "because all of our friends drink" or "to be a good sport." They concluded that drinking, at least until the point where it becomes a compulsive and destructive act, is carried on "for relaxation or for euphoric effect . . . as an escape from worries, responsibilities and frustration. . . ."[13]

Indeed, many forms of play or leisure activity represent self-destructiveness or harmful release of neurotic drives. Paul Haun has written extensively on so-called pathological play. In one form, an individual whose hate is self-directed may strive desperately *not* to win and may seek defeat, failure or even physical injury as a deserved punishment for feelings of guilt or personal crime. Beyond this, Haun saw play being distorted as a means of blotting out or resisting reality.

He described a number of forms of play that are extremely violent or dangerous, and afford almost completely unsublimated release for primitive drives, lending themselves "with exceptional ease to sadistic, masochistic, and compulsive distortion by the participant." Some of these types of play, such as speedboat and automobile racing, reckless mountain climbing, bullfighting or fencing with unprotected weapons, occupy a kind of twilight zone, slipping back and forth between pathology and wild adventure. Others are completely pathological in their self-destructive potential:

> *. . . the most notorious example being that of "Russian Roulette," which is played by spinning the cylinder of a revolver containing a single round of live ammunition, placing the muzzle of the gun at one's temple and pulling the trigger. Another example is the game of "Chicken," in which two contestants drive their automobiles toward each other at the highest possible speed on the same highway lane. The first to weaken and swerve out of the path of certain destruction is said to lose in this singular display of immaturity—and is accordingly labeled "chicken". . . .*[14]

Such examples reveal the ways in which play may serve as a release for harmful or self-destructive drives. In contrast, there are many forms of play that serve as a healthy and constructive means of maintaining emotional balance and preventing neurosis. As a single example that has become increasingly popular in recent years, one might cite the hobby of "back-packing" in the wilderness setting. This has become an enthusiastic interest of great numbers of Americans of all ages and walks of life; it has been estimated that, in recent years, no fewer than 20 million Americans have taken up this hobby. In part, the interest in wilderness hiking stems from a desire to get away from the artificiality and tension of city life. In part, it comes from the need to meet direct physical challenge and to find out what one is capable of doing and not doing.

The very fact of being able to play in constructive and self-enhancing ways is often an indicator of one's mental health and level of social adjustment.

---

[13] John W. Riley, Jr., Charles F. Marden and Marcia Lifshitz: *In* Eric Larrabee and Rolf Meyersohn: *Mass Leisure.* Glencoe, Illinois, The Free Press, 1958, pp. 327–330.
[14] Paul Haun, *op. cit.,* p. 26.

Typically, disturbed children and youth often show an inability to engage in normal forms of play activity; those committed to penal or correctional institutions often lack useful leisure skills. Play serves as a form of release for many kinds of drives that, if bottled up, might be seriously destructive to the individual. It represents a form of self-discovery, a way of knowing and, in its purest form, the opportunity to have fun for its own sake!

It is apparent, then, that for many persons who are not ill or disabled in any serious or permanent way, recreation serves to meet important psychosocial and physical needs. It may be constructively used or, when not understood and dealt with intelligently, may provide an outlet for harmful or dangerous drives that can result in great damage to the individual. For these reasons, it is essential that *all* individuals be aware of their leisure needs and behavior and that full opportunity be provided in the community at large for varied, creative and constructive recreational participation.

However, this problem is obviously far more acute for the ill or handicapped person than for those who do not suffer from any form of disability.

RECREATIONAL NEEDS OF THE DISABLED

As indicated earlier, the term "disability" is today regarded as preferable to "handicap" because it stresses the concept of disability, which may be overcome, rather than that of handicap, which has a negative connotation in our society. In this text, the term "disability" is used throughout, except in quotations from the past or titles of organizations or projects that continue to make use of the term "handicap."

A statement formulated by the 1960 White House Conference on Children and Youth defines the "handicapped" child as one who ". . . cannot play, learn, work or do the things other children his age can do; or is hindered in achieving his full physical, mental and social potentialities; whether by a disability which is initially small but potentially handicapping, or by a serious impairment involving several areas of function with the probability of life-long impairment."[15]

Disability may be mild or severe, single or multiple, and may affect persons of every age, socioeconomic condition, race, religion or region. It may stem from birth defects, environmental factors, illness, accident or a variety of other causes. Although the impairment may initially be of a purely physical nature, it may have secondary effects, or *sequelae*, that limit the individual's social involvement, affect him or her emotionally and create serious behavioral problems. The disabled person's potential as far as mobility, physical activity, education, holding a job and maintaining satisfying social relationships may all be seriously affected.

As indicated in Chapter 1, it has been estimated that as many as 68 million persons suffer from some significant degree of disability in American society. When one recognizes that for each such person there is also a family unit involved in the problem, it is apparent that meeting the total needs of disabled

---

[15] *Conference Proceedings.* White House Conference on Children and Youth. Washington, D.C., 1960, p. 381.

persons and helping them fit as successfully as possible into the total society represent crucial concerns in the United States and Canada today.

During the past several decades, there has been a radical shift in public concern about the disabled. Social work agencies today provide a variety of welfare services in community settings, youth houses, hospitals and residential centers for the disabled. The accent today has shifted to constructive, rehabilitative approaches in many of the most enlightened states.

To a large degree, the public has also shifted in its attitudes toward the disabled in society. In past centuries, the physically or mentally disabled were often seen as persons who had been cursed by the gods. Often they were cruelly rejected, hidden, ridiculed or even, in some cases, disposed of. We have not *totally* overcome these attitudes, either in the United States or elsewhere in the world. In a three-year study of attitudes toward the disabled, two German psychologists, Jansen and Esser, questioned several thousand adults and school-age children regarding their feelings toward disabled persons. They found a high incidence of continuing prejudice and aversion. Ignorance appeared to be a major obstacle to social contact with the disabled; those questioned did not seem to know how to approach or deal with the disabled realistically.

Jansen and Esser summarized their findings:

> *Although many of those questioned spoke sympathetically of their attitudes toward the handicapped . . . often they felt revulsion . . . few wished to be friends with them, or to marry one . . . most (63 percent) thought that severely disabled persons should be kept out of sight in institutions; while none recommended that they deserved to die, openly, actually some spoke carefully of the merits of euthanasia. . . .*[16]

It is apparent that many prejudices toward the disabled have not totally disappeared. Many people still have feelings that range from excessive pity (which overprotects the disabled person and makes him less likely to make independent efforts in his own behalf) to outright rejection and even fear. For example, a recent study by the New York State Department of Mental Hygiene revealed that the public feared former mental patients more than ex-convicts. Believing that they were dangerous and unpredictable, at least one-fourth of those surveyed said they would not want to live, work or socialize with former mental patients.

By and large, however, the view is becoming more widely accepted that disabled persons are in many ways like everybody else, with important physical, social and emotional needs that must be met if they are to reach their fullest potential as human beings. In many ways, federal, state and provincial governments have moved vigorously to promote total rehabilitation of the disabled. Increasingly, it has been recognized that disability tends to be linked with economic poverty. Mitchell and Hillman have written,

> *Evidence suggests that poverty has a direct relationship to higher than average percentages of illness and chronic disability. . . . A survey . . . by an agency of the U.S. Department of Health, Education and Welfare revealed that of persons receiving old age assistance 41 percent live in inadequate housing, 18 percent are blind or near blind, 29 percent have a disabling heart condition and 35 percent*

---

[16] "Hostility to the Handicapped." *Time*, December 20, 1971, p. 67.

live alone. . . . Damage done to a child by his environment during pregnancy will in most cases be permanent . . . the risks of the child of poverty are enormous and the expectant mother herself is usually a very poor risk for reproduction.[17]

Based on this knowledge, strenuous efforts were made in the 1960s to expand programs of vocational rehabilitation; federal support was given for research and training personnel and to the development of new facilities to serve the disabled. Demonstration projects were initiated for the physically disabled first and later for the mentally retarded, mentally ill, alcoholics, drug addicts, public offenders and disabled persons who were socially and culturally disadvantaged. Under the Rehabilitation Services Administration of the Department of Health, Education and Welfare, hundreds of thousands of disabled persons were served each year. Within this total context, recreation has become an increasingly recognized area of service for the disabled.

What is the specific justification for providing special therapeutic recreation service in community life? The answer is twofold.

1. Like all people, the disabled have a right to self-expression, social involvement, creative experience and the other important values that can be provided by recreation. They are human beings, and they and their families are taxpayers; thus, they should be served fully by public agencies in this field of service. This principle is illustrated by a statement in the "credo" of the American Recreation Society about the obligation of professional recreators:

That recreation is of, and for, all the people; and that therefore the purpose of [this] profession should be to administer Recreation as a public trust, so as to multiply opportunities for happiness regardless of age, race, sex, creed, or condition in life.[18]

2. The second principle is that many disabled individuals find most aspects of "normal" life, such as the opportunity to complete their education, marry and have a family, enter a profession and earn a livelihood or travel freely, closed to them. For this reason, recreation represents a particularly crucial need. If it is not provided, their lives are cruelly barren and empty. The author has pointed out elsewhere,

Those who suffer from disability . . . frequently find difficulty in meeting their recreative needs in constructive and varied ways, in part because serious physical handicaps obviously limit the extent of participation. . . . Much recreative deprivation of the disabled is, however, caused by the reluctance of society to permit them to engage in activity to the extent of their real potential. Sometimes communities or recreation agencies do not make the kinds of adaptations in the design of facilities needed for disabled persons to use them fully. Sometimes recreational and park agencies actively bar disabled persons from their programs because they feel that to serve them would require specialized leadership to a degree they could not afford.[19]

Frequently, park and recreation administrators fear that the presence of blind, retarded or orthopedically handicapped individuals might be distasteful

---

[17] Helen Jo Mitchell and William A. Hillman, Jr.: "Disability and the Disadvantaged." *In* Nesbitt, et al.: *Recreation and Leisure Service for the Disadvantaged.* Philadelphia, Lea and Febiger, 1971, p. 190.
[18] *Credo for the Recreation Profession.* Washington, D.C., American Recreation Society, n.d.
[19] Richard Kraus: *Recreation and Leisure in Modern Society.* Santa Monica, California, Goodyear, 1971, pp. 364–365.

to the public at large. Sometimes parents or relatives shelter disabled people excessively, and sometimes they are barred from recreational participation by their own lack of skill or fear of rejection by others. Whatever the reason, many disabled persons are therefore unable to make use of available community recreation resources.

The problem of acceptance in community life is particularly difficult for those who are visibly disabled. Those who suffer from a severe physical disability or crippling deformity are acutely aware of the reactions of others, the threat of social isolation and the direct limitations that are imposed in terms of one's capability for full and varied social involvement. Wright points out that while physical limitations themselves may cause frustration or suffering, the more serious deprivation comes from the attitudes of others:

> One of man's basic strivings is for acceptance by the group, for being important in the lives of others, and for having others count positively in his life. As long as physical disability is linked with shame and inferiority, realistic acceptance of one's position and one's self is precluded.[20]

The task of gaining acceptance for the disabled in community settings is primarily a matter of helping the public come to grips with its own attitudes about the disabled and to perceive them in a more accurate light. This can be accomplished in a variety of ways: through public meetings, demonstration projects, conferences and seminars and publication of articles and special reports. One ingenious approach used by first-year therapeutic recreation students at Mount Royal College, Calgary, Alberta, was to declare a community-wide Awareness Day to help focus public concern on the needs and capabilities of the disabled. All college students and faculty, as well as governmental officials and the public at large, were invited to take part in events concerning the disabled and to experience stimulated forms of disability, such as maneuvering about the college blindfolded or taking part in wheelchair sports. All local agencies were asked to set up information booths and to distribute literature. Killingsworth comments that

> . . . the primary purpose of the day was to try to make people aware . . . of the disabled and to let them experience a disability in the hope that this would help make them more empathetic of the disabled. Further, the assignment allowed the students the opportunity to find and utilize valuable community resources. . . .[21]

In all such efforts, it is important that the disabled be seen realistically, rather than in an exaggerated, overprotective way. Wright points out that people with disabilities are frequently considered to be compensating when they are merely interested in an activity; they may be regarded as showing a sense of inferiority when they are merely hesitating before committing themselves to an activity because of a realistic awareness of their own limitations. Thus, it becomes extremely important that our attitudes in general about the disabled be based on an intelligent comprehension of their needs and capabilities rather than on stereotyped and distorted attitudes.

---

[20] Beatrice Wright: *Physical Disability: A Psychological Approach.* New York, Harper and Row, 1960, p. 14.
[21] C. L. Killingsworth: "Awareness." *Therapeutic Recreation Journal*, 4th Quarter, 1975, p. 141.

This is particularly true with respect to the attitudes of families toward disabled members of the family unit. As pointed out earlier, relatives frequently tend to be overprotective and unconsciously limit the extent to which such individuals may strike out independently. A study carried out at the University of Pennsylvania, under a grant from the Social and Rehabilitation Service of the Department of Health, Education and Welfare, suggested that society sometimes has a vested interest in having its members remain disabled:

> *The disabled handicaps the family unit in many ways, most obviously economically and socially. Within the unit, the members attempt, with varying degrees of success, to "negotiate" a satisfying relationship. . . . Despite the sympathy that such a setup might draw from society . . . the interplay of dependent and helper often satisfies the deeper psychological needs of each individual, often retarding the handicapped person's rehabilitation.*[22]

In this study, it was found that the disabled person typically was not an independent entity but rather the hub of a complex set of family relationships that in effect creates a "disabled family." It was found that both the family and the larger society "use" the disabled, symbolically, to meet psychological needs and therefore are often reluctant to have them move toward true independent functioning.

For the sake of the disabled themselves and in the interest of their families and the larger society, it is essential that disabled persons become as independent as possible in terms of their social and recreational lives.

MAINSTREAMING AS A PRIMARY GOAL

In recent years, the effort to enable disabled persons to become integrated members of society on every level has become known as "mainstreaming." Gunn describes this as both a process and a goal and points out that it represents a major trend in modern life. Increasingly, we have sought to close down large, custodial facilities and serve disabled persons within the community wherever possible. More and more, they are becoming part of regular school classes and community programs—including integrated recreation activities. Gunn writes,

> *The principles of mainstreaming do not mean that handicapped people will be made "normal" but that they will have every opportunity to fit into society and that society will accept them. Handicapped people need to be moved as close as possible to the "norm" and those people who make up the norm must be educated about the needs of handicapped people.*[23]

Breaking down the prejudices and barriers that inhibit mainstreaming represents a twofold task. Obviously, it is necessary to educate the public at large, as Gunn suggests, to help them understand and accept the disabled more fully. However, it would be a mistake to assume that disabled persons themselves always *wish* to be integrated into ongoing community recreation programs. In

---

[22] Nancy Hicks: "Life of Disabled is Tied to Family." *New York Times*, September 14, 1969, p. 73.
[23] Scout Lee Gunn: "Mainstreaming is a Two-Way Street." *Journal of Physical Education and Recreation*, September, 1976, p. 48.

many cases, they are not psychologically ready for this step. Shivers and Fait write

> *The physically disabled individual may accept his permanent disability, but frequently he also feels fear, isolation, and sensitivity about the handicap. . . . He may view his disability as a shameful stigma, as a mark of inferiority, and something which must be kept from view. . . . Disabled people (may) feel that they are not really accepted as members of social groups. . . .*[24]

There are numerous examples of such attitudes. In many retirement communities for aged persons, residents actively resist having younger families—particularly those with children—live in the community. Frequently, when blind or deaf persons are encouraged to enter community recreation groups designed for the public at large, they respond with fear and resistance. Often, when discharged mental patients return to the hospital, it is because they feel unable to live independently in the community, whereas the hospital and its recreational and social programs represents a warm, accepting atmosphere to them. Geddes points out that, although the disabled person may *wish* to be accepted, previous negative life experiences may have resulted in poor psychosocial adjustment that makes it difficult to be accepted by others.

> *For example, previous frustration, difficulty and embarrassment due to an obvious physical deformity may develop into an adjustment mechanism such as aggression or withdrawal that interferes with group (acceptance). Sometimes the psychosocial problem ends up being a larger, more incapacitating handicap than the condition itself.*[25]

She also suggests that integration itself does not always result in desirable outcomes. For example, mentally retarded youngsters included in regular physical education or recreation activities are not always accepted and may have stronger feelings of rejection at the end of the experience than at the beginning. All this suggests that, although mainstreaming is a highly desirable goal, it cannot be easily or automatically achieved by administrative decisions or parental pressure alone. Instead, it requires a process of careful education, preparation and skilled leadership in order to succeed.

It is at this point that the interests of institutional or treatment centers and community-based recreational and social agencies coincide. Both must be dedicated to returning disabled persons to the community with skills and attitudes that will permit them to function as happily and effectively as possible within a broad range of relationships and interpersonal spheres.

This has led to the fundamental concept that therapeutic recreation cannot be viewed as a set of isolated services provided without overall direction but must be organized along a continuum in which all elements are effectively coordinated. In order to meet the needs of disabled persons at various levels of illness and recovery, it is necessary to develop a logical and orderly progression of services. In turn, these must be designed to fit within a meaningful model of therapeutic recreation service. Indeed, it would be a mistake to assume that *all* therapeutic recreation programs have a common or similar conceptual base.

---

[24] Jay S. Shivers and Hollis F. Fait: *Therapeutic and Adapted Recreational Services.* Philadelphia, Lea and Febiger, 1975, pp. 184–185.
[25] Dolores Geddes: "Physical Activity for Impaired, Disabled and Handicapped Individuals: What's Going On?" *In* Timothy Craig, ed.: *The Humanistic and Mental Health Aspects of Sports, Exercise and Recreation.* Chicago, American Medical Association, 1975, p. 105.

They differ widely, according to the sponsoring agency and its philosophy of service.

MODELS OF THERAPEUTIC RECREATION SERVICE

Authorities in this field have identified a number of sharply contrasting approaches to the provision of therapeutic recreation service. For example, Martin describes four such approaches: (1) *fun and games,* in which recreation is seen essentially as a casual or peripheral experience to be carried on outside of the significant therapeutic program of the treatment center; (2) *personal adjustment,* in which recreation is used to help the patient to adjust to his changed life circumstances, to understand and accept his illness or disability and to improve his morale and reduce anxiety; (3) *medical approach,* in which recreation is seen as an integral part of the therapeutic process, with careful prescription of areas of participation intended to contribute to recovery; and (4) *educative,* in which strong emphasis is given to helping the patient develop broader recreative horizons through teaching skills and counseling that will help to prevent residual disability and insure a successful return to community life.[26]

Similarly, O'Morrow has outlined five basic models of therapeutic recreation: (1) *custodial;* (2) *medical-clinical;* (3) *therapeutic milieu;* (4) *education and training;* and (5) *community models.*[27]

CUSTODIAL MODEL

The custodial model refers to maintaining or acting as guardian for special populations in such institutions as nursing homes, homes for the aged, mental hospitals, special schools for the mentally retarded and correctional centers. In such situations, there tends to be a strong effort to maintain order and conformity, to subordinate individual needs to institutional routines and to use varied forms of pressure, even punishment, to enforce administrative policies. In general, this model is no longer in vogue, although it persists to a degree in some large state institutions or in correctional and penal programs.

Recreation is not usually seen as a significant form of service in such settings; indeed, custodial programs tend to offer only limited forms of other rehabilitative modalities. Often, professionally qualified leaders are not employed, and activities consist primarily of movies, dances, mass entertainment and, as in penal institutions, team sports that tend to work off hostility and aggression. Goffman, in his analysis of mental hospitals, prisons and similar custodial structures, comments,

> *Every total institution can be seen as a kind of dead sea in which little islands of vivid, encapturing activity appear. Such activity can help the individual withstand the psychological stress usually engendered by assaults upon the self. Yet it is precisely in the insufficiency of these activities that an important deprivational effect of total institutions can be found.*[28]

---

[26] Fred W. Martin: "Therapeutic Recreation Practice: A Philosophic Overview." *Leisurability*, Ottawa, Canada, January, 1974, p. 22.

[27] Gerald S. O'Morrow: *Therapeutic Recreation: A Helping Profession.* Reston, Virginia, Reston, 1976, Chapter Seven.

[28] Erving Goffman: *Asylums.* Garden City, New York, Doubleday-Anchor, 1961, pp. 69–70.

In custodial institutions, therefore, recreation may be used to "kill time," as well as provide some sense of release from formality and task orientation that normally govern inmate-staff contacts. With voluntary participation, patients or prisoners are permitted to make choices and, to some degree, have a sense of being individuals within the overall institutional framework. Annual parties or Christmas celebrations also help to break down barriers and provide a favorable public image—particularly when the institution is being visited by relatives of inmates or government officials—that may have little to do with the normal, on-going life of the institution. Finally, recreation may serve to provide rewards or, when withdrawn, punishments, and reinforce the societal structure and behavioral expectations of the institution through varied forms of ceremonies, patient or prisoner councils, newspapers and similar activities.

MEDICAL-CLINICAL MODEL

Over the past several decades, this has been the most familiar model for institutionally based recreation service. It is characterized, in O'Morrow's words, by a "doctor-centered, illness-oriented approach to patient care and treatment." Emphasis is placed on illness or disease, rather than on the whole person, and recreation depends heavily on the diagnosis made by the physician and his prescriptions for needed activity. It is best illustrated within traditional psychiatric hospital settings, in which the doctor in charge of a ward or treatment unit works with the recreation therapist to design patient treatment plans that utilize recreation as a specific modality addressed to specific patient needs.

Rosen writes knowledgeably of the needs of psychiatric patients and the ways in which recreation may be used as a specific tool in their treatment. She makes clear that the characteristics of psychiatric patients are such that it is not possible to present activities to them as "normal" people might visualize recreation:

> Certainly anyone who has worked with paranoid patients or with guilt-ridden, self-destructive personalities knows that even the most common events of everyday life, eating and sleeping, are frequently connected with fearful and anxiety-provoking fantasies. . . . The peculiar defensive systems erected by psychotic patients shut out and distort the environment and the people in it so that ordinary channels for communication and social interaction are obstructed. Psychiatric treatment is first and foremost concerned with breaking down these barriers, with whatever means are available. It attempts to enable the patient to function within the framework of the social community. Recreative experiences can be utilized to serve this purpose only when they are adapted to the particular needs of the individual patient. Finding the areas of accessibility to psychotic and emotionally disturbed patients may involve a great deal of experimentation in a variety of media. Resourcefulness and imagination in the adaptation of techniques are required. . . .[29]

Although it is possible to make such generalized statements as "strenuous physical activities or certain arts and crafts activities are useful for the release of aggression and hostility" or "group social activities are indicated for withdrawn or isolated patients," these *are* just generalizations. Often, the need

---

[29] Elizabeth R. Rosen: "The Selection of Activities for Therapeutic Use." *Recreation in Treatment Centers*, September, 1962, p. 30.

to develop a convincing statement of the purpose of a field may lead to precise "laundry lists" of needs and recommended activities, that are superficial and misleading. Rosen points out that many of the personal elements intrinsic to the recreative experience defy a systematized method of cataloguing. She comments that it is hazardous to ascribe a specific therapeutic effect to a particular activity:

> *The practice of listing categories of activities into which patients with specific types of psychopathology can be neatly fitted is little more than a convenience devised by efficient management. In the hands of untrained personnel, the fallacies of such "systems" of selection are obvious.*[30]

The treatment of the patient must be directed by the psychiatrist who makes the diagnosis, charts the various techniques or modalities that are to be used with him and evaluates his progress. The recreation specialist must work as part of the treatment team, using the tools of his profession with sensitivity to psychological needs. He plans a sequence of recreation experiences, appraising the patient's reactions and behavior, modifying his approach to use those activities that evoke the most constructive behavior and abandoning those that are unsuccessful.

It is necessary in programming to identify the specific therapeutic objectives for each patient and to analyze the structure and characteristics of each activity. Rosen writes,

> *It is important to know what physical skills and what degree of emotional maturity each activity might require to ensure satisfying participation. Some activities allow for a wide range of abilities, and their organization, materials and methods of presentation can be altered to accommodate many different individual needs. Other activities have a definite structural form and pre-requisite skills which limit their potential accessibility.*[31]

It is necessary, when selecting activities for patient involvement, not to rely on classic diagnostic categories as much as on specific observable symptoms, such as disturbances in communication, social control, reality testing and interpersonal relationships.

THERAPEUTIC MILIEU MODEL

Although this approach also seeks to use recreation as a significant therapeutic tool in treatment programs, it stems from a markedly different philosophy. Instead of viewing mental illness as a distinct form of disease that can be cured by the physician, those who use the therapeutic milieu model tend to see it more as a problem stemming from the patient's inability to deal realistically and effectively with his or her environment.

In the therapeutic milieu, the patient is reeducated in terms of attitudes or modes of behavior that will equip him or her to return to the community, family, job and other environments. Every aspect of the hospital or mental health center environment is an important element in treatment, and all staff members play an important therapeutic role. Within this framework, patients

---

[30] *Ibid.*
[31] *Ibid.*, p. 31.

are responsible for their own healthy behavior. Instead of being prescribed *for*, they are encouraged to make choices and decisions for themselves. In contrast to the medical-clinical model of care, where the physician is the major source of decision-making, in the therapeutic milieu model, all staff members share meaningfully in discussing patient needs and planning programs with them.

EDUCATION AND TRAINING MODEL

In institutions following this model, various forms of activity therapy are used to overcome physical, psychological or social disability and to equip the patient or client for independent community living. This approach is followed in a wide range of rehabilitation settings, including special schools for the mentally retarded, sheltered workshops, homes for the disturbed and correctional and penal centers.

Strong emphasis is placed on occupational therapy, remedial education, vocational training and similar modalities in order to improve the patient's skills, self-concept and social values. Individuals must learn a range of useful skills and interests and must develop favorable attitudes about taking part in them. Bizarre behavior or appearance that tends to repel others (as in the case of many mentally retarded individuals) must be overcome and healthy forms of self-management substituted. Patients and clients learn to seek out appropriate activities and facilities, often with the help of recreation therapists. Particularly in the case of the physically disabled, an important component of therapeutic recreation services lies in helping them learn again to travel around the community to available recreational programs, events and facilities. In the case of such groups as the cerebral palsied, recreation may represent the area of service in which problems of human sexuality, courtship or family living are dealt with meaningfully, again as a means of helping the disabled enter as fully as possible into community life and realize their full potential as human beings (see Chapter 7).

COMMUNITY MODEL

A flaw in several of the models just described is that they describe the role of recreation within the institution as one of preparing individuals to return to community life, and fail to deal with the issue of the community's readiness to accept the disabled person. Realistically, patients are discharged from many institutions only to live in neighborhoods where there are *no* clubs, centers or special interest groups they can join—either on a segregated or integrated basis.

The community model, then, implies that a critical aspect of recreation service for the disabled lies in the provision of a wide range of leisure opportunities geared to meeting their needs. Essentially, these are provided by three types of sponsors: (a) public recreation and park departments (b) voluntary agencies with a specific concern for the disabled and (c) therapeutic agencies or institutions that develop their own "out-reach" or "satellite" programs to serve outpatients or other disabled persons living in the community. Such programs may operate on a segregated basis, serving the disabled in special groups, and may also promote mainstreaming by establishing integrated groups serving both normal and special populations. Leadership may come from varied sources—professional, lay and volunteer—and may perform a wide variety of functions, including those of planning, organizing, leading, teaching, public relations, fund-raising, promoting legislation and social action and a host of other needed tasks.

In general, none of the models just described exist exclusive of the others. Even custodial institutions today tend to provide some degree of education and training, and certainly the clinical-medical model has been markedly influenced in most settings by the therapeutic milieu approach. Within all such settings certain principles of therapeutic recreation tend to apply. One of the most important of these principles deals with the need to develop a logical continuum of recreation service in order to best meet patient or client needs.

THERAPEUTIC RECREATION AS A CONTINUUM

This concept may be illustrated in three ways: (a) a description of the *sequence of settings* for therapeutic recreation; (b) an analysis of the principles of *progressive patient care*; and (c) a presentation of *levels of involvement* by patients, with respect to voluntary choice of activity, and personal motivation.

Sequential Settings for Therapeutic Recreation

This may best be demonstrated with respect to psychiatric care. Today, every effort is made to prevent hospitalization in the first place, through the dispersal of community mental health centers that can lead to early diagnosis of illness and the provision of special clinic services that can assist in keeping the patient functioning in the community. However, if this approach does not work and if the patient must be hospitalized because of an acute condition, the following sequence of settings for therapeutic recreation may be developed.

1. *Full hospitalization.* While the patient is undergoing treatment on an inpatient basis, every effort is made to maintain contact with family and community groups through recreation programs. Outside organizations may provide parties, entertainments and similar programs. Patients themselves may move into the community on special trips and visits. At the same time, a process of recreation counseling is developed that helps the patient to become aware of the role of recreation and leisure in his own life and to develop a positive attitude—as well as knowledge and recreative skills—with respect to future participation.
2. *Partial hospitalization.* Increasingly, instead of discharging patients directly from a custodial setting into complete freedom, the practice is developing of having them visit their homes for weekends or work during the day and return to the hospital at night. An important ingredient in this process is to have patients who are undergoing this process of gradual resocialization take part in community-based recreation activities and social programs. Hospital personnel working closely with community leaders may refer patients directly, assist them with transportation, brief the receiving agency about them and continue to assist them in a variety of ways.
3. *Post-discharge arrangements.* In a number of communities, "halfway houses" or special social clubs have been provided for discharged mental patients or for those who are undergoing day-clinic treatment. In addition to other services, such as educational, counseling or vocational training, such programs may offer a variety of recreational activities to ease the transition of the former patient back into community life.

Similar sequences may be found in other types of disability groupings. Mentally retarded adolescents or young adults may move from a special school or home, to a sheltered workshop or residence in the community, to full social independence. At each stage along the way, therapeutic recreation may be designed to meet current needs for constructive leisure activity and to contribute to the process of education and growing capability for community living.

Principles of Progressive Patient Care

This concept is fundamental to every aspect of medical treatment or rehabilitation. It implies that at each stage of the patient's illness and recovery all aspects of treatment are geared to providing maximum benefit and moving him along constructively to the next stage. For example, in an early description of therapeutic recreation service in a military hospital for physically injured or orthopedic patients, service was carried on in the following way:

1. *Post-operative and post-traumatic phase. Here, the emphasis is placed on medical care, and on helping the patient make a healthy initial adjustment to the fact of his injury and the period of hospitalization that he must face. At this stage, the recreation specialist makes an early contact with the patient, and identifies interests that may be developed in the following stages.*
2. *Traction Phase. Here, the patient is confined to bed, and obviously limited in mobility, although not under intensive medical care. The emphasis is on providing individual attention to the patient, and helping him occupy his time creatively, by use of such activities as games, arts and crafts and other pursuits that may be carried on individually, with limited mobility.*
3. *Ambulatory Phase. In this stage, the patient is able to move around the hospital, and to take part in varied activities of an individual interest, small-group, or mass nature. The effort here should be on reinforcing old interests and developing new ones that may be appropriate to the residual handicap left by the injury suffered—building on the strengths of the patient, and opening up new areas of recreational involvement for him.*
4. *Disposition Phase. Here, the emphasis is placed on providing experiences that will strengthen the patient's ability to meet his own recreation needs independently, and to develop associations and community involvements that will carry over effectively, following discharge from the hospital. It is at this stage that the recreation counseling process described earlier is most important.*[32]

Although this analysis deals with the physically impaired, a similar approach would obviously apply to psychiatric patients—the distinction being that their process of recovery would not be as likely to fit into such easily categorized phases.

Levels of Patient Involvement

Initially, it is often difficult for patients to make appropriate leisure choices; they may lack skills and interests, which compels others to make choices for them.

---

[32] Staff of Oliver General Hospital: "We Prescribe Recreation." *Journal of Health, Physical Education and Recreation*, November, 1951, pp. 12–13.

When a patient is *required* to do something, it may not have the desired elements of free choice, self-discovery and pleasure that true recreation can provide. It is the subjective experience of the patient that is most important. As Haun points out, a ball game is not necessarily recreation, but the absorbed involvement of the patient is. Prescribing calisthenics, softball or dancing may simply result in the patient undergoing exercise without receiving the values to be derived from true recreation.

Yet, it often is not possible to rely on the patient's self-motivation to bring him into activity. Both psychiatric and physically disabled persons frequently tend to resist involvement. Streeter writes,

> It is terribly hard for seriously damaged people to reconcile themselves to their disabilities. Some of them spend months or years evading the issue by trying vainly to live as they did before their accident or illness. Families, struggling with their own feelings about a disabled patient, may drift away while he is in hospital. Permanent disability and long-term hospitalization often make for apathy and despair. . . . The complex pathology of the severely disabled, deeply troubled patient makes it specially urgent for him to take initiative and decide for himself what he wants to do.[33]

What solution is there for this dilemma? Obviously, recreation may be offered on different levels in institutional settings:

> Recreation can be offered as an informal, completely voluntary form of activity in the hospital program, often on a mass or large-group basis, without any close relationship to other adjunctive therapies or medical guidance and direction. In such situations, it clearly should not be designated as therapeutic. On the other hand, when it is medically oriented, guided, and approved, related to pathology, modified or adapted to meet individual patients' needs, interests, and capabilities, and when it has certain specific goals of rehabilitation in mind, it deserves the title.
>
> What is important is that, even when it is "prescribed" for a given patient, the activity should not be approached in a compulsory fashion. A patient may be introduced to the activity, encouraged to participate, and given help—but cannot be forced to take part—or it is no longer recreation. Thus, the recreation worker will need to be ingenious in his effort to motivate patients and (particularly with psychiatric patients, who often are extremely withdrawn and reluctant to take part in recreation) fairly strong in his efforts to persuade. In the final analysis, however, unless the patient comes to the point of selecting activities for participation voluntarily . . . the approach will not have been successful.[34]

This varied approach to "prescribed" versus "voluntary" participation is illustrated in the breakdown of recreation program activities found in Veterans Administration hospitals. There, three major phases of recreation have traditionally been provided:

> 1. General: both active and passive services throughout the hospital, in the auditorium, recreation lounge, outdoor areas, dayrooms and on wards. Only a general clearance for these activities is required, usually obtained from the Chief of Staff and the chiefs of clinical services.

---

[33] George Streeter: "Art Studio: Therapy in an Institutional Setting." *Information Center, Recreation for the Handicapped Newsletter*, July–August, 1971, p. 1.
[34] Richard Kraus: *Recreation Today: Program Planning and Leadership.* Santa Monica California, Goodyear, 1977, p. 184.

2. *Specialized:* activities designed to meet needs based on specific disabilities, particularly of long-term patients in groups. This phase of the program is developed by the cooperative efforts of the medical and recreation staff, usually with recreation workers being assigned to specific services and developing programs for them.
3. *Prescribed:* individualized services which may be provided for individual patients at the specific request of the patient's physician, based on his needs, progress, and past participation in recreation.[35]

To cite another specific example, in a large home for disturbed and dependent boys, recreational opportunities are provided on four levels of participation: (1) *leisure education,* consisting of classes in recreational skills provided during the school day as part of the actual curriculum; (2) *after-school group activities,* in which cottages or units of boys take part as a group in activities scheduled for them on a rotating basis by the recreation staff and cottage parents or unit directors; (3) *individual selection of workshops,* in which each youngster takes part in activities such as music, arts and crafts or nature activities based on his own wishes and conferences with his counselors as well as unit team recommendations; and (4) *voluntary campus-wide participation,* consisting of voluntary involvement in school programs, teams, trips or special events. The principle underlying this structure is that each child needs all four elements: required instruction in skills, participation as part of his living-unit group, activities specially suited to his needs and interests and totally voluntary involvement, or noninvolvement, if he wishes, in community-wide programs.

INNER AND OUTER MOTIVATION

Seen more abstractly, patient participation should be helped to move along a continuum that extends from outer-directed involvement toward self-motivated, voluntary activity. Ball has developed a model of this continuum:

EXPERIENCE	TYPE OF TIME	MAJOR MOTIVATION
1. Activity for sake of activity	Obligated time	Drive is outer directed
2. Recreation education	Obligated time	Drive is outer directed
3. Therapeutic recreation	Unobligated time	Motivation is inner directed but choice of experiences is limited
4. Recreation	Unobligated time	Motivation is inner directed

On the *first* level, the patient engages in any activity, such as music, games or art, without conscious goals or purpose other than to provide reality orientation or diversion. Activity is carried on in time scheduled for recreation, with choice determined by the therapeutic recreation specialist.

On the *second* level, the individual is specifically counseled into activities that are based on an assessment of his needs and interests; the purpose of this phase is to help him develop constructive attitudes, knowledge and skills with respect to recreation and leisure.

---

[35] *Orientation Manual, Physical Medicine and Rehabilitation.* Washington, D.C., Veterans Administration Department of Medicine and Surgery, March, 1966.

On the *third* level, the patient begins to select therapeutically oriented activities in which he wishes to participate, within the hospital setting.

Finally, on the *fourth* level, the individual is free to engage in whatever activity he wishes in his unobligated time; this is simply viewed as recreation, and is the ultimate goal of the entire process.

Similarly, Frye and Peters have presented a sequence of stages showing how participants move from a situation in the clinical setting, in which the therapeutic recreation specialist exerts primary authority, to involvement in the community in which they are free to select and carry on their own choice of activity. This model involves five stages:

1. *Recreator administers highly structured program under medical orders.*
2. *Recreator "sells" program to patient, motivates patient to participate.*
3. *Recreator and patient construct program together.*
4. *Recreator advises patient and community.*
5. *Patient free to participate in any activity available to him.*[36]

Obviously, in some situations, such as nursing home settings, with a number of severely regressed residents who have suffered organic brain deterioration, it may not be possible for participants to exercise meaningful choices; it may be necessary for the recreation leader to select and direct all activities.

THE SELECTION OF APPROPRIATE ACTIVITY

A final area of concern, with respect to the development of effective therapeutic recreation programs, has to do with the selection and provision of organized programs of activity. On what basis should activities be chosen? Obviously, they must be appropriate in terms of meeting the overall goals of rehabilitation and therapeutic recreation service. However, to what extent are they to be geared to meeting the needs of patients in specific diagnostic categories?

Shivers and Fait stress that the therapeutic process in general should not be regarded as a science in which regimens can be selected with an absolute confidence in their effect. Instead, it should be regarded as an art, dealing with "the vagaries of human nature and personality... without the precision... which permits valid and reliable conclusions to be drawn."[37] In essence, this is probably truer about recreation than other forms of therapy, chiefly because it represents such an indefinable, subjective kind of experience and depends so much on the individual participant's leisure tastes and psychosocial needs for its effect.

This question is related to the issue, discussed earlier, of whether recreation *should* be regarded as a form of therapy. It has two subelements: (a) whether recreation is *comparable* to other therapies and (b) whether placing emphasis on it as a therapy does not actually *diminish its value* for patients.

Paul Haun has taken the position that when recreation is conceived of and presented as a therapy, it may lose some of its key benefits and, further,

---

[36] Virginia Frye and Martha Peters: *Therapeutic Recreation: Its Theory, Philosophy, and Practice.* Harrisburg, Pennsylvania, Stackpole Books, 1972, p. 43.
[37] Shivers and Fait, *op. cit.,* p. 2.

that it is *not* comparable to other medical techniques. He writes,

> *The hospital recreation worker performs many services essential, in my opinion, to the welfare of the patient. I cannot, however, regard any of them as therapeutic, first because I have never been convinced that recreation in any of its forms is a specific instrument for the modification of a disease process comparable say to penicillin in the treatment of syphilis; second, because I am so fully persuaded of the psychiatric patient's need for recreation as recreation that I grudge any dilution of its potency through adulteration with alternative purposes. . . . It is because I believe that recreation is an essential human need that I want it for my patients.*[38]

On the other hand, an equally distinguished physician, Howard Rusk, has stated: "I firmly believe that both individual and group recreation for patients have a direct relationship upon their recovery—these, in my opinion, are definitely adjunctive therapy."[39]

Therapy has been defined as a "planned conscious intervention intended to produce a change." Such an intervention must involve techniques that are not passive, accidental or happenstance but are known, understood and demonstrable. It may be reasonably argued that a variety of widely used therapeutic techniques *do not have* predictable and measurable effects. For example, psychotherapy itself is applied in many forms and with varied degrees of success. Certainly, no psychiatrist or psychoanalyst is able to predict that a given patient will progress at a certain rate or that a particular approach will ensure recovery. It is probably less important to argue about whether recreation should be categorized as therapy than it is to plan and present recreation so that it offers maximum benefits to disabled persons—however it is described. This process typically follows a sequence of several stages:

1. Assessment or diagnosis of patient or client's overall status and need for recreational experiences or other forms of growth or service that may be provided by recreation.
2. Identification of specific goals for therapeutic recreation.
3. Selection of appropriate activities or experiences to meet these goals.
4. Planning and implementation of programs involving these activities or experiences.
5. On-going monitoring of participation and evaluation of program's effectiveness.

Within this sequence, which is described in more detail in Chapter 4, the actual selection of activities and experiences depends heavily on the goals identified. Therapeutic recreation, broadly speaking, may be said to have three major levels of service: *supportive, reeducative* and *reconstructive.* Avedon describes each of these:

> *As a supportive modality, therapeutic recreation service aims to strengthen personality aspects that are not yet affected. As a re-educative modality, focus is upon enabling an individual to make use of existing potentialities even though some limitation is present. As a reconstructive modality, service is tailored to an individual's condition and situation, and is usually part of an interprofessional effort.*[40]

---

[38] Paul Haun: "Hospital Recreation—A Medical Viewpoint." In *Recreation for the Mentally Ill.* Washington, D.C., American Association for Health, Physical Education and Recreation, 1958, pp. 57–58.
[39] Howard Rusk: *Basic Concepts of Hospital Recreation.* Washington, D.C., American Recreation Society, 1953, p. 7.
[40] Elliott M. Avedon: *Therapeutic Recreation Service: An Applied Behavioral Science Approach.* Englewood Cliffs, New Jersey, Prentice-Hall Inc., 1974, p. 24.

He goes on to point out that each level of service tends to be useful for a different category of disability. *Supportive* service, for example, is generally most useful for those with chronic physical or mental disabilities living in long-term residential settings or served by community agencies. *Reeducative* service is particularly useful with the retarded or those who have suffered a significant physical impairment and who must learn, or re-learn, to live in the community as independently as possible. *Reconstructive* service, in his view, is geared primarily to serving psychiatric patients.

In settings based on the clinical-medical model, the physician in charge tends to play a dominant role, although, once having made a broad assessment of the patient's needs, he may delegate the actual identification of needed activities to the appropriate therapist. In settings following the therapeutic milieu approach, patients and clients obviously have a stronger voice in activity selection and program planning—sometimes on an individual basis and sometimes through group planning or patient councils or committees. Within each major category of disability, then, both the activities themselves and their manner of selection may vary considerably, as shown in Chapters 5 through 9.

In any given situation, it is likely that those responsible for the institution or special program will define their objectives in written form before initiating programs. For example, a day camping program provided for retarded children by Camp Spindrift, a project of the Recreation Center for the Handicapped in San Francisco, has the following objectives:

1. To provide fun in the out-of-doors.
2. To offer satisfying contacts with nature, so that the camper may acquire a sense of being at home in the out-of-doors.
3. To provide opportunities for group and individual experiences in a natural environment; to join in and contribute to a plan of living for a day, a week, or more.
4. To foster the growth of independence and self-direction in each camper.
5. To acquire new skills, hobbies, and interests that have long-time values.
6. To arouse a sense of curiosity, stimulate spontaneous expression, provide enjoyment, and accelerate the learning process.
7. To provide opportunities for new experiences, for emotional satisfaction, and for spiritual growth.
8. To foster better mental and physical health, courage, and confidence and to exercise mind and body in healthful activity.
9. To offer a range of experiences that will help to prepare the campers for resident camping.
10. To provide opportunities for the development of initiative, leadership, and a sense of responsibility.[41]

It is apparent that these goals are identical to those that might be cited for *any* day camp program. However, in order to achieve them and to make the program meaningful in terms of the special needs of retarded children, it is necessary to provide a higher degree of skilled leadership, a better ratio of leaders to children, a modification of program activities and a much more individualized approach to supervision than in normal programs. For retarded children, these program goals are particularly vital and may contribute significantly to the socialization, growing maturity and improving self-concept of the campers.

---

[41] *Report on Camp Spindrift*, Recreation Center for the Handicapped, San Francisco, California, Summer, 1968, p. 22.

CONCLUDING STATEMENT OF PURPOSES

Summing up the rationale presented in this chapter, the following important goals of therapeutic recreation service may be listed. It is obvious that they vary widely, depending upon the group being served, the nature and degree of disability and the setting in which the service is provided.

General Objectives of Therapeutic Recreation Service

1. To provide constructive, enjoyable and creative leisure activities, seen as a general need for persons of all ages and backgrounds.
2. To improve morale and a sense of well-being and interest in life, as opposed to depression and disinterest or withdrawal.
3. To help individuals come to grips with their disabilities and build positively on their existing strengths and capabilities.
4. To help individuals gain security in being with others and develop healthy, outgoing social relationships and a feeling of group acceptance.
5. To emphasize positive self-concepts and feelings of individual worth through successful participation in activity.
6. To help individuals gain both skills and attitudes that will assist them in using their leisure in positive and constructive, as opposed to negative and pathological, ways.
7. To help hospitalized patients build bridges for the successful return to community life.
8. To contribute to a sense of community in the hospital or in group life and to promote an atmosphere in which it becomes possible to make progress toward recovery.
9. To give experience in mastering simple tasks and reality situations that may be of prevocational value.

Specific Objectives of Therapeutic Recreation Service

In addition to these universal goals, therapeutic recreation service also has very specific objectives that focus on the needs of the population being served. The following list suggests a number of the high-priority objectives of recreation service for specific populations; they are explored in more detail in Chapters 5 through 9.

1. For disabled persons living in the community, to provide activities that they can share constructively with their families or that they can carry on independently, thus minimizing their dependence on their families.
2. For psychiatric patients, to provide a positive means of releasing aggression or hostility harmlessly, relating to others constructively, coming to grips with reality and gaining leisure interests that will contribute to mental health.
3. For the mentally retarded, to promote both physical, social and intellectual functioning, to assist in developing social independence and to promote confidence and the ability to function in community settings.
4. For the physically disabled, to provide new skills and interests that compensate for lost functions or abilities, to provide practice in self-care skills and to assist in reintegration in community recreation programs.
5. For the socially maladjusted, to assist in learning to develop effective social relations with others, to use leisure constructively, to learn to accept the values and rules of the larger society and to teach qualities of good sportsmanship and fair play.
6. For aged persons, to provide continuing social involvement, creative satisfactions and the opportunity to be of community service.

GUIDELINES FOR THE PROVISION OF
THERAPEUTIC RECREATION SERVICE

Finally, a number of guidelines for the provision of therapeutic recreation service are provided here:

1. Whenever possible, self-choice rather than compulsion should be stressed in the selection of activities.
2. Individuals should be encouraged to develop their own philosophy of leisure involvement, as true expressions of their own personality.
3. Activities should be provided that can be carried over independently in the community, after the process of rehabilitation is completed.
4. Emphasis should be placed on activities that contribute to the participant's feeling of competence and accomplishment.
5. Whenever possible, programs should be planned with the full involvement of those who are to be served.
6. The disabled should be integrated with the nondisabled, whenever possible, in carrying on recreational activities.
7. Emphasis should be placed on the strengths and existing abilities of participants rather than on their impairments or pathological aspects.
8. Service must include far more than simply providing diversional activities; instead, it must include varied forms of group therapy or activities geared to develop competence in daily living, when appropriate. Similarly, therapeutic recreation specialists must be more than activity leaders; they must also be prepared to assume the role of counselors, community organizers, advocates and members of the treatment team.

Other guidelines dealing with the actual planning, organization and presentation of therapeutic recreation programs are presented in later chapters of this text.

SUGGESTED TOPICS FOR
CLASS DISCUSSIONS OR
STUDENT PAPERS

1. Outline the ways in which recreation is an important component of healthy living for all persons; relate these to the process of rehabilitation for ill and disabled persons.

2. Present the arguments for and against considering recreation as a specific form of therapy and take a position on this issue.

3. Show how therapeutic recreation operates as a continuum in both institutional and community-based settings.

4. Briefly summarize the characteristics of three of the different models of therapeutic recreation service presented in this chapter and show how they would apply to programming for a specific type of disability.

chapter 3

Professional Development in Therapeutic Recreation Service

This chapter examines therapeutic recreation service as a career field today. It outlines its background and origins and describes the settings in which therapeutic recreation personnel are employed, as well as their job functions. It describes the past and present roles of professional organizations in therapeutic recreation, with special emphasis being given to current efforts to improve the selection process through registration, certification and licensing and to present trends in higher education in the field. It explains the nature of other activity therapies whose personnel have close working relationships with recreation specialists and concludes with an appraisal of therapeutic recreation's present image and status as an area of professional service.

EARLY DEVELOPMENT OF EMPLOYMENT IN THERAPEUTIC RECREATION

Professional specialization in therapeutic recreation did not suddenly spring into being as an independent area of service. Instead, it gradually developed in a variety of settings, often with personnel with training in other fields assuming responsibility for it.

There were four major stages in the development of therapeutic recreation service:

1. *General responsibility*. During the early decades of this century, responsibility for supervising or providing recreation tended to be seen as a general responsibility, shared by such practitioners as adapted or corrective physical educators, occupational therapists, physical therapists, nurses, attendants and other ward personnel.
2. *Beginning specialization*. Beginning in the 1930s, but more pronouncedly after World War II, individuals were employed on a wide scale who had a *special* responsibility for recreation and were known as "hospital recreation workers," "medical recreation workers," or similar titles. They were employed chiefly in large federal and state

hospitals, particularly those concerned with mental illness and long-term care. In some settings, they had the title of "recreation therapist."

3. *Recognition of the field.* By the 1950s and 1960s, there began to be a much wider use of recreation specialists in institutions serving special populations. These institutions included homes and training schools for retarded or emotionally disturbed children and adolescents, centers for physical rehabilitation, nursing homes and, to a lesser degree, penal institutions. At the same time, the term "therapeutic recreation" became widely accepted. College and university training in this field was established.

4. *Extension to the community.* In the middle and late 1960s, therapeutic recreation service was extended to varied community settings. This trend was based on three factors: (a) the recognition that hospitals could only do their job properly if they were able to help discharged patients make successful transitions into community life, which compelled a concern with such settings; (b) the fact that an increasing number of city and county recreation and park departments began to establish special programs for, and in some cases hired specialists to serve, the disabled populations within their jurisdictions; and (c) the role of voluntary agencies serving such handicapped groups as the blind, deaf or cerebral palsied in providing expanded social services, including recreation, social activities and camping.

GROWING NUMBER OF PROFESSIONALS IN THE FIELD

As a consequence of these developments, the image of the therapeutic recreation worker became more sharply defined, and increasing numbers were employed in treatment centers and community agencies around the country. Although there has been no definitive survey of the number of specialists in recreation service for the ill and disabled, there have been a number of studies of recreation within a particular region or type of service.

For example, Phillips reported in 1958 on a study conducted by the National Recreation Association in psychiatric hospitals throughout the United States.[1] Organized recreation programs were found in 456 hospitals providing psychiatric services; approximately 2780 full-time personnel were employed to conduct recreation in these institutions. It was also found that, in smaller institutions, the ratio of patients to therapeutic recreation specialists was much more favorable than in the larger ones. In hospitals with under 300 beds, for example, there was one therapist for each 41 patients. In hospitals with between 700 and 3000 beds, the ration was one to 220.

A more extensive study of recreation personnel in hospitals was carried out by Silson, Cohen and Hill in 1959.[2] It was found that, in the 1486 hospitals of all types that had organized recreation programs throughout the nation, there were 5236 full-time recreation workers. There were sharply contrasting patterns of employment among different types of hospitals, however, and a considerable number that had no full-time recreation specialists. For example, while almost all Veterans Administration and state hospitals had full-time employees with recreation titles, only a small percentage of municipal, county and voluntary hospitals had such employees. It was found that 30.8 per cent of the hospitals had

[1] B. E. Phillips: *Recreation for the Mentally Ill.* Washington, D.C., Conference Report, American Association for Health, Physical Education and Recreation, 1958, p. 1.
[2] John E. Silson, Elliott M. Cohen and Beatrice H. Hill: *Recreation in Hospitals: Report of a Study of Organized Recreation Programs in Hospitals and the Personnel Conducting Them.* New York, National Recreation Association, 1959, pp. 35–39.

no full-time recreation personnel, and 20.6 per cent had only one such employee on a full-time basis.

A number of studies carried on in the 1960s indicated a severe shortage of trained therapeutic recreation specialists. Berryman, in 1964, summed up reports from such states as Illinois, Indiana, Pennsylvania, California and Minnesota, showing that they had more than 500 recreation staff vacancies in state hospitals alone.[3] With the growth of municipal and voluntary hospitals, nursing homes, homes for the aged and community-based agencies and departments providing therapeutic recreation services and with a limited number of students graduating from colleges with specializations in therapeutic recreation, Berryman concluded that only a handful of persons existed to fill thousands of existing and expected vacancies.

It was estimated in 1968 by the National Center for Health Statistics of the Public Health Service of the United States that there were approximately 4000 recreation therapists in hospitals and other treatment centers throughout the country.[4] This statistic was undoubtedly conservative, in that it did not include many individuals working in community agencies and did not cover those persons trained in other disciplines with a major responsibility for providing recreation programs.

As evidence of the growth in the number of therapeutic recreation workers in the United States, Kelley reports that in the early 1970s, over 800 full-time professionals were identified in the state of Illinois alone.[5] With Illinois having about one-twentieth of the population of the United States at this time, this meant that there were close to 16,000 therapeutic recreation workers in the country as a whole, assuming that similar levels of service were found elsewhere. Clearly, the number has grown dramatically in recent years. At the same time, the function of therapeutic recreation specialists has become more sharply defined.

EMERGING FUNCTIONS OF THERAPEUTIC RECREATION SPECIALISTS

In the late 1950s, Fred Chapman, professor of recreation at the University of Minnesota, carried out an analysis of the responsibilities of recreation workers in state, military, Veterans Administration and private hospitals.[6] The functions were grouped in three categories: *essential* duties, *highly desirable* duties and *desirable* duties:

Essential Duties
1. *Organizes, directs, and supervises a recreation program for rehabilitation of patients.*

---

[3] Doris Berryman: "Manpower for Therapeutic Recreation Service." *Recreation in Treatment Centers*, September, 1964, pp. 24–27.
[4] *Health Resource Statistics, 1968.* Washington, D.C., Public Health Service, U.S. Department of Health, Education and Welfare, 1968, p. 183.
[5] Jerry D. Kelley: "A Status Report on Therapeutic Recreation in the State of Illinois." *Expanding Horizons in Therapeutic Recreation II.* Champaign-Urbana, Illinois, University of Illinois, Office of Recreation and Park Resources, 1974, pp. 55–56.
[6] Fred Chapman, survey findings summarized in B. E. Phillips: "Recreational Therapy: Duties of Hospital Recreation Personnel." *Journal of Health, Physical Education and Recreation*, April, 1957, p. 60.

2. *Provides supervision for recreation staff (staff meetings, recruitment, recommendations, and evaluation).*
3. *Confers with medical staff or a physician in developing a recreational therapy program for patients.*
4. *Cooperates with other medical team members in the coordination of a program of activities for patients.*
5. *Directs and participates in an in-service training program for recreation staff.*
6. *Surveys program and makes recommendations for improvement.*

Highly Desirable Duties
7. *Prepares reports on progress of recreational program for staff meetings and other personnel.*
8. *Interprets recreation program to staff, volunteers, and the public.*
9. *Observes, interprets, and reports progress in the recreational therapy program.*
10. *Makes, reviews, and authorizes budget requests and expenditures within recreation department.*
11. *Addresses student nurses, other staff members, and interested community organizations on recreational therapy.*
12. *Orders and maintains necessary recreation supplies and equipment.*
13. *Interviews referred patients and plans recreation program modified for patients' limitations and needs.*
14. *Attends professional meetings away from the hospital.*
15. *Directs volunteers' activities, enlists their support and coordinates their efforts.*
16. *Keeps clinical notes, records, and reports on patients in recreation program.*
17. *Directs special holiday program for patients.*
18. *Assists in training of students from educational institutions.*
19. *Leads a planned recreation program for an intensive treatment unit of patients ("total push," selected groups, etc.)*
20. *Instructs individual patients in recreation (encourages participation, arranges schedules, and leads activities).*
21. *Arranges special entertainments for patients (circuses, plays, etc.)*

The *desirable* duties identified in the study consisted chiefly of leading specific recreation activities for patients in the following areas: sports and games; social and folk dancing; nature and outing; motion pictures; music; parties; dramatics; hospital radio station, newspaper and clubs; arts and crafts; assigning patients to activities; and working with relatives of discharged patients. It is worth noting that Chapman's analysis found that administrative and supervisory responsibilities of recreation therapists (and even such duties as preparing reports, addressing student nurses, ordering supplies or attending professional meetings) were seen as *more* important than providing direct leadership for patient activity programs. This may reflect, in part, a tendency for professionals working in medical settings under the supervision of doctors to be seen primarily as therapists and directors of program service rather than as activity leaders *per se*, a somewhat less prestigious role. It may also indicate that full-time professional workers essentially *are* supervisors in many situations, with direct leadership carried out by part-time workers, aides or volunteers from the community.

In 1961, an influential statement was issued on the changing functions and roles of therapeutic recreation specialists. This statement was developed by the National Curriculum Conference on Therapeutic Recreation and had important implications for the education of professional personnel in therapeutic recreation.[7] The expanding role of practitioners was seen as including the following elements:

1. *Providing activities which serve therapeutic purposes.*
2. *Supervising and administering recreation services in a variety of settings, including institutions, the home and the community.*
3. *Training aides and volunteers.*
4. *Counseling the ill and disabled, to assist them in meeting their needs through recreative experiences.*
5. *Providing consultation service to communities and institutions planning programs for the ill or disabled, and helping them to implement such programs.*
6. *Interpreting therapeutic recreation to the community and particularly to the medical and professional personnel in allied disciplines.*
7. *Providing a continuity of recreation experience as the patient moves from the hospital or institutional setting through the rehabilitation process and into the community.*
8. *Expanding community recreation services to handicapped people of all ages who are not under direct medical supervision and who live in the community.*

During the 1960s, in some treatment settings, there was less emphasis on the therapeutic recreation specialist's planning and carrying out of programs and the other functions that have been listed, and more emphasis on his serving as a therapeutic agent in a broad, interpersonal sense in the hospital environment. In the "open hospital" or "therapeutic community," emphasis shifted away from providing activities for their own sake to the psychodynamics of the personal relationship they were able to facilitate.

Simon described the concept of "therapeutic use of self" as follows:

. . . the hospital must offer a controlled milieu in which the transferences of the patient may be expressed. Psychodynamics teaches us that these transferences are repetitions of relationships which existed in the early life of the individual. It would seem, therefore, that the hospital should present a model of the outside world in which the transference could take place and corrective emotional experiences come about—that the essential difference between the mental hospital and the community should be the presence of personnel trained to understand the patient's reactions and to use themselves therapeutically. In this atmosphere there should exist replicas of all the activities normally experienced by the patient in his community. Whatever the size or structure of the hospital, it should offer the equivalent, in as nearly a similar form as possible, of home and community. This . . . involves basic functions of living, eating and sleeping. . . . Everything is oriented, ultimately, toward re-establishment in the external world.[8]

This approach had considerable influence on the way many recreation personnel functioned, particularly in psychiatric institutions, which represented the largest single area of service in which activity therapies were practiced. It also influenced other treatment centers that were concerned with behavioral change, such as special schools for the emotionally disturbed, alcohol or drug rehabilitation centers and correctional institutions. In general, however, formal

---

[7] *Report of Therapeutic Recreation Development Conference.* Sponsored by National Recreation Association's Consulting Service on Recreation for the Ill and Disabled. New York, Comeback, Inc., 1961.

[8] Benjamin Simon: "The New Trends in Rehabilitation." *Recreation's Contribution to the Patient.* North Carolina Recreation Commission, September, 1963, p. 11.

statements of the functions of therapeutic recreation specialists have not attempted to encompass this approach. Instead, they tend to describe the more clearly identifiable functions. This is particularly true of job descriptions. For example, a 1968 recruitment brochure published by the Veterans Administration described the role of recreation therapists under two major headings:

Patient Care and Treatment Program:
1. *Teaching patients how to manage their leisure time.*
2. *Planning and conducting rehabilitative recreation on a voluntary, guided, or prescribed basis.*
3. *Programming of adapted sports; arts, crafts, and hobbies; motion pictures; music; radio-TV; dramatics and social activities.*
4. *Conferences with physicians and other hospital personnel concerned with the patients' problems and rehabilitation potential.*

Administrative Responsibilities:
1. *Planning and organizing a department of Recreation Therapy for the ill and handicapped.*
2. *Supervision of personnel who are administering the therapy program.*
3. *Responsibility for proper operation and care of modern facilities and equipment and requisitioning supplies.*
4. *Interviewing and orienting new employees.*
5. *Preparation of budgets.*[9]

In some cases, authorities have attempted to define the elements of therapeutic recreation more abstractly as a way of categorizing the responsibilities of practitioners in this field. Avedon, for example, suggests that there are four major services that are provided: (1) *education* and *information*; (2) *stimulation* and *instruction*; (3) *resources manipulation*; and (4) *programming* and *activity leadership*.[10] In general, however, job descriptions are usually framed in terms of specific job responsibilities. The Recreation Center for the Handicapped in San Francisco describes the functions of its recreation supervisors under the following headings:

General Responsibilities:
1. *Plans, initiates, organizes and supervises an extensive program of recreation activities for an assigned group of mentally retarded and handicapped children, teens or adults.*
2. *Supervises, trains and evaluates recreation leaders and volunteers in the use of activities for the mentally retarded and handicapped.*
3. *Incorporates recreation for the retarded and handicapped into an acceptable total philosophy of recreation, and interprets this philosophy to participants, leaders and the public.*
4. *Consults with the Center Director and with other professional staff members on the place of recreation for the retarded and handicapped in relation to the total recreation program, the program in various segments of the community, and other specialized activity programs.*
5. *Seeks new programming ideas and adapts them for use in the recreation program for the mentally retarded and handicapped, and sees that they are carried out with appropriate groups.*

[9] *Recreation Therapists in V.A. Hospitals and Clinics.* Washington, D.C., V.A. Pamphlet No. 10–68, March, 1968, p. 1.
[10] Elliott M. Avedon: *Therapeutic Recreation Service: An Applied Behavioral Science Approach.* Englewood Cliffs, New Jersey, Prentice-Hall, 1974, p. 27 and Section II.

6. *Investigates, recommends, demonstrates, and explains techniques, proce-dures, adaptations, materials, equipment and supplies for use in the program.*
7. *Participates in inter-agency planning, research and training, as consultant, leader, or center representative.*
8. *Serves as community recreation consultant, and interprets recreation and the program for the handicapped and mentally retarded to the general public as well as to interested groups and organizations.*
9. *Cooperates in promoting, organizing, and directing community-wide pro-grams and events.*
10. *Prepares instructional materials, budget estimates, and work programs, for assigned groups.*[11]

Recently, curriculum development in therapeutic recreation has been based on the identification of specific practitioner competencies (see Appendix B).

PROFESSIONAL AND SERVICE ORGANIZATIONS IN THERAPEUTIC RECREATION

An integral part of the growing professionalization of therapeutic recre-ation has been the contribution made by professional and service organizations in promoting public awareness of this field, strengthening practices, improving curricula in higher education and developing standards for the selection of per-sonnel. Among the major organizations to have contributed in this field are the American Recreation Society, the American Association for Health, Physical Education and Recreation, the National Recreation Association and the National Association of Recreational Therapists. Their contributions are briefly detailed in the section that follows.

HOSPITAL SECTION, AMERICAN RECREATION SOCIETY

This organization was formed in Omaha, Nebraska, in 1948. It promoted hospital recreation programs in a variety of ways: by (a) sponsoring special meetings on therapeutic recreation at the annual National Recreation Congress; (b) pressing for improved standards of training and selection through its Stan-dards and Training Committee; (c) advocating or sponsoring special national or regional conferences on hospital recreation, either independently or in coopera-tion with other organizations; and (d) developing effective relationships with other organizations in the fields of rehabilitation or recreation.

RECREATIONAL THERAPY SECTION, AMERICAN ASSOCIATION FOR HEALTH, PHYSICAL EDUCATION AND RECREATION

This section of the overall organization serving health, physical educa-tion and recreation education was formed in Los Angeles, California, in 1952. The Recreation Division of the American Association for Health, Physical Educa-tion and Recreation (a department of the National Education Association) had

---

[11] *Staff Manual.* San Francisco Recreation Center for the Handicapped, 1974.

included three sections: *public recreation, voluntary and youth-serving agencies* and *institutional and industrial recreation*. The third one divided, in April, 1952, into two autonomous sections: *industrial recreation* and *recreational therapy*. The interests of members of the latter section tended to be more heavily in special schools or in adapted physical education programs than in hospital-based recreational therapy. However, the section cooperated closely with other professional groups and, because of its natural linkage with colleges and universities that prepared recreation majors, made an important contribution to the field. It also was active in developing conferences, stimulating research and attempting to improve professional standards.

NATIONAL ASSOCIATION OF RECREATIONAL THERAPISTS

This organization was founded at Bolivar, Tennessee, in February, 1953. Its initial membership consisted primarily of recreation therapists employed in state hospitals and schools, particularly in the southern and midwestern states. Although many were members of the American Recreation Society, they wished to develop a stronger professional focus on the role of the recreation therapist than was possible in that organization. This group worked closely with other organizations in promoting conferences, research and other action related to therapeutic recreation service. It published a quarterly journal, *Recreation for the Ill and Handicapped*.

CONSULTING SERVICE ON RECREATION FOR THE ILL AND HANDICAPPED, NATIONAL RECREATION ASSOCIATION

Although the National Recreation Association did not have a separate section or branch concerned with therapeutic recreation, it employed consultants who provided service in this field, working with hospitals and other agencies, beginning in 1953. The National Recreation Association's monthly magazine, *Recreation*, regularly contained a column, "Hospital Capsules," and the organization itself was represented in many professional meetings and conferences.

COUNCIL FOR THE ADVANCEMENT OF HOSPITAL RECREATION

The membership of the above four organizations realized that there was a strong need for more effective evaluation of hospital recreation programs and an upgrading of personnel standards, as well as a system of registration or certification that might enforce such standards. To meet this need, they formed the structure that became known as the Council for the Advancement of Hospital Recreation in November, 1953. This body was to serve as a vehicle for registration of qualified practitioners, to develop standards for training and clinical practice experience and to serve as a means for promoting communication among the other organizations in this field.

In 1956, the Council officially adopted personnel standards for Hospital Recreation Director, Leader and Aide and set out to promote a registration system for identifying those in the field who met these requirements. It also attempted to upgrade and improve the overall field of therapeutic recreation and to develop a merger of the existing organizations in this field.

Mrs. Beatrice Hill, formerly a consultant with the National Recreation Association, formed an organization titled Comeback, Inc. that was designed to promote professional therapeutic recreation service. She also made a sustained effort to unify the field of therapeutic recreation service. However, this was not to be accomplished until the separate organizations representing the field agreed to merge late in 1965, forming the National Recreation and Park Association. This organization established a number of separate branches as substructures to represent the varied interests of its members. One of these, the National Therapeutic Recreation Society, absorbed the existing organizations concerned with recreation for the ill and disabled and has functioned effectively in this area since that time.

NATIONAL THERAPEUTIC RECREATION SOCIETY

One of the key functions of this organization is to promote professional development by sponsoring or cosponsoring conferences and by developing programs and special institutes for the annual National Recreation Congress.

For example, it cooperated in the early 1970s in the cosponsorship of professional conferences on activity therapy with the Joint Commission on Accreditation of Hospitals, the Accreditation Council for Psychiatric Facilities and other organizations representing occupational, music, dance and art therapy and mental centers and psychiatric services for children. At various National Recreation Congresses, it has provided pre-Congress Institutes, with meetings devoted to such themes as the following:

> "Programs and Standards for Nursing Homes"
> "Psychodrama in Activities Programs"
> "Comprehensive Programming for Emotionally Disturbed Children"
> "Federal Supports for Therapeutic Recreation"
> "Recreation Counseling for the Ill and Disabled"
> "Therapeutic Recreation in Correctional Institutions"
> "Planning Community Facilities for the Ill and Disabled"
> "Recreation Services for Drug Abusers"

The National Therapeutic Recreation Society has appointed official delegates to represent the views of its members at important national meetings. It has conducted district workshops to develop guidelines for the recruitment, training and employment of disabled individuals in the recreation and park field and has sponsored research efforts with the financial assistance of federal agencies. In addition, it has published the quarterly journal, *Therapeutic Recreation Journal,* that today acts as a single spokesman for this united field.

An important function of the National Therapeutic Recreation Society has been to influence government policy and promote improved public awareness of the field. It has done this by vigorously presenting its views before government officials and committees and by pressing for support of special projects serving the ill and disabled. For example, an NTRS special task force on recreation in corrections, chaired by Carroll Hormachea of Virginia Commonwealth University, has fought energetically, through publications, conferences, position statements and similar efforts, to promote a fuller use of recreation as a vital aspect of rehabilitation in penal institutions in the United States.[12] Perhaps its strongest efforts, however, have been in the direction of identifying qualified professionals and upgrading standards of selection and hiring.

REGISTRATION, CERTIFICATION AND LICENSING

Each of these represents a method of screening qualified personnel for employment in a given professional field. *Registration* usually refers to the process through which a nongovernmental association or professional society establishes a series of qualifications for given job titles and screens individuals to determine if they have the stipulated qualifications. Those approved are then placed on a list, in this case of registered therapists (see p. 371). In contrast to registration, which involves voluntary compliance by hiring agencies, *licensing* is a legal process through which an agency of government screens qualifications and grants approval to persons to engage in certain occupations or professions. Just as one must have a license to drive a car, so one must have a license to practice in such fields. The term *certification* tends to be used ambiguously. In some cases, it is used synonymously with registration. In other health-related or educational fields, certification is established as a process by state law, and all public hiring agencies must comply with its regulations, just as in licensing.

The National Therapeutic Recreation Society maintains a voluntary registration plan that defines standards for various levels of professional functioning based chiefly on academic education and professional experience. Minimum qualifying criteria are involved in registering as *Therapeutic Recreation Assistant I* and *II, Technician I* and *II, Worker, Specialist* or *Master Specialist.* The registration process is carried out by a special review board that assesses qualifications for registration at each level and issues certificates to individuals meeting stated requirements. Park writes,

> *Through the efforts of NTRS-NRPA in promoting quality therapeutic recreation services, this program has gained national recognition. Some states and employing agencies are now requiring this registration before they will hire an individual. Others, while not requiring registration, are strongly encouraging it. The standards included in the Joint Commission on Accreditation of Hospitals manuals refer to the registration program when discussing qualified personnel. As a result of these efforts, the number of professionally registered persons (grew) from less than 300 in 1970 to over 1,000 in 1973.*[13]

Despite these efforts, uniform standards of professional selection have not yet been applied to the bulk of practitioners in this field. In part, this is because there is such a diversity of employing agencies that it would be almost

---

[12] See David C. Park: "NTRS Task Force Reports." *Parks and Recreation*, September, 1974, pp. 44–45, 67.
[13] David C. Park: "Professionalism in the '70's." *In* Jerry D. Kelley (ed.): *op. cit.*, p. 67.

impossible to devise any system of certification or licensing that would apply to all positions and be readily enforceable. It also reflects the situation of the overall recreation and park field, in which certification has been approved in only a few states and Civil Service hiring requirements are generally quite flexible.

State Society Standards

In addition to the registration program of the National Therapeutic Recreation Society, a number of state recreation and park societies have developed their own registration plans. As an example, the California Board of Parks and Recreation Personnel established a general program of registration for recreation and park professionals in 1955; in 1970, special registration requirements were established for recreation therapists. With guidance from the Therapeutic Section of the California Park and Recreation Society, these requirements have been modified and strengthened. By 1975, they included the following:

> *A baccalaureate or graduate degree with specialization in Therapeutic Recreation, including 18 semester hours in upper-division courses in areas such as psychology, sociology, or the physical and biological sciences. Specific course requirements in aspects of disability, and a survey of recreation for the ill and handicapped, as well as 400 hours of supervised field work, were instituted, accompanied by a special examination administered by the California Board of Parks and Recreation Personnel.[14]*

In addition, the Therapeutic Section of the California Park and Recreation Society voted to endorse legislation calling for licensure in therapeutic recreation. They succeeded in having therapeutic recreation made part of a bill to certify occupational therapists, but it was vetoed by the state governor. Now, members of the state society are striving to achieve a separate status for their own discipline. Lawrence describes this growing effort in California as "a new maturity in the profession, a political coming of age," pointing out that

> *It represented a realization that existing federal and state laws appear to favor licensed health professionals and that medical insurance and reimbursement through use of public funds tends more and more to cover those services offered to consumers by state certified or licensed professionals. . . . (according to the) HEW Report on Licensure and Related Health Personnel Credentialing: "Under present statutes and regulations when a health profession is licensed by a state, federal health insurance programs typically link qualification for reimbursement to state licensure requirements."[15]*

The only state thus far to have approved formal licensing or certification in therapeutic recreation is Utah; it passed a "Recreational Therapy Practice Act" (H.B. No. 361, 1975) outlining requirements for several levels of therapeutic

---

[14] Patricia J. Lawrence: *Position Statement of AB4428 to Include Recreation Therapists.* Legislative Recommendation to Certify Recreation Therapists, to Therapeutic Recreation Section and Board of Directors, California Park and Recreation Society, 1976, p. 1.

[15] Patricia J. Lawrence: *Certification: The Time is Now.* Report of Therapeutic Section to California Park and Recreation Society, 1976, p. 1.

recreation service, with statements of purpose, definitions, exemptions, basis for license suspension or revocation and examples of unauthorized or unlawful practice. This pioneer licensing law has been extremely effective. According to Clark Thorstenson of Brigham Young University, it has had a positive effect upon employment opportunities for professionally qualified personnel in Utah:

> *We have had excellent cooperation from all agencies who have been involved with therapeutic recreation and we have successfully encouraged them to hire only those who are trained in the field . . . we have many more positions in therapeutic recreation than we are able to fill because of lack of (qualified) students. An additional benefit is that those who are licensed have often had an increase in salary. . . . We feel, in general, our image as a profession is increasing and we are much more unified as a group than we previously were.*[16]

Obviously, all such efforts to upgrade the profession are heavily dependent on college and university programs of professional preparation in therapeutic recreation service. Before describing these in detail, however, it should be noted that, in addition to the National Therapeutic Recreation Society, a number of other national organizations in the United States have promoted the overall rehabilitation movement and, through joint projects, have cooperated with therapeutic recreation specialists. Among these organizations have been the American National Red Cross, American Occupational Therapy Association, American Physical Therapy Association, Association for Physical and Mental Rehabilitation, National Association for Music Therapy, American Association of Rehabilitation Therapists, American Art Therapy Association, American Dance Therapy Association and the National Association of State Activity Therapy and Rehabilitation Program Directors.

In particular, the American Association for Health, Physical Education, and Recreation (now known as the American Alliance for Health, Physical Education and Recreation) (AAHPER) has been active in promoting recreation services in general, leisure education and adapted physical education and recreation for the disabled. It has sponsored conferences and curriculum development task forces, published literature and encouraged research and demonstration projects in this field. One of its most important recent contributions has been the Information and Research Utilization Center (IRUC) on Physical Education and Recreation for the Handicapped, a comprehensive center for information, referral services and other forms of assistance in this field.[17] This project was supported for three years in the mid-1970s by the U.S. Department of Health, Education and Welfare's Bureau of Education for the Handicapped as a special demonstration project under the direction of Julian U. Stein, with follow-up grants extending into the late 1970s.

The branch of AAHPER most directly concerned with recreation is the American Association for Leisure and Recreation (AALR), which has done much to promote professional development in camping and outdoor education, education for leisure and leisure research and varied forms of professional recreation service. Because of their shared concern with general aspects of health, fitness, physical activity, leisure education and needs of special populations, both

---

[16] Clark T. Thorstenson, letter to author, March 11, 1977.
[17] See American Alliance for Physical Education and Recreation Newsletter, *Update*, March, 1976, p. 1.

AAHPER and AALR have done much to complement and work with the National Therapeutic Recreation Society.

PROFESSIONAL EDUCATION IN
THERAPEUTIC RECREATION SERVICE

The development of special curricula in therapeutic recreation did not get fully under way until after World War II. In August, 1953, the Standards and Training Committee of the Hospital Recreation Section of the American Recreation Society reported that of the 44 colleges and universities that offered degrees in recreation only six had graduate or undergraduate degrees in "hospital" recreation. These were Teachers College, Columbia University; New York University; Springfield College; the University of Minnesota; Purdue University; and Sacramento State College.

However, a number of other colleges offered special courses in this field or sponsored workshops and institutes that contributed significantly to professional practice. For example, the University of North Carolina hosted a series of Regional Conferences on Hospital Recreation, beginning in the mid-1950s, that brought together representatives of Veterans Administration, state, county and private and municipal hospitals to discuss theory and present innovative practices in therapeutic recreation.

An important step in developing special curricula was the conference on graduate curricula in therapeutic recreation sponsored by the National Recreation Association's Consulting Service on Recreation for the Ill and Handicapped, held in New York in 1961. This meeting brought together leading recreation educators and practitioners and sought to identify the changing competencies required of professional specialists in therapeutic recreation and suggest curriculum models based on these competencies.

It made a number of recommendations, chiefly to the effect that professional practitioners required graduate education in a specially designed program that followed an undergraduate major in general recreation. On the graduate level, it recommended that emphasis be placed on mastery of medical and psychiatric nomenclature, ability to adapt activities for the ill and disabled and competence to meet new demands that went beyond the traditional function of providing activities, such as training of personnel, providing consultation services, interpreting the field to the community and to other disciplines and developing strong links to community agencies.

It recommended that such programs include a strong component of clinical experience (including observation, involvement in programs, record-keeping and evaluation). The graduate program should not be fragmented into such areas as psychiatric, orthopedic or general medical options and should include a common core of information related to medical understandings and knowledge of other therapeutic disciplines.

During the 1960s, as the rapid growth in therapeutic recreation programs created a shortage of qualified personnel and as interest grew in this field as a specialized concern, the number of colleges and universities offering curricula in therapeutic recreation grew steadily.

In 1969, the Society of Park and Recreation Educators carried out a study of recreation curricula in the United States that revealed that of 114 institutions identified as having a recreation or recreation and park program, 35 offered a major in therapeutic recreation service.[18] It was found that the largest number of such curricula were in the Great Lakes and Southwest Pacific regions of the country. They tended to be located in departments or schools of health, physical education and recreation—logically so because of the emphasis on physiology, kinesiology, physical activities, psychology and special education in such schools or departments. No therapeutic recreation majors were found in curricula housed in colleges or schools of agriculture, forestry or natural resources.

It was reported in 1975 that, as a result of increasing interest in professional recreation service in general, the number of colleges and universities in the United States and Canada offering undergraduate and graduate degree programs in this overall field had expanded to 345.[19] The third largest area of specialization was therapeutic recreation, with 95 institutions offering degree options in this field. This rapid growth reflected, in part, increasing interest on the part of Canadian colleges and universities. Until comparatively recently, there were few Canadian college or university programs in recreation. Many Canadian therapeutic recreation specialists were receiving their training at such institutions as the University of Illinois or the University of Indiana. Within the past several years, however, a substantial number of Canadian colleges and universities have initiated special programs in therapeutic recreation, particularly on the two-year and baccalaureate levels.

Courses Offered in Therapeutic Recreation Curricula

In 1970, Donald Lindley reported on a study revealing the types of courses offered in therapeutic recreation curricula, and their relative importance, as rated by college educators and practitioners in the field.[20] In an initial study of 30 colleges and universities offering therapeutic recreation curricula, he found that courses tended to be grouped in nine major areas: (a) communication arts-public relations; (b) community institutions and organizations; (c) social science and psychology; (d) medical and psychiatric information; (e) recreation philosophy; (f) recreation administration; (g) recreation programs; (h) evaluation and research; and (i) clinical experience.

On the *undergraduate* level, the most valuable courses were rated in order of importance as follows: field work, introduction to therapeutic recreation, philosophy of recreation, social psychology, community organization in recreation, small group dynamics, foundations of recreation, internship, programming in therapeutic recreation and methods of recreation leadership. Courses dealing with other rehabilitation services, psychiatric and medical information or program elements for specific disabilities fell far below the first ten.

On the *graduate* level, the most valuable courses, in rank order of importance, were: research methods, readings in therapeutic recreation, psy-

---

[18] Thomas A. Stein: "Therapeutic Recreation Education: 1969 Survey." *Therapeutic Recreation Journal*, 2nd Quarter, 1970, pp. 4–7.

[19] See Thomas A. Stein: *Report on the State of Recreation and Park Education in Canada and the United States.* Arlington, Virginia, Society of Park and Recreation Educators, 1975.

[20] Donald Lindley: "Relative Importance of College Courses in Therapeutic Recreation." *Therapeutic Recreation Journal*, 2nd Quarter, 1970, pp. 8–12.

chological aspects of disability, readings in recreation, research seminars, professional seminars, psychiatric and medical information and administration in therapeutic recreation.

The actual development of therapeutic recreation curricula has been influenced by the recommendations of task forces established by professional organizations, by federally funded projects intended to develop superior models of professional preparation and by the guidelines for accreditation prepared by the National Recreation and Park Association and the National Therapeutic Recreation Society.

For example, in 1973 the Information and Research Utilization Center (IRUC) in Physical Education and Recreation for the Handicapped, a special service unit of the American Association for Health, Physical Education and Recreation, published a set of guidelines for college and university curricula in physical education and recreation serving special populations.[21] Funded by the Bureau of Education for the Handicapped of the U.S. Department of Health, Education and Welfare, this publication provided a rationale for therapeutic recreation service, identified roles of practitioners and outlined needed competencies for professional personnel within specific areas of function. It described major curriculum areas and needed college resources, giving particular stress to the development of strong practicum experiences ranging from observation to full employment in settings staffed by qualified professional leaders.

Similarly, beginning in the early 1970s the Bureau of Education for the Handicapped gave substantial support to a number of colleges and universities providing professional education in physical education and recreation for the disabled under Public Law 91–230, Title VI, Education of the Handicapped. Eight grants were solely or predominantly recreation oriented and supported master's level or doctoral programs at the University of Illinois, University of Oregon, University of Kentucky, New York University, San Jose State College, North Carolina Central University, Pennsylvania State University and the University of North Carolina.[22] In general, these grants were intended to improve the quality of professional preparation in this field and to help create a pool of high-quality personnel for upper-level positions as administrators, consultants, researchers or educators in therapeutic recreation. A number of more recent grants from the Bureau of Education for the Handicapped have included a *Therapeutic Recreation Curriculum Development Project for Community Colleges* being carried out at the University of Illinois[23] and a *Competency-Based Curriculum Project in Therapeutic Recreation* sponsored by Temple University in Philadelphia[24] (see Appendix B). The latter project in particular has focused on the identification of tasks and needed competencies of therapeutic recreation professionals and methods of analyzing levels of successful performance, as well as assessing present practices and manpower patterns in the field.

---

[21] Julian U. Stein, Project Director: *Guidelines for Professional Preparation Programs for Personnel Involved in Physical Education and Recreation for the Handicapped.* Washington, D.C., American Association for Health, Physical Education and Recreation and U.S. Bureau of Education for the Handicapped, 1973.

[22] National Therapeutic Recreation Society: "Impact." In *Communique* (National Recreation and Park Association Newsletter), September, 1971, pp. 17–18.

[23] *Therapeutic Recreation Newsletter.* University of Illinois Department of Leisure Studies, October, 1975.

[24] *Therapeutic Recreation Project Newsletter: Competency-Based Curriculum.* Temple University Department of Recreation and Leisure Studies, September, 1976.

Community College Curricula

A significant trend in professional preparation in therapeutic recreation has been the steady growth in two-year, community college curricula. This has stemmed from two basic sources: (a) an awareness of the shortage of trained personnel in the field during the late 1960s and early 1970s and (b) the general expansion of community college programs around the United States and Canada, many of which sought to prepare young people for positions in the health services or other technically oriented fields. At an early point, Hutchinson described the rationale for such programs:

> Those students entering junior (community) colleges who seek a terminal education at the end of two years should be given the opportunity to prepare themselves as assistants in therapeutic recreation settings. A two-year course could develop some to become valuable technicians who, under professional supervision, could contribute much to the recreation program. The functional roles which seem appropriate for them are: movie projector operators and visual aids experts; radio operators, and/or television repairmen; games rooms operators; designers of posters, notices, and other visual materials; organizers of outings, picnics and camp trips; storeroom and equipment attendants; and program assistants.[25]

Despite the original conception of community college programs as terminal, two trends have developed among many community college graduates:

1. Those who found employment tended to move into actual leadership or supervisory roles rather than be restricted to the kinds of limited tasks described by Hutchinson. Thus, they represented a threat to those already in the profession, who felt that opening up job levels that had formerly required a bachelor's degree to community college graduates represented a lowering of professional standards.

2. The great number of positions expected to materialize for two-year graduates did not appear, and promotional opportunities were sharply limited. Thus, the bulk of community college students sought to transfer following graduation to four-year colleges, where they might complete their bachelor's degrees and become fully eligible for Civil Service and other professional positions.

This in turn created a problem of articulation between two-year and four-year colleges. In many cases, the community college curriculum had an extensive range of recreation courses, with comparatively few liberal arts or general academic courses. When students sought to transfer to baccalaureate programs, they found that they were required to take a substantial number of liberal arts credits and, in some cases, certain recreation major courses again on the senior college level. In a number of states, articulation agreements have been worked out between two-year and four-year colleges with the assistance of state recreation and park societies. Another problem has been that, in many community colleges, faculty with limited backgrounds in recreation and parks were assigned to this field. Gradually, however, community college curricula

---

[25] John L. Hutchinson: "Therapeutic Recreation Education: Programs and Proposals For Sub-Professionals." *Recreation in Treatment Centers*, September, 1964, p. 29.

have been upgraded, and today there are many excellent two-year recreation majors, including a number with a strong therapeutic option.

Hutchinson also urged that—in order to relieve the shortage of therapeutic recreation personnel—intensive three-month training institutes be given to prepare recreation aides, including retired persons, to work in hospitals and other treatment settings. Generally, such institutes have not been developed, with the exception of short courses that have been used to prepare recreation aides for nursing homes (an area of extreme shortage of personnel, in which the salaries have not been attractive enough to justify employing full-time, professionally trained individuals). In some cases, specially funded federal grants have been given to train minority group persons from disadvantaged backgrounds in therapeutic recreation leadership. In general, however, only a limited number of positions have been created to employ such persons.

Personnel-Sharing Plans

Other attempts to meet the personnel shortage have included an experimental approach to having several institutions share the costs of employing a professional recreation director who would supervise the work of subprofessionals and volunteers.

Another approach that has been used in many nursing homes has been to have several institutions employ a consultant on therapeutic recreation who then visits each of them regularly, supervising aides, nurses and other part-time or nonprofessional personnel conducting actual program activities. In most cases, such arrangements do not constitute an actual cooperative plan on the part of the nursing homes. Instead, they simply represent a convenient means of hiring part of the time of a professional consultant to assist in program development and meeting state-imposed requirements for activity programs in nursing homes.

Another attempt to relieve the shortage of personnel consisted of a 750-hour training program approved by the NTRS Board in 1975 to prepare individuals who would be qualified to work at Recreation Assistant or Recreation Technician levels. It should be stressed that despite the fact that a much greater number of qualified individuals are being prepared today by colleges and universities, the personnel shortage in therapeutic recreation continues. Many hospitals, community mental health centers and especially penal and corrective institutions are greatly understaffed! The reason is the general economic decline of the mid-1970s that caused the budgets of many state agencies, municipal departments and voluntary institutions to be frozen.

In other words, instead of the situation that prevailed earlier, with many openings for qualified therapeutic recreation personnel and comparatively few persons holding degrees in this field, today there are relatively fewer openings and a much greater number of individuals with specialized degrees. This situation makes it all the more necessary to develop stricter licensing, certification and registration procedures and strengthen Civil Service codes to insure that only qualified individuals are employed in the field. In the past, it was argued that it was unrealistic to require applicants to have degrees in therapeutic recreation because not enough such individuals were graduated each year to fill the demand. Today, it clearly can and should be done, and, as indicated earlier, both national and state societies are pressing vigorously for such action.

Accreditation of College and University Programs

Traditionally, recreation education has been most closely attached to departments of health and physical education, with the exception of a relatively smaller number of departments found in schools of forestry, landscape architecture and agriculture. In the past, such curricula have been accredited through the National Council on Accreditation of Teacher Education (NCATE). Since the mid-1960s, an effort has been made to develop a more specialized and meaningful accreditation procedure to scrutinize recreation and park curricula thoroughly instead of permitting them to "slide by" almost unnoticed as part of stronger health and physical education programs or schools of education. Several sets of guidelines for accreditation were developed, and in 1975 the National Recreation and Park Association, in cooperation with the American Association for Leisure and Recreation, developed a final draft of evaluative criteria on two levels (baccalaureate and master's degrees) and a set of procedural guidelines. In the following years, a number of pilot accreditation procedures were carried out, and by the late 1970s, the accreditation process was well under way.[26]

Use of Volunteers

A final means of dealing with the personnel shortage is using volunteers to carry on actual programs. Clark sums up the values to be gained by the use of volunteers in a Veterans Administration hospital:

> We believe that volunteers under medical staff leadership and guidance can make a valuable contribution to the care and treatment of patients. We believe the volunteer's contribution is made in two basic types of supplemental service to the patients; first, direct service in which the volunteers participate in hospital-approved programs with and for the patients; secondly, direct service in which the volunteers provide equally valuable assistance as public relations ambassadors to the community, informing friends and neighbors about the care and treatment programs and the role of the community in assisting in these programs.[27]

In addition to these values, volunteers are able to relieve professional staff members of many time-consuming tasks that do not require a high level of training. They may provide specialized leadership skills lacking in the regular staff, thus extending the program and offering more highly individualized activities. The fact that they are offering their time without payment, because they *care*, is undoubtedly an important morale "booster" for patients. However, volunteers may constitute a serious adminstrative problem if they are not

---

[26] Ira G. Shapiro: "The Path to Accreditation." *Parks and Recreation*, January, 1977, pp. 29, 112.

[27] Thomas J. Clark: "The Administration of Voluntary Services in a Recreation Program." *Recreation in Treatment Centers*, September, 1962, pp. 13–17.

properly guided and supervised. Clark suggests a set of guidelines for this process:

1. Organization. *It is necessary to have one individual who will coordinate and direct the volunteer program, acting as a liaison with community organizations which are the source of volunteers, and assuming this entire responsibility.*
2. Climate. *It is necessary, as a first step, to establish a climate for the constructive use of volunteers within the total scope and philosophy of the agency. Staff members—who may feel threatened by the use of volunteers who work for nothing and may have highly developed skills—should be helped to accept volunteers, and assured that they do not represent a danger to professional, paid personnel.*
3. Establish Need. *Before any volunteers are recruited or accepted, the agency should carry out a survey of its need for volunteers. After these have been established, "job" descriptions might be written for each possible volunteer assignment.*
4. Recruitment. *Generally this is carried on most effectively if there is an advisory council for voluntary services in the community. If not, contact must be made with service organizations that provide volunteers, and all forms of communication (radio, television, announcements, newspapers, and personal contact) should be used to reach potential volunteers.*
5. Screening and Selection. *The potential volunteer should fill out appropriate background forms and be interviewed by the member of the staff responsible for coordinating volunteer services. Such qualities as sincere interest, the ability to work with people and to accept the policies of the agency, dependability, and personal stability should be assessed in this meeting. Then the volunteer should be interviewed by the member of the staff responsible for the program to which he would be assigned.*
6. Orientation and Training. *All volunteers who are accepted should be given a thorough introduction to the agency, in which they are helped to understand its objectives and philosophy, and learn about its structure and operation. Such a process helps to develop an effective rapport between staff members and volunteers. There should also be a preliminary period of instruction of specific skills or methods of carrying out the assignment.*
7. Supervision. *This is a key element in the use of volunteers. A properly qualified, capable supervisor should observe the work of the volunteer, meet with him regularly, offer assistance when needed, help him recognize and solve his problems—and, if necessary, make recommendations for re-assigning or terminating the employment of the volunteer.*
8. Recognition. *Most volunteers do contribute an important service, which should be recognized. This may be done regularly through the year, by praise and recognition of achievements at staff meetings. Providing identification cards or other formal symbols of volunteer roles may be helpful. In addition, it is desirable to give volunteers scrolls or other concrete statements of appreciation, or to hold volunteer dinners or other formal ceremonies in which they are publicly recognized.*

THERAPEUTIC RECREATION WITHIN THE TREATMENT TEAM

Another important consideration in this chapter is the place of therapeutic recreation within the treatment team and its relationship with other treatment modalities generally described under the broad heading of *activity therapies.* In many hospitals and treatment centers, recreation has been made a part of larger rehabilitation departments in which recreation specialists must work in close cooperation with occupational therapists, physical therapists and similar personnel. The following section provides concise descriptions of the different disciplines found in the hospital setting that may be provided as part of the rehabilitation process.

Activity and Adjunctive Therapies

Before it is possible to meaningfully consider the role of the activity therapies, or adjunctive therapies as they are sometimes called, it is essential to examine how they relate to the physician and the role he plays. This may be done with respect to two major types of medical settings: *physical medicine and rehabilitation* and *psychiatric care.* Both are part of the broad process of rehabilitation that involves the "cooperative efforts of various medical specialists and their associates in other health fields to improve the physical, mental, social and vocational aptitudes of persons who are handicapped, with the objective of preserving their ability to live happily and productively on the same level and with the same opportunities as their neighbors."[28]

The physician's responsibility today goes far beyond diagnosing, providing necessary surgical or drug treatment and then dismissing his patient. Instead, he must concern himself not only with the physical disability but also with the psychological, social and vocational problems of his patient.

How is this whole person to be treated in the field of physical medicine? Krusen writes that rehabilitation, as practiced in modern treatment centers, is a multidisciplinary service directed by the specialist in physical medicine and rehabilitation, assisted by other specialists in internal medicine, pediatrics, orthopedic surgery, neurology, neurosurgery and plastic surgery. These physicians in turn are assisted by a team of associates in the allied health professions, which might include various types of therapists, as well as social workers, clinical psychologists and vocational counselors.[29]

Within the field of psychiatric treatment, occupational and recreational therapy have, since the 1930s, been operating under a model of prescribing individualized activities designed to meet patients' specific psychodynamic needs during the treatment process. Although there had been examples of the use of varied types of patient activities in psychiatric treatment facilities over a century before, it was not until the beginning of the 20th century that such programs were widely accepted. The rationale for them, quite simply, was that activity was necessary to combat the demoralizing condition of being "invalided" and institutionalized. Activity was viewed as a valuable antidote to "idleness," which in turn was seen as worsening the condition of the ill and retarding treatment progress.[30] Positive forms of activity—at this time, largely consisting of beginning forms of occupational therapy and recreation—were seen as helping to channel the patient's "attitude toward life," in healthy directions. A leading psychiatrist of this early period, Adolf Meyer of the Phipps Clinic in Baltimore, stressed the need to appeal to what was "sane and wholesome and natural in patients" and to lead "that healthy core along the road of simple activity."

---

[28] Frank H. Krusen, Frederick J. Kottke and Paul M. Ellwood (eds.): *Handbook of Physical Medicine and Rehabilitation.* Philadelphia, W. B. Saunders Co., 1971, p. 1.

[29] Max Pinner: *In* Krusen et al.: *op. cit.,* p. 2.

[30] Joan M. Erikson: *Activity, Recovery and Growth: The Communal Role of Planned Activities.* New York, W. W. Norton, 1976, p. 20.

Erikson writes,

> *Meyer's emphasis was on the intact areas of strength and normal functioning in every patient and on the hospital's responsibility, not only to preserve but to nourish and maximize these aspects in treatment.*[31]

Furthermore, he stressed the importance of activity in the hospital regimen as a way of encouraging patients to work within the defined limits of reality, balancing self-absorption and fantasy and acting as a remedial normative influence against other distorting factors in their lives. As the use of occupational and recreational therapy spread in hospitals after World War I, Erikson points out that

> *...two views of activity or occupation as part of psychiatric treatment were juxtaposed and debated. The scientific emphasis meant research and a systematic theory, to be applied in prescribing activity specifically to alleviate or correct symptoms. The humanist emphasis, on the other hand, meant advocacy of all that was normal and wholesome in the patient and claimed that any productive or socially acceptable activity is beneficial, irrespective of diagnosis or symptomatology.*[32]

Supporting the first position, in order to gain status within the medical setting, training in occupational therapy was expanded to include psychiatric principles and nomenclature, along with survey and introduction to diagnosis and symptomatology. On the other hand, as the milieu therapy approach became more widely accepted in many institutions, activities came to be seen as broadly socializing and normalizing forms of experience, rather than a specifically prescriptive treatment service. Following World War II, and particularly during the 1960s, the term "activity therapies," or "activities," came to be used widely, including both occupational and recreational therapy. At the same time, greater stress was given to a variety of other forms of adjunctive therapy related to work, education and creative expression that also tended to be included under the administrative umbrella of "activity therapies." In each case, however, the training for a given therapy remained separate, and Civil Service titles or job descriptions continued to specify the exact nature of the service (such as occupational, physical or recreation therapy) rather than to describe all such workers as activity therapists.

The clinical-medical approach to the use of recreation in psychiatric settings was popularized at the Menninger Clinic in particular and involved guiding members of the staff in precisely how to deal with specific patients. Activities themselves became a means of making psychodynamic diagnoses, and the adjunctive therapist developed elaborate schemes for prescribing specific activities for patients. Pattison comments that this model persists as a dominant model for the adjunctive therapies in psychiatric institutions for two reasons:

> *For one, it adheres closely to the traditional model of psychodynamic psychotherapy which focuses solely on the one-to-one therapeutic relationship. The adjunctive therapist in his occupational or recreational therapy represents an extension of the one-to-one model of therapy. The activities of the adjunctive*

---

[31] *Ibid.*, p. 27.
[32] *Ibid.*, p. 29.

therapist are intended to indeed be "therapy"; and the adjunctive therapist becomes a junior psychiatrist of sorts. Thus the work of the adjunctive therapist is determined and controlled by the psychiatrist who is the ultimate authority on the diagnosis and psychodynamic treatment of the patient . . . .[33]

The second reason, in Pattison's view, for this model's continued use is that it supports the professionalization of the various adjunctive therapies. Typically, adjunctive therapists look to the psychiatrist to achieve identity and gain social and professional status. Thus, adjunctive therapists are urged to become educated in psychiatric diagnosis and in psychotherapeutic techniques. However, it is no longer taken for granted that the major value of the adjunctive therapies lies in their specific psychodynamic meanings. Instead, in many institutions, their contribution is seen chiefly as being in the area of creating a therapeutic environment.

The concept of "milieu" therapy implies that treatment consists chiefly of providing, guiding and maintaining activities that are therapeutic and thus promoting healthy patterns of social interaction. Specifically, then, the adjunctive therapies should *not* be regarded as therapy in a literal sense but rather as elements of the total treatment process that contribute to varied aspects of the patient's growth and recovery.

With this background, the following section describes a number of activities or adjunctive therapies prominent in the field of rehabilitation today.

OCCUPATIONAL THERAPY

The field of occupational therapy has been broadly defined by the American Occupational Therapy Association as "any activity, mental or physical, prescribed by a physician as a valuable adjunct in contributing to and hastening recovery. Physically, its function is to increase muscle strength and joint motion as well as to improve the general bodily health; mentally, its function is to supply as nearly as possible normal activity through avocational projects and prevocational studies and training." More recently, the U.S. Public Health Service described occupational therapy in these terms:

Occupational therapy (is) the use of purposeful activity in the rehabilitation of persons with physical or emotional disability. The occupational therapist, as a vital member of the rehabilitation team, determines the objectives of the treatment program according to the individual needs of each patient. This may include decreasing disability during the patient's initial phases of recovery following injury or illness, increasing the individual's capability for independence and improving his physical, emotional, and social well-being and developing his total function to a maximum level through early evaluation and experimentation for future job training and employment.[34]

Occupational therapy may be prescribed to accomplish any of the following objectives:

1. *Specific treatment for psychiatric patients—to structure opportunities for the development of more satisfying relationships, to assist in releasing or sublimating emotional drives, to aid as a diagnostic tool.*

---

[33] E. Mansell Pattison: "The Relationship of the Adjunctive and Therapeutic Recreation Services to Community Mental Health Programs." *Therapeutic Recreation Journal*, 1st Quarter, 1969, p. 17.

[34] *Health Resource Statistics, 1968: op. cit.*, p. 145.

2. *Specific treatment for restoration of physical function—to increase joint motion, muscle strength, and coordination.*
3. *To teach self-help activities—those of daily living such as eating, dressing, writing, the use of adapted equipment, and prostheses.*
4. *To help the disabled homemaker readjust to home routines with advice and instruction as to the adaptation of household equipment and work simplification.*
5. *To develop work tolerance and maintenance of special skills as required by the patient's job.*
6. *To provide prevocational exploration—to determine the patient's physical and mental capacities, social adjustment, interests, work habits, skills, and potential employability.*
7. *A supportive measure—help the patient to accept and utilize constructively a prolonged period of hospitalization and convalescence.*
8. *Redirection of recreational and avocational interests.*[35]

Stated differently, the official Manual for Occupational Therapy Programs in Pennsylvania State Mental Hospitals in the Department of Public Welfare stresses that occupational therapy is involved in a wide range of disability areas, and its goals vary considerably from setting to setting:

> *Typical non-psychiatric goals are prevocational exploration and evaluation, selective muscle strengthening, and developing performance capacity through positioning, practice and adaptive devices. In the latter instance, activities used may be vocationally oriented, or activities of daily living—dressing, eating, locomotion et al. These complex activities are often broken down into component motions which are practiced intensively and individually.*[36]

On the other hand, in psychiatric programs, the Pennsylvania manual suggests that occupational therapy emphasizes the patient's interaction with the human and nonhuman environment. Goals relate generally to feelings, attitudes, habits, insights, interpersonal skills and general behavior, with patients being expected to move gradually through higher stages of decision-making, responsibility and interpersonal relationships.

It is apparent that a number of these goals are very similar to those of therapeutic recreation service. This is supported by the actual content of occupational therapy, which includes many clearly recreational activities.

However, a clear distinction must be made between therapeutic recreation and occupational therapy in terms of professional preparation. Occupational therapists must graduate from a college or university accredited by the Council on Medical Education of the American Medical Association, in collaboration with the American Occupational Therapy Association. Such programs may have as a minimum requirement a four-year bachelor's degree, a one-year certification program following the bachelor's degree or a two-year Master's degree program. Normally, they include considerable work in the biological sciences, particularly human anatomy and physiology, behavioral sciences and physical and psychosocial dysfunction, as well as courses in occupational therapy principles and skills.

---

[35] Helen S. Willard and Clare S. Speckman: *Occupational Therapy.* Philadelphia, J. B. Lippincott, 1971, p. 2.
[36] *Manual for Evaluation of Occupational Therapy Programs in Pennsylvania State Mental Hospitals.* Pennsylvania Department of Public Welfare, 1974, p. 1.

As indicated, most occupational therapy programs place a heavy emphasis on the use of manual activities, such as crafts or industrial skills, to help patients recover function with respect to writing, reading, function with respect to writing, reading, self-care, homemaking and the use of prosthetic equipment in order to increase mobility and the ability to function in various spheres of living.

PHYSICAL THERAPY

Physical therapy is concerned with the restoration of function and prevention of disability following disease, injury or loss of a bodily part. It seeks to aid the normal progression of the healing process by serving to relieve symptoms and speed recovery.

Among the types of patients served by physical therapy are those suffering from chronic arthritis, rheumatism, forms of paralysis, organic and functional affections of the nervous system, digestive disturbances and various other severe trauma. Generally, physical therapy employs the following types of treatment:

1. *Thermotherapy:* radiant heat; artificially induced fever.
2. *Light therapy:* heliotherapy; artificial ultraviolet radiation.
3. *Electrotherapy:* Galvanic current; low-frequency currents (electrodiagnosis); high-frequency currents (long-and-short wave diathermy); static electricity.
4. *Hydrotherapy:* hot and cold, medicated, electric baths; douches and showers; whirlpool bath, therapeutic pool; colonic irrigation.
5. *Mechanotherapy:* massage; general and special exercise; occupational therapy.[37]

In addition, physical therapy includes the process of instruction, in that it is often necessary to teach patients or their families, or both, about the use of prosthetic and orthopedic appliances and the use of continuing therapeutic exercises and other home treatment procedures. Physical therapy generally is regarded as having three major phases or applications:

1. *Prevention:* to prevent deformity or disability, instruction and practice may be given in corrective posture and movement techniques, muscle reeducation or progressive relaxation as well as preoperative exercises given before surgical procedures.
2. *Diagnosis and treatment:* use of physical therapy as a form of testing, to assist the physician in establishing the diagnosis of certain conditions and in determining prognosis and the treatment required; treatment by medically prescribed physical therapy procedures and techniques.
3. *Rehabilitation:* this should begin the day the patient enters a hospital or rehabilitation center and continue until maximum functional or organic recovery is achieved. It includes instruction in functional training, ambulation and self-care activities leading to maximum social and vocational independence.

Physical therapy is based on medical guidance and precisely stated objectives. It is normally applied on a one-to-one basis in which the patient is, for the most part, in a passive or recipient role; it has comparatively little effect

---

[37] Richard Kovacs: *A Manual of Physical Therapy.* 4th Ed. Philadelphia, Lea and Febiger, 1949, pp. 13–14.

on his social or emotional development. As in the case of occupational therapy, this field normally requires graduation from an approved school or department of physical therapy and the passing of a state board examination.

CORRECTIVE THERAPY

Corrective therapy is the treatment of patients by medically prescribed physical exercises and activities designed to strengthen and coordinate functions and to prevent muscular decline resulting from lengthy convalescence or inactivity due to illness.[38] It places emphasis on functional training and practice in the more advanced stages of rehabilitation and makes use of various types of exercises and modified sports activities. In addition, it may provide instruction in the use of orthopedic and prosthetic appliances.

The Veterans Administration employs the largest number of personnel specifically identified as corrective therapists. Generally, corrective therapy in the V.A. hospitals includes the following types of treatment activities:

1. Conditioning exercises to develop strength, endurance, neuromuscular coordination and agility; reconditioning exercise to prevent both physical and psychological deconditioning.
2. Exercises and resocialization activities for psychiatric patients, specifically oriented toward the accomplishment of psychiatric objectives.
3. Teaching self-care activities, including personal hygiene.
4. Teaching of functional ambulation and elevation techniques, including the use of all types of prosthetic devices.
5. Therapeutic swimming (hydrogymnastic) programs.
6. Corrective and postural exercises prescribed and administered for specific conditions.
7. Conditioning, reconditioning, self-care and motivation activities for aged and infirm patients.
8. Special activities in the reorientation of the blind.
9. Training in the operation of manually controlled motor vehicles, where appropriate.

Corrective therapy may be provided in ward or clinic situations or in outdoor exercise or games areas. Normally, prescription for corrective therapy is given on an individual basis, although the program of activity itself may be carried on in a group setting.

The title "corrective therapist" is normally given to persons who work in this field in hospitals, nursing homes and rehabilitation centers. The minimum educational requirement is a baccalaureate in physical education from an accredited school, which should include a strong component of courses in anatomy, kinesiology and related courses, followed by a period of clinical training involving 400 to 600 hours in an affiliated hospital approved by the American Corrective Therapy Association.

ADAPTED PHYSICAL EDUCATION

A field that is closely related to corrective therapy is *adapted physical education.* This term is normally applied to programs of modified physical activity provided in educational settings to meet the needs of atypical students with

---

[38] *Orientation Manual, Physical Medicine and Rehabilitation.* Washington, D.C., Veterans Administration Department of Medicine and Surgery, March, 1966, p. 183.

physical or psychological disability. In some settings, the term "corrective physical education" is used.

In adapted or corrective physical education, the activities of students should be highly individualized, with the choice and modification of activity based on medical diagnosis, prescription and supervision. Its application should mean that all students in a school setting are able to engage in some form of physical education:

> Adapted physical education is for every student who cannot safely or successfully participate in the regular program. Adapted physical education should not be limited to students with postural, orthopedic, and organic conditions. The program should include students with visual handicaps and hearing impairment, as well as those with intellectual limitations, behavior problems, perceptual-motor difficulties, and (other) physical impairments. In addition to students with chronic conditions, adapted programs should provide for those recuperating from injuries and accidents and those convalescing from long or short term illnesses.[39]

In general, corrective therapy and adapted physical education tend to share similar objectives and employ the same types of activities. Adapted physical educators make greater use of modified games and sports, while corrective therapists rely more heavily on various types of individualized exercises and functional training activities.

Other Activity Therapies

In addition to the therapies just described, a number of other therapies are used in various rehabilitation settings and are frequently included under the general heading of "activity therapies."

EDUCATIONAL THERAPY

Educational therapy is the conscious utilization of instruction in academic areas of education to develop the mental and physical capabilities of hospitalized patients. Instruction given at various levels may be accredited by recognized educational authorities. It may be restricted to classwork in such subjects as English, mathematics and the physical or social sciences—all carefully geared to the capabilities of those taking part and with teaching methods designed to meet individual needs.

In addition, in some programs of educational therapy, discussion groups serve to promote motivation and social involvement. Such sessions may include current events discussions, travelogues, seminars on problems of aging, human relations and similar topics. Educational programs of this type are becoming increasingly important in treatment plans for chronic, long-term geriatric patients and in some cases have been blended with "sensitivity training" or "encounter group" methods to promote interaction, awareness and involvement on the part of aged patients. One approach to using discussion groups in this way has been titled "remotivation therapy."

---

[39] See *Journal of Health, Physical Education and Recreation*, May, 1969, p. 45.

Educational therapists normally are people who hold a college degree with a major in education, combined with several months of training in a clinical setting.

MANUAL ARTS THERAPY

Manual arts therapy is the use of industrial arts activities of vocational value in programs of actual or simulated work situations that help patients prepare for return to community life and successful vocational adjustment.

In part, such therapy is used to appraise patients' reactions, functional ability, emotional status and aptitudes in order to help them in planning realistic rehabilitation goals relating to post-hospitalization employment or involvement in a sheltered workshop. In addition, manual arts therapy may have the same goals as occupational therapy, in terms of direct stimulation and improvement of the patient's physical and mental functioning. Typically, seven broad categories of manual arts therapy are metalworking, woodworking, electrical work, graphic and applied arts, agriculture and hospital industries. Within these categories, the demands of many types of job operations can be duplicated and the patient's level of performance evaluated.

The normal preparation of a manual arts therapist consists of a college degree with a major in industrial arts, agriculture or some other related field, followed by a period of between two and seven months training at an approved hospital or rehabilitation center.

INDUSTRIAL THERAPY

This field consists of the therapeutic use of activities related to the operation of the hospital. Formerly, it was known as "hospital industry"; it involves the patient working in such capacities as laborer, carpenter, kitchen worker, electrician, plumber, clerk-typist, laboratory technician, psychiatric aide or nursing aide. In some settings, such assignments of patients (e.g., unskilled labor, laundry help, grounds maintenance and the like) have represented little more than a form of cheap labor that helps to keep the hospital going. However, when properly supervised, industrial therapy has real value for patients. A Veterans Administration statement to this effect holds that

> The motivation provided, the acceptance engendered, the socialization encouraged, the psychodynamics observed provide definite therapeutic benefits for the patient which far outweigh the benefits the hospital may receive from the patient's efforts.[40]

The distinction between industrial arts and manual arts therapy is that the former generally involves performing a real work function that is significant in the operation of the hospital, while the latter is basically a form of modified instruction and treatment within a clinic or workshop setting. Industrial therapy is not normally carried on under the guidance of specially trained therapists but

---

[40] *Orientation Manual. op. cit.*, p. 27.

is most valuable when selective placement techniques are used and patients are carefully observed and evaluated.

There is a growing body of opinion that work in itself is an important form of therapeutic experience and makes a significant contribution to the patient's feeling of self-worth and importance, as well as to his growing readiness for discharge to the community and ultimate vocational adjustment. This view is based in part on the high value that modern society places on work as a human endeavor. It also is based on the nature of work that relates patients to reality-based situations, providing a structure to their lives and a sense of concrete accomplishment.

VOCATIONAL ADJUSTMENT

In some situations, manual arts and industrial therapy are combined with vocational or career counseling in a treatment program designed, when possible, to enable patients to return to the community and to hold a meaningful job. According to the Pennsylvania State Mental Hospital Manual cited earlier, Vocational Adjustment Services are intended to help patients find productive work roles satisfying to them that permit realization of their highest vocational potential, either in the outside society or the institutional community:

> Vocational Adjustment is the planned utilization of work activities in a realistic manner to meet the needs of the patient/resident, who for some reason is presently not able to compete in the normal work role expected by society. Its operation is based on planned work activity that combines a variety of learning and counseling techniques to provide the motivation to foster the development of goals (emotional, social, academic, financial, and vocational), appropriate to the individual.

> The vocational adjustment program involves finding, developing, and providing the opportunity for realistic and therapeutic work experiences based on the current needs of the individual patient/resident, and utilizing existing work and training areas throughout the institution and community.[41]

ACTIVITIES OF DAILY LIVING

A closely linked form of activity therapy found in many rehabilitation programs today is called A.D.L., or activities of daily living. It involves group and individual experiences in self-care, home management, shopping, cleaning, cooking and similar tasks. In some hospital situations, for example, patients may live in a special apartment unit where they take on responsibility for self-care before being discharged completely or moved to an off-grounds semi-independent residential location. In some cases, A.D.L. is made one of the assigned responsibilities of the activity therapist, who might be an occupational therapist or therapeutic recreation worker. In other situations, it might be defined more specifically as "homemaking therapy," and assigned to a specialist known as the "homemaking rehabilitation consultant." Such individuals are usually college graduates with a degree in home economics or occupational therapy, followed by in-service or graduate training in work with the physically or mentally dis-

---

[41] *Pennsylvania State Mental Hospital Manual. op. cit.*, section on Vocational Adjustment, p. 3.

abled. Degrees or work experience in such fields as dietetics, nutrition or home economics or practical experience in homemaking and child care are also valuable attributes.

The homemaking rehabilitation consultant adapts knowledge of home management, family finance, nutrition and similar subjects to meet the needs of disabled persons who have housekeeping responsibilities to which they will return on discharge. The specialist may either provide direct retraining experiences in these areas to patients or may, as a resource specialist, counsel other persons on the rehabilitation team. His goals should be to strengthen the skills of patients in these areas and to help restore their confidence in being able to handle family problems, at which they may have failed in the past.

MUSIC THERAPY

The use of music for therapeutic purposes is found more widely in psychiatric treatment programs than in physical rehabilitation settings. Emphasis is placed on the use of music as a means of promoting group dynamics, nonverbal communication and individual expression. Both improvisation and instruction in technical skills are stressed, with the emphasis usually on instrumental music.

Music is generally viewed as a medium through which disturbed patients may be reached and involved and in which they may find not only emotional expression and release but also a growing sense of self-worth. It is regarded as a supportive therapy that facilitates other treatment methods. A number of colleges offer degree programs in music therapy today. To meet the standards of the National Association for Music Therapy, qualified music therapists must complete a six-month internship in approved psychiatric hospitals affiliated with their institution.

ART THERAPY

Like the field of music therapy, art therapy is generally regarded as a form of treatment that provides the opportunity for healthy self-expression and growth, self-awareness, communication and relation to society. Art has been widely used in the past as a means of understanding the dynamic elements in a patient's illness (it is chiefly used in psychiatric therapy) and helping him express himself and recognize the source of some of his own difficulties through nonverbal forms of expression.

In recent years, there has been a growing recognition of the value of creative expression in healthy personality development and integration. Art therapy generally focuses on the freer forms of artistic expression, such as drawing, painting, modeling and sculpture. It is commonly seen as a highly flexible, individualized experience in which patients select their own project and proceed at their own pace, with the encouragement and help of the art therapist. In some settings, an art studio is simply made available for the voluntary use of patients, unlike other forms of therapy that may be prescribed and carefully structured for them.

Art therapy may also be used for specific hospital projects, such as the design of Christmas cards and the provision of posters or other art work for departments of public information, recreation or volunteers. A number of colleges and special schools have initiated special training programs for art therapists that include course work in psychology, psychopathology, rehabilitation and therapeutic methods, as well as art techniques.

DANCE THERAPY

Like art and music therapy, dance therapy is based on the view that expressed feeling, meaningfully shared, can aid in the integration of the personality and growth in the ability to relate to others. It is particularly useful in work with individuals for whom words are difficult or impossible.

Dance therapy utilizes the tools of basic dance movement and rhythmic action as a means toward nonverbal communication. In many hospitals, both psychiatric and physically disabled patients may be involved in social forms of dance, such as folk, square and social dancing, as part of the overall recreation program. When it is applied as dance therapy, it consists of a simplified and unstructured form of modern or creative dance, permitting highly individualized, free personal movement. The dance therapist aids individuals or groups of patients in discovering their own capabilities for expressive movement, using simple music, drum rhythms or even vocalization and other improvised sounds, as accompaniment.

At its most effective, dance therapy is carried on in close consultation with psychiatrists and other hospital personnel, with close attention being paid to the psychodynamic needs and recovery process of individual participants. There has been an increasing amount of research and special training in this field, encouraged by the American Dance Therapy Association.

PLAY THERAPY

This form of therapy is generally carried on with younger children in hospital or psychiatric treatment settings. In the hospital, it may be used with both general medical and psychiatric patients. In one general hospital setting it has been described as having the following goals:

1. *To offer diversional activity to the child while undergoing medical treatment, thus continuing as much normal play as possible.*
2. *To help alleviate tension or feeling of homesickness, thus aiding orientation by establishing a better rapport with hospital personnel and other children.*
3. *To promote normal development, in spite of physical, mental or emotional disability.*
4. *To promote staff and parental understanding of the purpose, use and selection of play experiences and equipment.*[42]

When used as a form of treatment with disturbed children, play therapy is normally carried on by specially trained therapists with a strong background in guidance and psychotherapeutic principles and techniques. Usually, it is unstructured; children are encouraged to use a variety of media—toys, play equipment, clay, finger-paints, construction materials, dolls, clothing and similar

---

[42] Eloise C. Parker: "Play Therapy." *American Journal of Occupational .Therapy*, September–October, 1952.

free-expression materials—in a completely free way. They play either individually or in small groups, with a therapist who encourages them, helps them resolve difficulties and talks with them about what they are doing and why but does *not* instruct or guide them in any formal way. Play therapy is used as a means of understanding disturbed children and diagnosing the bases of their illness and also of helping them express themselves in nonverbal ways. For severely disturbed children, play may represent the only way to encourage self-expression and communication and may represent the first step in the process of communicating with a therapist and beginning the treatment process.

BIBLIOTHERAPY

This field consists of the guided use of reading to promote patient recovery. Normally, it is carried on by hospital librarians who become specialists in understanding patient needs and who help them in selecting books, magazines or stories that will meet their interests and promote specific aspects of reintegration. Generally, it does not constitute a separate professional field with its own area of training but represents the work of librarians who become knowledgeable in the area of psychodynamics and who work closely with medical personnel in understanding and guiding patients in their reading programs.

Other Group Therapies

Each of the activity therapies just described may, to some degree, be part of the responsibility of therapeutic recreation specialists or may overlap with therapeutic recreation service. For example, in some hospitals or treatment centers, recreation workers conduct arts and crafts, music or dance programs and activities of daily living. Similarly, adapted sports may be provided in some situations by recreation specialists, although they would not normally be responsible for the kinds of one-to-one, medically prescribed services provided by physical therapists.

In addition to the services presented here, numerous other special forms of activity therapy may be found, such as "poetry therapy," "gardening therapy," and other unique areas of participation. Activity therapists in general may also be expected to conduct special programs like "remotivation therapy," "reality orientation" and "sensory training" and to apply principles of behavior modification or reality therapy in their regular activities. In such cases, they may be given in-service training or encouraged to attend outside institutes to become qualified to use these special methods.

STATUS AND ROLE OF THE THERAPEUTIC RECREATION SPECIALIST

This chapter has thus far examined the early development and functions of and professional education in therapeutic recreation service. It has examined a number of allied treatment disciplines, or activity therapies, and made clear that in many institutional settings, therapeutic recreation does not function as a separate department or service but is an integral part of a department of rehabilitation or department of activity or adjunctive therapies. Within this framework, it is important to stress that the therapeutic recreation specialist *must* be prepared to work knowledgeably and cooperatively as part of the treatment team.

Working Within the Treatment Team

In addition to working closely with other activity therapists, the therapeutic recreation specialist must also coordinate his or her efforts with medical practitioners, dietetic and nutritional services, other health aides or health educators, nursing and related care services, psychological and social services, speech pathologists, the clergy and, of course, representatives of the community or concerned voluntary organizations. Within many hospitals, five or six of these disciplines may work closely on the treatment team in diagnosing patient needs, determining their program and formulating treatment plans. It is essential that therapeutic recreation specialists be accepted on this team and that they play a significant role if they are to gain respect for their field of service and make a significant contribution to the overall treatment process. Witt describes alternative approaches to playing the team "game," suggesting that the most appropriate concept is one in which

> . . . the client's needs are directly served and he is viewed as the focal point of all team interactions. Assessment, objective setting, programming to meet objectives and on-going evaluation are areas in which all team members contribute skills and ideas to facilitate the delivery of services. Open communication, fostering a varied exchange of viewpoints and resources are essential to selecting and implementing a program with optimal potential for meeting the client's needs.[43]

To make the team work effectively, Witt writes, it is necessary for the specialist to provide accurate and clearly written or verbal information to other team numbers and to collaborate closely with them in order to provide consistent and meaningful service and avoid duplication of efforts. It is helpful for each member of the team to gain a broad familiarity with basic medical terminology and concepts and, when possible, to extend his or her own area of special competence by developing secondary therapeutic skills, as well as generalized skills of team management and administration. Above all, it is necessary to put the overall success of the team before all matters of individual prestige or dominance by avoiding personal or professional biases or defensiveness.

Status of the Field

The question must now be asked—what is the present degree of recognition of therapeutic recreation as a specialized field of rehabilitation of community service? As the earlier chapters of this text have indicated, there has been a

---

[43] Jody Witt: "The Team Concept as Interpersonal Ping Pong." *Journal of Leisurability*, Ontario, Canada, April, 1974, n.p.

steady growth of therapeutic recreation, at first in hospitals and other treatment centers and more recently in community-based programs. David C. Park writes,

> *During the first twenty-five years of our development, we have grown a great deal and have experienced significant changes. We began as a profession that was almost exclusively hospital oriented, but we have since developed and declared a broader interpretation of therapeutic recreation. We have recognized the needs of all disabled individuals regardless of where they may reside, including such new areas as nursing homes, day care centers, and penal institutions. We were a profession that was split by semantics and even, to a degree, by philosophy. We now agree that therapeutic recreation is a process which is applicable in many different types of settings. Finally, we began as a profession that included several professional groups, but now there is one strong central organization that is becoming instrumental in bringing about acceptance and the realization that therapeutic recreation is a significant part of the rehabilitation process.*[44]

However, this recognition is still on a somewhat tenuous basis. Community recreators too often tend to see their function with respect to therapeutic recreation service as limited to sponsoring Senior Citizens clubs or providing an occasional special program for the mentally retarded or physically disabled. Few have fully accepted the view that this area of service represents a major responsibility of municipal recreation and park departments. Fewer still have developed meaningful links with institutions in order to facilitate post-discharge or outpatient programming for disabled persons.

In too many hospitals, the view held by administrators or key medical personnel is that recreation is chiefly a diversional activity and thus deserves lower priority than other services that are more closely related to treatment goals. In part, this attitude stems from the fact that, unlike occupational therapy and physical therapy, both of which are certified fields requiring clinical training under medical supervision, the field of therapeutic recreation does *not* require such training. In many institutions, those working in recreation have come from other disciplines and have little specialized preparation for their work.

This problem is made more complex by the fact that many therapeutic recreation specialists today work in settings in which medically oriented training is *not* essential. The recreation leader who works in a Senior Center, a home or school for the retarded, a correctional institution or similar setting may require varied kinds of information related to that disability and its treatment goals and procedures, but it is not basically medical information.

Thus, it is essential that fuller attention be given to the nature of professional education in therapeutic recreation service today, as well as to the kinds of selection, accreditation, registration or certification procedures that might be used to insure a higher standard of professionalism among workers in this field.

Reimbursement and Effect on Recognition

Since so many treatment programs today are largely supported by federal funding sources, such as Medicare, it is important to understand the place of recreation within such structures. For example, Park points out that for a

---

[44] David C. Park, *op. cit.*, p. 63.

number of years, federal Medicare regulations stipulated that such institutions as nursing homes had to have activity programs and activity directors to be eligible for Medicare funds. However, for years no regulations stipulated minimal standards for programs or professional staff, and it was only through the effort of the National Therapeutic Recreation Society in cooperation with the Public Health Service that guidelines were developed that recognized therapeutic recreation as a professional discipline and included meaningful personnel classifications. Despite this progress, in many institutions throughout the United States in which occupational therapy and physical therapy represent reimbursable services, to be paid for by Medicare funds, recreation is *not* billed as a significant medical service. As a consequence, in such treatment centers, it is treated as an unimportant aspect of the overall rehabilitation program and poorly supported.

The fact is, however, that "recreation therapy" service *is* reimbursable through Medicare, Medicaid and third-party carriers in the hospital setting. The Medicare-Medicaid Guide states the following under Regulation Section 6095.75 (Determination of Cost of Services to Beneficiaries):

> *For reimbursement purposes, the reasonable cost of recreational therapy furnished by a hospital to inpatients where such services are ordinarily furnished by the hospital to its inpatients should be included in computing the cost for routine services.*[45]

Therapeutic recreation is also reimbursable in the psychiatric setting as an "active treatment," defined in the Government Programs Reimbursement Manual as a service furnished while the patient is receiving either active treatment or admission and related services necessary for diagnostic study and meeting the following criteria: (a) provided under an individualized treatment or diagnostic plan; (b) reasonably expected to improve the patient's condition or for the purpose of diagnosis; and (c) supervised and evaluated by a physician. Richard Patterson, Director of Activity Therapy at Mercy Hospital and Medical Center in San Diego, California has done a systematic study of federal reimbursement procedures and points out that therapeutic recreation may be billed, just like occupational therapy, physical therapy or electroconvulsive or drug therapy, provided that it is planned for a particular patient and is prescribed, supervised and evaluated by a physician. In addition, it is necessary to document the treatment in medical records, giving progress notes, program descriptions and treatment plans in the accepted style of the regulatory agency and with such frequency as to give a full picture of the therapy administered.

Patterson concludes that, by following reimbursement guidelines properly, it is possible to lay the foundation for an income-producing, self-sufficient therapeutic recreation program within the general or psychiatric hospital. At the same time, he points out that there are certain pitfalls or dangers in this process, and that although it may upgrade the status of therapeutic recreation as a service and improve the morale of recreation practitioners, it may have a negative effect on the provision of recreation in the treatment setting.[46]

---

[45] Richard Patterson: *The Development of a Self-Sufficient Therapeutic Recreation Service.* Mercy Hospital and Medical Center, San Diego, California, unpublished report, March, 1977, pp. 1–2.

[46] *Ibid.*, pp. 3–5. See also *Medicare and Medicaid Guide.* Blue Cross Association, Chicago, June 11, 1974, pp. 6097, 8063, 8066.

PROFESSIONAL EDUCATION AND THE
WORK OF PROFESSIONAL ORGANIZATIONS

Another priority in upgrading therapeutic recreation as a field of professional service is to improve the quality of major curricula in colleges and universities. Many of the programs that have been recently developed are minimal in terms of staffing, courses offered and, particularly, clinical affiliations with practicum agencies. Although the accreditation process recently initiated by NRPA Council on Accreditation is seeking to improve this situation by identifying high-quality institutions as well as those that fail to meet minimal standards, it will be difficult for it to screen several hundred curricula in the years ahead, given its limited resources and recognition. It may therefore be up to the colleges and universities themselves, working cooperatively on the local level and with the help of state societies, to improve their curricula. A roadblock here is the declining enrollment picture and budgetary crisis that has affected many public and private colleges, forcing them to cut back on staffing and other services and making it difficult for them to put additional resources into new program areas. Nonetheless, it seems clear that such efforts constitute the most promising means of upgrading professional education in the years ahead, producing more highly qualified practitioners and improving the status of workers in this field.

Need to Clarify Roles, Functions and
Accomplishments

Just as in the overall field of recreation, the roles and functions of therapeutic recreation specialists are extremely complex and varied. Unlike the physical therapist, who has a clearly defined set of objectives and techniques, the recreation worker may have goals and methods that vary widely according to the setting in which he is employed and the patients he is serving.

Therefore, it is necessary to define more sharply each of these specialized areas of service as to the needs of those served and the unique responsibilities or functions of the therapeutic recreation specialist in each of them. It is quite apparent that this varies widely from institution to institution—even within a particular area of service, such as psychiatric care. It is clear also that the other fields of professional service described earlier also impinge on recreation. Occupational therapists frequently assume major responsibility for recreation in their institutions. Corrective therapists frequently conduct modified games and sports activities. Music, art and dance therapists often provide services that might be regarded as recreational.

This confusion of role is made more complex by the fact that in an increasing number of departments of activity therapies, especially those committed to the "milieu therapy" approach, the functions of *all* practitioners have become blurred.

Again, it should be the responsibility of college and university educators in this field and of those in professional organizations to carry on systematic research to clarify roles and functions. Following this, it would be appropriate for them to make recommendations regarding the assignment of responsibilities that might be helpful to those responsible for organizing services in institutions, communities or in federal or statewide systems of rehabilitation. Closely attached to this is the need to conduct more effective research related to effective methodology in therapeutic recreation service, and to the legitimate outcomes of such programs.

SUGGESTED TOPICS FOR CLASS DISCUSSION, EXAMINATIONS OR STUDENT PAPERS

1. Identify and describe several of the major functions carried out by therapeutic recreation specialists in hospitals or other treatment settings today. In what ways do these extend beyond the direct provision of activity programs?

2. How does the National Therapeutic Recreation Society promote professional development in this field today?

3. Contrast the work of specialists in other fields of activity therapy (such as occupational or physical therapy) with that of therapeutic recreation specialists. How do these fields differ? How do they overlap?

4. Therapeutic recreation was formerly regarded as a hospital-based or institutionally based field, quite separate from the broader field of community recreation. How is it regarded today?

chapter 4
Program Planning and Therapeutic Techniques

This chapter is concerned with the process of program development in therapeutic recreation service. It presents general guidelines for program planning and summarizes several basic approaches for identifying goals and selecting appropriate activities. In addition, it examines methods of organizing and scheduling activities in various types of settings and concludes by describing a number of recently developed forms of therapeutic intervention that may be used with individuals or groups in activity therapy programs.

GUIDELINES FOR PROGRAM PLANNING

Therapeutic recreation program planning depends on certain key factors, such as (a) the type of sponsoring agency or agencies; (b) the service model being followed (*medical-clinical, education and training*, and so on); (c) the exact nature of the population being served, in terms of type and degree of disability, age, diversity, stage of recovery or rehabilitation, and so on; (d) the overall philosophy of the treatment staff and the services being provided by other disciplines; (e) the resources of the program, including leadership, facilities, equipment and assisting community groups; and (f) the nature of patient or client involvement in program development.

There is no single pattern of program development that is followed in all settings. In some cases, when a new program is being initiated, the recreation worker in charge begins with the tentative introduction of a few obviously needed activities or services and gradually adds to them, building up a more comprehensive program structure. In other situations, program activities are clearly delineated by a set of guidelines that may have been developed in a large hospital or rehabilitation system over a period of time and are set forth in manuals or in-service training programs. Just as in the planning of community recreation programs, several influences help to determine the choice of activities, such as traditional practices within the field, the expressed desires of those being served, current practices or innovative services and the views of the program director or supervisor. Unlike community recreation programs, however, there *must* be a clear emphasis on achieving distinctly stated goals, as far as the treatment or rehabilitation needs of patients are concerned.

On one level, the therapeutic recreation specialist may simply seek to identify the most important goals of the population he or she is serving.

In many new situations, it is necessary to work in close cooperation with other professionals and to solicit their advice and suggestions. For example, Evans writes of the process of developing a diversified recreation program in a 217-bed active treatment hospital concerned with short-term patient care in Guelph, Ontario. Here, it was necessary to develop appropriate treatment goals and activities for a wide range of patients, including postoperative, stroke and burn patients, diabetics, cardiac convalescents, pediatric and geriatric populations and those in other categories of treatment service. The bulk of the case load was obtained via referrals from doctors and head nurses, and it was necessary to work closely with the Director of Nursing, the occupational therapist and the physical therapist, as well as volunteers and representatives of community agencies.[1] Obviously, within this framework no single set of goals could easily be developed, and it was necessary to be highly flexible in adapting to the needs and expressed interests of patients, as well as the recommendations of medical and other staff members.

A number of examples of objectives for program service are presented in Chapters 1 and 2, with others appearing in later chapters of this text. To make sure that these goals are comprehensive and realistic, it is important to analyze them systematically. Avedon suggests that program activities are generally directed in relation to one of the following five objectives:

1. Diagnosis and Evaluation. *Recreation personnel are in a position to contribute to the treatment team's understanding of a patient's social behavior, self-concept, leisure skills and interests, or other important areas of personal functioning. Such information, gathered through interviews, informal conversation, or direct observation, is useful both to other staff members and to the therapeutic recreation specialist, in developing further program goals or suggestions for needed involvement.*

2. Programming for Treatment and Care Purposes. *Here, participation is specifically geared to achieve direct therapeutic outcomes, such as providing a release for aggression, developing confidence in social situations, or helping to develop useful recreation or self-care skills. Frequently, at this stage, activities must be directly attuned to medically-imposed needs and limitations, such as the need to divert the patient's attention from discomfort, or to help him begin to adjust to a disability.*

3. Contribute to Pre-Discharge Counseling. *This aspect of therapeutic recreation service in the institutional setting is generally described by the term "leisure counseling" [see p. 117]. It involves helping the patient understand the place of leisure and recreation in his life, and begin to develop improved attitudes and motivations, as well as improved skills, that will permit him to use leisure positively in the community setting after discharge. It may also involve direct referral to community programs, or post-discharge counseling and assistance.*

---

[1] Lorna Evans: "The Guelph General Hospital Story." *Journal of Leisurability*, Ontario, Canada, January, 1974, pp. 27–31.

4. Adjustment to Altered Life Situations. *Here, the emphasis is on helping the patient or client ventilate feelings of anger against a recent loss or disability, and begin to strengthen feelings of self-worth and independence. Following this, the effort is to help the patient determine what his residual skills are, reawake dormant skills or interests, and learn new interests or leisure capabilities, in order to live as fully as possible within the reality of his changed life circumstances.*

5. Programming for Sheltered Experience. *Assuming that the patient or client will continue to require special supportive services, or will live in an institution, special residence or other sheltered setting, this final area of therapeutic recreation programming involves providing appropriate leisure opportunities geared to the individual's level of social and physical capability. Avedon describes five such levels:* isolated, secluded, limited, included *and* independent, *and suggests guidelines for serving each level. Throughout, of course, the overriding goal is to help the client achieve the maximum level of independence and autonomous social functioning.*[2]

Numerous examples of appropriate programs for different types of disability categories are provided in Chapters 5 through 9. The purpose here is to analyze the *process* of program planning, rather than to recommend specific *kinds* of programs, or examples of indicated activities for special populations. Over the past several years, a number of authorities have evolved scientific approaches to program planning in therapeutic settings. Several examples of such approaches will be presented here.

Systems Analysis in Therapeutic Recreation

Peterson has presented a model of program planning in therapeutic recreation service with three basic elements: *input* (combination of clients, resources, personnel and materials), *transformation process* (involving in this case some form of service or program involvement) and *output* (referring to changed patient or client behavior).[3] The key to this sequence is the element of *feedback*, in which the programmer seeks ongoing information to determine whether the system is working as anticipated or desired or whether it needs to be modified or redesigned.

Peterson devised a matrix, or grid, of therapeutic recreation services of three types (preventative, sustaining and remedial) that in turn are provided on administrative, supervisory, leadership and educational levels. She points out that specific therapeutic recreation systems must function within the framework of a larger agency, institution or department that in turn exists within the suprasystem of the overall society. These surrounding or higher systems provide the input to the therapeutic recreation system in the form of patients or clients, staffing and other resources at the same time that they impose agency or societal expectations, values and constraints. The heart of Peterson's method is based

---

[2] Elliott M. Avedon: *Therapeutic Recreation Service: An Applied Behavioral Science Approach.* Englewood Cliffs, New Jersey, Prentice-Hall, 1974, pp. 80–103.
[3] Carol A. Peterson: "Application of Systems Analysis Procedures to Program Planning in Therapeutic Recreation Service." *In* Avedon, *Ibid.*, pp. 128–155.

on the definition of systems analysis as

> *a systematic approach to helping a decision maker choose a course of action by investigating his full problem, searching out his objectives and alternatives, using an appropriate framework—insofar as possible analytic—to bring judgment and intuition to bear on the problem.*[4]

Based on this understanding, Peterson has designed a program planning procedure founded on fundamental principles of systems analysis and applied to the actual problems and situations found in therapeutic recreation service. She describes it as a flexible tool rather than a totally fixed procedure. It contains seven stages that might be applied, with some degree of elaboration or modification, to any therapeutic recreation setting:

1. *Conceptualization and formulation.* Here, the planner or analyst identifies the components in the process (agency, clients, resources, current status of program and purposes or objectives).
2. *Investigation.* This stage involves fuller study of the clients, the agency and the environment in relation to program goals and identification of the most promising alternative program elements or strategies to achieve objectives.
3. *Analysis of Alternatives.* The planner analyzes the probable outcomes of each alternative program element or strategy based on known factors in the situation or overall system. In some types of systems, this is done with computer analysis; this tends to be done less frequently in therapeutic recreation service.
4. *Determination of Strategy or Course of Action.* Here, the planner selects an appropriate course of action and identifies needed service components, resources, leadership, facilities and so forth.
5. *Design of Program.* In this key stage, the planner formulates specific goals and objectives of the program (usually stated in clearly measurable and quantifiable behavioral terms). He or she also designs the actual program sequence, activities, schedules and so on and constructs criteria and evaluation methods for each element of service.
6. *Operations Planning.* As a continuation of the previous stage, detailed schedules, staff assignment and training, preparation of facilities, acquisition of needed supplies or equipment and similar operations are planned and put in motion.
7. *Implementation.* The plan is put into action. As in all systems operations, it is continually reviewed and needed improvements or changes are carried out. If feedback indicates that elements need to be redesigned, or objectives rethought, this is done. Full evaluation would be carried out after a period of time in order to give the operation sufficient time to achieve its stated goals.[5]

Peterson's approach, which she illustrates specifically with the example of a nursing home's therapeutic recreation program, may be applied to many other types of settings. It may be used to design an entire program structure or to solve a single limited problem in an agency.

Computer-Based Activity Analysis and Prescriptive Programming

A second line of development for providing a more rational and scientific basis for selecting and prescribing appropriate recreation activities for disabled

---

[4] E. S. Quade; Cited in Peterson, *Ibid.*, p. 136.
[5] Adapted from Peterson, *Ibid.*, pp. 137–155.

populations has explored the use of the computer. In the past, activities have been selected and used with a limited concern about their specific elements, applications and outcomes. Similarly, behavioral objectives for patients and clients have been stated in extremely broad terms. A number of studies during the past several years, however, have sought to sharpen both the understanding of the specific elements inherent in recreational activities and the methods for modifying them for varying levels of skill or making them progressively more demanding or challenging. Recently, investigators have explored the potential of computer analysis in determining program goals, client needs and appropriate forms of activity prescription. Such approaches show considerable promise for providing more precise and sophisticated methods of designing programs in order to meet specific treatment, rehabilitative or educational goals.

Under a three-year grant from the Bureau of Education for the Handicapped of the U.S. Office of Education, Doris Berryman and Claudette Lefebvre of New York University have developed preliminary models intended to assist institutions or community agencies provide effective and comprehensive therapeutic recreation services for disabled children and youth. In the investigators' words,

> . . . there is a great need to systematically analyze and organize existing information on utilization of play and recreation activities to achieve specific education, learning and/or treatment goals; develop a conceptual model for comprehensive analysis of play and recreation activities to determine the sensory-motor, cognitive, affective and social dimensions inherent in those activities; and, utilizing the information derived from these analyses, design a therapeutically-oriented recreation program for disabled children and youth which will assist in developing perceptual-motor, cognitive and social skills and abilities.[6]

Following the design of these models and computer programs storing activity analysis data and client demographic and behavioral assessment information, Berryman and Lefebvre moved ahead to carry out pilot demonstrations of the project in the town of Hempstead, New York. Clearly, this approach offers significant promise for helping to make therapeutic recreation a more significant and respected form of service, particularly within institutions or agencies operating under the *medical-clinical* or *education and training* models. Like the Peterson systems analysis method, however, it does raise a serious question as to whether it is possible to reduce an area of human service to a computerized model with precise diagnoses and quantifiable, measurable outcomes. Certainly, within such fields as psychotherapy or social work, although the broad directions of treatment may be indicated, it would be unlikely that the exact outcomes of treatment or the effects of different types of therapeutic strategies could be either predicted or measured objectively as a practical form of everyday programming. Beyond this, as earlier chapters have shown, a major thrust in recent years has been *away* from prescriptive programming by therapists and in the direction of

---

[6] Doris L. Berryman and Claudette B. Lefebvre: "A Computer Based System for Comprehensive Activity Analysis and Prescriptive Recreation Programming for Disabled Children and Youth." *In* Betty van der Smissen (ed.): *Indicators of Change in the Recreation Environment—A National Research Symposium.* State College, Pennsylvania, Penn State HPER Series No. 6, 1975, pp. 99–116.

milieu therapy, in which all concerned (patients and staff alike) serve as therapeutic agents, chiefly through a process of social interaction and overcoming problems of self-management and group living.

Nonetheless, it seems clear that within the *medical-clinical* model of service there will be continuing efforts to develop new and more effective models of therapeutic recreation service delivery. One such model has been developed by David Compton and Donna Price. Entitled the *Linear Model for Individual Treatment in Recreation* (LMIT), it represents a detailed model for planning, implementing, recording and evaluating program service for an individual client and has seven stages.[7] The stages, or phases, are similar to those in other systems approaches, including developing a personal profile of the client, determining objectives and planning activities for the treatment unit, implementing the unit treatment plan and evaluating its results.

Its unique element is the utilization of a rating system that evaluates performance over time in six developmental areas: cognitive, communicative, motor, self-help, social-emotional and expressive. The important point about the use of this type of performance evaluation is that it specifies exactly the types of tasks to be performed, as well as the exact behavioral outcomes of planned or prescribed activity. Use of such instruments is essential if systems analysis or computer-based planning are to contribute to the successful development of therapeutic recreation programs. Compton describes the essential purpose of LMIT or similar models:

> . . . to provide the practitioner with a greater degree of accountability for the "purposive intervention" in therapeutic recreation; to utilize the most current and relevant techniques from related areas; to develop precision in the delivery of therapeutic recreation services; to provide the therapist with a step-by-step systems analysis of the delivery of therapeutic recreation services to individuals; for application primarily to those individuals who have accentuated needs, especially the more profoundly handicapped; and for application to clients regardless of their age, sex, diagnostic category or severity of dysfunction.[8]

Despite the fact that Compton and Price's model is primarily concerned with young children, a similar approach might be used with any age group or type of disability. Peterson's major illustration, for example, was the development of an activity program for a nursing home. It is important to stress that the initiation of such a program is expensive. Although it is possible to employ computer experts, train observers and mount a substantial budget in a program-planning process in a federally funded project, such as Berryman and Lefebvre's, in most situations, this would not be feasible.

Realistically, it is likely that, through experimental work done by leading researchers and theorists in this field, new program principles and uses of activity with specific disability categories will be developed and will then be applied directly by practitioners in treatment settings. New guidelines or formulations for developing programs tend to be disseminated through the professional literature, by professional organizations, or, in many cases, through networks of organizations that guide member agencies or institutions in their basic directions and policies.

---

[7] David M. Compton and Donna Price: "Individualizing Your Treatment Program: A Case Study Using LMIT." *Therapeutic Recreation Journal*, 4th Quarter, 1975, pp. 127–134.
[8] *Ibid.*

As an example, in the State of Pennsylvania, the State Department of Public Welfare operates 20 hospitals for the mentally ill, 9 schools and hospitals for the mentally retarded, 10 youth development centers, 10 general hospitals and a number of additional diagnostic, evaluation, restoration and mental health centers—a total of 55 different institutions. Through policy guidelines, training programs, use of state consultants and development of manuals, strong direction is given to each of these programs by state officials. As new and promising methods or treatment approaches are developed, they tend to be channeled by central offices to all appropriate institutions, and their use is encouraged.

ORGANIZATION OF THERAPEUTIC RECREATION SERVICE

The actual organization of therapeutic recreation service within an institution or agency involves a number of aspects: (a) staff and administrative structure, (b) available facilities, (c) scheduling of activities and (d) patterns of patient or client involvement.

Staff and Administrative Structure

This varies considerably from institution to institution. In terms of administrative locations, recreation may be provided as a separate service, with its own departmental title, or may be part of a larger department of service. In a regional study of recreation in psychiatric institutions, it was found that recreation was most frequently located within a separate department (42.7 per cent) and next as a service within a department of psychiatry (13.3 per cent), occupational therapy (12.0 per cent), activity therapies (10.7 per cent), rehabilitation service (5.3 per cent) and within several other, less frequently found, types of structures.[9]

It may be provided as an institution-wide service, with a single centralized recreation staff organizing and providing services for the entire patient or client population, *or* it may be on a decentralized basis, in which each separate unit of the institution has its own treatment staff (usually including medical, nursing, activity therapy and social service personnel).

Staff members in turn are normally identified by professional titles and Civil Service grades in all governmental institutions and agencies, although within an actual hospital or rehabilitation center, they may be assigned a different title within the table of organization. For example, a Civil Service title might be *Recreation Therapist II*, while within a given institution the title might be *Senior Activity Leader*. Program responsibilities are customarily assigned to personnel according to rank, with upper-level staff members, such as directors, supervisors or senior therapists, assuming major responsibility for planning, coordinating and directing services while lower-level personnel provide direct program service and activity leadership. The numbers of recreation staff

---

[9] Richard Kraus: *Recreation and Related Therapies in Psychiatric Rehabilitation.* New York, Herbert Lehman College and Faculty Research Foundation, November, 1972, p. 17.

members may vary greatly, with as many as 50 or 60 activity therapists, including 15 or 20 recreation specialists, in a large state psychiatric hospital or physical rehabilitation center and as few as one or two leaders in a small nursing home or sheltered workshop program.

Available Facilities

Obviously, the number and type of available facilities play a major role in helping to determine program services. Many large psychiatric or chronic disease hospitals have auditoriums, lounges, music rooms and even swimming pools, arts and crafts shops, outdoor ballfields, picnic areas and tennis courts. On the other hand, it is not uncommon to find some hospitals in which all activities are carried on within the ward or in a crowded day room.

Although it is clearly much easier to run a rich activity program in a well-endowed complex, this is not the sole criterion in determining a program's effectiveness. In some penal and correctional institutions, for example, there may be facilities that are hardly used because of lack of staff or administrative support or because problems of security and staff coverage militate against diversified programming. Even though it is important to make the fullest possible use of available resources, it is also possible to "make do." In many nursing homes, for example, cafeterias or dining rooms are also used as meeting rooms, and auditoriums also double as gymnasiums in many agencies. In addition, many hospitals or special schools make use of other public, voluntary or commercially owned facilities in the community at large.

What is critical is that facilities be obtained, improvised or borrowed to serve all of the major elements of a diversified program. The use of facilities must be carefully coordinated with other hospital or agency services to avoid overlap and confusion of use and to insure safety and administrative efficiency. For example, arts and crafts rooms, swimming pools, meeting rooms or other facilities may be used by more than one discipline or by different units of a hospital. These are usually assigned according to schedules worked out by the administrative heads or supervisors of various units or services and cleared by the institution's buildings and grounds staff. When off-grounds facilities are to be used or when patients take a trip to attend some community event, it usually must be cleared through administrative channels, with, in some cases, medical clearance or the permission of parents or guardians.

In addition, there are usually clearly stated hospital or agency guidelines or procedures governing the use of all facilities or the scheduling of all trips. These may include (a) permissions and approval from administration and authorization from parents or guardians; (b) regulations regarding staff members of one sex taking patients or clients of the opposite sex off grounds; (c) nature of transportation, including use of hospital-owned or private vehicles; role of volunteers in assisting with transportation and supervision; (e) required ratios of accompanying staff; (f) regulations controlling participation of patients in outside activities, as opposed to involvement as spectators; (g) regulations governing emergency situations, accidents or lost or runaway patients or clients; and (h) cooperative parties, picnics or other special events sponsored with parents, community groups or other assisting groups.

Activity Scheduling

In the past, many institutions tended to follow an extremely rigid and segmentalized schedule of activities, with weekly schedules posted in all locations and patients assigned to activities at regular times during the day or evening. Today, scheduling tends to be much more flexible in many settings, with a much higher degree of patient choice in the selection of involvements. Schedules are normally worked out through the cooperative effort of all team members in order to meet their particular needs and avoid overlapping and duplication. In most situations, certain services—particularly those connected with medical treatment or prescribed physical therapy—are given the key priority when assigning blocks of time. It is important, however, that other services be given significant blocks of time and that these scheduling commitments then be respected, rather than arbitrarily changed or canceled because of the decision of medical or nursing staff members.

TIME BLOCKS

These are usually worked out in terms of morning, afternoon and evening sessions in which certain key activities are offered each day. Other, more specialized, program elements may be offered less frequently. Each of the major elements in the overall activity program should be assigned appropriate times, including (a) scheduled time for small-group activity; (b) open hours for informal arts and crafts or sports involvement; (c) time for social programs and group discussions; (d) time for religious activity, either on-site or off-grounds; (e) appropriate time for trips and community involvement; (f) time for major events or institution-wide programs, such as large parties, carnivals or bazaars; (g) assigned hours for special therapies, like *sensory training* or *remotivation*; and (h) opportunities for one-to-one or small-group leisure-counseling sessions.

Time blocks must be fitted to availability of facilities as well as to staff schedules. For example, leaders or therapists must have hours assigned to group or team meetings, filling out reports or records, in-service training and other administrative duties. Some of these must be assigned to regular weekly time slots; others may be fitted into gaps between other leadership activities. In developing schedules, it is important not to have major blocks of time, such as evenings and weekends, when *no* activities are offered. In some institutions, Civil Service personnel are employed on a weekday schedule from 9 A.M. to 5 P.M., leaving only part-time workers or aides assigned to evening hours or weekends and these periods extremely barren of activity. This is particularly true because other therapeutic services are not usually scheduled at these times—resulting in a great bulk of empty time for patients. To deal with this problem constructively, some institutions stipulate that activity therapists must work an alternating schedule so that they will have some evening session responsibilities—or duty every third weekend, with days off *during* that week.

Such scheduling should provide both a skeletal framework of regular activities with participation of a prescribed or voluntary nature and enough flexibility to permit the introduction of new activities, events or groups on relatively short notice. As much as possible, patients' needs should be the primary

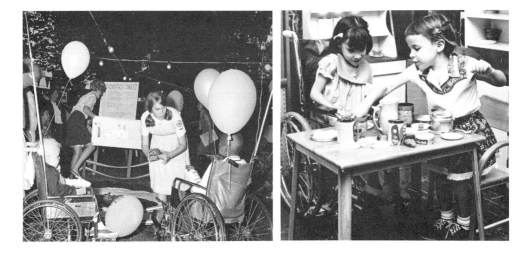

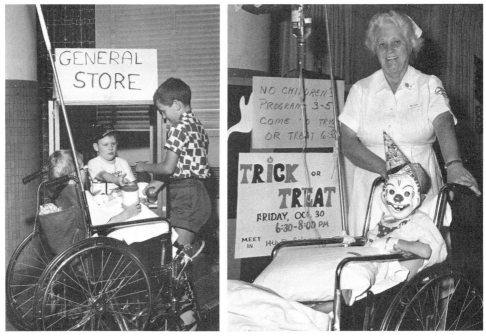

Children enjoy the annual patients' carnival, a Halloween party, creative play with "pots and pans" and a "general store" at the federal National Institute of Health Clinical Center in Bethesda, Maryland.

basis for scheduling decisions—rather than the convenience of staff members or the goal of administrative efficiency.

Patterns of Patient or Client Involvement

There is no single system or structure that gives a representative picture of typical types of patient or client program involvement. As an example of the varied patterns of involvement, the regional study of recreation in psychiatric facilities, described earlier, found that there was an almost equal incidence of hospitals reporting that patients were involved in activities through "complete free choice" (40.0 per cent), "assigned individually" (38.7 per cent) or "assigned by group" (46.7 per cent), with many institutions using a combination of several methods.[10] Although it might appear that the most desirable situation would be one in which patients took part in only those activities that they chose for themselves, in many cases, the nature of their illness is such that if given complete free choice they would engage in *no* recreational, social, work or educational activities at all. The rationale for this approach is expressed in the following passage:

> . . . disruptive, asocial and socially unacceptable behavior, often called emotional disorder, may perhaps best be seen as chronic social disruption. For these people, perhaps, a living and learning program of activities might best meet their needs. . . . An answer then seems to be that the disabled would benefit most from a structured learning situation. The activity therapies can be seen as a part of milieu therapy, which definitely implies a structuring of the environment. Structure involves certain regulations, directions and control, and in a sense at least, certain limitations of freedom for the individual. Such limitations . . . have the very purpose of giving greater freedoms in certain other directions. . . . Various kinds of structure and prescribed activities, with the proper kinds of supervision, have a therapeutic effect.[11]

Optimally, over the course of treatment patients move from a situation in which much of their participation in activity therapy is prescribed for them to one in which they operate primarily through free choice and, indeed, through group action, plan and conduct many aspects of the activity program themselves. Certainly, in community settings, such as Senior Centers or clubs for the physically disabled, the most successful ventures are those in which the participants play a major role in program development.

MODIFICATION AND ADAPTATION OF ACTIVITY

A final key element to be considered in program planning is not just what activities are to be provided but also the form that they should take. In other words, it is not enough to decide that retarded children should have gymnastics or swimming—it is also necessary to determine what the current status of the participants are in these areas, what their potential is and what the goals for the

---

[10] *Ibid.*, pp. 21–22.
[11] *Activity Therapy Manual.* Longview, Ohio, State Hospital, 1973, p. 21.

activity should be. Given these factors, it may be necessary to modify the activities and place them within a sequence that will permit gradual mastery of limited objectives over a period of time. Numerous examples of how activities may be modified to meet the needs of specific disability groups are found in Chapter 10 as well as in other chapters dealing with special populations.

In addition to recreational activities as such, many activity therapy programs include special techniques or approaches that are not clearly recreational but help to promote the therapeutic aspects of participation. In the following section, a number of such methods are described in detail. It might be noted that all of them appear to be concerned with behavior and thus most appropriate for populations with psychiatric disability or social deviance. However, any serious disability has important emotional and psychological overtones and effects, and therefore these methods may in some cases be useful with patients or clients who have physical impairments. All of them represent ways of strengthening the self-concept and social involvement of patients and clients and of developing constructive attitudes, values and habits of participation in positive forms of leisure—among other important goals.

SENSORY TRAINING

This represents a form of group experience specially designed to assist residents in nursing homes or geriatric units in hospitals who are classified as suffering from organic brain syndrome or institutional neurosis. Organic brain syndrome, often called *senile dementia* in the aged, is "commonly due either to vascular degeneration interfering with the blood supply to the brain, or to senile degeneration of the brain substance itself. Its manifestations include memory defect, intellectual deterioration, uninhibited behavior and loss of emotional control."[12]

Institutional neurosis is the term applied by Whitehead to effects of institutionalization on patients who, on admission to a nursing home or hospital and on being subjected to regimentation and loss of their sense of individuality and independence, suffer an erosion of personality.[13] Geriatric patients, who are particularly vulnerable, tend to reduce their sensory input by refusing to respond to the limited stimuli in their isolated environments. Such individuals commonly referred to as "disoriented," seem to have little or no awareness of time or space; often, they do not respond to even the most simple occupational or recreational tasks. The rationale for sensory training, according to Leona Richman, who helped to develop the method, is to make use of participation in a closely knit group and the impact of selected stimuli, guided exercises and social interaction to prevent further atrophy of the senses and, hopefully, to improve alertness of levels of functioning. She describes the method in the following terms:

> 1. *Sensory training is designed for the patient who is regressed, blind, or wheelchair-bound, and does not participate in off-ward activities.*

---

[12] Anthony Whitehead: *In the Service of Old Age: The Welfare of Psychogeriatric Patients.* Baltimore, Penguin Books, 1970, p. 33.
[13] Sylvia Carlson: "Communication and Social Interaction in the Aged." *Nursing Clinics of North America,* June, 1972, p. 254.

2. *Sensory training is a structured, sequential process, which is a shared group/individual experience.*
3. *The program provides the person with differentiated stimuli to improve his/her perception and response to the environment.*
4. *All sense receptors are stimulated: auditory, olfactory, tactile, vision, taste, proprioception, and kinesthetic.*
5. *Sensory training is specifically ordered, structured and designed to increase sensitivity to stimuli by the individual's discrimination, and response to stimuli. A "response-feedback" system is inherent in the group interactional setting.*[14]

The method, as formulated by Richman, formerly an occupational therapist at Bronx State Hospital in New York City, involves a group situation in which patients are brought to a room available at the same time on a daily basis and relatively free from distractions. Patients should be comfortable in the familiar environment. The sessions themselves involve from four to seven patients at a time and last from a half hour to an hour. Patients are greeted by the leader, who introduces herself to them and encourages them patiently to respond; if they do not know their names, they are helped to reply. Patients are encouraged to greet each other by their first names. The leader shakes hands with each patient, since touching is an important form of communication. She also speaks loudly, slowly and clearly, with as much repetition as necessary. When the introductions are over, the leader helps orient group members to the time, place, date and the fact that they are in the hospital or nursing home to be helped; a blackboard or bulletin board may be used for this purpose.

Body image training becomes an important part of the session in order to give patients a fuller sense of self and to lay the groundwork for later perceptual-motor development. Each group member is asked to identify and move various parts of his or her body—naming and bending the joints, for example, or having them move in imitation of the leader. In a sitting position, they go through various flexion and extension movements. Next, in order to stimulate their awareness of the environment, the leader provides a number of *tactile* stimuli. Material or objects of various kinds are passed around one at a time, so patients have an opportunity to handle them and describe the feeling of touching them in their own words. The leader stimulates them with questions: "Is it hard? Soft? Is the surface smooth? Rough? How does it feel? What do you call it?"

In turn, the leader introduces a number of stimuli that are then identified and discussed: *olfactory* stimuli—smells from liquids, foods or other objects (perfume, coffee, garlic, etc.); *auditory* stimuli—various sounds; *visual* stimuli—various objects or pictures (they may be asked to look at themselves in mirrors and say what they see, or they may be asked to describe other patients and what they are wearing); and *taste* stimuli—candy, cookies, or other forms of food or seasoning.

Throughout the session, verbal exercises or questions are used to encourage alertness, awareness and communication. During *hearing* exercises, for example, the leader may bounce a ball and ask group members to count and tell how often it was bounced. Throwing a ball gently from patient to patient may be used to encourage them to remember and call out each other's names. Songs and rhythm instruments may be used, always with the goal of stimulating group

---

[14] Leona Richman: *Manual of Sensory Training Techniques.* Geriatric Unit, Bronx State Hospital, New York, 1968.

members to respond, to interact with each other and to become aware of what is happening. It is generally believed that at least 10 or more sensory training sessions are needed before concrete progress begins to show. As patients improve, they may be moved on to a more advanced sensory training group, in which, rather than simply responding by repeating the leader's words, they express their individual ideas, engage in discussion and take part in more complex body movements, songs, dances or group interaction activities.

This therapeutic method, like others described in this chapter, may be seen both as a technique of therapy and as a recreational experience with value of its own. It makes use of basic recreational activities and often has a playlike and enjoyable atmosphere, particularly when patients begin to be more fully involved, to respond and to laugh.

REMOTIVATION

Remotivation represents a somewhat similar technique that promotes interaction. It may be used by recreation leaders, nursing personnel or aides in the nursing home or hospital situation to help disoriented geriatric or mentally ill patients improve their cognitive and social functioning.

Remotivation, which is closely linked to the "reality orientation" approach, is a method evolved by Dorothy Hoskins Smith at the Philadelphia State Hospital in 1956 and assisted by Smith, Kline and French Laboratories as it spread rapidly to other hospitals and nursing homes throughout the United States and Canada. Before long, it was recognized by the American Psychiatric Association as a valuable technique for use with disoriented aged persons and chronically ill mental patients. Through the 1960s, the American Psychiatric Association provided workshops, seminars and demonstrations to train leaders in remotivation, with assistance from Smith, Kline and French. By the late 1960s over 15,000 leaders were trained in the method.

Remotivation consists of a series of meetings involving between 10 and 15 patients and a leader that last from 45 minutes to an hour. Meetings are held once or twice a week and are usually designated for patients who have not responded to other hospital therapies. Patients are encouraged to attend but are not forced to do so. The essential goal of remotivation is to help disoriented or regressed patients begin to be aware of their environment and relate to the hospital staff and other individuals. Remotivation meetings are highly structured and follow a five-step sequence, shown below with the approximate amount of time given to each phase:

1. Climate of Acceptance (5 min.). *The leader addresses the group and expresses appreciation to its members for coming to the meeting. The leader moves around the group greeting each member, calling them by name, or introducing herself to them. She compliments them on their appearance, and attempts to establish contact or arouse response in other ways. The purpose of the first step is to help the patient to realize that he or she is in a new different setting, away from the regular daily routine, and to establish a comfortable, relaxed social atmosphere.*
2. Bridge to Reality (15 min.). *The leader uses a clipping, poem, article, or other piece of printed material, which is intended to gain the interest and attention of the group. She may read from it, slowly and clearly, or may move around the circle asking other participants to read a line or two, if they are able to*

do so. Patients are asked to comment on, or respond to this statement. In some "bridges," a theme is presented which may reflect the patient's past experience, and they may be asked to discuss it, based on the past. Photographs may be helpful in arousing such interest.

3. Sharing the World We Live In *(15 min.). Here the leader develops a topic for group discussion and response. The theme may stem from the idea presented in step 2, or may be different. It should have to do with awareness of what things are like today, and should involve information close to patients' experiences or personal interests. Ideally, it should be interesting enough to arouse different views and ideas, but should not be a disturbing or highly controversial subject. The leader should be prepared with specific questions and information, and should encourage all group members to contribute to the discussion.*

4. The World of Work *(15 min.). Extending the previous step's emphasis on the reality of present-day life, the intent is to discuss work as a form of human activity. The patient is encouraged to think of work in relation to his or her own life—either in terms of work he or she has done, or is presently doing in the hospital, or might do in the future. This step is particularly useful with psychiatric patients who might return to community life, and less so to disoriented geriatric patients who are not likely to do so.*

5. Climate of Appreciation *(5 min.). The leader thanks each group member in turn for coming to the session, and tells them that she is pleased with them. She announces when the next meeting will be held, and urges them all to attend.*[15]

Records of the participation of individual patients in remotivation sessions are kept, with detailed information as to their involvement, understanding and reaction to different aspects of the experience. As patients progress, such records may provide the basis for recommending that they be moved along to a higher functioning group or encouraged to become involved in other hospital programs.

REALITY ORIENTATION

Reality orientation is a very similar kind of approach that is used with disoriented or chronic patients in an effort to help them focus on reality and relate meaningfully to their physical and social environment. Gladin points out that it has two separate aspects: (a) a 24-hour-a-day method basing all contacts with the patient on an "attitude therapy" approach that is part of reality orientation and (b) specific therapeutic sessions carried on in a classroom-like situation. In the first aspect, patients are dealt with in a consistent, interpersonal style that emphasizes the reality of who they are and why they are there and points out what their behavior is like, how they affect others and why the institution operates as it does. Gladin indicates that the following therapeutic attitudes are helpful in this respect:

Kind firmness *used with depressed or uncooperative patient.*

No demand *made on the patient who is out of control.*

Active friendliness *used with the withdrawn and apathetic patient.*

Passive friendliness *used with the suspicious patient.*

---

[15] M. Alice Robinson: *Remotivation Technique: A Manual for Use in Nursing Homes.* American Psychiatric Association and Smith, Kline and Fench Laboratories, n.d.

Matter-of-fact *manner used with patients who are manipulative, seductive, and those approaching more "normal" behavior.*[16]

This approach is very similar to reality therapy developed by William Glasser, which places emphasis on patients' accepting reality, responsibility and awareness of right and wrong.[17] It deals concretely with the individual's present behavior and seeks to correct and improve it rather than to delve into the past causes of illness or deal with problems through a traditional psychoanalytic approach (see Chapter 5). The second aspect of reality orientation consists of classes held to help small groups of disoriented or confused patients become aware of the present and the reality of their life situation and surroundings. Structured on two levels (basic and advanced), the classes use a "reality orientation board" as a teaching tool; this contains such information as:

Title card (name of agency or institution)
Location card (city or state)
Today is—
The date is—
The year is—
The next meal is—
The weather is—
The next holiday is—
Today's activity is—
Activity director is—

As Gladin describes the method, patients are drilled in learning and reciting accurate information, based on such categories of knowledge as those listed above. In more advanced classes, they would deal with other aspects of the hospital or nursing home situation—the daily schedule, their living circumstances, their family and home background or other relevant information. As indicated, this method is similar to remotivation but more specific and limited in the areas of information covered.

BEHAVIOR MODIFICATION

In a sense, all activity therapies are designed to be a form of behavior modification, since it is their purpose to substitute new, more constructive values and forms of behavior for past negative, limited or destructive attitudes and behaviors. However, the term "behavior modification" has become popular in recent years as a distinct form of treatment. Dunn defines it as

... *the systematic use of the theories of learning to weaken, maintain, or strengthen behavior through the use of selected reinforcers and under specified conditions.*[18]

---

[16] Catherine B. Gladin: "Reality Orientation and Remotivation in Health Care Facilities." *In* Jerry D. Kelley (ed.): *Expanding Horizons in Therapeutic Recreation II.* Champaign-Urbana, Illinois, University of Illinois, Office of Recreation and Park Resources, 1974, pp. 111–114.
[17] William Glasser: *Reality Therapy: A New Approach to Psychiatry.* New York, Harper and Row, 1965.
[18] John M. Dunn: "Behavior Modification with Emotionally Disturbed Children." *Journal of Physical Education and Recreation,* March, 1975, p. 67.

Behavior modification may be used to describe a wide range of techniques, including brainwashing of prisoners, the use of aversive conditioners to work with sex criminals, addicts or alcoholics and many other methods—some of which have a dubious reputation among the public at large. As it is most commonly used in therapeutic settings with the emotionally disturbed or socially deviant, behavior modification places heavy reliance on the use of positive reinforcement, which may be defined as "any pleasant event which follows a behavior that strengthens the future frequency of that behavior," or, more simply stated—a reward. Obviously, a reward need not simply be an object, such as money or a piece of candy, but can involve privileges, verbal praise, a hug, a smile or other forms of positive reinforcement. Modeling, or demonstration of appropriate behavior, is also a useful behavior modification technique.

In order to discourage inappropriate or undesired behavior, negative reinforcement such as withdrawal of privileges, criticism or other penalties, may be used. Rawson describes the rationale of behavior modification:

> Behavior modification theory places heavy emphasis upon the early extinction of socially maladaptive behaviors and immediate and consistent reinforcement of socially appropriate behavior. Put in its simplest terms, the basic assumption of this theory is that most behavior, good or bad, is in fact learned, and it was originally learned because it was reinforced socially or otherwise. Therefore, deliberate, consistent manipulation of reinforcements as a consequence of specific behaviors leads to unlearning of previous behaviors (which no longer lead to positive reinforcements) and simultaneous learning of new alternate behaviors which now lead to positive reinforcements.[19]

In another setting, the author describes the program of behavior modification at the Englishtown Park therapeutic camp, a residential short-term camp in Indiana for children with behavioral problems. It demonstrates how behavior modification cannot simply be a casual dispensing of praise and blame, rewards and punishments, but must instead be based on a systematic identification of the behavioral problems of each subject and determination of appropriate therapeutic goals:

> Before each child arrived at camp, an intensive "behavior prescription" was drawn up for him, based upon study of family case histories, school and teacher reports, psychometric case findings, and parental reports. Based on this, the teacher-therapists sought to achieve specific behavior modification goals, using a number of positive and negative reinforcements to either reward or inhibit behavior. Positive reinforcements were: (a) verbal praise; (b) physical gestures of affection and approval; (c) award of candy pellets; (d) award of gummed stars on name badges, which could be traded for candy bars, soft drinks, or ice cream; (e) fancy certificates of merit given in public ceremonials; and (f) the right to participate in highly desired activities, such as evening swimming or overnight campouts. Negative reinforcements were: (a) complete ignoral (turning one's back on a child, despite his attention-getting pleas); and (b) withdrawal from a highly desired activity for a period of several minutes.[20]

A prescription is written for each child, outlining major problems, desired and undesired behavior and suggesting appropriate forms of reinforcement

---

[19] Harve E. Rawson: "Residential Short-Term Camping for Children With Behavior Problems: A Behavior-Modification Approach." *Child Welfare*, October, 1973, p. 513.
[20] See: Richard Kraus and Barbara Bates: *Recreation Leadership and Supervision: Guidelines for Professional Development.* Philadelphia, W. B. Saunders Co., 1975, pp. 276–277.

to modify behavior in desired directions. A typical prescription, after outlining goals and methods, stated, "Be very firm and consistent with this camper at all times and make sure he understands your expectations, repeating them often; utilize maximum peer pressure where possible to alter inappropriate behavior, including halt of coveted activity for entire group."

Behavior modification can obviously be applied in all types of settings, but it is at its most effective in situations of sustained contact and interpersonal involvement—as in a camp or other residential situation, as opposed to a community mental health center where clients may come only for a few hours a week. In some cases, the method used is a contract outlining specific desired behaviors as well as behaviors or deficits to be eliminated. Based on whether the client lives up to the contract, certain rewards or other positive reinforcers are given. As in reality therapy, behavior modification is not concerned with exploring and understanding the past roots of the individual's disturbance. Instead, emphasis is on the here and now, and it is assumed that if the client is helped to behave constructively and rationally, this will help to reduce his problems significantly.

TOKEN ECONOMY

A somewhat similar approach, used in a number of large psychiatric hospitals, is the "token economy" system. Maxmen, Tucker and Lebow describe the token economy method as a treatment modality that systematically applies certain principles derived from general experimental psychology, particularly operant learning. It seeks

> . . . to strengthen the patient's desirable behaviors and weaken his socially maladaptive ones by utilizing tokens as tangible and serviceable intermediaries between the patient's desirable activities and the positive reinforcers that are available to him. For example, a withdrawn patient may receive tokens for socializing with other patients, which he can then exchange for privileges or commodities he desires, such as watching television.[21]

In a hospital residential unit, the patient may receive tokens for carrying out assigned responsibilities, such as bedmaking, washing or other service functions. He may also display adaptive behavior in other areas of social interaction or activity therapy that is rewarded and reinforced by tokens. Tokens themselves are positive reinforcers and are generally concrete objects that have little or no inherent value, such as paper money or "scrip," colored poker chips and foreign coins of low value. They must be easy to carry and difficult to counterfeit. They gain their power as reinforcers by being essential in acquiring other positive consequences, such as buying tobacco or going on a trip or to a movie. It is desirable to give immediate reinforcement for most patients in psychiatric situations, and since there are limited ways in which this can be done directly, the use of tokens (which can be granted immediately) acts as an intermediary between the desired behavior and the deferred reward.

In hospitals employing this method, tokens are used as a means of structuring an entire network of recreational involvements, as well as other

---

[21] Jerrold S. Maxmen, Gary J. Tucker and Michael LeBow: *Rational Hospital Psychiatry: The Reactive Environment.* New York, Brunner, Mazel, 1974, p. 26.

conveniences or amenities of living. The approach is therefore known as the "token economy" method because it represents an entire economy of exchange within the institution. In addition to serving as a means for channeling reinforcers, tokens serve as a continuing form of motivation, a stimulus to think in terms of deferred rewards and to plan for the future. Finally, as preparation for returning to community life, they represent working for wages and an experience in saving and spending—all important areas of preconditioning for independent community living.

LEISURE COUNSELING

A final important therapeutic approach to be discussed in this chapter is leisure counseling. Although not a specific form of recreational activity in itself, leisure counseling is directly concerned with attitudes, values and habits of participation in recreation and can make a major contribution to the readiness of patients or clients to function successfully in community life. Pointing out that leisure counseling is fast becoming an integral part of the total therapeutic recreation program in psychiatric institutions, McLellan and Pellett state,

> The objective of leisure counseling is to determine the patients' leisure interests and then to assist in locating activities in the home community to meet their interests. The leisure counselor also helps the patients examine the feasibility of their activity choices in terms of cost, accessibility, and personal skills and capabilities.[22]

Extending this description somewhat, it should be stressed that not only psychiatric patients but also other special populations are normally in need of effective leisure counseling. Although much of the literature, as summarized by O'Morrow and McDowell, refers to leisure counseling as a form of therapy used in an institutional setting, it has also been widely used with the physically disabled, the mentally retarded, the socially deviant and, indeed, with nondisabled populations as well. A precise definition of leisure counseling, then, is provided by Gunn, who characterizes it as

> a helping process which uses specific verbal facilitation techniques to promote and increase self-awareness, awareness of leisure attitudes, values, and feelings, as well as the development of decision-making and problem-solving skills related to leisure participation with self, others, and environmental factors.[23]

Leisure counseling may be carried out in a variety of ways: through informal, one-to-one interchange between activity staff members and patients or clients; through regularly scheduled counseling sessions with individuals; or through group counseling meetings. It should include procedures designed to evaluate each patient or client's recreational interests and planned efforts to expand and enrich these interests and skills during the treatment process. It should also include a conscious effort to have patients engage in community

---

[22] Robert W. McLellan and Lane Pellett: "Leisure Counseling—The First Step." *Therapeutic Recreation Journal*, 4th Quarter, 1976, pp. 161–165.
[23] Scout Lee Gunn: "A Systems Approach to Leisure Counseling." *Journal of Physical Education and Recreation*, Leisure Today, April, 1977, p. 8.

recreation programs while institutionalized and the involvement of community groups in recreation activities carried on within the hospital or treatment setting. Finally, it should provide not only guidance to help discharged patients find desirable leisure outlets in the community but also follow-up assistance to help them function effectively in such settings.

Six component parts, or phases, may be identified in this process:

1. *Procedures designed to evaluate each patient or client's present and past recreational interests.* This involves such techniques as reading the case record, using a "recreation inventory" during an initial leisure counseling interview and interviewing family, friends and associates. The inventory (see p. 156) might include such categories as games and sports, social activities, cultural events, hobbies and arts and crafts and might deal not only with established interests but also other leisure interests the individual would like to engage in.

2. *Planned efforts to expand and enrich interests and skills and to examine values and outcomes during the treatment process.* Most frequently, this phase involves regular small-group meetings that focus on the problem of leisure use. They may be under the leadership of a multidisciplinary counseling team but are most often directed by a single staff member. Social workers or activity therapists, including recreation specialists, are frequently given this responsibility. In group discussions, they explore leisure interests and opportunities and examine problems they may have had using leisure in the past as well as their present involvements and future plans. At the same time, according to Olson and McCormack, patients in recreation counseling groups go to group activities together

> . . . and thus accumulate a backing of common social experiences. They ordinarily bring these experiences into the group discussions and comment on their reactions to them. This serves as a point of departure for observations about their pre-hospital experiences in the social-recreational area and of expectations about the future.[24]

Hitzhusen also emphasizes the importance of learning by doing and of the interaction between recreation experiences and counseling.[25] Along with group-centered activities, patients should also be guided in their choice of hospital recreation programs in order to enrich skills and build positive attitudes of participation.

3. *Efforts to have patients engage in community recreation programs while institutionalized.* To the greatest degree possible, patients should become directly involved in community recreation activities while still in the institution or treatment program in order to build a bridge to the future and give them a realistic exposure to available community programs. Olson and McCormack, for example, describe one patient who was referred to and became part of a community orchestra before discharge and remained with it after leaving the hospital.

4. *Involvement of community groups in recreation activities carried on within the hospital setting.* Mobilizing community resources is important to the success of any leisure counseling service. Many institutions, therefore,

---

[24] W. E. Olson and J. B. McCormack: "Recreation Counseling in the Psychiatric Service of a General Hospital." *Journal of Nervous and Mental Diseases*, April–June, 1957, p. 237.
[25] G. Hitzhusen: "Recreation and Leisure Counseling for Adult Psychiatric and Alcoholic Patients." *Therapeutic Recreation Journal*, 1st Quarter, 1973, p. 19.

encourage community groups to become involved in the hospital or other rehabilitation center program by sponsoring regular events or programs in which patients may take part. Again, this serves as a means of building a bridge to the community by establishing favorable personal contacts and confidence on the part of the patient or client.

5. *Guidance to help discharged patients find desirable leisure outlets in the community.* Throughout this process, the patient's leisure attitudes, values and goals for future leisure participation are being clarified. Based on this, while still in the treatment program, he or she develops a conscious plan of involvement for the future—identifying programs, groups, clubs and hobby interests. To make this work, it is essential that hospital personnel become thoroughly familiar with potential recreational resources. O'Morrow lists "a directory of community recreation resources" as one of the "usual missing ingredients" in a recreation counseling program.

6. *Follow-up assistance to help patients function effectively in the community.* Referral, initial visits to a community recreation program while still hospitalized and follow-up observation and counseling are the final step to insure that patients make a satisfactory adjustment to community programs. Despite the fact that some institutions do not feel this is a necessary or appropriate step, it is often critical that disabled persons be given this type of temporary assistance in returning to the community. In some cases, as shown in Chapter 5, they may attend a community-based mental health center or other day-clinic program through which they can continue to receive leisure counseling assistance. However, the effort should be on breaking the dependency link and encouraging them to establish their own independent interests and group affiliations.

In another text, the author describes examples of comprehensive leisure counseling programs at the Binghamton, New York, State Hospital and at the Mental Health Centre in Penetanguishene, Ontario, Canada. The latter program in particular places strong stress on the use of a variety of diagnostic and exploratory procedures, including videotaped interviews, the use of printed recreation interest inventories, administration of psychological projective tests and specially designed sessions to measure the patient's actual behavior in a variety of different social and recreational settings.[26]

It should be stressed that, although chief emphasis has been given to the need for leisure counseling in psychiatric settings, it is obviously of considerable importance for those with other forms of disability as well. It is being used today, for example, in penal and correctional settings.[27] Within the past several years, realization has grown that many individuals who have no specific psychological or physical impairment at all can benefit greatly from leisure counseling. Cross describes several community-based programs of leisure counseling that approach it not so much as a therapeutic service but as a developmental learning experience and serve both the disabled and the nondisabled in Los Angeles, Milwaukee and the Borough of Etobicoke, Ontario, Canada. The Milwaukee program in particular has become known as a leading community-based center for leisure education for a general population.[28]

---

[26] Kraus and Bates, *op. cit.*, pp. 289–293.
[27] Bob Brayshaw: "Leisure Counseling for People in Correctional Institutions." *Journal of Leisurability*, Ontario, Canada, January, 1974, pp. 10–14.
[28] Ken Cross: "Leisure Counseling: An Overview with a Community Center Emphasis." *Recreation Review*, July, 1976, pp. 22–26.

Thus far, this chapter has outlined a number of basic approaches to planning therapeutic recreation programs and has presented several special approaches that may be used in such programs. It should be recognized that many other types of activities may be presented. For example, in senior centers daily activities may include a hot-lunch program; seminars, discussion groups or social action programs dealing with problems of aging in society; legal, family or housing counseling; or other special health, dental or vision services—all as a part of the overall program.

GUIDELINES FOR THERAPEUTIC RECREATION PROGRAM PLANNING

In conclusion, a number of important guidelines for program planning in therapeutic recreation are presented. Obviously, these may vary somewhat in their application according to the type of disability being served or the setting or resources of the agency under consideration. As a general picture of *how* programs should be planned and implemented, however, they serve as a practical model.

1. Program planning should be based on a coherent philosophy of the place of leisure and recreation in human life. At the same time that specific therapeutic objectives are identified, it should also be the purpose of program activities to provide such general values of recreation as pleasure, emotional release, sociability, healthy physical exercise and creative self-expression.

2. Emphasis should be placed on using and serving the healthy, positive aspects of each patient or client's personality and physical make-up rather than focusing only on disability or pathological aspects of behavior.

3. Although there is an important place for prescribed or assigned participation in activity, patients should also be given the opportunity for free choice within a flexible therapeutic recreation program structure. Regimentation that contributes to institutionalization and dependency should be avoided.

4. Program activities should cover a wide range of social, physical, creative, intellectual and service involvements of both an active and passive nature. Patients or clients should be encouraged to begin at their present level of skill and interest and should be helped to move toward more deeply involving and challenging activities.

5. Through both participation and leisure counseling sessions, the program should help patients and clients become aware of the place of leisure and recreation in their lives and help them develop more constructive plans for their own involvement, either in the community or in a continued residential setting.

6. Programs should be planned with the help of other disciplines represented on the treatment team or should, at least, be made thoroughly familiar to them in terms of rationale, schedules and outcomes. This can be done through regular reports, invitations to events and input from recreation and activity staff members at team meetings.

7. Programs should be scheduled at appropriate times, both to allow for other hospital or treatment services to be provided without conflict and to space needed leisure activities through the day, evenings and weekends.

8. Important health and safety principles should be observed, with medical supervision in all necessary areas, such as use of medication, effects of

exercise on physical disability or appropriate ways of dealing with patients in acute phases of illness and treatment.

9. Whenever possible, programs should not be limited to the institution or treatment setting but should involve community resources. This may mean carrying on activities in community settings or agencies or inviting members of community groups to take part in or to assist programs in the hospital or agency setting.

10. Program planning should involve and encourage patient or client initiative to the fullest. This may be done by having individuals or small groups of patients take responsibility for planning activities, contributing to policy decisions or leading their own activities. It may also involve, on a broader scale, patient councils that help to set priorities and make policy decisions on activity programs.

11. Just as the therapeutic recreation specialist is more than an activity leader, so the activity program should include varied special treatment methods, as described in this chapter, or other nonrecreation services when appropriate.

12. There should be an ongoing, consistent and systematic effort to assess patient needs and capabilities, define program objectives and measure outcomes of participation regularly. To the extent that therapeutic recreation specialists are made accountable and demonstrate what they have accomplished, their status within the overall rehabilitative structure will be enhanced, and it will be possible to continue to modify and improve the program.

Each of these guidelines is illustrated and reinforced in the chapters dealing with specific disability areas, the modification of activity, community-based programs and services and research and evaluation.

SUGGESTED QUESTIONS FOR CLASS DISCUSSION, EXAMINATIONS OR STUDENT PAPERS

1. Outline the key elements that come into play in the program-planning process in therapeutic recreation.

2. Apply the systems analysis approach described in this chapter to program development in a specific hypothetical setting. How does this method relate to the *milieu therapy* model presented in Chapter 2?

3. What are several of the ways in which patients or clients may be involved in programs (i.e., through assigned groups, individual prescription, voluntary attendance at mass activity, etc.)? Show how these might be combined in a total program schedule in a given institution or community setting.

4. Summarize the goals and steps involved in one of the special techniques, such as *sensory training*, described in this chapter.

chapter 5

Recreation and Mental Illness

Mental illness is a complex form of human disorder. Medical authorities have at best only limited knowledge of the causes and symptomatology of functional mental illness. Indeed, there are no clear-cut criteria for defining this disorder or for characterizing a person as mentally ill. Despite these facts, it is clear that mental illness constitutes a major social problem today. In the early 1970s, it was said to affect one out of every 10 persons in the United States, with psychiatric patients occupying almost half of all hospital beds at an estimated economic cost of about $3 billion a year.

A substantial number of persons who are mentally ill are not hospitalized. For example, the National Institute of Mental Health estimates that between four and eight million Americans each year suffer depressions severe enough to keep them from performing their regular activities or to compel them to seek medical help. In addition, an estimated 10 to 15 million have less severe depressions; the majority of both groups, however, are not institutionalized.[1]

There is a widely held belief that mental illness is most prevalent in large cities, due to the stress of urban life and the high incidence of other social pathologies. A recent report to the American Psychiatric Association based on community mental health statistics gathered by the National Center for Health Statistics, however, found that people in rural areas and small cities reported 20 per cent more symptoms of psychological disturbance than did big-city residents.[2] Indeed, the estimated mental-morbidity rate of a rural Canadian area, to which the researchers gave the name Stirling County, was higher than that of midtown Manhattan, in New York City, by a substantial margin. Thus, mental illness may be seen as affecting all ages, classes and geographical areas. Statistical evidence has shown that it is closely related to economic factors—whenever the economy declines, with resultant unemployment, psychiatric admission to mental hospitals arises dramatically. Depression in particular is subject to economic factors, as evidenced by recent studies by the National Institute of Mental Health in California, New Jersey and Missouri.

---

[1] Jane E. Brody: "Mental Depression: The Recurring Nightmare." *New York Times*, January 19, 1977.
[2] "Mentally, the Urban Life Beats the Rural." *New York Times*, May 8, 1977, p. E-7.

CONCEPTS OF MENTAL ILLNESS

In modern psychiatry, there are two conflicting approaches to characterizing mental illness.

The older approach, which might be characterized as the *disease model*, suggests that the psychotic behavior of a disturbed individual unfolds inevitably from a defective psychological or neurological system that is essentially contained within the person. Symptoms of mental disorder are not caused by the social system in which the individual exists; mental illness is considered in the same manner as a virus infection or other physical illness might be.

The more recent approach, which might be described as the *maladaptive model*, takes into account the social environment—including the family, neighborhood and larger community—of those persons who are described as mentally ill. The mentally ill, according to this viewpoint, should not be thought of or treated as diseased persons but rather as individuals with severe problems of adjustment. Thus, disturbed behavior is simply seen as maladaptive and often caused by stresses of the social environment and the inability of the individual to meet these stresses—rather than by pathology as such.

There is no clear line of distinction between so-called normal and abnormal behavior. Unlike physical illness, in which the norm is the structural or functional integrity of the body and in which medical science has little difficulty in identifying "illness," it is difficult to identify, along the range of possible actions, the point at which human behavior shifts from a normal to an abnormal form of expression.

For example, it was recently reported by the National Institute of Mental Health that violence was surprisingly endemic in American families. It was estimated, based on the study of a demographic cross-section of families, that parents kicked, bit or "beat up" well over 2 million children each year and that almost 50,000 attacked their children with knives and guns. In addition, 7.5 million couples a year went through a violent episode of trying to do each other bodily harm, and 2.3 million children wielded knives or guns against a brother or sister.[3] Should such violence be classified as a sign of mental illness? Surprisingly, the reported mayhem was found in intact families, among "apparently normal, average Americans, and took place as often among the well educated as among those with little schooling."

Lee Meyer puts the question bluntly:

> *... are deviations from "normal" therefore indicative of mental illness? One problem is the difficulty in determining the appropriateness or inappropriateness of someone's behavior in a given situation due to the variations in social norms and values that exist and the range of possible responses. Usually, digressions from the normal are not regarded as mental illness unless they are persistent or so extreme that no other explanation is possible.*[4]

Medical science has, however, suggested certain criteria for identifying the mental health of individuals. These criteria are rather broadly stated as per-

---

[3] For a recent discussion of violence in modern life, see Erich Fromm: *The Anatomy of Human Destructiveness.* New York, Holt, Rinehart and Winston, 1973.
[4] Lee E. Meyer: "Recreation and the Mentally Ill." *In* Thomas A. Stein and H. Douglas Sessoms (eds.): *Recreation and Special Populations.* Boston, Holbrook, 1977, p. 138.

sonal adjustment, personality integration, personal maturity and growth and social or group involvement. The actions of persons, in terms of whether or not they are able to function effectively in terms of family, vocational responsibility or other interpersonal relationships, are used to determine whether they are mentally healthy.

Physicians have established two major divisions in the classification of the mentally ill: disorders associated with organic brain disturbance and disorders of psychogenic origin.

Chronic brain disorders, which result from severe, lasting damage to cerebral tissue, may effect impairment of judgment, memory or orientation. Epilepsy is an example of a brain disorder usually caused by physical injury to a tiny but critical part of the brain. Temporary injury to brain tissue may result in acute behavioral malfunction from which the patient recovers. These two examples fall within the realm of organic brain disturbance.

In contrast, disorders of psychogenic origin have no apparent physical cause. Temporary personality disorders may be triggered by acute stress and tend to involve previously normal individuals who have a good potential for recovery. Another form of disorder is the presence of neurosis or psychoneurosis that is related to acute anxiety and partial inability to function effectively; this normally does not require hospitalization, although psychotherapeutic treatment may be helpful. Frequently, psychosomatic illnesses, such as migraine headaches or hypertension, may be connected to such neuroses. Other forms of character disorders may result in various symptoms, such as alcoholism, drug addiction or severely antisocial behavior.

Functional psychosis is the most severe and disabling psychogenic disorder, and it is to this category that the term mental illness is most frequently applied.

Functional psychosis usually involves a severe degree of personality disorganization and a progressive loss of contact with reality. It is customarily classified today under one of four headings: *schizophrenia, manic depression, involutional states* and *senility*. These represent the major disabilities of patients in mental hospitals today. It should be recognized, however, that such diagnostic terms should not be viewed as precise or permanent labels of varied forms of mental disorder. For example, more than one set of symptoms may be present at a given time, and patterns of behavior may shift from one diagnostic category to another. Shivers and Fait write, "Precise diagnoses of patient's syndromes may not be forthcoming due to differences of diagnostic technique, individual variables of behavior, and differences of symptom evaluation or interpretation."[5] Despite such reservations, there is fairly widespread agreement as to the following major diagnostic categories, both in the literature and in professional practice.

Schizophrenia

Schizophrenics are characterized by a striking withdrawal from society and from emotional ties with other persons. This may be caused by the general social alienation of the person or loss of the ability to think in meaningful and

---

[5] Jay S. Shivers and Hollis F. Fait: *Therapeutic and Adapted Recreational Services.* Philadelphia, Lea and Febiger, 1975, p. 114.

logical terms. Five common characteristics of schizophrenics are (a) withdrawal from reality; (b) autism; (c) emotional distortion; (d) delusions and hallucinations; and (e) abnormal or bizarre behavior.

Persons suffering from schizophrenia often have a history of social inadequacy. They tend to be disorganized persons who have never developed adequate roles or self-concepts. In the face of emotional difficulties or disappointments, they tend to withdraw into a fantasy world. They no longer communicate meaningfully with others and their thought processes become disorganized and unreal. As a consequence, schizophrenics are unable to relate to or understand others, take meaningful social roles or function meaningfully in their families in society at large.

Brody describes schizophrenia as a "weird, seductive, baffling form of madness that has long been a source of fear, fascination and contempt." Although other forms of mental illness have faded from prominence or yielded to scientific discovery, she writes, schizophrenia continues to afflict about 1 per cent of the American population:

> *As a worldwide problem and the westernized societies' most common severe mental disorder, schizophrenia has little respect for race, creed, intelligence, wealth or breeding. In the United States, schizophrenics comprise half the patients in mental institutions. Many more live in society, but must return occasionally to hospitals for treatment. On the average, one-third of the schizophrenics get better, one-third get worse, and one-third stay the same indefinitely.*[6]

Schizophrenia has often been referred to as evidence of a "split" personality, with a sharp split, or contrast, between the outer and inner self of the individual. Based on recent studies, it is now evident that schizophrenia has a strong genetic component. A child with one schizophrenic parent, even if adopted and brought up by others, has a 10 times greater chance of becoming schizophrenic than the general population; with two schizophrenic parents, the risk is 40 times greater.

Schizophrenic disturbance can be further categorized into the following groups.

SIMPLE SCHIZOPHRENIA

Persons suffering from this disorder are not always confined to mental hospitals but may simply lead undemanding, socially withdrawn lives. Simple schizophrenics are generally isolated, with few friends and with jobs requiring only superficial contact with others; they often have peculiar habits of dress or speech.

HEBEPHRENIC SCHIZOPHRENIA

This frequently emerges at puberty, a time of physical change and emotional stress. The individual's thoughts become confused and his language unintelligible; he may be prone to hysteria or uncontrollable laughter or rage. Hebephrenic schizophrenics often report hearing voices or other forms of halluci-

---

[6] Jane E. Brody: "Schizophrenia is Unyielding." *New York Times*, May 19, 1974, p. 6-E.

nations. They may ritualize their lives in great detail, apparently as a means of controlling their environment and avoiding ambiguous or threatening situations.

PARANOID SCHIZOPHRENIA

This common disorder often involves patients having a strong sense of persecution. They may feel that their entire environment is hostile and threatening, that people are plotting against them and even that they are inhabited by, or controlled by, other persons. Paranoid schizophrenics tend to be suspicious of others and to resist social communication or emotional contact.

Manic Depression

Many persons experience mild depressions. These deepen markedly in the psychotic form of this disorder. The patient feels sad and lonely; his thought processes and behavior slow down. He refuses to respond to others, and the entire functioning of his mind, memory and thought processes is retarded. Depressive persons may become suspicious and irritable and have frightening hallucinations, but, most commonly, they become slow and drowsy, sitting or lying in one spot for hours on end. Ultimately, the patient may become suicidal as a result of his feelings of hopelessness and lack of worth.

It is the nature of the manic-depressive patient to swing violently in emotional mood from extreme elation to severe depressive states. In the manic, or "high" state, he may have feelings of great optimism and become extremely energetic and overexcited, talking incessantly. He may develop unreal, grandiose images of himself. His judgment becomes faulty; he is easily distracted and may readily fly into sudden rages. When exhausted, he may then swing into a state of severe depression.

Many individuals do not experience the manic phase of this form of mental illness and instead appear to vacillate between a relatively normal state of functioning and a mild or acute state of depression. Depression can be caused by many factors, including stressful events, organic diseases, drugs or even childbirth or the completion of a major creative effort. In addition to being a severe problem itself, when the depressed individual becomes almost totally incapacitated and withdrawn, depression may also lead some victims to seek escape through excessive drinking, marital infidelity, gambling or other forms of compulsive behavior—which in turn create further problems.

Involutional Psychosis

This disorder is similar to the extreme state of depression found in those with manic-depressive psychoses. It tends to occur for the first time in later middle age, along with general physical and intellectual decline. Patients complain of insomnia, excessive anxiety, restlessness and concern about unimportant matters; often they fall into spontaneous periods of weeping. Suicidal impulses and delusions of hypochondria are also frequently seen in involutional states. Those with involutional psychosis tend to remain in the depressive state and do not recover spontaneously, as sometimes occurs with manic-depressive individuals.

Senility

In senile patients, progressive mental deterioration occurs as a result of the degenerative brain changes and arteriosclerosis that affect many older persons. Withdrawal from social contacts, a narrowing of interests and a general lessening of alertness and awareness of the environment are typical of senile patients. Often they become extremely confused, with severe memory impairment, even of recent events. Today, it is recognized that, in addition to organic causes, social isolation and the lack of environmental stimuli may also lead to what is generally described as senility.

CAUSES OF MENTAL ILLNESS

In attempting to identify the causes of mental illness, it is first necessary to recognize that this term has never been precisely defined. Even today, the exact nature of mental illness in terms of personal behavior or psychological state has not been given a universally acceptable description, and diagnostic categories like those just presented are frequently modified or changed in the literature.

In past centuries, physicians tended to accept the view that all mental illness resulted from anatomical lesions of the brain or nervous system. This view, which dominated the practice of neurology and psychiatry in the United States until the turn of the 20th century, held that only the body could become diseased; the mind could not. As a result, only those who had suffered organic brain damage were regarded as legitimately mentally ill. All other disturbed persons were held to blame for their actions and often prosecuted as willful criminals.

Sigmund Freud was responsible for the view that mental illness should be regarded as a functional maladjustment, without discernible anatomical basis. He conceived of the role of the psychiatrist or psychoanalyst as a practitioner of the science of the mind rather than of the brain and nervous system. According to Freud, all persons—even those who are considered mentally healthy—tend to adjust to life's problems by creating subtle delusions of reality and employing defence mechanisms to deal with stress and problems of human relationships.

Freud sought to eliminate the sharp differentiation between neurotics and so-called normal people. It was his view that abnormal psychology merely represented an exaggerated picture of processes that were at work among all human beings; the mentally ill were seen as caricatures of their more smoothly functioning brethren and the state of the disturbed constituted a mirror held up to human nature in general.[7]

Despite the influence of Freudian theory in discouraging the doctrines of 19th century pathology, the view that mental illness is the result of biochemical inbalance or disturbance has been repeatedly presented during the present cen-

---

[7] Donald Fleming: "The Meaning of Mental Illness." *The Atlantic Monthly*, July, 1964, p. 73.

tury. Pavlov, the Russian physiologist, drew a connection between schizophrenia and physiology in the overdevelopment of the process of cortical-based inhibitions that resulted in the individual's withdrawing from the outside world.

Recent scientific research has indeed demonstrated that biochemical and electrochemical disturbances accompany certain clinical manifestations of mental illness. Scientists have found that the brain encompasses a complicated system of nerve connections between arousal structures in the brain stems and the many areas of the cerebral cortex. Specific chemicals are employed in these connections to transmit impulses. They either arouse or retard the operation of brain processes, and their proper functioning is the basis of balanced behavior, including the generation of moods, appetites, desires and drives. Other pathways in the brain are concerned with countering such arousal activities by diminishing or inhibiting their effects.

In clinical cases of severe psychosis, it has been shown that the excitatory pathways and their chemicals have sharply increased their activities. This results in an increased state of arousal, which becomes difficult to handle. The patient becomes distracted and confused and often overwhelmed by hallucinations, rages and other disorders of mental functions. In contrast, in depressed states, the patient does not appear to be properly aroused, with the likelihood that the arousal pathways in his brain are not sufficiently stimulated. In short, it is hypothesized today that both the explosive thought processes and behavior of the manic patient and the extreme withdrawal of the severely depressed individual are caused by physiological malfunctions.

It has still not been determined whether biochemical malfunctions of this type are the *cause* or the *result* of functional mental disturbance. Certainly, there is a strong body of professional medical opinion that holds that the primary cause of mental illness lies in environmental and social factors and that psychosis results not from a chemical malfunction but from inability to handle the stresses of daily living.

Those who take this position stress that mental illness is, in fact, a problem that all persons have to some degree. It is not seen as a disease in the classic sense but rather as the result of the inability to cope with life in the fashion that social norms accept as mentally healthy. Since all persons deviate occasionally from what is considered normal behavior, some authorities have argued that it is wrong to classify such deviation as mental illness. Meyer writes,

> *We are all in fact, at times mentally ill. Most, however, are never so far down on the continuum, or for long enough periods of time as to require professional assistance. The number requiring professional assistance varies by definition. If you define mental illness as needing 24-hour-a-day residential care, the number is indeed small. If you define mental illness as a condition which interferes with maximum performance and a reduction in happiness and self-fulfillment, you are talking about a massive number of people, perhaps 50 to 75 per cent of our total population.*[8]

Some authorities, critical of current psychiatric treatment processes, hold, in fact, that there is no such thing as mental illness in a medical sense.

Thomas Szasz, for example, characterizes mental illness as the impersonation of society's stereotype of madness by individuals whose real impairment

---

[8] Martin W. Meyer: "Recreation and Mental Health." In *Dialogue with Doctors.* North Carolina Recreation Commission, Bulletin No. 41, April, 1968, p. 18.

concerns a problem in living. Mental illness, unlike a physical disease or defect, is perceived as a strategy of the individual to help himself cope with a psychological crisis or to get help from others. Since the behavior norm upon which the diagnosis of mental illness is based is a psychosocial and ethical standard, Szasz argues that it is illogical to attempt to "cure" it by medical means.

Carrying the argument further, Szasz argues that mental illness is a false concept that serves to hide and disguise, behind the facade of the term "mental illness," certain real problems in human needs, aspirations and values.

It is his position that it is wrong to diagnose cases of "mental illness" as forms of disease that should be treated. He argues vigorously against the present system of treatment by forced custodial care in mental hospitals. Szasz regards mentally ill persons as those who have broken out of their normal social role classifications and tried to define their own identities; and he sees the normal process of psychiatric treatment as forced repression by an organized society of individuals who are socially deviant.[9]

Other authors have presented similar points of view. Thomas Scheff, for example, suggests that most chronic mental illness represents a form of role playing in response to stereotypes that are established by society. He points out that at times of stress, severe depression or so-called psychological "crisis" states many persons tend to be unsure of their own feelings and to behave in ways that deviate from normal behavior. They tend to be in a highly suggestible state and are vulnerable to the suggestion by others that something is wrong with them, that they are "sick" or "going mad."

To support this argument, Scheff points out that the images of insanity in our society are continually reaffirmed and stereotyped through childhood games, mass media imagery and ordinary social interaction. The process of becoming a confirmed deviant, of being "mentally ill," is completed when the traditional imagery of insanity becomes part of the disturbed person's own orientation and he accepts it as a basis for guiding his own behavior.

Scheff suggests that the assumption of the role of being "crazy" is used as a means of adjustment by the patient, because he is just as confused about his own behavior as are the observers. He prefers the role of insanity as a replacement for his normal self image, which has broken down under stress; the label of "I'm going mad" is preferable to the feelings of nothingness that the severely depressed person feels. He concludes that the mentally ill person has in a sense become a forcibly type-cast actor, forced into this role by society's reaction to his personal crisis. Ultimately, he cannot control his behavior; chronic mental illness is on the border between the volitional and the nonvolitional.[10]

The arguments made by Szasz and Scheff have been strongly supported by other authorities. Erving Goffman, for example, writes,

> . . . I want to stress that perception of losing one's mind is based on culturally derived and socially engrained stereotypes as to the significance of symptoms such as hearing voices, losing temporal and spatial orientation, and sensing that one is being followed, and that many of the most spectacular and convincing of these symptoms in some instances psychiatrically signify merely a temporary emotional upset in a stressful situation, however terrifying to the person at the time. Similarly, the anxiety consequent upon this perception of oneself, and the

---

[9] See Thomas S. Szasz: *Law, Liberty, and Psychiatry: An Inquiry into the Social Uses of Mental Health Practices.* New York, Macmillan, 1963.
[10] Thomas Scheff: *Being Mentally Ill—A Sociological Theory.* Chicago, Aldine, 1966.

strategies devised to reduce this anxiety, are not a product of abnormal psychology, but would be exhibited by any person socialized into our culture who came to conceive of himself as someone losing his mind.[11]

A final eloquent spokesman for this point of view has been R. D. Laing, who has gone the furthest in criticizing the disease model of mental illness and has implied that there is nothing really wrong with the person described as "mentally ill." Instead, Laing holds, it is the environment that has somehow gone wrong.

He argues that madness is not a disease to be cured but results from the conflict between an outer "false" self and an inner "true" self. He suggests that this split is begun in childhood, when children have certain needs and feelings that they wish to express but are taught by parents to suppress or change in order to be socially acceptable. By sheer social force, Laing argues, this inner self is compelled to become isolated from the false outer state that arises in compliance with society and gradually becomes alienated from relatedness to the outside world.

In what is frequently referred to as a "nervous breakdown," the individual experiences the sudden removal of the veil of the false self, which served to maintain an appearance of outer normality but did not reflect the true feelings of the inner self.

In Laing's view, getting a person to behave in a conforming way, acting adaptively to the norms of society, is not a "cure" for what is disturbing him. He suggests that the traditional mental hospital approach attempts merely to restore the split between the true, inner, and the false, outer self. Although it produces an outward compliance in the individual and an apparent "cure," it has merely denied the validity of the inner self.

In response to this, Laing developed a radical new approach that was carried out in an institution in England called Kingsley Hall. This involved an experiment in communal living, in which residents, all of whom had come from traditional mental institutions, were permitted to make up their own rules of operation instead of accepting old ones. The purpose of the Kingsley Hall experiment was to see what would happen if disturbed people were allowed to completely abandon their outer selves and let their "inner selves," which emerge during psychosis, take over. They were urged to follow their impulses completely rather than attempt to curb them, so that they could live and grow through their own "madness." No attempts at all were made to urge them to return to "normality," and no restrictions were placed on the behavior of members.

Kingsley Hall yielded some remarkable results. Many of its members, who had not been "cured" by years of treatment in traditional programs of psychiatric therapy and who had been locked up for sustained periods in mental wards, were able to leave therapy and lead emotionally happy lives.[12]

The arguments offered by Szasz, Scheff and Laing—that mental illness is essentially a form of deviant social behavior or unwillingness to accept societal norms or a form of semi-volitional self-labeling, which society controls by forced treatment in mental hospitals—have considerable appeal. Several years ago, a Stanford University psychology professor, David Rosenhan, reported a study in

---

[11] Erving Goffman: *Asylums: Essays on the Social Situation of Mental Patients and Other Inmates.* New York, Doubleday and Co., Inc., 1961, p. 132.

[12] See R. D. Laing: *The Politics of Experience.* New York, Ballantine Books, Inc., 1967.

which several perfectly sane researchers had themselves committed to 12 different mental hospitals in five states over a three-year period by temporarily faking one symptom of mental illness, hearing hollow-sounding voices.[13]

At none of the institutions did the staff suspect the sanity of any pseudo-patient, although other patients frequently did. The hospitals were of several types, large and small, public, private and voluntary, but in all cases the researchers were treated the same—in a totally depersonalized way. When they sought to ask reasonable questions about their status, staff members refused to talk to them, often without even making eye contact. The stereotypic view that they were insane *because* they were in mental hospitals was invariable, and although the researchers stopped reporting hallucinations as soon as they were admitted to the hospitals and behaved perfectly normally, it took them from seven to 52 days to get out. The very fact that the researchers (themselves skilled social scientists) began to insist that they were really sane was taken as convincing evidence that they were insane. When the staff of one research hospital heard that they had so consistently misjudged patients and that a follow-up study would be made, they went on the lookout for new pseudopatients—with the result that of 193 patients legitimately admitted, staff members tagged at least 41 as faking.

In addition to the consistent finding that mental patients were not treated as human beings but dehumanized and ignored in the 12 hospitals investigated, the study also came to the conclusion that any diagnostic process that could be so easily fooled and then sustained in its massive error by an immovable and unresponsive bureaucratic structure could not be a very trustworthy one.

Despite the arguments of Szasz, Scheff and Laing and such evidence, however, there continues to be widespread agreement that there *is* such a phenomenon as mental illness—and that it is a disorder that prevents or inhibits happy and effective living in society. While treatment approaches vary considerably, an increasing number of therapists today are moving toward a "behaviorist" view of mental illness.

The Behavioral Psychology Viewpoint

The behaviorist holds that all human behavior is the result of learned associations of stimulus and response that the individual has been conditioned to adopt. Behavior generally is seen as coming about as a response to external pressures rather than coming from within as a coherent unfolding of the personality.

In this approach, human behavior is seen as adaptive; the actions of even the "strangest" individual are perceived as the long-term result of social influences to which he has learned to adapt. Therefore, his behavior is neither normal nor abnormal, neither right nor wrong; it is simply how the individual has *learned to* act. The goal of behavior therapy today is to get the mentally ill person to re-adapt to society's norms by learning to act in ways that are considered normal. Only the part of the person's self that comes into contact with the outside world is important for the behaviorist. The so-called inner self is nonobservable and therefore meaningless.

---

[13] David L. Rosenhan: "On Being Sane in Insane Places." *Science Magazine*, January 19, 1973, pp. 250–257.

The behavioral therapist rules out any introspective report by the patient on his own mental processes and instead is concerned solely with his observable external behavior. It is the behaviorist view that if the symptoms of abnormality can be arrested, then the person has been cured. Neurotic or even psychotic behavior is seen as the product of defective learning and can be unlearned by intensive reconditioning and reeducation processes.

Freudian psychotherapists see this approach as dealing superficially with the surface manifestations of underlying neurosis. They argue that if the therapy succeeds in removing or repressing a specific symptom, it will be re-placed by another symptom until the neurosis itself is uncovered and dealt with. Freudians see behavior therapy as a form of symptomatic relief that removes the outward evidences of disturbance without attacking the essential disturbance in personality or giving the patient any real insight into his own needs.

In contrast, William Glasser, a leading proponent of "reality therapy," stresses that each patient must learn to face reality and assume responsibility for his or her own behavior in the present:

> The past has certainly contributed to what he is now, but we cannot change the past, only the present. . . . Why become involved with the irresponsible person he was? We want to become involved with the responsible person we know he can be.[14]

The emphasis is placed not on blaming others or asking where things went wrong but rather on what is happening now. Within this treatment frame-work, Glasser suggests that there are three separate but intimately interwoven procedures. First, the patient must begin to face reality with the therapist's help and see how his behavior is unrealistic. Next, the therapist must reject the patient's unrealistic behavior, while at the same time accepting the patient as a person and maintaining a trusting relationship with him. Finally, the patient must begin to learn better ways of fulfilling his needs within the confines of reality—rather than by denying it, which in Glasser's view, is the key element in all mental illness.

Before examining other treatment approaches in fuller detail, it is helpful to gain a perspective of past methods of treating the mentally ill.

TRENDS IN PSYCHIATRIC CARE

Humanitarian attempts to care for and heal the mentally ill began about 150 years ago. Prior to that time, mental illness had been considered to be a result of witchcraft or possession by spirits, and its treatment had been carried on by such primitive measures as flagellation, confinement in dark cells and severe contrivances for mechanical restraint, shock treatments and purging the sick person through emetics or bleeding.

The first half of the 19th century saw a new philosophy of treatment titled "moral therapy." This method emphasized kinder treatment of the insane, as well as the view that they should become involved in occupational and recreational activity.

---

[14] William Glasser: *Reality Therapy: A New Approach to Psychiatry.* New York, Harper and Row, 1965, p. 32.

Moral therapy also emphasized the need to keep institutions small, so that personal contact between the patients and the supervisor could be maintained. During this period, high rates of curability, often as high as 90 per cent, were reported for hospitals that had adopted this approach.

By the 1870s, a new approach replaced the moral therapy method. Mental institutions became largely custodial in nature. Recoveries and discharge rates declined to below 10 per cent in many hospitals during the first two decades of the 20th century. Many psychiatrists believed that less than 5 per cent of schizophrenics could be expected to recover. Tourney attributes the growing therapeutic nihilism—as this period has been termed—to "personnel problems, budgetary difficulties, hospital overcowding, the large proportion of chronic cases, and a dogmatic depersonalized theoretic approach to insanity."[15]

During this period, however, a number of the basic principles underlying modern care for the mentally ill were first developed. Individual patient treatment, open-door policies, patient freedom, voluntary admissions, home and after-care services and sheltered or specially arranged employment for patients were all experimented with during this period.

Before the end of the 19th century, owing chiefly to the efforts of Sigmund Freud, attention was given to the effectiveness of the new method of psychotherapy in treating the mentally ill. This approach gave emphasis to the direct relationship between the physician and the patient rather than reliance on medical or surgical procedures. Techniques of dream analysis, exploration of the unconscious, free association and the use of transference were developed, based on a growing body of theory of psychoneurosis as the cause of mental illness. Psychotherapy tended to be offered chiefly in clinics and private practice and to devote itself to the treatment of psychoneurosis, while its success with psychotic patients in mental hospitals was limited.

During the 1930s, new approaches in the field of somatic therapies were employed, including the use of insulin coma, convulsive therapy and lobotomy. Tourney writes,

> *Two broad schools of psychiatry emerged, the organic-physical treatment oriented, and the psychodynamic-psychotherapeutic group. The former focused on psychotic patients, and the latter largely on the psychoneurotic and characteriologic problems.*[16]

Somatic therapy as developed in the 1930s survives today in the use of electro-convulsive therapy for the treatment of depression. However, it aroused interest in the use of physical therapies and drugs in the treatment of psychotic patients; this paved the way for the two most recent and promising developments psychiatry, *psychopharmacotherapy* and *community psychiatry*.

Psychopharmacotherapy

The recent revolution in drug-based psychotherapy began in 1951, when the French scientist Laborit synthesized chlorpromazine (Thorazine). This became widely used as a tranquilizer and accounts for the major portion of drug

[15] Garfield Tourney: "Psychiatric Therapies: 1880–1968." *In* Theodore Rothman (ed.): *Changing Patterns in Psychiatric Care.* New York, Crown, 1970, p. 12.
[16] *Ibid.*, p. 35.

treatment today. Along with similar drugs, such as reserpine, chlorpromazine is used in such conditions as anxiety states, agitated depressions, manic states and schizophrenia. The effect of these drugs is to calm the overly aroused nerve systems in the brain.

The second phase of the psychopharmacological movement began in 1954, when iproniazid (Marsilid) was found useful with severely depressed patients. This drug and other "psychic energizers" that stimulate the arousal pathways in the mind began to replace convulsive therapies—particularly electroconvulsive treatment—in the care of depressive illness.

Since the mid-1950s, the increase in the use of drugs in the treatment of the mentally ill has been tremendous. As an example, the total number of psychopharmaceutical tablets dispensed by the Boston State Hospital grew from 113,503 tablets in 1955 to 1,675,190 tablets in 1965—a more than tenfold increase. Similarly, the use of tablets in outpatient care has grown tremendously.

Many investigators regard psychopharmacology as palliative rather than curative. They claim that although drugs are useful in the reduction of symptoms they do not hit at the basic causes of mental illness. The value of psychopharmacology appears to lie chiefly in its use with other therapeutic methods. It has made a great number of patients more accessible and amenable to treatment and has been used in combination with psychotherapy, milieu therapy and other specific treatments.

An immediate and outstanding value is the control of tension and of disturbed behavior, reflected in the virtual elimination of restraint and seclusion in the department's institutions.[17]

The psychopharmacologic revolution has done much to change the nature of mental hospitals and of psychiatric care in general. In recent years, there has been a marked shift from large, impersonal mental hospitals devoted chiefly to custodial care, to smaller institutions based on the therapeutic community model and, most recently, to the development of community mental health centers.

Within institutions, because it is no longer necessary to confine many patients, a new emphasis on activity therapy has been made possible. In general, there is a stronger push toward treating patients and getting them out of the hospital—or avoiding institutionalization in the first place. Fewer patients are neglected, and the total resources of the hospital may be used for therapeutic purposes. Emphasis is placed on helping patients return to community life by a combination of resocialization, living skills and work readiness experiences.

It should be made clear that medical opinion is still somewhat divided regarding drug therapy. Some psychiatrists regard psychopharmacotherapy as a "chemical strait jacket," in that it simply serves to make patients more docile, allowing overburdened hospital staffs to control them easily. In their view, doctors simply tend to do things *to* patients rather than work meaningfully *with* them. However, it is clear that one major benefit of this therapeutic innovation has been the sharp decrease in the number of patients confined on a long-term basis in large, isolated, custodial-type asylums and the corresponding increase in the use of community mental health centers or small local hospitals or units in

---

[17] *Treatment in the Modern Mental Hospital.* Albany, New York, New York State Department of Mental Hygiene, 1966, p. 1.

general hospitals. To illustrate this change, during the period from 1954 to 1970, the number of patients in state mental hospitals declined by almost a third; it was reported in the mid-1970s by several large insurance companies that the average stay for their policyholders in mental hospitals was only 16 days. Although not representative of all psychiatric treatment statistics, this is a revealing figure.

Community Psychiatry

This represents the most important and promising recent trend in psychiatric care. Its purpose is to prevent hospitalization by maintaining disturbed patients in the community or to reintegrate them after hospitalization as rapidly and effectively as possible. Deriving its principles from the idea of social causation of mental illness, community psychiatry stresses the need to understand the familial, social and cultural milieu of each patient. The community psychiatry approach also defines mental illness broadly and includes, as part of its concern, delinquency and crime, sex offenders, addicts and alcoholics, as well as mentally retarded and isolated senile persons.

Community psychiatry works through decentralized mental health centers to prevent hospitalization or, when it is necessary, to get patients back into the community as rapidly as possible. Emphasis is placed on using a variety of groups or resources in the community, such as family, friends, employers, health and welfare agencies or sociorecreational organizations to support and work with patients. Thus, the problem of isolation and resistance against treatment that often occurs when patients are taken a great distance from home and institutionalized may be minimized.

> Emphasis is placed ... on treatment in the community, the utilization of clinic resources, day and night hospital units, crisis-oriented therapy, rehabilitation and aftercare, hospitalization in psychiatric units in general hospitals, earlier discharge, use of halfway houses, and the establishment of special programs for the mentally retarded, aged, alcoholics, and addicts. The education of the public regarding mental illness becomes paramount in helping change community attitudes toward the mentally ill.[18]

The community psychiatry movement was given a strong impetus by the Mental Retardation Facilities and Community Mental Health Centers Construction Act of 1963. This legislation stipulated that, in order to qualify for federal funds, a community mental health center must provide at least five essential services: (a) inpatient services; (b) outpatient services; (c) partial hospitalization services, including at least day-care; (d) emergency services provided 24 hours per day within at least one of these three categories; and (e) consultation and education services available to community agencies and professional personnel. In addition, adequate services were defined as including such other components as diagnostic services, rehabilitation programs (including vocational and educational activities), and pre-care and after-care services (including foster home placements, training and research and evaluation). In many states, new legislation and reorganization of mental health treatment services made it

---

[18] Tourney, *op. cit.*, p. 32.

possible to release large numbers of patients to the community for treatment in community mental health centers. In New York State, for example, after the passage of the Progressive Mental Hygiene Law of January, 1973, the number of outpatients climbed to 84,000 in the following year, surpassing for the first time the inpatient psychiatric population of the state. Many community mental health centers today maintain social groups to which patients can be referred, either by hospitals, psychiatrists, outpatient community clinics or other social agencies. In most cases, such clubs serve as an intermediary step for the patient to move from a treatment center to a more active social life. Another technique of helping patients in their return to community life is the halfway house. These are places where discharged persons can live in the company of professional staff members and other former patients. It provides a means of helping them adjust to community life before attempting to live independently. Halfway houses offer alternatives to living alone in run-down hotels or having to return to unsympathetic or overanxious relatives.

RECREATION IN PSYCHIATRIC TREATMENT

Although it has not been possible to develop valid scientific evidence to show that recreation can either prevent or cure mental illness, it has been widely accepted that recreation makes an important contribution to psychological well-being. Meyer writes,

> *Basically, recreation is an experience which leaves one refreshed, rejuvenated, fulfilled, happy, content and at peace with oneself and the world. It reinforces companionship, group belonging and esteem, mutual interests, concern for our fellow human beings. It is a happy, productive, creative and positive experience, fostering a feeling of well-being. It does not leave us isolated, withdrawn, anxious, apprehensive, suspicious, hostile, fearful and totally sick inside. The outcomes of recreation, the very experience itself, are so closely related to positive mental health that one may consider them as almost synonymous.*[19]

Individuals with poor mental health often have exaggerated feelings of worthlessness, inferiority, deficiency in body structure, athletic ability, intellectual performance and other personal characteristics. Unable to achieve normal relationships, they frequently become supersensitive to social slights, apprehensive about failure and rejection and ultimately withdraw from social contacts.

Recreation has the capability for providing such individuals with the opportunity to be successful and to develop feelings of self-worth. It has other important functions as well, in terms of maintaining healthy emotional status. One of these is its potential for providing a release for the socially acceptable discharge of violent or hostile emotions. Recreation may be used to strengthen or develop such defense mechanisms as repression, displacement of affect, substitution, sublimation and compensation. Although it may be argued that these mechanisms do not deal with the fundamental neurotic problems that affect emotionally unstable persons, the fact is that they make it possible for many

---

[19] Martin W. Meyer: "Recreation, A Positive Force for Mental Health." *American Recreation Journal*, September–October, 1964, p. 140.

such individuals to live with themselves and others in a reasonably happy and constructive way.

Thus, recreation provides a means of dealing with one's antisocial or unhealthy impulses. Meyer writes,

> *A classic example is the "substitution" of dangerous aggressive impulses, such as the desire to destroy or kill, to a more acceptable, but none-the-less aggressive activity. Kicking a ball, striking at a punching bag, chopping wood, throwing a rock at a target, can serve as initial substitutions. These impersonal and socially harmless acts can be further redirected or refined to more meaningful releases, with rules established as controls, such as in the organized sports of soccer, handball, archery, football and tennis. As aggressive impulses are brought under control or redirected . . . important defense mechanisms can thus be established which may serve as a safety valve when dangerous aggressive impulses are ready to explode. . . .*[20]

Art, music, dance and similar activities may also serve as desirable forms of release or sublimation. The kinds of pathologic, high-risk, destructive play described earlier can be made less appealing by providing more constructive and self-enhancing activity.

Typically, recreation programs in psychiatric institutions have been designed to achieve the goals of helping to improve patient morale, provide constructive outlets, promote resocialization, redevelop capacities for creative self-expression and the enjoyable use of leisure and promote the patient's capability for independent community living following discharge from the hospital.

Programs, as described earlier, have been designed on a variety of levels: for mass participation on a voluntary, nonprescribed basis; group or ward activities with specially designed components to meet the needs of patients in certain classifications of illness; and individually prescribed activities geared to meet the unique needs of each patient. Many hospitals have developed extensive schedules of activities throughout the week, with the opportunity for patients to engage in them on a varied basis, depending on their own capability and need.

Activity Therapy Approach

As described in Chapter 3, the activity therapy approach includes various types of rehabilitative therapies, such as occupational therapy, physical therapy, recreational therapy, educational therapy and work therapy. The basic premise underlying this method is that, by prescribing a diversified program of manual and creative activities, patients are given incentives, outlets and means of creative satisfactions. Pertinent data are provided to the psychiatric treatment team regarding the patients' reactions, aptitudes, interests and social adjustment.

Woloshin and Tamura point out that within the rehabilitative-adjustive model, support is given for productive instead of inappropriate behavior. Essentially, the method is geared to the behavioral psychology viewpoint described earlier:

> *The message that should be clearly communicated is that staff respects the patient enough to expect something of him. He is expected to participate in his*

---

[20] *Ibid.*

Psychiatric patients of varied ages take part in a fishing expedition, a picnic at a nearby lake and a cookout in the snow at the Traverse City, Michigan, State Hospital.

Other Traverse City patients take part in a bowling tournament. At the Saskatchewan Hospital at Weyburn, varied craft activities are offered, along with typical Canadian winter sports, like hockey and curling.

program and activities, to contribute to his community, and be productive rather than "crazy." ... *the rehabilitative-adjustive approach is based upon those things which are tangible and easily seen....* *The staff and patient can chart progress more readily through tangible accomplishments* ... *than through therapeutic gains in a one hour interview. If a person indeed can be productive and see the results of his productivity, it is an assumption that behavior modification takes place. Deep insight need not occur within this model for behavior modification to begin. An enhanced self-image and a greater belief in one's ability to be productive, to trust oneself and to trust others can result in further ego strengthening and social growth.*[21]

This approach has generally been accepted throughout the country. As an example, in 1964, the Joint Information Service of the American Psychiatric Association and National Association for Mental Health, in conjunction with the Division of Community Psychiatry of Columbia University and the Department of Mental Health of the American Medical Association, published a survey titled "The Community Mental Health Center—An Analysis of Existing Models." Ten mental health centers in the United States and one in Saskatchewan, Canada, were studied in depth. All of these centers were reported as putting a strong emphasis on occupational and recreational therapy, with considerable emphasis on the resocializing aspects of these programs. In addition to the use of formally trained recreation therapists, these centers made use of other personnel, such as social workers, occupational therapists, rehabilitation counselors, nurses and volunteers, to assist in program development.

Within the activity therapy program, the primary thrust today is toward the maximum "push" in helping "rapid-recovery" patients move toward discharge. Because of the use of drugs, many patients are able to move freely around hospital grounds or even to go into the community on trips or work sessions—this would not have been possible in the past. Almost every aspect of programs in many of the newer mental hospitals is geared directly toward developing competence for community living.

LEISURE COUNSELING

As described in Chapter 4, many hospitals have developed new leisure or recreation counseling programs intended to (a) help patients maintain and strengthen their existing affiliations with family, friends, churches, lodges and civic groups; (b) help patients form new ties with individuals and groups and make effective use of available community resources for recreation; and (c) mobilize community resources for fostering mental health. Similarly, the *token economy* method, also described in Chapter 4, is an important element in many activity therapy programs, with tokens being used to reward patients for responsible behavior and serving both as a way of "purchasing" recreational opportunities and as a means of recording involvement.

Increasingly, the movement in this field has been away from emphasis on *treating* patients with recreation toward *making use* of recreation as a social interaction medium. The major value of recreation with mental patients is seen not as the opportunity to provide individualized psychodynamic prescriptions of activity but rather as the opportunity to play and create in a manner that allows the patient to recapture his own sense of individuality and meaningfulness.

---

[21] Arthur Woloshin and Robert Tamura: "Activities Therapy in a Community Mental Health Center." *Therapeutic Recreation Journal*, 1st Quarter, 1969, p. 31.

Milieu Therapy

It has become widely accepted that psychiatric disorder is integrally related to the social milieu in which it has developed. As a consequence, the conviction has grown that the community in which he is *treated* must be a healthy and constructive one if the patient is to regain a positive relationship with his family and community. This viewpoint is the basis of "milieu therapy," which stresses the importance of the total physical and social climate in which the patient is treated. Stanton has written,

> The onset, symptoms, and recovery rates of major psychiatric illness are deci-
> sively influenced by the environment within which the patient is observed and
> treated. . . . There is no patient "untreated" by his environment—only patients
> "treated," well or ill.[22]

Milieu therapy or, as it is often referred to, the therapeutic community approach is concerned with *all* aspects of the hospital environment, including its physical structure, the opportunity for patients and staff to interact with each other in emotionally supportive ways and the provision of a wide range of important experiences and activities that support meaningful change. In short, the total philosophy of the hospital must be therapeutic, and in every aspect of hospital life, therapeutic agents must be at work:

> The concept of the therapeutic or curative community may be described as an
> arrangement in which all of a patient's time in the hospital—not just the time he
> spends in therapy—is thought of as treatment. The milieu in which he finds
> himself—i.e., the hospital, is seen as exerting a powerful influence upon his
> emotional life and behavior. Every contact, every casual conversation with a
> fellow patient, a nurse, even a kitchen helper, is regarded as potentially thera-
> peutic. Milieu therapy . . . is an attempt to take into account what psychiatrists
> have called "the other 23 hours in the day"—to treat mental illness through a
> careful restructuring of the social environment.[23]

Interest in the patient's environment as an important element in treat-ment was heavily influenced by the British social psychiatrist, Maxwell Jones, who established in 1947 what was later to be called the "therapeutic community." Instead of the authoritarian, hierarchic structure that had been commonly found in mental hospitals, Jones encouraged a treatment system with permissive, democratic and communal values:

> Everybody in the community, both staff and patients, was encouraged to maximize
> his therapeutic potential. Furthermore, all ward activities were deliberately
> integrated so as to be part of the total treatment program.[24]

Maxmen, Tucker and LeBow point out that the terms "milieu therapy" and "therapeutic community" have been used synonymously with a number

---

[22] Alfred Stanton: *In* V. Cumming and E. Cumming: *Ego and Milieu.* New York, Atherton Press, 1969, p. v.
[23] Maggie Scarf: "In the Therapeutic Community Patients Are Doctors." *New York Times Magazine,* May 25, 1969, p. 109.
[24] Jerrold S. Maxmen, Gary J. Tucker and Michael LeBow: *Rational Hospital Psychiatry: The Reactive Environment.* New York, Brunner, Mazel, 1974, p. 17.

of similar terms, such as "sociotherapy," "social psychiatry" or "psychotherapeutic community." Although the specific examples of this approach may vary considerably in practice, they define the concept as

> . . . a treatment modality which attempts not only to utilize maximally the therapeutic potential of the entire staff, but also to place a major responsibility upon patients to serve as change agents. In other words the unit's structure facilitates patients having a significant therapeutic role in the rehabilitation of other patients. Thus, all staff and patients meaningfully participate in the unit's decision-making processes about patient care as well as in the implementation of these plans.[25]

The therapeutic community concept represents a radical departure from the traditional view of a mental hospital as a custodial institution or "asylum." The asylum was deliberately located at a place far from the community to afford the patient protection from the stress of daily life or the problems that had beset him and probably also to "remove" him from the family as a source of grief or shame. Within such hospitals there was little sense of community life or interaction; patients were not expected to make decisions, exercise judgment or function responsibly.

The proponents of the milieu therapy approach claim that removing patients from social stress and meaningful community roles serves to make their return to society more difficult because of the prolonged period of dependence they have experienced. Their social skills and ability to face the outside world may have atrophied during hospitalization, and they may understandably fear that there is no longer a place for them among family and friends and in the vocational world.

Milieu therapy, therefore, is committed to making a patient's stay in the hospital a replica of the social interactions of ordinary life—in terms of social and recreational activities, work, civic or community responsibility, human relationships and other significant aspects of life. Within the therapeutic community, patients, while being treated for their illness, are encouraged to function as fully as possible in settings that are realistic and make real demands on them.

Typically, many mental hospitals maintain an open-door policy for large numbers of patients. Patients are encouraged to have frequent contacts with the outside community:

> The principle of the open door was established as a general policy for New York State hospitals, and patients responded by taking new interest in their surroundings, their personal appearance, and other members of the hospital community. This was the beginning of an overall liberalization program that permitted patients to move freely about the institution, that encouraged them to choose their companions, their activities, their clothes, to assume responsibilities for themselves and others—in short, to function as normally as possible while being treated for illness. . . .

> A new flexibility in hospital management is also developing. Patients are encouraged to go home for brief visits, weekends and "vacations." In addition to the full time resident patient, there is now the "day patient," who lives at home and spends his days at the hospital participating in regular treatment programs, and the "night patient" who lives in the protected environment of the hospital but goes out to work during the day. As the average length of hospitalization decreases,

---

[25] *Ibid.*, p. 25.

families are urged to keep a place for the patient in the home and help him main-tain his community ties.

The community itself, evincing a more understanding and accepting attitude, has made it possible for many more patients to leave the hospital and continue their treatment in the department's outpatient clinics. Treatment in the community has become more feasible because convalescent patients may be maintained on sustaining doses of the tranquilizing drugs.[26]

CURRENT TRENDS IN THERAPEUTIC RECREATION

What has been the total impact of the milieu therapy and decentralized mental health centers movements upon therapeutic recreation service? First, it should be made clear that theoretical statements of philosophy, or of idealized programs, do not always portray the reality of what goes on in institutions. The reality is that many institutions are badly overcrowded and that many patients still exist in chronic wards or "extended-care" facilities for older, highly regressed patients, while newer, smaller centers situated in and around cities represent the big push for patients with more hopeful prognoses.

The very notion of the therapeutic community, with the idea that every staff member, every aspect of living, every physical or social element of hospital life serves as a supportive therapeutic agent, belies the reality of crowded wards, overworked personnel who may be moonlighting because of poor salaries and a lack of cooperation among disciplines or the difficulty in developing meaningful relationships with community groups. Nonetheless, the new approaches are exciting ones. They have had a significant impact on therapeutic recreation service in the following ways.

Shifting of Emphasis in Activities

In the traditional psychiatric hospital recreation program, in addition to numbers of special events or other mass activities, there were normally a va-riety of regularly scheduled sports and games, arts and crafts, music, dance or other social programs that patients were, in effect, assigned to as part of regular ward or building unit schedules. Today, the emphasis has shifted away from this type of clearly recreational activity, frequently in the direction of activities that have an informal, less structured, social-learning kind of orientation.

Instead of learning dances, games or crafts or playing sports or music— with the emphasis on the activity involvement—many departments are today providing activities in which patients become involved in self-discovery processes that are heavily based on "encounter or sensitivity group" activities. As an example, one such program in a New York State Department of Mental Hygiene mental hospital schedules the following kinds of activities throughout the week:

grooming (male)	newspaper group
grooming (female)	coffee and conversation
bowling	psychodrama

---

[26] *Treatment in the Modern Mental Hospital, op. cit.*, pp. 2–3.

open shop

dance therapy

drama and poetry

cooking

small crafts

"psychogymnastics"

hootenanny

self-expression

exercise group

small groups

ward clean-up

movies

Such activities are more personally involving, less demanding of skills and much freer in terms of permitting expressive behavior than more traditionally oriented recreational activities. Whether they are more or less valuable in terms of the fundamental goals of therapeutic recreation than the traditional kinds of activities is not easy to measure.

Another example of innovative program service in psychiatric treatment involves therapeutic camping. More and more state and private mental hospitals, for example, have experimented in recent years with camping programs, even for extremely sick and unresponsive patients. A leading example is Oregon State Hospital, which has taken as many as 50 patients at a time on wilderness camping trips involving white-water boating, rock climbing and survival-ecology activities.[27] In a similar program involving a modified version of Outward Bound, the private psychiatric division of the Massachusetts General Hospital in Belmont, Massachusetts, has involved patients in activities such as long distance bicycling, rock-climbing, cross country skiing, a confidence-building ropes course, group initiative tests and two to five day backpacking expeditions in the White Mountain National Forest.[28] Such ventures have challenged mental patients to deal with reality, test their own capabilities and act as mature, responsible adults, with surprisingly positive effects in most cases. In addition, camping provides an intimate "social structure and feedback system that builds closer interpersonal ties and presents a reflective backdrop on behavior."[29]

Another growing area of interest in psychiatric rehabilitation is movement therapy, a creative and expressive technique that has been widely used as a way of reaching and involving highly regressed mental patients. This method is described, along with other innovative treatment approaches, in Chapter 10. In addition to the development of new kinds of program elements, therapeutic recreation has also been administratively restructured in many mental health systems, typically through what has been called the "unitization" approach.

Unitization and the Blurring of Professional Roles

In a number of large mental hospitals in which unitization has gone into effect, patients are grouped in terms of housing and treatment services, according to their original residence or "catchment area." The purpose of this is to strengthen the element of community affiliation and, presumably, to facilitate

---

[27] David M. Graham and James B. Ingersoll: "Helping Adolescents Get Moving: The Reality Therapy Approach." *Journal of Physical Education and Recreation*, May, 1975, pp. 32–33.
[28] John Shank: "Therapeutic Recreation Through Contrived Stress." *Therapeutic Recreation Journal*, 1st Quarter, 1975, pp. 21–25. See also "Roughing It Back Toward Sanity." *Life*, October 27, 1972.
[29] Robert H. Jones: "An Alternative to the Ward: Wilderness Camping." *Journal of Physical Education and Recreation*, May, 1975, p. 24.

planning for return to the community, recreation counseling and community-patient interaction. What it has meant in a practical sense is that patients with all degrees of illness or recovery stages, and of various ages and backgrounds, are lumped together in hospital units rather than housed according to age and type or severity of illness, as in the past. In this type of structure, staff members no longer serve their hospitals on a system-wide basis, planning overall hospital activities and acting as specialists within their areas of competence. Instead, they are attached solely to their units and assume roles that contribute generally to the therapeutic community process—but in which they do not specialize in their fields of particular training or skill.

In an increasing number of hospitals, staff members working in such programs are no longer identified according to their professional specialities but are simply titled activity therapists. The implication of this is that they no longer will be presenting specific areas of activity in which they are highly competent leaders but instead will simply be promoting group process and the therapeutic interaction of patients and staff. The notion of recreation *as* recreation appears to have suffered a decline in such settings. Instead, the group process and the experience of living, planning and sharing decision-making together appear to be the primary emphases.

Development of Community-Based Facilities

The community mental health movement has had a profound impact in breaking down the rigid walls that have separated psychiatric patients from community life in the past. Recreation has become a part of special day-care and night-care programs. In many communities, it is now provided as part of day-center programs that, operating as satellites to a hospital structure or existing independently in the community, meet the needs of discharged mental patients who require a protected setting or are living at home and are receiving psychiatric clinical counseling for part of the day.

For example, in Rockland County, New York, the Elmwood Club for discharged mental patients serves over 100 members with 11 part-time workers on staff, aided by 35 volunteers and student leaders. The goals of this program are the following:

> . . . *individual self-fulfillment; development of a sense of self-worth; creative use of self; emphasis on healthy aspects of personality, focusing on strengths, development of new skills and encouraging the emergence of old ones; belief in the ability to manipulate one's environment, to change undesirable parts of it; to participate fully in what life has to offer; and a positive approach to life based on day-to-day existence, but one with careful planning of activities over an extended period of time with concrete goals in mind.*[30]

Many of the members of the club work either full-time or part-time while others attend a local community college or work in a sheltered workshop. The club meets for parts of three days or evenings each week and engages in social

---

[30] *Annual Report, Elmwood Club.* Rockland County, New York, Mental Health Association, 1970.

recreation activities, home crafts, discussion groups, grooming activities, community service programs (dramatics, dancing and singing), parties, trips, cooking, exercise and games and similar activities.

In addition to such activities, the members of the staff work closely with social workers and other staff members at nearby state or veterans hospitals and with social workers from the Rockland County Department of Social Services. Many other community mental health centers have begun to sponsor such services.

In some communities, such as East St. Louis, the provision of such social clubs and after-care units in community mental health centers has been seen as instrumental in sharply reducing the return of discharged patients to psychiatric hospitals.[31] Particularly when foster communities are developed— in which patients, rather than return to their original homes and families, are located in residential "halfway-houses" or helped to set up apartments with other discharged patients—it has been found that ongoing social and vocational assistance is needed to help them move effectively back into the overall community structure. This is particularly true of ex-patients who are placed in "welfare" hotels, S.R.O. (single room occupancy) units or similar environments and who run a high risk of being totally isolated if special services and programs are not designed for them.

MENTAL HOSPITAL PROGRAMS

This chapter concludes by providing descriptions of the activity therapy or recreation programs in a number of hospitals in the United States and Canada. Obviously, it is not possible to give full details of such programs. In each case, some of the more interesting aspects of the program are provided, along with examples of rating or evaluation forms, personnel assignments and program schedules.

Athens Mental Health Center, Athens, Ohio

This center provides both inpatient and outpatient services, assisting persons in a 15-county area of southeastern Ohio who have a "major" mental illness and less severely ill persons in a five-county area. Multidisciplinary teams of mental health workers operate through four major treatment units: (a) Community Services, for outpatients and acutely disturbed inpatients; (b) Adolescent, for inpatients up to 18 years of age; (c) Geriatric, for inpatients 65 years of age and older; and (d) Continued Care, for patients requiring long-term hospitalization.

The history of this hospital reflects changing trends in psychiatric care throughout the United States. Founded in 1874 as the "Athens Lunatic Asylum," its name changed to the "Athens Asylum for the Insane," the "Athens State Hospital" and finally the "Athens Mental Health Center." Its treatment procedures also shifted through the years, from a primary emphasis in the 1950s to

---

[31] C. R. Gilpin and Edward Neufield: "Community Cooperation and a Shoestring Budget: R_x for an Activity Program." *Mental Hygiene*, July, 1970, pp. 397–400.

work on the farms and hydrotherapy, to a heavy use of lobotomies and finally to the use of psychiatric drugs coupled with a strong emphasis on the activity therapies and the therapeutic community approach. The inpatient population has been reduced from 1800 to about 600; in addition, several hundred outpatients are treated monthly.

The treatment staff is organized into several departments (Fig. 5–1). Of these, the Activity Therapy Department includes the following services: Volunteer Services, Patients' Library, Beauty Shop, Recreation Therapy, Music Therapy, Physical Therapy, Education Therapy, Industrial Therapy, Arts Therapy and Occupational Therapy (including Arts and Crafts shop and Home Management).

A key element in this program is provided by an evaluation committee that is responsible for appraising patients (based on past history, medical record admission information and personal interview), determining the needs and interests of clients and assigning them to appropriate placement groups or patients. This committee also is responsible for reporting periodically on each patient's progress and for recommending changes in assignments. The goals of all elements of the Activity Therapy Program are clearly outlined. For example, the Vocational and Work Training Center seeks to meet the following goals:

1. Develop ego, strength, and self-worth.
2. Provide maximum reality contact through work.
3. Learn to establish standards and techniques.
4. Learn to follow a routine by use of verbal or written instruction.
5. Learn to use already established methods and procedures.
6. Learn to recognize limits set by a given task.
7. Use those work structures that are good in serving the client's dependency needs.
8. Permit client some control of his situation by the use of structure and control implicit in jobs.
9. Encourage decision making and planning.
10. Teach responsibility through care of equipment and tools. . . .[32]

This department provides work assignments in several categories: maintenance department (power house, pulling ashes, shoveling coal and cleaning), dietary department, farm, store room and sewing room, laundry, commissary and paint shop. Similarly, each service within the Activity Therapy Department has clearly outlined goals and procedures.

Recreation is offered in conjunction with other creative activities, such as art, music and drama therapy. Activities are divided into two classes, based on the nature of participation required:

1. Passive participation
   (a) Movies
   (b) Theatre
   (c) Church services
   (d) Art exhibit
   (e) Bus rides
   (f) Concerts
   (g) Trips to Columbus Zoo
   (h) Spectator sports

---

[32] *Activity Therapy Manual.* Athens, Ohio, Mental Health Center, 1971.

Figure 5-1. Organization of Athens, Ohio, Mental Health Center.

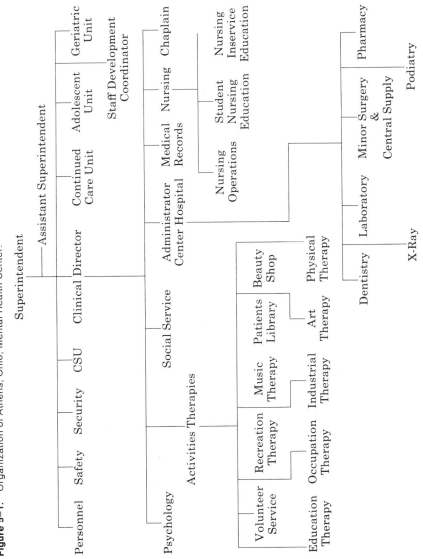

2. Active participation
  (a) Club activities (press club, garden club, cooking club, literary club, drama and radio club)
  (b) Adapted sports (softball, basketball, shuffleboard, horseshoes, touch football and bowling)
  (c) Glee club and choir activities
  (d) Individual music lessons (voice, piano, organ, guitar and brass instruments)
  (e) Music appreciation groups
  (f) Art therapy groups
  (g) Social recreation (dances, parties, teas and picnics)
  (h) Tournaments (pool, checkers, bowling, ping-pong, table shuffleboard, cards and horseshoes)
  (i) Camping (overnight and day camping)
  (j) Library (regular lending services, literary and current events groups, for both leisure time and educational purposes.

The facilities used include an extensive variety of shops, studios and other recreation areas at the hospital itself, as well as other resources in the community, such as schools and colleges, hobby groups, service clubs, fraternal organizations, families and friends.

Mt. Sinai Hospital, New York, New York

The psychiatric unit within Mt. Sinai Hospital in New York City provides a useful example of activity therapists employed as fully integrated members of the psychiatric treatment team. The rationale for this role is stated thus:

The Activity Therapist is responsible for full-time in-patient psychiatric care. The patients involved are not confined to bed; yet they must remain within the hospital for an average stay of 35 days. The patient generally spends only one-and-a-half hours a week with his resident psychiatrist; if he has a private psychiatrist, he will usually spend five hours a week with him at best. The balance of the patient's time, a considerable part of the day and the entire evening and weekend time, the patient's treatment plan is implemented by his Activity Therapist. There is considerable need for this care; in psychiatric illness, the constructive use of this time is of the utmost importance toward the patient's recovery. An Activity Therapist must be professionally trained for this responsibility. His activities must facilitate the patient's recovery, and bring him back to healthy functioning, by restoring an interest in life and constructive action; and guiding the patient to an awareness of his unhealthy mental habits, pointing the way to a positive change toward healthful balanced attitudes. This must be done with the cooperation of the nursing staff, regarding medication and medical problems; and the programs must complement the doctor's long-range treatment goals for the patient.[33]

The time of Activity Therapists at Mt. Sinai is about equally divided between servicing an inpatient unit and working on the ninth floor of the hospital, where activities and programs are provided on an all-hospital basis. They have the following specific responsibilities for their own units:

1. Supervision of patient government-type meetings.
2. Leading activity planning sessions for events that will take place on weekends or evenings when Activity Therapists are not present.

---

[33] *Departmental Manual.* Mt. Sinai Hospital, New York, 1971.

3. Attendance and participation in daily morning group meeting with patients and staff and follow-up discussion meetings with medical and nursing staff.
4. Attendance and participation in twice- or thrice-weekly unit conferences with medical, nursing and social work personnel at which new admissions are interviewed and discussed.
5. Staff meetings with medical, nursing and social work personnel to bring out and discuss inter-staff problems.
6. Meetings between the chief resident and Activity Therapists, and the unit chief and Activity Therapists, to keep each of these individuals aware of patients' progress.
7. Meetings with nursing staffs of individual units to exchange information regarding patients.

In addition, Activity Therapists attend weekly staff meetings of their own group, in which they deal with the mechanics of running the program, such as scheduling, planning of special events, problems relating to equipment, supplies and similar matters. They also meet in regular inservice seminars concerned with evolving new types of programs designed to best serve psychiatric patients today. Essentially, Activity Therapists are responsible for three types of group experiences: leisure-time groups, prevocational groups and rehabilitative groups. In each situation, they must serve as resource persons (with emphasis on skills involved in the activity) and as facilitators of group process. The team approach to the use of the Activity Therapist is illustrated in the listing of meetings to which he is committed, as well as in the following statement:

> Since his function is that of a professional within the Department of Psychiatry, it is necessary for the Activity Therapist to have a working double professional vocabulary; one relating to activities, and one involving psychodynamics, psychopathology, and psychopharmacology. The foregoing knowledge is essential when writing in nursing report books on the individual units, and in filling out evaluation sheets on patients in . . . ninth-floor activity groups, and in verbally sharing information on patients with the medical staff. . . .[34]

Each form of activity in which patients engage is seen as providing a particular kind of challenge and a special opportunity to observe and evaluate patient skill and response.

In general, the emphasis is on open-ended, creative kinds of activities or projects and on experiences that are rooted in feeling and fluid group relationships and that provide self-discovery opportunities. Various forms are used in evaluating patient performance and in making recommendations for activity. An example of such a form used in the Mt. Sinai psychiatric treatment program is shown in Figure 5–2.

Various inventories, forms or rating scales are used as part of the evaluation and counseling process in Activity Therapy at Mt. Sinai. For example, this department has patients fill out (if they are not able to do so independently, they are assisted) a comprehensive background profile. Excerpts from this form are seen in Figure 5–3.

A final example of program development taken from the Mt. Sinai program is a sample schedule for a period of several weeks in February and March, 1972, listing activities and the times they are offered, the location and the criteria for admission to the group. The schedule is prepared for the entire week; however, only a portion of it is presented here (Fig. 5–4).

---

[34] *Ibid.*

Figure 5–2. Performance evaluation summary and program recommendations.

Patient's name: _____ Date: _____

Unit: _____

I. Evaluation summary: Performance deficits and strengths related to
  (A) Self-concept and identity
  (B) Need-drive adaptation
  (C) Interpersonal and social relations
  (D) Cognition and problem solving
  (E) Perceptual—Motor functions
  (F) Life tasks skills and vocational adjustment
II. Program focus and recommendations:
  (A) Program focus
    1. Remedial:
      (a) deficits in performance skills around which program is to be structured
      (b) essential characteristics of remedial activities
    2. Supportive:
      (a) existing skills, capacities and interest which should be sustained and/or protected
      (b) essential characteristics of supportive activities
    3. Life tasks skills and vocational adjustment
      (a) areas and level of daily life tasks skills and vocational adjustment needs toward which rehabilitation program should be directed.
      (b) activity and/or task assignment recommendations
      Staff: _____

Figure 5–3. Educational, vocational and interest profile.

I. Identification: Name _____ Address _____
  Age _____ Family Members _____
II. Education (includes dates, diplomas or degrees, type of program, courses most enjoyed and most disliked, etc.)
III. Avocational experiences:
  Hobbies: What activities or hobbies do you enjoy doing during your leisure time? Please list. How did you become interested in each?

  Check your special skills, talents or outstanding abilities and state whether skillful or average in each case:

Singing _____	Sports
Debating _____	Teams: Baseball _____
Dancing _____	Volleyball _____
Photography _____	Individual: Tennis _____
Sewing _____	Skiing _____
Arts and crafts _____	Swimming _____
Playing instrument _____	
Needlework _____	
Woodworking _____	
Painting _____	

IV. Family occupational inventory: (includes questions about age, educational background, major area of work or occupation, interests and hobbies of father, mother, sisters, brothers, spouses or other close relatives)
  (The profile also asks specific questions regarding:)
  Hobbies, work or other activities as part of early background of patient or shared with family.
  Total vocational experience record. Attitudes toward various jobs, qualities of employer, special vocational skills and work experience.
  Personal ambitions and self-perceived abilities, strong points, weaknesses and interpersonal relationships.

Figure 5-4. Department of Psychiatry, Mt. Sinai Hospital, Therapeutic Activities Division: February–March activity schedule.

Monday

TIME	GROUP	ROOM	CRITERIA FOR ADMISSION TO GROUP
Morning			
10:15–11:15 A.M.	Painting group	Room 3 OT area	By referral only
10:15–11:15 A.M.	Sewing workshop	Room 1 OT area	By referral only
Afternoon			
1:30–2:00 P.M.	Body awareness		
2:00–3:30 P.M.	Current events Discussion group	Music room gym area	Voluntary
2:00–4:00 P.M.	Clay workshop	Room 4 OT area	By referral only
2:30–3:30 P.M.	Gym for pediatrics	Gym	Pediatrics only
5:00–6:00 P.M.	Planning for leisure time	Room 2 OT area	By referral only
Evening			
7:00–8:00 P.M.	Gym for child psychiatry	Gym	Child psychiatry only

Tuesday

TIME	GROUP	ROOM	CRITERIA FOR ADMISSION TO GROUP
Morning			
10:15–11:30 A.M.	Crafts workshop	Room 3 OT area	By referral only
10:15–11:30 A.M.	Food a la carte		By referral only
10:15–11:30 A.M.	Production lines	Room 4 OT area	Two separate groups—tie dye workshop and candle making workshop. By referral only
Afternoon			
2:00–3:30 P.M.	Painting group	Room 3 OT area	By referral only
Evening			
6:00–7:00 P.M.	Gym-free time	Gym	Voluntary
7:00–8:00 P.M.	Gym for child psychiatry	Gym	Child psychiatry only
8:00–9:00 P.M.	Gym—volleyball, basketball, table tennis	Gym	Voluntary

Wednesday

TIME	GROUP	ROOM	CRITERIA FOR ADMISSION TO GROUP
Morning			
10:00–10:45 A.M.	Social dance instruction	Gym	By referral only
10:15–11:30 A.M.	Crafts workshop	Room 3 OT area	By referral only
10:15–11:15 A.M.	Food nutrition group	Room 5 OT area	By referral only
10:15–11:30 A.M.	Production lines	Room 4 OT area	By referral only
Afternoon			
2:00–4:00 P.M.	Sewing workshop	Room 1 OT area	By referral only
2:30–3:30 P.M.	Gym for pediatrics	Gym	Pediatrics only
Evening			
5:30–6:00 P.M.	Coed body movement and exercise group	Gym	Voluntary
6:00–7:00 P.M.	Volleyball instruction	Gym	Voluntary
7:00–8:00 P.M.	Men's physical fitness group	Gym	By referral only
8:00–9:00 P.M.	Gym—volleyball, basketball, table tennis	Gym	Voluntary

Saskatchewan Hospital, Weyburn, Saskatchewan, Canada

For a period of years, this hospital represented one of the major institutions for psychiatric care in Western Canada, with a patient count in the late 1950s of well over 1500. As part of the shift to smaller, community-based institutions and more flexible treatment services, the patient load was reduced to 350, chiefly extended-care (long-term, chronic) patients. The following section describes the recreation program of the hospital *prior* to its shift in focus. It is deliberately included here to show how large, traditionally conceived mental hospitals have operated in the past and, in some cases, continue to do so today. A number of the elements in its program, such as the "voucher" system (token economy), evaluation of patients' interests and participation and role of the patient council, illustrate principles presented earlier in this and preceding chapters.

STAFF

Two staff members, a recreation supervisor and an assistant, both of whom hold diplomas in psychiatric nursing and have completed three-year certification courses in recreation, are responsible for this program. They are assisted by nurses who encourage patients to take part in activity, while the recreation staff members act as providers, guides and enablers.

FACILITIES

Compared to a municipal institution like Mt. Sinai, the Saskatchewan hospital has extensive facilities that, in turn, make possible an extremely varied program. These areas and buildings include a curling and skating rink, poolroom, shuffleboard areas, music rooms, hobby rooms, game rooms, sports field, auditorium, gymnasium, picnic areas, miniature golf course, lawn bowling courts, croquet courts, horseshoe pits, library and other specialized facilities. In addition, the recreation department uses buses and camp rental procedures to provide vacations for both in- and outpatients.

GOALS OF HOSPITAL

To facilitate the discharge of larger numbers of patients, the recreation department has placed emphasis on three major goals: (a) retraining in social and recreational skills; (b) fostering independence; and (c) exposing the patient to the community. It has structured its operation so that it is similar to the normal model of citizens living in the community. During the hours of 9 to 5, patients engage either in occupational therapy or in work assignments, either in a sheltered workshop manufacturing wood products or in hospital departments, such as the laundry, gardens or plumbing shop. Recreation is provided after 5 P.M. or, by prescription with special patients, between 9 and 5 P.M.

PROGRAM ORGANIZATION

This is carried out in the following ways:

1. By assigning several facilities and activities to each patient unit of the hospital.
2. Through the general function or core program, which is scheduled five nights a week for those patients who are able to attend them independently.

3. Providing equipment and activities for unit-building living rooms (day rooms) to serve patients who are too sick to leave this area.
4. Services for outpatients. The recreation staff of the hospital is also active in planning and setting up programs for youth, the physically disabled or elderly people in the adjacent community, by providing consultation, offering workshops and helping to establish youth coffeehouses and sports programs, nursing home activities and other events.

Figure 5–5. Recreation interest questionnaire.

Date:
Name _____ Age _____ Occupation _____
Home Address _____ Town _____ Rural _____

In your community,

do you have:	*did you ever:*	*would you like to learn:*
_____ a rink	_____ curl	
_____ a bowling alley	_____ bowl	
_____ a theatre	_____ attend shows,	
_____ a pool hall	_____ dances, bingo	
_____ a swimming pool	_____ play pool	
_____ a golf course	_____ swim	
_____ a community hall	_____ golf	

Do you belong to any clubs such as:

_____ a home makers club   did you ever _____ would you like to _____
_____ a square dance club
_____ a Legion society   Do you have any hobbies?
_____ a church organization   What games or instruments have you enjoyed playing?
_____ a craft club (What?)

What types of activities would you enjoy (Yes, No, Don't know):

Quiet Games	*Active Games*	*Social Activities*
_____ playing cards	_____ volleyball	_____ community singing
_____	_____ darts	_____ tours
_____	_____ shuffleboard	_____ picnics
_____	_____ croquet	_____ parties
_____ table games	_____ horseshoes	_____
_____	_____ ring toss	_____
_____	_____	_____
_____		

Entertainment	*Hobbies and Clubs*
_____ bands	_____ drawing and painting
_____ plays	_____ leathercraft
_____ slides	_____ wood carving
_____ variety shows	_____ rug making
_____ television	_____ needlework
_____ sports events	_____ gardening
_____ speakers	_____ cooking and baking
_____ discussion groups	_____ reading

When you return to your home would you like help from anyone to join in any activities or clubs there may be in your town? _____>
Comments:

EVALUATION OF PATIENTS

Both in the assignment of patients to activities and in the evaluation of their continuing participation and progress, a five-point rating scale is used by staff. The patients are rated with respect to their attendance and participation in recreation and social activities on the following scale:

5. Attends willingly and participates in activity as it would be expected of someone in a similar situation in the community. _____
4. Attends willingly but is mostly a passive observer. ____
3. Will attend, but only after protesting about it. _____
2. Usually refuses to attend. _____
1. Considered too ill to attend. _____

Patients are rated each week on these points, and their status is charted on an overall graph that extends over a preiod of several weeks or months, thus providing a longitudinal view of their progress as seen by recreation therapists and nurses.

In addition, two other devices are used to ascertain patient needs and interests and to evaluate systematically their participation in recreation activities. The first is a Recreation Interest Questionnaire (Fig. 5–5), and the second is an Evaluation Form for Patient Participation and Interaction (Fig. 5–6).

Figure 5–6. Evaluation form for patient interaction and participation.

NAME		ATTENDANCE			PARTICIPATION AND INTEREST						VERBAL INTERACTION DURING ACTIVITY				WARD—
Date	Group Act. (1) Spont. Act. (2) Voucher Act. (3) Activity	Refuses	With Persua-sion	Will-ingly	Does Not Partici-pate	Spec-tator (Shows In-terest)	Partici-pates with Persua-sion	Partici-pates Freely	Assists in Start-ing Activity	Assists Others	None	Some When Spoken to	Some Spon-taneous Inter-action	Inter-acts Freely	Comments

The second form (Fig. 5–6) is used to measure patient involvement in three types of activities: group activities, spontaneous or individual activities and "voucher activities." This refers to activities that the patient attends, for which he pays with vouchers that have been paid him as a reward for work. The entire hospital operates with a system of such vouchers or "chits" through which the patients may purchase merchandise, candy, clothing and similar articles or gain admission to special events at the hospital. The purpose of this device is to encourage appropriate spending within areas of personal responsibility. Patients are expected to spend a certain minimal amount each month in certain recreation activities as evidence of social involvement.

PROGRAM ACTIVITIES

This includes a substantial number of activities, both inside and outside of the hospital setting. In a recent year-end report, the following were listed (partial listing):

Social Activities
Coffee groups in city
Dances
White Cross socials
Seasonal parties
Whist tournaments
Scavenger hunts
Darts tournaments
Barbecues
Wiener roasts
Music listing
Bingo in hospital and city
Checker tournaments
Pool and pool tournaments
Picnics
Ping pong tournaments

Education and Cultural Activities
Films
Art contests
Magazine subscriptions
Weekly newspaper
Library services
Craft sessions
Musical sessions
Talent shows
Cooking contests

Physical Activities
Archery
Curling

Broomball
Shuffleboard
Miniature golf
Fishing
Ice fishing
Bowling in city
Gymnasium activities
Lawn bowling
Horseshoes
Croquet
Volleyball
Floor hockey and tournaments
Badminton
Soccer
Tobogganing and sleigh riding

Audience Activities
Weekly movies (popular)
Weekly educational films
Curling matches in city
Band performances
Caroling
Hockey games in city
Television sports watching
Softball in city
Fair in city
Karate performances
Tours of city sites of interest

Substantial numbers of hospital patients also have been taken on one-week vacations, based on satisfactory performance in the industrial therapy (work program), satisfactory social behavior and payment of vouchers at an approved level. In addition, a selected group of outpatients have been taken on trips to scenic sites, parks, picnic areas and spectator events in various parts of southeastern Saskatchewan.

PATIENT COUNCIL

A final interesting aspect of the Saskatchewan Hospital has been its patient council, which functions in the following ways: (a) as a patient union in dealing with problems related to patient employment in the industrial therapy program; (b) helping to plan and critically evaluate the recreational services in the hospital; and (c) dealing with patient complaints regarding individual treatment programs or general ward affairs.

The officers of the patient council are elected from the general patient population every three months, or whenever a presiding officer is discharged or regarded as too ill to hold office. General meetings are held weekly and deal with a variety of problems; they also hear reports from various patient committees set up to deal with aspects of hospital life. Once a month, 25 patient representatives of all the units in the hospital meet with the recreation staff to discuss and critically evaluate recreation activities. Their suggestions are implemented, unless they are regarded as detrimental to hospital or treatment goals. Reports are made regularly to the general meeting of the patient council.

As mentioned earlier, the Saskatchewan Hospital has been converted from an institution serving the general mentally ill population to a "level four" facility, designed to serve older patients (chiefly in the 45 to 70 age range). As described in the official guidelines,

> *This level of care is for persons of all ages who do not require acute hospital care and treatment but do require regular and continuous medical attention, highly skilled technical nursing provided under appropriate supervision on a 24-hour basis, and, in addition, special techniques for the improvement or maintenance of function. Patients at this level require initial and continuing medical assessment involving investigation and diagnosis for which appropriate facilities must be readily available. The aims of treatment are to control the disease process, to achieve maximum recovery of function, to prevent further disability, to retard deterioration, and to alleviate pain and distress.* [35]

Realistically, these patients are regarded as poor-prognosis, long-term care patients, who have little or no prospect for recovery and will probably spend the remainder of their days within the facility. It is believed that when such patients are permitted to become completely passive, they deteriorate sharply, both physically and mentally. However, "where there is a therapeutic environment in which there is motivation and stimulation for patients to be as independent as possible, even those with poor prognoses may improve."

Obviously, as some large institutions (like the Saskatchewan Hospital) have been transformed into smaller settings for chronic-care patients, others have been created or strengthened to provide more active treatment programs and strong community linkages for patients who are regarded as candidates for quick recovery and discharge. An excellent example of this is the Mental Health Centre at Penetanguishene, Ontario, Canada, operated by the Province of

---

[35] *Annual Report.* Saskatchewan Hospital, Weyburn, Saskatchewan, Canada, 1971.

Ontario. This institution places special emphasis on a meaningful program of leisure counseling (see p. 117). The rationale for this program is described by James Montagnes, Director of Vocational, Recreational and Volunteer Services in the Penetanguishene Mental Health Centre:

> *Since the beginning of our department in 1968 we have been moving toward developing a Recreational Service which offers both a treatment modality and rehabilitative avenue for a patient's avocational time upon discharge. It has been our experience . . . that regardless of the abilities an ex-patient has upon discharge, it is generally the hours during which he is not working when difficulties arise and he is no longer able to cope. In order to overcome this problem we have developed a number of programs . . . which assist us in overcoming these difficulties. Not only do we provide for the avocational needs of the patients while they are in the Centre, but actively utilize both institutional and community facilities to reintegrate and rehabilitate the patients to community leisure activities.[36]*

There are two units within the overall structure of the facility: a Regional Hospital to serve residents of three contiguous counties or districts, with 370 beds and a 304-bed maximum security psychiatric hospital, which serves the entire Province of Ontario. For this patient population, there was in the mid-1970s a recreation staff of 12 full-time workers, all with extensive experience or professional training in the field, as well as additional summer staff leaders. It should be noted that, in many institutions, recreation staff members feel that they are not sufficiently valued or supported by administrative or medical directors; in others, they are an important element in the treatment team. Recreation staff members at Penetanguishene clearly belong in the second category. Montagnes writes,

> *Our services are well recognized by the Senior Management of the Centre and I believe this is what makes us somewhat unique within the Province of Ontario, if not the country of Canada. I know of no other institution . . . where acceptance by the total professional group within the Centre is such that referrals are made consistently and recommendations followed very closely by the Clinical Teams in their dealings with our recreational professionals. . . . We have a well-established assessment and counseling program which not only provides service to the inpatients of our institutions, but is also available upon request to local community facilities. In order to do this, we have used the expertise of many professionals in psychology, social work, and vocational services, as well as recreationists.*

> *At the Senior Management level we are regarded as a senior department within the Centre and therefore have our equal say in matters pertaining to the total institution and its philosophy. . . . We have many new ideas which we are presently investigating, and in fact will be initiating very shortly in our Ward VI Geriatric Program, a pub which will be open two half-days a week serving alcoholic beverages. I feel most of the success we have enjoyed can be summarized by saying that we have a very dedicated and interested staff, who have as an objective the continuing development of programs which are useful to the patients we serve. Programming and the patient needs are the major interests of the staff, rather than the attainment and programming of the usual "white elephants" which we find in many institutions.[37]*

---

[36] Letter to author from James M. Montagnes, Director of Vocational, Recreational and Volunteer Services, Penetanguishene Mental Health Centre, January 16, 1974.
[37] *Ibid.*

In this, as in other psychiatric treatment centers in which therapeutic recreation service has achieved a significant and respected place as a treatment modality, the key factors seem to be the following: (a) having a solid philosophical base; (b) developing an intelligent, well-organized and professionally-staffed service; (c) being able to develop effective cooperative relationships with members of other rehabilitative disciplines in the institution; and (d) using varied communication media to influence and inform team members, the overall institutional staff, Provincial officials and the public and community groups at large. The value of effective communication in defining a service's goals and describing its programs cannot be overestimated.

COMMUNITY SERVICES: AN APPRAISAL

In this chapter, it has been made clear that there has been a tremendous push toward serving those who are capable of quick recovery and discharge and toward the development of the therapeutic community and community-based programs serving the mentally ill in a variety of ways. It also is apparent that there is a substantial population of mentally ill patients who are *not* candidates for discharge. These individuals must be served, and the risk is that, in the pressure toward using intensified services to treat those with more favorable prognoses, the needs of the chronic or long-term patient will be ignored. It seems clear that, in the years ahead, there will continue to be an important need for services for such patients and that new techniques and approaches for serving them effectively in custodial situations will have to be developed.

Beyond this, however, the question must be raised—how effective are the community services that have been established to serve the mentally ill in community life?

First, it should be made clear that many of the sweeping reforms or innovations proposed during the 1960s were either naive or uncritical in their assumptions. For example, the "open door" policy, under which many large state institutions unlocked all or almost all gates inside and outside their buildings, turned out in some cases to be a disaster. Patients at various levels of illness roamed through buildings, in some cases committing violent acts or stealing; in other cases, they fled from hospitals, frequently creating problems in nearby communities or neighborhoods. In many hospitals that initiated "open door" policies at that time, the practice has now been largely curtailed.

It also became apparent that the assumption that patients could, after discharge, readily assume or reassume roles of responsibility in a vocational sense or within their own families was often based on tenuous ground. It was increasingly evident that many psychiatric patients were not simply people who had undergone a mental breakdown and who, after treatment, were "cured" and ready to assume a normal life. Instead, it was recognized that many such individuals are not really psychotic as such but rather simply disorganized, weak and unable to cope with the demands of community living, particularly in neighborhoods that are dangerous, disorganized and exploitative. In a study of recidivist patients, investigators of the New York State Department of Mental Hygiene found that many patients return chiefly because they are familiar with the hospital and feel comfortable there.

Such patients, report Rosenblatt and Mayer, are not primarily seeking psychiatric treatment. Instead, they write,

> These patients are weary sojourners in a hostile world. They want a place to rest For example, one patient began sleeping under a bridge because his family refused to shelter him any longer. He gave this account of his return to the hospital:
>
> "I returned because I had no place to sleep. I had nowhere to stay. And I was hungry and wanted something to eat. I tried to sleep in the emergency room (but this didn't work). I thought to myself that if I go to the hospital I will eat."[38]

Another patient, who was receiving welfare benefits, could not find a safe place to live; he was in an old building about to be torn down, and he feared drug addicts in the new place he would be sent. With his life in danger, he returned to the hospital. Another patient, separated from her husband and worn by the hassle of raising children alone, said, "I needed a rest period in the hospital. Maybe I would have done better on a vacation, but, then, I couldn't afford one. . . ." Still other patients return in part because they have pleasant memories of the social life and recreational program in the hospital. One returned individual explained,

> I went swimming and picnicking. We went on trips to the movies and to the zoo. . . . I felt that it was good being in the hospital.

And another,

> I liked the hospital. I enjoyed it very much. I used to go to the game room and play a lot of pool. And there were parties. I really enjoyed myself when I was there.

Still another stressed the social life and friendships found in the hospital:

> It's beautiful the way we get along together. We eat together. We sit down. We have conversations. We express ourselves—no arguments. I think it's wonderful how a group of people on the ward can get together and live together from day to day and there's no confusion.

The message from this study is clear. In part, it is that hospitals cannot afford to let themselves simply become safe refuges for society's weaker members—providing food, shelter and an enjoyable, problem-free recreational life. It is also that the goal of discharging patients into the community cannot be realized unless the community is prepared to accept them and unless adequate housing, therapy, medication and other supportive services, including vocational and activity therapy, are provided. The after-care centers and social clubs described earlier in this chapter are all too few. At a 1976 conference of mental health authorities in Washington, it was pointed out that because of sharp federal cutbacks only a fraction of the mental health centers that had originally been scheduled for construction were actually built.

Residential plans for outpatients, which were intended to include such varied accommodations as dormitory housing with "live-in" therapists, supervised apartment units and unsupervised apartment units, also were greatly

---

[38] Aaron Rosenblatt and John E. Mayer: "Patients Who Return: A Consideration of Some Neglected Influences." *Journal of Bronx, New York, State Hospital,* Spring, 1974, pp. 73–74.

limited in their development. As a consequence, many discharged mental patients have been "warehoused" in single-room occupancy units or in welfare hotels that provide only the bare necessities of living and represent a shameful exploitation of this population. Often they live in dangerous slums where they are preyed on by the criminal elements around them. When they are placed in special group homes that tend to be clustered in certain neighborhoods where cheap housing or substandard hotels are available, there is often sharp resistance to them by community residents. In planning the phasedown of mental hospitals in Massachusetts, Scholberg, Becker and McGrath found that

> *Abstract expression of support for the policy of deinstitutionalization rapidly evaporates when citizens become aware of plans to establish halfway houses or family type residences in their midst; formidable opposition coalesces overnight when a specific site is suggested. Fears of physical or sexual assault are invariably expressed, along with anxiety about bizarre behavior in the neighborhood, a lowering of property values, noisy disruptures, destruction of property, panhandling, prostitution, and so forth. . . . Public outcries have mounted against the dumping of helpless persons and (one town) has even passed a constitutionally questionable ordinance (later overturned in Federal court) barring former patients from residing there.*[39]

In some communities, such as Long Beach, New York, large seaside hotels that once catered to summer vacationists now provide housing for large numbers of discharged psychiatric patients from the chronic wards of state mental hospitals. Anderson, writing about such hotels as "the new snake pits," describes the attitudes of the owners of such hotels:

> *This neglect arises from the fact that the facilities to which most former patients are transferred are privately operated and, for the most part, subject to few legal controls in terms of accountability. For most owners, each new resident merely represents a potential profit. The less that is spent on him in the way of food, therapy, recreation, medical and psychiatric care, the greater the profit will be.*[40]

The original plan for remodeling state or provincial mental health services throughout the United States and Canada was based largely on the assumption that huge mental institutions had outlived their usefulness and that for those who might require long-range or lifetime care, smaller, more specialized facilities were needed. For most mental patients, it was considered that rehabilitation would best be effected by placing them back in the community, in small, well-staffed intermediate facilities, such as halfway houses, sheltered workshops and evening hospitals. With the lack of such facilities, however, and with a disagreement between state and local agencies as to the responsibility for such populations, many patients are left in limbo, in exploitative or inadequate facilities as described above, and with almost no meaningful rehabilitation.

The need is clear. If the community mental health concept is to be made workable, it will have to be supported with a large-scale development of effective neighborhood or community centers. These, in turn, will have to provide badly needed rehabilitative services, including not only drug maintenance medication

---

[39] Herbert C. Scholberg, Alvin Becker and Mark McGrath: "Planning the Phasedown of Mental Hospitals." *Community Mental Health Journal*, Spring, 1976, pp. 9–10.
[40] George M. Anderson: "Ex-Mental Patients and the New Snake Pits." *America*, September 4, 1976, p. 90.

that helps to make it possible for mental patients to live in the community on a reasonable level of responsible functioning but also educational, counseling, vocational and recreational service. Within this spectrum of needed services and programs, therapeutic recreation specialists employed by a variety of institutional and community agencies must play an increasingly important role.

**SUGGESTED TOPICS FOR CLASS
DISCUSSION, EXAMINATIONS OR
STUDENT PAPERS**

1. Summarize and discuss the two basic positions regarding mental illness: (a) that it is a distinct form of illness to be treated by medical practitioners and (b) that it represents a form of social disturbance or role-playing that should be treated by other means.

2. What are the special values and appropriate methods of recreation service in programs operating under the *therapeutic community* or *milieu therapy* approaches?

3. Outline an imaginative and comprehensive recreation program for a modern psychiatric hospital or community-based mental health center.

4. In the terms of the goals that were established for community mental health programs and the break-up of large custodial institutions, what progress has been made and what problems are now being faced?

chapter 6

Recreation for the Mentally Retarded and Learning-Disabled

This chapter provides an understanding of the scope, causes and effects of mental retardation and of the place of recreation in institutional or community programs designed to meet the needs of the mentally retarded. Emphasis is placed on the role of recreation in promoting social independence and job capability for the moderately or mildly retarded and on recreation's function in minimizing disability and in enriching the lives of *all* retarded children, youth and adults.

THE NATURE OF MENTAL RETARDATION

Although mental retardation has traditionally been defined as a function of intelligence (with an I.Q. of below 75 identifying the retardate), this is an unfortunately narrow view. A more sophisticated definition of the mentally retarded, who encompass a varied and complex population, would be likely to include the following elements:

1. It is generally agreed that mental retardation is a condition that *originates during the developmental period*, i.e., before the age of 18.
2. The key concept in many definitions is that of *mental or cognitive subnormality*. This is not the sole criterion of mental retardation however, and a second significant element must be *social inadequacy*—the inability of the mentally retarded person to function effectively in a social setting.
3. Although there has been a traditional belief that mental retardation must have an *organic cause*, such as a defect in the brain or some other significant pathology of the central nervous system, it has been accepted more recently that *environmental factors* are responsible for a substantial amount of mental retardation.
4. It is believed that mental retardation *cannot be cured* in the sense of a total reversal of the impairment. With appropriate education and supportive services, however, its effects can be markedly reduced; many individuals who are classified as mentally

retarded are able to enter community life, hold jobs, raise families and live as responsible citizens.

Recognizing the difficulty of defining the term, the *Manual on Terminology and Classification in Mental Retardation* of the American Association on Mental Deficiency offers the following definition:

> *Mental Retardation refers to significantly subaverage general intellectual functioning existing concurrently with deficits in adaptive behavior and manifested during the developmental period.*[1]

In this definition, *significantly subaverage general intellectual functioning* refers to scores that are more than two standard deviations below the mean of either the Stanford-Binet or Wechsler intelligence tests (I.Q. scores of 67 and 69 respectively). *Adaptive behavior* refers to the individual's ability to function independently in the family, neighborhood, school or community setting. It includes a set of appropriate functional areas at each age level; for example, during infancy and early childhood, adaptive behavior would encompass sensory-motor skills development, communication skills, self-help skills and socialization.

If a person has a low I.Q. but is socially adequate, he is not to be regarded as mentally retarded. If a person lacks social competence but has a high I.Q., he is similarly not to be considered mentally retarded. Only when both elements are present is one considered mentally retarded.

NUMBERS AND TYPES OF MENTALLY RETARDED

According to a 1976 report of the President's Committee on Mental Retardation, there are believed to be about six million retarded persons in the United States today. Past estimates have indicated that half of the retarded are children and youth below the age of 20. Mildly retarded are 89 per cent of the total number, and moderate retardates are about 6 per cent. Only about 5 per cent of the overall number are considered to be severely or profoundly impaired.

The life expectancy of the mildly retarded is about the same as that of normal persons. Although the development of antibiotic drugs that reduce fatal pulmonary illness in the severely and profoundly retarded has resulted in more of these individuals living to adulthood, their life expectancy is still shorter than that of the overall population.

Once he has lived to the age of five or six, the retarded child has a reasonable expectancy of living to adulthood. Following the school years, many mildly retarded individuals gain an adequate level of socially adaptive behavior and a degree of economic independence and are able to blend into community life. Thus, a proportion of persons who were identified as mentally retarded in childhood are no longer classified in this way as adults.

---

[1] See Herbert J. Prehm: *In* Larry L. Neal: *Recreation's Role in the Rehabilitation of the Mentally Retarded.* University of Oregon, 1970, pp. 9–11.

The causes of mental retardation are many. They include the following: (a) genetic or hereditary factors; (b) problems incurred during pregnancy or in childbirth; (c) illness, disease or accident; and (d) social or environmental deprivation.

Among the hereditary and genetic factors is the chromosomal imbalance that causes Down's syndrome, commonly known as mongolism, which affects 1 out of 600 children. There are several other metabolic or chemical factors inherited from the mother that can cause retardation; a mixture of incompatible Rh factors may also be responsible.

Other illnesses, such as meningitis, or injuries incurred in childhood may lead to mental retardation. Lead poisoning and malnutrition are believed to be frequent causes of retardation among young children in poverty-stricken areas.

There is increased awareness of the role of the social environment in causing mental retardation. Lack of stimulation and cognitive input in the family setting means that a much higher proportion of children in extremely poor neighborhoods are classified as mentally deficient than those in middle- and upper-class families. This differentiation becomes increasingly marked during the elementary grades, as does the actual percentage of children classified as mentally retarded.

There are some 200 diseases a woman can have during pregnancy that may lead to mental retardation in her child. Loss of oxygen during childbirth, the mother's diet or medication and accidents during pregnancy or childbirth may all result in brain injury causing retardation. Fortunately, modern science is developing preventive measures, and mothers are being taught more effective approaches to pre- and postnatal care, so that retardation stemming from such causes can be prevented or minimized. Indeed, the President's Committee on Mental Retardation estimated in 1976 that the number of severely retarded persons in the United States could be cut in half by the end of the century by better prenatal care and planned parenthood.

Categories of Retardation

There are a number of different systems under which the mentally retarded may be classified. Prehm points out that these include (a) the *legal-administrative* system found in the laws of most states and cities that judges which children, youths or adults are eligible for educational, residential or other forms of special social services; (b) the *educational* system, which customarily classifies the retarded into three groups—educable, trainable and custodial (totally dependent); and (c) the *psychiatric* classification system.[2]

In the past, the psychiatric system divided mental retardates into categories called *morons, imbeciles* and *idiots*. Today, these demeaning terms are seldom used.

Instead, the most common classification systems are those that relate to educational potential and capability for independent living. Generally, these two factors appear to be highly correlated. In terms of potential for independent

---

[2] *Ibid.*, p. 13.

living, as a wage-earner, member of a family or resident in community life, adaptive capability is an extremely important factor. The following terms are widely used today to classify the retarded:[3]

LEVELS	DEGREE OF IMPAIRMENT	EDUCATIONAL	I.Q. RANGE	PERCENTAGE OF RETARDED POPULATION
I	Borderline or mild	Educable	52–67	89.0
II	Moderate	Trainable	36–51	6.0
III	Severe	Custodial	20–35	3.5
IV	Profound	Totally dependent	Under 20	1.5

Of these groups, it has been estimated that approximately 95 per cent, composed chiefly of mild and moderate retardates, live in the community, primarily with their families. The 5 per cent who are classified as severely or profoundly retarded are heavily dependent on others for even the most basic forms of care (most cannot dress or feed themselves or attend to toilet needs without help) and are often institutionalized.

Hayes points out, based on the American Association on Mental Deficiency's most recent manual on classification in mental retardation, that it is extremely difficult to establish distinct categories within this overall population for the following reasons: (a) mental retardation is not a single disease or syndrome but instead is a general state of impairment; (b) individuals with the same medical diagnosis and comparable I.Q. and adaptive behavior levels may still vary widely in specific abilities; (c) mental retardation may be difficult to distinguish from autism, emotional disturbance or learning disability; (d) it may also coexist with other forms of mental or physical disability, particularly in more severely impaired individuals; and (e) there is a lack of consistency of terminology and classification among different professional groups and in different countries.[4]

Adaptive Characteristics of the Retarded

Keeping these difficulties in mind, behavioral traits within the four levels of impairment cited earlier have been classified (Fig. 6–1).

Heber suggests that each retardate should be evaluated with respect to the following behavioral impairments:[5]

1. *Personal-Social Factors.*
   a. *Impairment in cultural conformity, involving dependable or reliable social behavior, as opposed to behavior which is persistently anti-social or asocial.*
   b. *Impairment in interpersonal relations, implying inadequate ways for relating to peers and/or authority figures, or for recognizing the needs and feelings of other persons in interpersonal situations.*

---

[3] Adapted from Larry L. Neal: "Recreation for the Mentally Retarded." *Therapeutic Recreation Journal*, 1st Quarter, 1968, p.11.
[4] Gene A. Hayes: "Recreation and the Mentally Retarded." *In* Thomas A. Stein and H. Douglas Sessoms: *Recreation and Special Populations.* Boston, Holbrook, 1977, pp. 70–72.
[5] Larry L. Neal: "Recreation for the Mentally Retarded." pp. 16–17.

Figure 6–1. Levels of adaptive behavior of the mentally retarded. (From Larry L. Neal: "Recreation for the Mentally Retarded." *Therapeutic Recreation Journal*, 1st quarter, 1968, pp. 14–15.)

	PRE-SCHOOL AGE 0–5 MATURATION AND DEVELOPMENT	SCHOOL AGE 6–21 TRAINING AND EDUCATION	ADULT 21 SOCIAL AND VOCATIONAL ADEQUACY
Level I	Can develop social and communication skills; minimal retardation in sensori-motor areas; rarely distinguished from normal until later age.	Can learn academic skills to approximately 6th grade level by late teens. Cannot learn general high school subjects. Needs special education particularly at secondary school age levels.	Capable of social and vocational adequacy with proper education and training. Frequently needs supervision and guidance under serious social or economic stress.
Level II	Can talk or learn to communicate; poor social awareness; fair motor development; may profit from self-help; can be managed with moderate supervision.	Can learn functional academic skills to approximately 4th grade level by late teens if given special education.	Capable of self-maintenance in unskilled or semi-skilled occupations; needs supervision and guidance under serious social or economic stress.
Level III	Poor motor development; speech is minimal; generally unable to profit from training in self-help; little or no communication skills.	Can talk or learn to communicate; can be trained in elemental health habits; cannot learn functional academic skills, profits from systematic habit training.	Can contribute partially to self-support under complete supervision; can develop self-protection skills to a minimal useful level in controlled environment.
Level IV	Gross retardation; minimal capacity for functional in sensori-motor areas; needs nursing care.	Some motor development present; cannot profit from training in self-help; needs total care.	Some motor and speech development; totally incapable of self-maintenance; needs complete care and supervision.

    c. Impairment in responsiveness and consistent motivation, involving typical inability to resist short-term gratification of needs, and to strive for long-range goals.
2. Sensory-Motor Skill Impairment.
    a. Motor skills, involving disability in large and fine motor movements.
    b. Speech skills—including such disabilities as stuttering, lisping, or other poor vocalization patterns.
    c. Auditory limitations, in understanding and responding to the speech of others, beyond what might be expected on the basis of measured intelligence.
    d. Visual limitations, involving inadequate response to visual stimulation, beyond what might be expected on the basis of measured intelligence.

    In concluding this section, it should be pointed out that the mentally retarded are sometimes referred to as the "developmentally disabled" today, particularly in school systems where they are being served in special education classes. In some cases, they may be confused with or served jointly with the learning-disabled. This, however, is a distinctly separate population (see p. 196).

NEEDS OF THE MENTALLY RETARDED

    Often, the retarded person is set aside from the rest of society and is heavily dependent on his family. It is clear, however, that with intensive training, care and personal attention, a high proportion of retarded persons can develop a reasonable level of adaptive and, in some cases, even academic skills and can be enabled to function as useful, contributing citizens.

In the past, the mentally retarded were cruelly treated by society, locked in attics, hidden away from the world, confined in prisons and madhouses or— too often—completely ignored. Even today, many parents view their retarded children with a mixture of apathy and shame. Particularly among families in disadvantaged areas, the signs of retardation are ignored until it is too late to provide remedial services that might have minimized disability. Often, needed educational and community services are not provided.

However, over the past 15 or 20 years, there has been a growing realization of the scope of this problem, as well as of the fact that retardation is a disability stemming from identifiable causes and may be minimized and dealt with constructively.

It is now widely understood that the mentally retarded have the same basic needs as all other human beings. They have very strong human needs for love and understanding. They require food, shelter, work, if they are capable of it, and other interests and involvements that will provide their lives with meaningful activity and a sense of accomplishment. Although those who do not know the mentally retarded sometimes fear them or believe that they are capable of wild or irrational acts, those who have observed mentally retarded individuals who have been brought up with affection and care have seen that they are gentle and friendly, capable of giving and receiving love.

Programs Serving the Retarded

For many years, the only programs serving the retarded were those of custodial institutions—either publicly operated homes and schools for the most severely impaired or private homes or schools. In recent years, a number of public and voluntary organizations have been established to promote needed services for the mentally retarded. These organizations include the following:

1. The National Association for Retarded Children, a private organization involved in a comprehensive program, including research, education, counseling, recreation and promoting public awareness of the needs of the retarded. This body operates both on a national level and through local or regional chapters.
2. The American Association for Mental Deficiency, a voluntary, nonprofit organization involved primarily in research concerning causes and effects of mental retardation.
3. The Federal Department of Health, Education and Welfare, which operates through a Mental Retardation Branch, promotes research and professional training in special education and other services for the retarded and provides financial assistance to special projects.
4. The Division of Mental Retardation of the Council for Exceptional Children, which promotes research, education and special community services for the retarded.
5. The Kennedy Foundation, a philanthropic organization that operates institutions for the retarded, supports research and demonstration projects and promotes innovation in the field of institutional care and community services.
6. The American Alliance for Health, Physical Education and Recreation, which has designed tests for the retarded and promoted broad programs of adapted physical education and recreation for this population. With Federal funding, it has sponsored a special Project on Recreation and Fitness for the Mentally Retarded and published a newsletter, *Challenge*, which presents developments in this field.

In addition to these national bodies, there are many state and municipal organizations that have promoted a variety of services and programs, including education, vocational rehabilitation, sheltered workshops, recreation and legislation to serve the needs of the retarded. They have focused on research for the causes and prevention of mental retardation, on the development of new forms of rehabilitation that might succeed in helping retarded persons live independently in the community and on providing programs of public relations that might improve public understanding of this problem.

A major breakthrough was achieved in 1962 when the President's Panel on Mental Retardation, instituted by President John F. Kennedy, recommended a new, comprehensive program to serve the mentally retarded. This program made specific recommendations dealing with research, manpower, treatment, education, vocational preparation, legal protection and the development of federal, state and local programs for the mentally retarded. This was the first large-scale effort to come to grips nationally with the problem of mental retardation. It began a decade of development during which many of the goals that private organizations had been working for over a period of years were realized.

An example of legislation developed in this period was Title V, the Mental Retardation Amendment of 1967. This federal act provided $10 million over a period of three years to assist in the training of personnel and provide aid to programs already established. Another federal contribution was the Hospital Improvement Program, designed originally by the National Institutes for Mental Health and then shifted to the Office for Mental Retardation, which was designed to upgrade the care of the mentally retarded in state institutions.

RECREATION IN THE REHABILITATION OF THE MENTALLY RETARDED

One of the significant outcomes of the President's Panel on Mental Retardation was the recognition of the vital role played by recreation in working with the mentally retarded. It had already been recognized by many professionals that recreation served a variety of useful purposes with the retarded, but the Panel was the first influential national body to affirm this value:

> The retarded child, like other children, needs opportunity for healthy, growth-promoting play. The adolescent's vital need for successful social interaction and recreational experience is frequently intensified by isolation resulting from parental overprotection, the numerous failures he experiences in school and occupational pursuits, and by his exclusion by normal groups from everyday play group and social activities. For the retarded adult, opportunity and constructive use of leisure time may prove a major factor in maintaining community adjustment.[6]

During the 1970s, formal recognition was given to this need through legal authorization of recreation services as part of overall community services for the mentally retarded within Federal Developmental Disabilities legislation. Similarly, the *Standards for Community Agencies Serving Persons with Mental*

---

[6] President's Panel on Mental Retardation: *A Proposed Program for National Action to Combat Mental Retardation.* Washington, D.C., U.S. Government Printing Office, October, 1962.

Retardation and Other Developmental Disabilities manual states that if adequate community recreation is not available for disabled persons, public agencies are required to offer consultation and training services to special agencies for the development and implementation of recreation programs.[7]

The specific values of recreation for retardates lie in four major areas: (a) physical capacity and development; (b) social maturity and group adjustment; (c) contribution to vocational adjustment; and (d) constructive use of leisure time.

Physical Development

The physical appearance, strength, stamina, motor skills and overall development of the mentally retarded are often inferior. Often the mentally retarded have not even mastered the basic skills of self-care. Since physical development is important not only for its own sake and because it contributes to the health of the individual but also because one's physical status is an important factor in having a positive self-concept, it is essential that retarded individuals be given full opportunity to gain physical skills and experience leisure pursuits.

Often these individuals are not involved in school-sponsored physical education programs, and they may be excluded from sports programs that serve children and youth in the community at large. An important contribution of recreation, therefore, is to provide games, sports, aquatics, conditioning programs and self-testing activities that help the mentally retarded reach their full potential of physical development. When such programs are provided, many retarded children and youth are able to compete with nonretarded youngsters on an equal basis in team and individual sports.

Social Development

Many retardates are isolated from the mainstream of community life. Perceived by others as "different" because of their appearance and behavior, they are often excluded from peer groups and find it difficult to establish meaningful social relationships with others.

Often they are unmotivated in terms of social involvement and are overprotected by their families. Childish and immature behavior is frequently considered to be an inevitable part of their make-up, and they often are tremendously insecure in group settings—partly because of repeated failures and rejection by others. Carefully planned recreational activities, either in segregated or integrated group settings (in which they share social contact with the nondisabled), may do much to overcome these limitations.

Vocational Adjustment

Many retardates find it difficult to function well in a regular educational environment. They are often able to function more effectively in special voca-

---

[7] Julie Gleason Burmeister: "Leisure Services and the Cultural Arts as Therapy for the Mentally Retarded Individual." *Therapeutic Recreation Journal*, 4th Quarter, 1976, p. 139.

tional classes that are geared to their capabilities and that equip them to hold jobs, either in regular industry or service trades or in sheltered workshops in the community.

Even when the retarded youth is successful in mastering the skills necessary to hold a job, he may fail to hold one down and function independently in the community. Francis Kelley, Superintendent of the Mansfield, Connecticut, State Training School and Hospital, states,

> *It has been confirmed that many young retarded people have not been able to adjust in the community and have had to be placed in institutions because they have not been able to adjust during leisure, rather than because they failed to perform satisfactorily on the job, or . . . in the home . . . . As we provide for the education, vocational training, occupational and spiritual needs of the retarded, it is equally imperative that we do not overlook (their) recreational rehabilitation and social needs . . . . The presence of this "plus factor" often makes the difference between a happy life in the community or commitment to an institution.*[8]

Constructive Use of Leisure

One of the major problems of the mentally retarded is the use of the leisure time that, for many, constitutes the entire day. Burghardt comments,

> *We must realize the fact that in some instances the recreational skills mastered by the mentally retarded will constitute their major achievements and their most important assets. There is slim hope that their reading, writing, arithmetic and vocational aptitudes will assure them of acceptance by society. Thus, the skills they acquire as a result of the recreational program could mean more to them than they ever would to a normal person, insuring a reasonably successful social life.*[9]

For many retardates, the empty hours in their day are characterized by lethargy, frustration and a feeling of uselessness. Too often, they spend their waking hours sitting alone or watching television endlessly. Higher-performing retardates in the adolescent age bracket may become involved in delinquent behavior because of a lack of other stimulation or interesting involvements. Thus, carefully planned recreation programs can do much to provide a useful and pleasurable existence for the retarded.

Finally, recreation may greatly help to promote the *mental development* of retarded children and youth. Broadly conceived, recreation may involve creative activities, hobbies, learning experiences, trips and similar experiences that broaden the range of knowledge and personal involvement of participants. Since retardates are so often deprived of the normal range of developmental experiences, it is essential to enrich their lives in this way.

Even programs of physical activity may do much to improve the mental performance of the mentally retarded. A British researcher, Dr. J. N. Oliver, reported dramatic results from a specially designed physical activity program for

---

[8] Francis P. Kelley: "Recreational Services for the Retarded—An Urgent Need." *Recreation in Treatment Centers*, September, 1964, pp. 12–13.

[9] Edward T. Burghardt: "Recreation for the Retarded: An Aid to Balanced Living." *Recreation in Treatment Centers*, September, 1964, p. 12.

the retarded. All subjects improved significantly in physical ability, fitness and strength, and 25 per cent showed marked gains in intellectual performance.[10]

Realistically, it is difficult to identify any single type of outcome and to demonstrate that it is the result of a single form of recreational involvement. Most recreation activities involve varied kinds of personal growth. Burmeister, for example, describes the multiple values of cultural activities, such as music, drama and dance, with the mentally retarded:

> ... the cultural arts may be viewed as a therapeutic medium, a multi-faceted, audio-visual, kinesthetic teaching modality, a means of promoting socialization and normalization, and a safety valve for psychological and physiological cathar- sis. Objectives should be stated for mentally retarded persons participating in cultural arts programs. Broad objectives might include freedom of expression, increased independent functioning, the development of individual skills, and cognizance of the cooperation required of individuals working together as a group.[11]

Substantial evidence has been gained of the value of physical activity and other forms of recreation for the mentally retarded. In addition to the Oliver study cited earlier, a number of studies showing the positive effect of varied forms of play and exercise programs on trainable and educable mentally retarded children were summarized in a publication of the Pennsylvania State University.[12]

Goals of Recreation Programs for the Retarded

Summed up, then, the goals of recreation programs for the mentally retarded are the following:

1. To improve physical growth and development, enhance motor skills and lend confidence to participants by improving bodily build and physical fitness.
2. To minimize or prevent social isolation by helping the mentally retarded gain friends and adjust to social situations, minimizing atypical behavior and appearance and teaching social interaction skills.
3. To teach skills for the creative and constructive use of leisure and to provide regular opportunity for hobbies, pastimes and other leisure involvements, either at home or in institutional or community settings.
4. To contribute to the retardate's ability to function independently in the community and thus to hold down a job, where other ability levels permit this.
5. To improve language skills and develop other cognitive abilities and to broaden the range of knowledge and environment contacts of the retarded.
6. To provide practice in self-care activities, thus enhancing the individual's capability for independent living.
7. To improve the morale and quality of family living by helping to make the retardate less of a burden and a more capable and autonomous individual.

---

[10] J. N. Oliver: "The Effect of Physical Conditioning Exercises and Activities on the Mental Characteristics of Educationally Sub-Normal Boys." *British Journal of Educational Psychology, 28*:155–165, 1958.

[11] Burmeister, *op. cit.*, p. 141.

[12] Herberta M. Lundegren, ed.: *Physical Education and Recreation for the Mentally Retarded.* State College, Pennsylvania, Penn State HPER Series No. 7, 1975.

PLANNING SERVICES FOR AGE AND
FUNCTIONAL LEVELS

Obviously, the kinds of recreational programs that may be provided for the mentally retarded must be geared closely to their capabilities. These, in turn, may be classified in two ways: (a) on the basis of chronological age and (b) in terms of functional performance levels.

Planning on the Basis of Chronological Age

There is a temptation, in working with the retarded, to give excessive weight to demonstrated levels of social immaturity or limited mental development and to treat ten or twelve-year-olds as if they were children of primary-grade age. However, as much as possible, it is desirable to carry on activities suitable for each age level, with whatever modifications may be necessary to make it possible for participants to be successful in them.

PRE-SCHOOL AGE

During this period of early childhood, it is essential that children who have been diagnosed as mentally retarded be given as wide a range as possible of those developmental play experiences that normal children receive. The emphasis should be on providing equipment, settings and structured leadership in games, environmental play, music, dance, drama and other creative experiences, simple arts and crafts, hobbies, group activities, neighborhood trips and similar program elements. The emphasis is on providing activities that will build on the existing capabilities of the child and prevent further disability and that will provide a healthy self-concept.

ELEMENTARY SCHOOL AGE

This is generally considered a key stage of growth in helping the retarded child realize his full potential and in developing a healthy and well-adjusted personality. Play programs should be designed that promote physical vigor and well-being, a range of leisure interests, and satisfying and confidence-giving social adjustment and that make the retarded child as independent as possible. All the activities that are normally provided for children in this age range may be offered, although many may be modified to permit successful accomplishment.

ADOLESCENCE

During this period of growth, it is essential that teen-age retardates be helped to adjust to the fact of their disability and to gain a realistic picture of their strengths and weaknesses. A considerable amount of emotional and practical support should be given to this age group, whose members face the problem affecting all teen-agers—making the transition from childhood to adulthood—complicated by their unique status in society. Although they require adult guidance, adolescent retardates may assume a considerable degree of leadership in their own recreation and social activities.

EARLY ADULTHOOD

Recreation programs established for this age group in community settings should continue to offer skills instruction and general participation in activity, including remedial help in developing appropriate behavior and appearance, social adjustment and other elements of personal guidance. As much as possible, however, the emphasis should be placed on informational and counseling services, which help young retarded adults develop their own leisure activities and social groups. Not infrequently, a community center will act as host to such a group, with an advisor provided by a local chapter of the voluntary association serving the mental retardation field.

In addition to chronological age, another useful way of developing program services is by assessing the degree of social independence of the children who are to be served. Avedon and Arje outline four descriptive categories that provide a basis for making such determinations. These categories are as follows: *socially-independent*, *semi-independent*, *semi-dependent* and *dependent*.

For those in the first two classifications, it is essential to provide the kinds of counseling and community involvements that strengthen the retarded individual's capability for living and working in the community, thus preventing social isolation. Semi-dependent children, who generally are not able to hold positions, even in sheltered workshops, should be given the opportunity for community contacts through trips and other forms of recreational involvement. Dependent children, who usually are in institutions, should have a strong stress on physical development and self-care programs. On this level, although past practices have been almost completely custodial, it is important to provide intensive treatment services that may bring about improvement in functioning. In some situations, when even severely retarded children have become involved in intensive programs of physical recreation, they have progressed to the point that they were able to be reassigned to higher-functioning levels.[13]

INSTITUTIONAL RECREATION PROGRAMS

It is a curious commentary that, in contrast to many communities in which very limited special programs are provided for the mentally retarded and in which they are not permitted or discouraged from entering programs serving the public at large, many state-operated or privately operated residential schools and homes for the mentally retarded offer an impressive range of leisure programs. Examples of such programs follow.

State Training School and Hospital, Southbury, Connecticut

This state-sponsored institution provides excellent recreation facilities, including outdoor ponds and pools, sports fields, a large auditorium, gymnasiums,

---

[13] Elliott M. Avedon and Frances B. Arje: *Socio-Recreative Programing for the Retarded, a Handbook for Sponsoring Groups.* New York, Teachers College, Columbia, Bureau of Publications, 1964, pp. 15–18.

a bowling alley and play areas or rooms in each of its cottages.[14] Emphasis is given to program activities that improve socialization, teach skills, motivate interest and increase body awareness and balance. Among the major program areas are the following:

Intramural activities, such as checkers, regular and wheelchair bowling (as indicated earlier, many of the most severely retarded individuals have multiple disabilities), pool and kickball.

Special events, such as a Fourth of July parade, Easter egg hunt, amateur night, athletic banquet and soap-box derby race.

Visiting entertainment by outside groups that provide circuses, rock, country and western bands, variety shows, plays and snow-mobiling.

Scouting, including Boy Scout, Girl Scout and Sea Scout troops and participation in the New England Scout Jamboree.

Camping and outdoor activities, according to season, including boating, fishing, picnicking, swimming, miniature golf, sledding, skating and tent camping.

Excursions into the community for activities such as plays, movies, athletic events, Connecticut River boat rides, circuses and carnivals.

In addition to a recreation staff of four full-time and two part-time workers, many attendants in the cottage units are involved in program leadership and bus transportation of residents to community recreation activities. Crafts, sports and hobby activities, along with various leagues and tournaments, compose much of the program on the cottage level. Intensive, small-group recreation skills training, along with self-care management, has been carried out in small groups of severely retarded adults with the aid of personnel skilled in behavior modification techniques.

In another Connecticut institution, the Mansfield State Training School and Hospital, considerable stress is placed on developing social training and recreational opportunity for all residents, at whatever level of retardation.[15] With the help of volunteer college students from the nearby University of Connecticut, teen-age girls are involved in a good grooming project that has a marked effect on their appearance and social behavior.

Physical activities, including softball, swimming, baseball, basketball and even football (played competitively with other high schools), serve to counteract the common obese and physically weak appearance of many retarded children. Other recreational activities at the Mansfield school include dances for the residents every Saturday, birthday parties, picnics, field trips, a swimming and camping program and special seasonal activities to celebrate holidays like Christmas, Halloween and Easter. Children from both educable and trainable classifications are admitted to the school program at an early age and are trained for eventual return to the community whenever possible.

Many other institutions have developed elaborate programs of recreation service, both for discharge-bound residents and for those whose prognosis is lifelong custodial care. However, it should be stressed that the majority of mentally retarded children and youth are not institutionalized, but live with their families.

---

[14] Nicholas Rusiniak: "Recreation for the Retarded—One Institution's Approach." *Journal of Health, Physical Education and Recreation,* April, 1974, pp. 85–87.
[15] Francis P. Kelley, *op. cit.*

LEISURE COUNSELING FOR THE RETARDED

It is therefore critical that the mentally retarded be provided with adequate leisure education and counseling sessions to enhance their awareness of the role of recreation in their lives and to assist them in making appropriate choices of involvement. In many institutions, this has become a significant aspect of therapeutic recreation service for the mentally retarded. At the Parsons State Hospital and Training Center in Kansas, for example, Hayes succeeded in having each resident's involvement in recreation made the concern of the institution's vocational evaluation committee. This included such activities as

> . . . weekly individual and group leisure education and counseling sessions, day-long trips to discharge locations which included a variety of experiences pertinent to community leisure living, and cooperative efforts with other staff members in the education, vocational rehabilitation, social work, and nursing services.[16]

Without such preparation, it is all too probable that the individual who is discharged to the community will be unable to make use of available community recreation resources. Ramm describes the problem of many mentally retarded children who live at home, including the mildly and moderately retarded:

> The retarded child living at home has little recreation opportunity. He may make friends with the children in his special class at school, but unlike the normal children who can play with their school chums in the neighborhood after school hours, retarded children are transported from their homes in different parts of town and have few friends in their own neighborhoods. A similar situation exists with mentally retarded adults who work in a centrally-located sheltered workshop, or who do not work at all. These people are victims of enforced leisure. They have a six-to-eight-hour time block each weekday and more on weekends or holidays during which little or no activity is available to them. Many just sit and watch television.[17]

Recognizing this need, an increasing number of city and country recreation departments provide extensive recreation services for the mentally retarded, often in cooperation with voluntary organizations or parents' clubs concerned with this special population.

Too often, retarded persons living in the community have a consistent past record of failure; they have disappointed their parents, have few friends, if any, and have been rejected in many areas of life. Even when they enter special training centers as young adults, they tend to feel lonely and inadequate, unable to cope with the pressures of the interpersonal experience and with a high degree of expectation of further rejection and failure. The purpose of recreation in the community setting then would be to help the mentally retarded individual develop interests that would improve his or her social relationships and provide a sense of social competence and acceptance. Studies have shown that mentally retarded children and youth are able to gain markedly in their recreational interests and readiness to initiate activities and invite others to participate and to con-

---

[16] Gene A. Hayes, *In* Jerry D. Kelley, ed.: *Expanding Horizons in Therapeutic Recreation II.* Champaign-Urbana, Illinois, University of Illinois, Office of Recreation and Park Resources, 1974, pp. 35–37.

[17] Joan Ramm: "Challenge: Recreation and Fitness for the Mentally Retarded." Washington, D.C., American Association for Health, Physical Education and Recreation, 1966, p. 1.

tinue participation even though unsuccessful. In a study of 24 mentally retarded children and adults taking part in a special summer program provided by the Anaheim, California, Parks and Recreation Department, Seaman found significant improvement in such areas of behavior and in the self-esteem of participants.[18]

A number of communities throughout the United States and Canada have established comprehensive recreation programs for the retarded. In Washington, D.C., for example, a special program was set in motion several years ago, with the following goals: (a) to develop a comprehensive set of recreation programs and services for the retarded and (b) to develop a number of principles and procedures as guidelines in the promotion of multiagency cooperation in this field.

In carrying on this program, the city is divided into nine areas, each with a center where a variety of activities are provided for the retarded, such as arts and crafts, music, bowling, nature pastimes, golf, trips, self-help classes and aquatics. The program is staffed by 46 members of the city's recreation staff, who have received in-service training at the University of Maryland and who are assisted by volunteers. Serving approximately 450 retardates, the program receives the cooperation of varied community agencies and parents' clubs, and departments of the federal government as well. The program is carefully monitored and assessed to determine its effectiveness and has succeeded in arousing a high level of community concern about the needs of the retarded.[19]

Another leading program that has been developed to serve the retarded in the community is the Recreation Center for the Handicapped in San Francisco. This nonprofit corporation has been influential in bringing happiness and companionship to mentally retarded and physically disabled children, youth and adults of varied races and creeds in the San Francisco, California, metropolitan area.

With assistance from both private and public agencies and with appropriations from the city and special federal grants, the Recreation Center for the Handicapped operates both integrated and segregated services for the mentally retarded. It also operates a laboratory that assists in the training of college students and others in the field of therapeutic recreation. As an example of its work, in a recent year, out of 500 children served, 225 had made sufficient progress to be accepted in city schools for the retarded or in special classes in regular schools. The Center also provides educational talks, films and lecture series designed to educate the public on mental retardation.

One of its special projects is Camp Spindrift, a program sponsored with the assistance of the Kennedy Foundation and other community organizations. Operating in a wooded environment as a day camp, Camp Spindrift places stress on developing living skills and social independence. Many of the campers who formerly had been extremely dependent on their families have been able to take part in special overnight camping programs; others have shown remarkable progress in varied activities and in being able to communicate effectively, take social responsibilities and make friends.

---

[18] Janet A. Seaman: "Effects of Municipal Recreation on the Social Self-Esteem of the Mentally Retarded." *Therapeutic Recreation Journal*, 2nd Quarter, 1975, pp. 75–78.
[19] Helen Jo Mitchell: "A Community Recreation Program for the Mentally Retarded." *Therapeutic Recreation Journal*, 1st Quarter, 1971, pp. 3–8.

In some cases, camping programs for the retarded have been sponsored by school systems or by state schools or hospitals for the retarded. For example, San Diego, California, has been one of the pioneers in school camping for elementary age children. For a number of years, it has included a special unit for retarded boys and girls in its program at Camp Cuyamaca. Within an integrated social structure, it was found that many of the anticipated problems did not exist, and retarded youngsters were able to function effectively in the camp setting.

Camping is of particular importance because it changes the environment of the retarded child radically and puts him in a living situation where he is much more dependent on his own efforts. Camp Confidence, a year-round camping operation for the retarded operated in connection with Brainerd State Hospital in Northern Minnesota, stresses the need for young retardates to develop self-confidence, social adjustment and specific skills in the areas of camp living, nature and crafts, sports and conservation education. The keynote of the camp is "learning by doing." Endres writes,

> If our primary objective . . . is to develop social adjustment within the individual, the camp setting and outdoor education [offer] a natural laboratory . . . . The mentally retarded do not basically learn best by being "told" or "shown" what to do. They must physically experience a given situation to attain comprehension and understanding. Within the aesthetic setting of a camp, they are able to experience things first hand, through outdoor education classes. Such a relaxed atmosphere usually allows for better individual and group counseling. Nature has a way of relieving our tension and anxieties and as such we are better able to live with ourselves, as well as being more considerate of our fellow man.[20]

It is essential that activities be carefully geared to the capabilities of participants. The following section describes a number of activity categories widely used with the mentally retarded and shows how they are organized and modified where necessary.

In selecting activities, it is wise to bear the following principles in mind:

1. The mentally retarded have the same basic needs as other individuals for self-respect and a feeling of accomplishment.
2. Whenever possible, activities chosen should be appropriate for the chronological age level of retarded participants.
3. Retardates tend to have a short attention span; activities should therefore be diversified and should have a time limit determined by the behavior of the individuals taking part.
4. The mentally retarded also tend to have a low level of frustration. Therefore, games and other activities should be simplified, where necessary, and the teaching process should be done in stages.
5. The mentally retarded usually do not respond well to "talking about" an activity but learn better from direct participation.
6. Repetition is essential for retardates in learning most activities and skills.
7. Recreation can serve as an important stabilizing factor in the lives of the mentally retarded and should be organized in an orderly fashion, following a familiar schedule.
8. While the leader may have other social or educational goals in mind, activities must provide fun and a sense of enjoyment for participants.

---

[20] For a description of Camp Confidence see Richard Endres: "Northern Minnesota Therapeutic Camp." *Journal of Health, Physical Education and Recreation*, May, 1971, p. 75.

USEFUL ACTIVITIES FOR THE RETARDED

Recreation programs for the mentally retarded have tended to emphasize the following areas of activity: (a) sports and physical fitness activity; (b) creative experiences: arts and crafts, music, dance and drama; (c) games; (d) social activities; (e) training in living skills; (f) special events and trips; and (g) camping.

Sports and Physical Fitness Activity

Some of the most successful programs for the retarded include such activities as bowling, skating, swimming, volleyball, track and field and similar activities. In addition to the physical benefits of sport, these activities provide the opportunity to engage in healthy competition, to strive toward a goal, to gain a sense of accomplishment and to feel that one is part of a group.

In general, when a given sport is presented to a group of retardates, it is necessary to teach the basic skills much more painstakingly and slowly than with other children of similar chronological age. It may be necessary to simplify the rules, and even modify the structure of the game, in order to insure success and enjoyment for the participants.

One of the sports programs that has received considerable attention in recent years has been the Special Olympics—national competition that brings together teams of retarded children and youth from cities throughout the United States. They engage in various sports and fitness events, and, ultimately, national champions are selected. Carried on with funding by the Kennedy Foundation and other public and private sources, the Special Olympics have been sponsored by major cities throughout the United States, such as Chicago, and have had thousands of retarded participants.

In some cases, major athletic programs have been promoted for the mentally retarded on a state-wide level. In Ohio, for example, the Ohio Athletic Association coordinates sports and physical activities in schools and institutions for the retarded. It arranges competitions and assists in providing transportation for visiting teams; it also provides modified rules and procedures for the more complicated sports in order to standardize practices throughout the state.

In many institutions, physical conditioning programs, such as stunts and tumbling, gymnastics or systematic exercise routines, have been developed for retarded residents. In general, there is widespread support for all forms of physical activity for the retarded, although some have warned of the dangers inherent in overemphasis on competitive sport. A report issued by the American Association for Health, Physical Education and Recreation commented,

Undue emphasis is often placed upon participation in complex and complicated sports or athletic events in physical education and recreation programs for the mentally retarded. Frequently the retarded are placed in sports activities they don't understand, and in which their chances for success are minimized because of the intellectual function required by the activities themselves. An inadequate foundation of fundamental motor skills combined with too-early introduction to complicated sports skills also promotes failure for the retarded.[21]

---

[21] *Guidelines for Programing in Recreation and Physical Education for the Mentally Retarded.* Washington, D.C., American Association for Health, Physical Education and Recreation, 1968, p. 13.

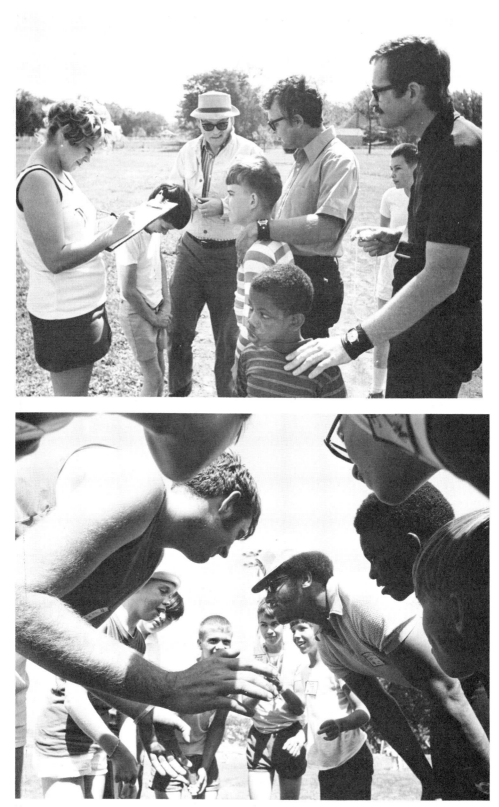

Young mentally retarded athletes at Parsons State Hospital in Winfield, Kansas, sign up for competition in local Special Olympics, while others receive special coaching from Buck Buchanan, pro football star. One young lady is proud of her second-place ribbon (see facing page)!

182

Recognizing this, many institutions place stress only on the informal and casual use of sports activities, usually for higher-functioning retardates. Many activities are approached in an exploratory, "fun" way, as well as other activities that involve the mastery of a single, fairly basic skill. For example, resistive weight training has been used successfully with severely mentally retarded youth. Based on six different exercises (presses, pulls, curls and so on) on a single-unit adult-station multipurpose weight training machine, various adaptations were used to help students carry out the exercises correctly: (a) since none of the students was able to count, or understood the concept of numbers, loud rhythmic music was used to mark the length of time an exercise or lifting period should last; (b) instructors gave manual assistance, with minimal pressure, to help participant fully extend arms or legs in certain exercises when they did not understand the need to do this; and (c) progress was noted by marking scores in colored ink, which the participants could understand, thus knowing when they were making progress.[22]

Other activities typically used with the retarded are bowling, skating and swimming. To demonstrate how such activities are presented in an institution serving the retarded, the following descriptions of objectives of activity are

[22] Richard A. Ness: "Weight Training for Severely Mentally Retarded Persons." *Journal of Health, Physical Education and Recreation*, April, 1974, pp. 87–88.

excerpted from the leadership manual of the Plymouth State Home and Training School in Northville, Michigan. They deal with *roller skating* and *swimming.*[23]

ROLLER SKATING

Objectives. *Roller skating is used to help develop the balance and motor coordination of the residents. Their sense of accomplishment is increased with mastery of skating skills, and they have a way to use their leisure time constructively. Residents need to learn the following skills:*

1. *Feeling comfortable with skates on.*
2. *Standing and moving about with a skate on one foot and the other foot on the floor.*
3. *Using side rails or rolling stand to initiate movement around the gym or day room.*
4. *Propelling themselves around the room.*
5. *Balancing themselves well enough to walk or glide around the room on two skates.*
6. *Using alternate leg movements to move about on skates.*
7. *Attempting to skate to music.*
8. *Participating in a skating party with residents from other buildings.*

Structure. *Most ambulatory residents can learn and enjoy skating. From ten to 15 residents can be in a group for instruction. Fifty to 75 residents can participate in a skating party. Instruction is scheduled for twice a week for one hour at a time.*

SWIMMING

Objectives: *The swimming program for the physically handicapped (many retarded residents in institutions have physical handicaps as well as mental) is planned to meet the following objectives:*

1. *Build or maintain organic strength and vigor.*
   a. *Increase the range of movement within joints.*
   b. *Lengthen periods of sustained activity.*
   c. *Improve circulation.*
   d. *Promote deeper breathing.*
   e. *Improve control of body movements.*
   f. *Relax the body (sedative effect of immersion).*
   g. *Promote better elimination.*
2. *Improve the morale of the participants by:*
   a. *Socializing in fun activities with persons not physically handicapped.*
   b. *Developing a feeling of satisfaction in achievement.*
   c. *Satisfying their desire for physical activities (buoyancy effect of water enhances movement).*
   d. *Projecting thoughts beyond themselves to concentrate on the movement task.*
   e. *Reducing the appearance of the handicap.*

Instruction in swimming *is used to help all residents overcome their fear of water, and learn basic water safety skills, including:*

1. *Holding their breath for ten seconds.*
2. *Breathing rhythmically ten times.*
3. *Floating on their stomach.*
4. *Floating on their back.*
5. *Treading water.*

---

[23] *Activity Therapy Manual.* Plymouth State Home and Training School, Northville, Michigan, 1971, pp. 7, 19, 21.

All residents except the severely physically handicapped receive recreational benefits from swimming. The wide and varied range of swimming skills challenges even the more physically capable residents. Competitive swimming offers an opportunity for them to socialize and increase their ability to take the win or loss in a sportsmanly manner.

Structure. Therapeutic use of the pool is appropriate for any resident recommended by the doctor in charge. Swimming instructions are appropriate for all residents who are able to follow simple instructions and are somewhat mobile. Competitive swimming is appropriate for those residents with swimming skills on a competitive level and the desire to compete.

Each resident in the program should participate for one hour, including dressing time, and should be scheduled at least once a week. Therapeutic swimming can be provided for those residents who need one-to-one assistance in numbers no greater than 15 scheduled for the pool area at one time. Swimming instruction should be given to groups of ten or less per instructor. Competitive swimming should be in groups of six or less.

Creative Experiences: Arts and Crafts, Music, Dance and Drama

A second major aspect of recreation programming for the mentally retarded is in the area of cultural and creative activities. These can be adapted to meet the needs of residents at all levels of ability in institutional settings or to provide engrossing and enjoyable hobbies for the mentally retarded in community life. In general, the same kinds of activities that normal children would engage in are provided for the retarded. As in the case of sports, however, it is necessary to teach them at a slower pace, to keep projects simpler and to provide a fuller level of supervision.

Arts and crafts may range from the use of crayon and paper in drawing, finger painting, play with clay and similar unstructured kinds of activities to more elaborate forms of painting or craft activities, such as block-printing, leatherwork, weaving and metalwork or ceramics.

Dance activities may range from simple singing games and rhythmic exploration to more complicated folk and square dances, creative or modern dance and, for older retardates, social dancing as a popular coeducational activity.

Dramatics may include puppetry, creative or informal dramatics or actually putting on plays. Since it may be difficult for many mentally retarded children and youth to memorize and deliver lines effectively, the emphasis may be on improvised dialogue in some dramatic ventures. However, it *is* possible to do much more elaborate dramatic productions with mentally retarded children As an example, 65 children and young adults from Letchworth Village for the Mentally Retarded in Thiells, New York, a state institution, put on a full-scale performance of the musical "Oklahoma" before 3000 guests at the New York City Hilton Hotel. The individuals, with a chronological age of between eight and 35 and an I.Q. range between 30 and 79, prepared the show as a climax to a fund-raising campaign for the school. The residents rehearsed steadily for the performance for six months and did an almost professional job of remembering their lines and cues.

Creative activities lend themselves to specific therapeutic uses. For example, simple musical activities may be used to promote reading readiness. In a year-long experimental program with 18 teenage boys with I.Q.s ranging from

17 to 56 at Northern State Hospital in Bellingham, Washington, such a process was carried out effectively.[24]

In a more general way, music may be used to provide a release for tension and emotional expression, to encourage and stimulate language and communication, to improve group interaction and to enhance the self-image of residents. Additionally, it strives to improve the musical abilities of the residents and to promote their sense of accomplishment and ability to use their leisure constructively. At the Plymouth State School, it is presented in two forms: music therapy and music education. Program content in each of these includes the following:[25]

Listening Behavior
1. *Sitting quietly and attentively listening to music played on a phonograph, tape recorder or instrument.*
2. *Improving the attention span until the resident can participate in a classroom setting for 30 to 45 minutes.*
3. *Discussing what has been heard.*
4. *Improving comprehension of instructions.*
5. *Giving creative interpretations of what has been heard.*

Gross Motor Activities, Coordination and Rhythm
1. *Developing basic movements of walking, marching, running, jumping, tiptoeing, hopping, galloping, skipping, and skating.*
2. *Clapping hands to strong rhythmic music.*
3. *Using rhythm instruments for marking simple and compound meters.*
4. *Participating in a rhythm band (playing when music begins, stopping when music stops, playing alternately and at different times).*

Musical Games
1. *Understanding the idea of the game by verbal or demonstrative instructions.*
2. *Taking turns.*
3. *Group participation.*
4. *Heading the group.*

Singing
1. *Humming.*
2. *Singing parts of songs.*
3. *Singing song in correct melody and rhythm.*
4. *Singing a song within the proper key.*
5. *Singing with the correct words.*
6. *Singing a complete song with a group.*
7. *Singing a complete song alone.*
8. *Leading others in song.*

Ear Training
1. *Recognizing various recorded sounds.*
2. *Differentiating stop and go.*
3. *Differentiating between high and low, fast and slow, loud and soft, musical and non-musical sounds.*
4. *Describing musical moods (happy, sad, funny, serious, etc.)*

Instrumental Music
1. *Playing simple musical instruments, (kazoos, hum-a-zoos, harmonicas, drums).*

---

[24] John De Blasio: "Teaching Pre-Academic Concepts with Music." *In* Larry L. Neal: *Recreation's Role in the Rehabilitation of the Mentally Retarded.* pp. 55–56.
[25] *Plymouth State Activity Therapy Manual. op. cit.,* pp. 8–13, 19–20, 21–23.

2. *Learning the names of various instruments and recognizing them by sight.*
3. *Learning to play the more difficult instruments (tonettes, recorders, guitar, autoharp, piano).*
4. *Learning to play chords.*
5. *Playing by ear.*
6. *Reading music.*

In some cases, different forms of creative activity may be combined with each other in integrated learning experiences. For example, "Orff-Schulwerk," a creative process involving elements of music, movement and language that was originated by Carl Orff, a German composer, has been used successfully as a form of creative dramatics with mentally retarded children at the San Francisco Center for the Handicapped.[26] Morgan describes an improvisational, open approach to acting out or moving to themes based on familiar surroundings in the "real" world, children's songs, fairy tales, adventure stories or simple exploration of concepts and ideas. Appropriate themes are selected according to participants' chronological ages and levels of comprehension, and children participate with considerable enthusiasm.

Use of Games

Games are extremely useful in recreational programs for retarded children, youth and adults. They may include quiet table games, more active equipment games, social games and mixers carried on in group situations and active outdoor or gymnasium games.

Games provide an important environment for the learning of social skills, as well as the opportunity to have fun in simple ways. Many retardates who have never really learned to play can have this experience for the first time in a game situation. Games provide the opportunity both to compete against others and to cooperate closely with others in a team effort. Specific games may require participants to learn and obey rules, to work with number concepts, to develop alertness, to practice memory or to dramatize roles.

Obviously, games that involve complex rules or highly developed skills are not appropriate for the mentally retarded. It is important, in leading games, not to use those activities that depend on all participants functioning correctly. Thus, even if one or two players do not understand the point of a game, or are not able to carry it on successfully, it should be possible for the overall group to continue to play it with enjoyment.

Some institutions, such as the Rainier State School in Buckley, Washington, have published pamphlets in which they list the needed equipment, teaching procedures and time required to play specific games. Richard Endres, Patient Program Supervisor of the Brainerd State Hospital, Brainerd, Minnesota, has compiled a collection of basic games (relays, tag games, simple ball games, follow-the-leader and elimination games) that he has used successfully with the retarded.[27]

---

[26] David Morgan: "Combining ORFF-Schulwerk With Creative Dramatics for the Retarded." *Therapeutic Recreation Journal*, 2nd Quarter, 1975, pp. 54–56.
[27] Richard Endres: *Modified Game Activities: Improvisation is the Key.* Brainerd, Minnesota, State School Manual, 1971.

Social Activities

One of the most important elements of an overall program serving mentally retarded teen-agers and adults is the social program. Most retardates find it extremely difficult to mingle and be accepted by other people in their same age range who are not retarded. Often, their social skills and confidence are extremely limited because of this exclusion.

Therefore, it is essential to provide club activities, dances, parties, trip programs and similar activities to meet the important social needs of retarded youth and adults and to prevent isolation and withdrawal. These may vary according to the setting. In an institutional program, such social activities should not only provide fun and social contact, but also should contribute to the overall social development of participants.

At the Rainier School, for example, social recreation is used to develop social skills and to learn to use leisure independently and creatively. Hough writes that "exchange dinners" between halls and units of the school are popular on a coeducational basis. Often these are followed by games, dancing and informal conversation. Proper table manners and social behavior are encouraged by the supervising staff. She continues,

> A social atmosphere is also provided through parties and entertainment planned and carried out by staff and/or volunteer groups. . . . The Residents' Canteen is another medium wherein skills learned . . . include: money handling, purchasing refreshments by name and cost, dancing, table games, social etiquette, group activity participation and interaction, and facility rules. Essentially, this is a place for the practice of skills. However, the recreation leader offers a reinforcing element by correcting inappropriate behavior, assisting each person who may have trouble with reading the name of an item he or she desires to purchase, and helping the person in recognizing the value of money. The program is primarily for use in one's leisure time and not structured as a class.[28]

Other social activities at the Rainier School are geared to the same objectives of achieving personal growth for teen-age retardates. For example, one program designed for the Placement Unit (youth and adults who might be discharged but who lack the skills needed for community living) is the Holly and Cedar Leisure Time Activity Club. Hough describes this program as an extremely popular one that deals not only with activity but also with exploration and group discussion of the following areas:

> Program content developed with the participants to include: grooming and care of clothing; personal hygiene; physical conditioning and posture; boy-girl relationships and dating procedures (with supervision); party and picnic planning; behavior problems discussions for correction and understanding of right and wrong; self-motivating hobbies; service projects; community based functions and other special items as brought up by the membership. . . . Special emphasis is made on the development of each individual's attitudes toward responsibility in work and play, as fellow men and women, and in general, life itself.[29]

Within this program, the development of potential leadership abilities receives special attention, and members of the club are encouraged to act as activity leaders and planners.

---

[28] Barbara A. Hough: "Activities for Youth." *In* Larry L. Neal: *Recreation's Role in the Rehabilitation of the Mentally Retarded*, p. 65.

[29] *Ibid.*, p. 66.

In the community, as indicated earlier, many public recreation and park departments and voluntary agencies provide services for the retarded. As an example, the Nassau County, New York, Association for the Help of Retarded Children provides after-school and evening recreation for 200 retarded adolescents and adults in several locations around the county. Programs include eight bowling leagues that meet weekly in eight communities and additional weeknight programs that include general recreation (ping-pong, social dancing, outdoor ball games when weather permits and dramatics). One group is organized as a club, electing its own officers and conducting its own agenda and carrying out its own recreational events. In addition, social dances for adults, with music, refreshments, dancing and talent shows, are held each month for about 150 retarded adults.

A number of voluntary organizations in the community, such as the Y.M.C.A. or Y.W.C.A., also conduct social programs for this population. For example, since the mid-1960s, the San Bernardino, California, Y.W.C.A. has co-operated with the San Bernardino County Council of Community Service to sponsor a recreation club for educable retarded men and women over 18. Known as the Y.W. "Merri-Mixers," the club meets weekly, and its members take part in social activities such as arts and crafts, games, refreshments or ping-pong, along with trips, parties and other special events. Programming is flexible and changes from year to year, according to the interests of the group members. In turn, the membership continues to rotate as some young members take jobs or enter job training and new members are referred to the group.

Living Skills

Many recreation or activity therapy programs in state and private institutions include a strong component of special living skills. As indicated earlier, some of these—particularly those related to social behavior—are included in club and other social programs for teen-agers and adults. Not infrequently, special classes or workshops may be held in such activities as cooking, sewing or the repair of simple equipment.

As groups of retarded persons go out on trips, they learn to handle money and admission tickets, to find their way to needed facilities and to gain confidence in the community setting that will serve them in good stead at a later point. Although these concepts and skills may be learned in a recreation activity, they are useful throughout the entire life of the participant. Having gained the ability to take a bus to a recreation event or sports program, the teen-age retardate has also gained the ability needed to take a bus every day to a job.

CAMPING PROGRAMS FOR RETARDED

There is a rapidly growing interest in camping for the retarded. One of the pioneer programs in this field has been Camp Confidence, the Northern Minnesota Therapeutic Camp, an independent organization intended primarily to provide year-round camping and outdoor recreation facilities for mentally retarded residents at Brainerd State Hospital that also serves groups sent by Daytime Activity Centers in the hospital's receiving area and families of the retarded. Camp Confidence is unique, not only in its program but also in the way

Winter sports like skiing, snow-mobiling and snowshoeing are enjoyed by participants of all ages at Camp Confidence, in Brainerd, Minnesota.

it has gained support and assistance from local businessmen, parents' groups and other auxiliary organizations and even from a U.S. Army Reserve Engineer Battalion located in Brainerd.

Tent sites, picnic areas, cabins and a lodge have been constructed on a 140 acre wilderness site with over half a mile of lakeshore frontage. Program activities include winter sports (ice-fishing, snow-mobiling and tobogganing), archery, swimming, boating, nature study and other activities suited to the natural setting. Richard Endres has outlined a number of categories to show how camps of this type may serve different classifications of mentally retarded persons, both institutionalized and living in the community. On a year-round basis, a number of the following programs might well be conducted simultaneously:

1. One-week programs for individuals considered capable of *independent or semi-independent community living*. Emphasis on outdoor education curriculum, with participants coming to camp approximately every six weeks.
2. Two- or three-day *vacation camping*. Primarily intended for hospital residents working in industrial programs, who have little or no vacation opportunity. Less emphasis on outdoor education and more on recreational programs. Participation for such individuals suggested every three to four months.
3. *Day camping programs*. Primarily intended for children participating in special education classes at the parent facility (hospital). Instructors would serve as the major counselors for day camping experiences.
4. Two- or three-day *independent living skills camp*. Operated in separate units (away from the main camp complex), with six to eight individuals and one counselor living together with emphasis on home and camp living skills (cooking, clean-up, and so on).

In addition, as campers become proficient in various phases of the outdoor education curriculum, they might take part in two-or three-day *overnight tent camping* programs. Also, families of the retarded might enjoy meeting and camping together with similar families in a *family tent and trailer camping area.*[30]

For retarded children and youth living in the community, such special camping programs might serve as a preliminary experience that would then equip them to move into integrated camping programs with nondisabled peers. In writing about "habilitative camping," Marilyn Herb, Recreation Director of the Fairview Hospital and Training Center in Salem, Oregon, stresses the need to give campers real responsibilities in planning and carrying out program activities. Only if this is done can camping produce the maximum results in terms of positive social, emotional, physical and intellectual growth in retarded participants. The stress must be on the camper's abilities, not disabilities. She asks,

1. *What responsibilities can be assumed by the camper?*
2. *How do these responsibilities affect the function of the camp?*
3. *Are duties and activities geared to camper abilities?*
4. *Who assigns these duties, you or campers?*
5. *Do your activities have carry-over values?*
6. *Are the activities new, or have campers been involved in like programs before?*
7. *What is the potential for camper planning, executing, and evaluating programs?*
8. *Do activities stress anticipation, participation, and reflection?*
9. *How can activities be broken down to meet the needs of varied levels of participants?*
10. *Is the program the result of direct or indirect professional involvement?*[31]

In some cases, camping programs may be eligible for special federal funding support. For example, the Porterville State Hospital in Porterville, California, operates an extensive on-grounds camping program for mentally retarded residents at Camp Vandalia, an 18 acre site on the hospital property, and other varied camping experiences made possible with the help of the District VII California Council for Retarded Children, Boy Scouts and Girl Scouts, Y.W.C.A., Easter Seal and other, more rustic, sites. The Camp Vandalia program is financed primarily by a Federal Title I grant as an "Outdoor Education for the Handicapped" project, with assistance by a strong parents association. The site itself is also made available to outside community groups, particularly those affiliated with the hospital, involved in service to special populations or assisting in its development and maintenance.[32]

SCOPE OF THERAPEUTIC RECREATION FOR THE RETARDED

This chapter has given examples of recreation programs and activities designed to meet the needs of the mentally retarded. How widespread *are* such programs? No fully comprehensive information has been gathered about all in-

---

[30] Richard Endres: "Northern Minnesota Therapeutic Camp." *Journal of Health, Physical Education and Recreation*, May, 1971, p. 75.

[31] Marilyn Herb: "Habilitative Camping." *In* Larry L. Neal: *Recreation's Role in the Rehabilitation of the Mentally Retarded*, p. 53.

[32] *Bulletin on Camp Vandalia.* State Hospital, Porterville, California, July, 1970, pp. 1–17.

stitutions and community programs. It is obvious, however, that practices vary widely around the United States and in Canada today.

In many cases, inadequate staffing and funds have limited the total provision of care for severely and profoundly retarded patients in state hospitals. Often they are extremely overcrowded, and it is all that staff can do to keep up with their minimal physical needs. Aroused public opinion has, in some cases, resulted in improved funding and program development in such institutions.

For the last several years, there has been a ground swell of evidence that large institutional systems represent neither economical nor humane approaches to the care and habilitation of the mentally retarded. The March, 1976, report of the President's Committee on Mental Retardation actually took the position that institutional commitment, either voluntary or involuntary, should be prohibited except in extreme cases and through due process. More and more states are developing networks of group homes in the community setting. In terms of cost, it was reported in 1977 that Pennsylvania, which operates the largest group home program in the United States, was able to care for 2100 residents in homes and apartments throughout the state at a cost of $15 million a year, approximately $7300 per person. In contrast, in the same state, one institution's budget for the fiscal year 1976 to 1977 for 1430 residents was $34 million, a cost of almost $24,000 per person. Recognizing that those in institutions are probably more severely disabled than those in group homes, thus requiring a fuller level of care, the disparity in cost is still striking.

Clearly, more and more cities and states are moving toward community-based services for the mentally retarded. In the growing number of group homes, it will not be possible to provide the full range of needed services (typically, such a residential unit might have from 10 to 15 residents, thus making it difficult to have enough specialized staff to provide all needed programs). Thus, such units are likely to depend more heavily upon recreation facilities and programs in the community itself and to "mainstream" their residents, whenever possible, in integrated leisure settings.

Realistically, if this is to be accomplished, public and voluntary agencies in the community will need to have a fuller level of expertise in serving special populations and will, in many cases, need to design programs specifically for them. Much progress needs to be made in this area. Stracke, in a survey of 500 community recreation agencies in the United States, found that only 37 per cent of the 365 responding departments had assigned full- or part-time staff members to working with the disabled.[33] Mitchell and Hillman have commented,

The overall picture of recreation services for the mentally retarded in municipal recreation agencies suggests that a wide gap exists between the services provided and the services needed. Studies reveal that far too many recreation departments are not engaged in providing programs for which they should be basically responsible.[34]

Hillman stresses the need for improved coordination and intra-agency cooperation in the provision of services, as well as for improved research programs to determine needs and effective programs, better information services,

[33] Richard Stracke: "The Role of the Therapeutic Recreator in Relation to the Community Recreator." *Therapeutic Recreation Journal*, 1st Quarter, 1969, pp. 26–29.

[34] Helene Jo Mitchell and William A. Hillman, Jr.: "The Municipal Recreation Department and Recreation Services for the Mentally Retarded." *Therapeutic Recreation Journal*, 4th Quarter, 1969, p. 35.

training for staff, parent education and involvement and evaluation of participants. He writes,

> . . . the overall effort to provide information services related to recreation and mental retardation has been sporadic. The need to consolidate efforts and planning in this area is reflected along with other prevalent needs. . . . Vital to the delivery of any service is that of planning. The contributions to either comprehensive planning for mental retardation or planning for recreation services to the retarded have been scant. . . . The need to collect data on such topics as residential areas, transportation methods, building, commercial and public recreation areas, along with the demographic aspects of the population, is often completely overlooked.[35]

Berryman, Logan and Lander urge the need for research and demonstration programs in the following areas, if community and institutional recreation programs are to be improved throughout the United States:

1. Strategies for training and utilization of para-professional personnel to help reduce the current shortage of available trained manpower.
2. Methods of fostering inter-agency cooperation in the development of comprehensive recreation services to disabled children and youth.
3. Design and implementation of transportation services for disabled children and youth.
4. Community and parent-education programs concerning the importance of early play experiences for disabled children.
5. Analysis of play and recreation activities in relation to sensory-motor, cognitive, and affective behaviors, and their development in the handicapped child.
6. Design and demonstration of methods for integrating disabled youngsters into recreation programs with normal peers.[36]

This statement is especially meaningful for service to mentally retarded children, youth and adults. Within the community setting, a number of alternatives exist for serving the retarded. Programs may be sponsored by separate voluntary organizations or public recreation departments or by joint efforts of both. When no program exists and interested parents or community leaders seek to initiate one, a process of community education, identification of need and organization is required. Avedon and Arje have developed a handbook for sponsoring groups that presents useful guidelines for carrying on this process.

Guidelines for Developing Community-Based Programs[37]

1. *Assess retarded population and existing programs*. As a first step, it is necessary to determine the size and make-up of the retarded population and the existing facilities and services within the area concerned. Usually such information can be gathered through the local chapter of the National Association for Retarded Children, public agencies such as the Board of Education or private agencies or welfare organizations serving the disabled.

---

[35] William A. Hillman, Jr.: "Federal Support of Recreation Services Related to Mental Retardation." *Therapeutic Recreation Journal*, 3rd Quarter, 1969, p. 10.
[36] Doris L. Berryman, Annette Logan and Dorothy Lander: *Enhancement of Recreation Service to Disabled Children.* New York, New York University School of Education, Report of Children's Bureau Project, 1971, pp. 65–66.
[37] This section has been adapted from Elliott M. Avedon and Frances B. Arje, *op. cit.*

2. *Assemble "framework" committee*. After determining the extent of need within a community, Avedon and Arje suggest that it is essential to develop a steering committee or "framework" of sponsors to plan and initiate action. This may include active parents of retarded children, representatives of community agencies, specialists in recreation and related rehabilitative services and similar individuals.

3. *Mobilize community interest and support*. To arouse community concern and promote involvement, it is desirable to have an initial, well-attended community meeting to discuss the need for, and ways of sponsoring, an interagency program. Those to be invited might include representatives of the public school system, public recreation and park department, voluntary social and recreational agencies, civic clubs, government, churches and synagogues and the general public. If successful, this meeting should evoke concern, gain the support of community leaders and agencies in beginning a recreation program for the retarded and result in the formation of an advisory and programming committee to form the program and publicize and gather funds for it.

4. *Developing funding support*. Potential sources of financial support for such programs include: federal and state grants, Community Chest or other charitable funds, civic and service clubs, the municipal recreation and park department or the local chapter of the Association for Retarded Children. Not infrequently, money may be gathered from several sources (including fees from the families of retarded participants, if they can afford to pay them); at the same time, one agency may provide facilities free of charge, while another provides trained leadership and another provides equipment or transportation. Special fund-raising efforts, such as rummage sales, carnivals, theater parties or charity balls, may be used to raise initial funds and thereafter be repeated yearly.

An effective public relations program is necessary from the outset, both to support fund-raising efforts and to stimulate public awareness of the needs of the mentally retarded.

5. *Developing staff resources*. This is one of the most important considerations in getting a new program under way. Ideally, it is desirable to have the program directed by a recreation leader who has had direct experience with the mentally retarded and professional training in the field of therapeutic services. Since such persons are not always available, it is a reasonable solution to have the program directed by a qualified recreation leader, who is assisted by consultants or representatives of community organizations who are quite expert in the field of mental retardation—although not in recreation.

In addition, it is necessary to make considerable use of volunteers—since the ratio of staff to participants must necessarily be high, in working with the retarded. Young college students and even high school students often provide an excellent resource. Other volunteers may be recruited from civic groups, women's auxiliaries, fraternal orders, religious groups or service clubs. A program of orientation, in-service training and on-the-job supervision should be established for all workers, professional and volunteer alike.

Programs should include not only a wide variety of activities but also counseling and personal guidance for participants that will serve them in the various areas of development described earlier. When possible, program activities should be carried on in integrated settings with the nondisabled. This is most feasible when done with educable retardates, who are capable of functioning socially on a higher level.

This chapter has dealt with the nature of the mentally retarded and presented a number of guidelines for developing recreation program services for this group, both in institutional and in community settings. It should be stressed that in many cases—particularly among the more severely retarded institutional residents—mental and social disability is complicated by other physical factors. A substantial percentage of such retarded persons have visual, auditory or other physical disabilities that hamper their overall development and their participation in such programs.

PROGRAMS FOR THOSE WITH LEARNING DISABILITY

A final concern of this chapter is the problem of children and youth with learning disability and the kinds of leisure programs and services that should be designed to meet their needs. The term "children with specific learning disabilities" refers to

> ... those children who have a disorder in one or more of the basic psychological processes involved in understanding or in using language, spoken or written, which disorder may manifest itself in imperfect ability to listen, think, speak, read, write, spell, or do mathematical calculations. Such disorders include such conditions as perceptual handicaps, brain injury, minimal brain dysfunction, dyslexia and developmental aphasia.[38]

It should be understood that learning disabilities stem primarily from neurological origins and not from a visual, hearing or motor handicap, mental retardation or emotional disturbance. It should be stressed that learning-disabled children are *not* mentally retarded; indeed, such children, despite their frequent inability to read, write, speak or move with appropriate control, often have intellectual potential that is normal or better than the general population. The list of famous world figures who had some form of learning disability includes General George Patton, President Woodrow Wilson, Thomas Alva Edison and Albert Einstein. Nonetheless, many individuals with learning disability are misdiagnosed as mentally retarded or emotionally disturbed, chiefly because their behavioral impairment bears a surface resemblance to these other broad categories of disability. It has been conservatively estimated by the U.S. Office of Education that there are slightly more than two million children with learning disability in the United States, about 3 per cent of the population in this age group from birth to age 19. In 1970, Congress designated learning disabilities as a separate category of the disabled, funding a wide variety of special educational programs to meet their needs.

Mangel writes,

> Most of these boys and girls have the potential to lead fulfilling, productive lives. They are intellectually competent. With skilled and compassionate handling by parents and professionals, they can overcome much or all of their handicaps.[39]

---

[38] U.S. Department of Health, Education and Welfare, 1970, *cited in* Rhona Shulman: "Recreational Programming for Children with Specific Learning Disabilities." *Journal of Leisurability*, Ontario, Canada, January, 1976, p. 13.

[39] Charles Mangel: "The Puzzle of Learning Disabilities." *New York Times*, April 25, 1976, p. E-S 21.

Nonetheless, great numbers of the learning-disabled are not provided such assistance. Often, their continuing failure in school and in social activities, as well as increasing criticism, scorn and rejection by teachers, families and peers, results in devastating damage to the child's basic image of himself or herself. Maturational lag within various spheres of activity means that the disabled child falls far behind others, becomes socially isolated and often develops significant emotional problems. Recreation's unique role within this area is that it can provide both a sheltered and encouraging environment in which the learning-disabled can experience success for the first time in their lives and can also undertake new kinds of directed learning tasks, both conceptual and psychomotor in nature, that help them function more effectively.

Recently, a number of voluntary agencies and public recreation and park departments have initiated programs designed either to meet the specific needs of the learning-disabled or to integrate them into general recreation and camping activities. In many cases, the sheltered experience is most desirable at the outset. For example, in a special summer camping program operated by the Westchester County, New York, Association for Children with Learning Disabilities, a high ratio of skilled staff to campers provides careful, individualized instruction in arts and crafts, music, swimming, varied sports, perceptual and motor training and a variety of other nature-oriented activities and special events. In a study of recreation programs for children with specific learning disabilities in Toronto, Canada, Schulman found the following general rationale underlying the development of such programs: (a) children with specific learning disabilities require remedial attention outside the classroom, much of which can be provided in a recreational atmosphere; (b) these children cannot function adequately in a regular community recreation program because they lack the necessary physical, social and/or behavioral skills; and (c) special programs can help develop the skills needed for later integration into regular recreation programs.[40]

Schulman's study showed considerable contrast, both in parents' and professionals' attitudes about whether learning-disabled children needed to be placed in special settings and in the extent to which many of these children had already taken part in some regular community recreation programs. She concluded,

> . . . a great deal of the ambivalence experienced by parents and recreational personnel regarding recreational programs for these children is a reflection of the present lack of knowledge, imprecision and lack of direction in the field of learning disabilities as a whole.[41]

Given the extent of this special problem, however, as well as the considerable difficulty that many learning-disabled children have in taking part successfully in community recreation activities (in part because those who attend special schools are, in effect, isolated from normal neighborhood associations and play friendships), it seems clear that recreational professionals must pay increased attention to serving those with specific learning disabilities.

It was pointed out earlier that many mentally retarded children are multiply disabled, with more or less severe physical impairments. The chapter

---

[40] Schulman, *op. cit.*, pp. 13–30.
[41] *Ibid.*, p. 18.

that follows deals specifically with the nature of recreation service for various categories of physically disabled children, youth and adults.

**SUGGESTED TOPICS FOR CLASS
DISCUSSION, EXAMINATIONS OR
STUDENT PAPERS**

1. What are the unique characteristics of the mentally retarded that influence the planning of a recreation program for this special population?

2. Select a specific area of program activity and show how it would be modified and planned in order to meet the needs of the mentally retarded (example: sports or camping).

3. Develop a set of guidelines for the establishment of a community-based program of recreation service for the mentally retarded, including such elements as finance, public relations, leadership, and scheduling.

4. There appears to be marked indecision as to whether the learning-disabled require special, separate recreation programs. What are the key elements to be considered in programming for this population?

chapter 7
Recreation for the Physically Disabled

This chapter deals with major forms of physical disability as they affect both children and adults. Each type of disability is described, together with its effects on the individual afflicted, the consequent needs for recreation service and suggested program activities.

PHYSICAL DISABILITY IN MODERN SOCIETY

As previous chapters have indicated, it has been estimated that as many as 68 million Americans have some form of significant disability that limits their participation in varied life experiences, including recreation. A substantial number have a serious physical impairment or chronic condition. For example, it was reported in 1974 by the National Center for Health Statistics in the United States that 409,000 Americans were in wheelchairs, 1.1 million used heavy leg braces, 2.1 million used canes, 404,000 used walkers, 443,000 used crutches and 172,000 had artificial limbs.[1] Millions of others are blind, deaf or have other forms of physically limiting illnesses. Although precise figures were not available for Canada, it is likely that similar statistics of physical disability exist in proportion to that nation's smaller population.

Such statistics do not give a true picture of disability and its effects. Because of the lack of uniformity in defining the conditions of crippling and orthopedic handicaps, Fait points out that

> . . . statistics of incidence are neither very meaningful nor very accurate. The number can be doubled or cut in half by the inclusion or exclusion of certain conditions.[2]

What this implies is that both the degree of physical disability and the extent to which it has proven to be a major limitation to the individual suffering

---

[1] *Trends for the Handicapped*. Washington, D.C., National Park Service and National Society for Park Resources, 1974, p. 4.

[2] Hollis F. Fait: *Special Physical Education*. Philadelphia, W. B. Saunders Co., 1972, p. 98.

from it vary very widely within *each* disability. The great majority of physically disabled persons live within the community, either with their families or independently. Many of them, even those with extremely serious physical limitations, are able to engage in a wide range of recreational and social interests. Unlike the mentally ill person who tends to be withdrawn and to avoid social contact or challenges that may be psychologically threatening, the physically disabled person is often eager to test himself among the nondisabled. Unlike the mentally retarded individual, who has great difficulty in establishing a meaningful bond of friendship with his nondisabled peers, those with physical limitations are often well-integrated members of other social groups.

However, to provide adequate program service for the physically disabled, it *is* necessary to plan specifically for them, to provide programs geared to their needs and abilities, to modify activities and facilities and to provide sympathetic and capable leadership.

GOALS OF RECREATION FOR THE PHYSICALLY DISABLED

These goals are quite similar to those that have been described earlier for the mentally ill and mentally retarded. They include the following:

1. To contribute to the positive morale and favorable adjustment to the hospital situation of those who are being actively treated, as in the case of an individual who has suffered a stroke, heart attack or serious accident.
2. To contribute directly to the process of rehabilitation within the treatment setting by providing a range of physical activities involving exercise that restores or helps to maintain functions of affected parts.
3. To provide opportunities for the constructive, creative and pleasurable use of leisure for individuals who are not in active treatment and are either in a special residential setting or in the community.
4. To enhance the social independence of the individual and, when possible, give him satisfying group experiences in socially integrated settings.
5. To relieve the families of the disabled, both psychologically and in terms of time commitment, from the need for unremitting care for the physically disabled member of the family.
6. To help physically disabled persons compensate for their specific disability by mastering and finding personal achievement in other areas of activity in which the disability is not an important factor.
7. To promote healthful physical involvement and so prevent further physical deterioration because of disuse.
8. To expand the disabled person's involvement in community life and complement other social, vocational, educational or civic involvements in a rounded schedule of activity.

As earlier chapters have pointed out, efforts to improve the lives of the physically disabled became widespread only in the 20th century and after World Wars I and II, when public awareness of the needs of disabled war veterans led to a broad concern for the total rehabilitation of the physically disabled. Efforts were made to establish programs that would permit vocational and social reintegration into the mainstream of community life. In addition to programs established by the federal government, many municipal governments and voluntary organizations developed multiservice programs for the physically disabled. Among these programs have been a variety of recreation-oriented services.

A number of states have taken significant steps to provide needed recreation services for the disabled. In Massachusetts, for example, a state law was passed in 1958 to promote and foster recreation for the physically disabled and mentally retarded. Although responsibility for this overall function was assigned to the Director of Special Education in the Massachusetts State Department of Education, it was specified that the responsibility for actually organizing programs would rest with recreation and park departments in municipalities throughout the state. The state reimburses local departments that provide day camping, swimming and various adapted indoor recreation activities for children and youth with a wide variety of disabilities.

In addition, there are a variety of voluntary organizations in American communities that have recognized the need of the physically disabled for recreation and are concerned with meeting their overall needs. As an example, the Easter Seal Society for Crippled Children and Adults is a national organization that operates through local chapters in cities throughout the nation. It provides special clubs and recreational programs in community centers, and in some cities also sponsors programs for the homebound physically disabled person.

In some cases, disabled adults themselves have organized to provide programs to meet their recreational and social needs. An excellent example is the Metropolitan Activities Club in Birmingham, Michigan. The members of this club range in age from 18 to 72, and all have serious physical disabilities;

Camp Kysoc, sponsored by the Kentucky Society for Crippled Children, offers hundreds of disabled youngsters the opportunity for swimming, picnicking, fishing and other outdoor pastimes (see also p. 202).

A wide variety of organizations, such as hospitals and special schools, municipal recreation and park departments, and community agencies serving the disabled, provide special camping programs. Here, a youngster checks the mailbox of Camp Courage, run by the Minnesota Society for Crippled Children and Adults. On p. 204, Parsons State Hospital Boy Scouts take part in an outing. Greensboro, North Carolina's Camp Joy offers many special activities for the disabled, including horseback riding.

many are in wheelchairs or on crutches. Members of the Metropolitan Activities Club assume total responsibility for fund-raising and the organization of activities. These include bowling, basketball, swimming, square dancing, singing, arts and crafts and such special activities as parties and outings. Members also publicize their activities through a newsletter and yearbook and through radio and television appearances.

On a national level, such organizations as the National Wheelchair Athletic Association promote specific forms of activity for the orthopedically disabled. Many other organizations designed primarily to serve the nondisabled, such as the Boy Scouts of America, also provide special programs for the physically disabled.

Although in many programs groups with various types of physical impairment are combined, it is helpful to be able to understand each major category of disability in order to be able to plan to meet needs most effectively.

RECREATION FOR THOSE WITH ORTHOPEDIC DISABILITY

Orthopedic disabilities are those that prevent individuals from properly performing the motor and locomotor functions of their body and limbs. Such disabilities may be concerned with the functions of joints, tendons, bones, nerves or peripheral blood vessels and may be caused by trauma, congenital conditions or infection.

Traumatic causes consist most frequently of amputation or peripheral nerve injury. Amputations may result from a number of reasons: accidents, illnesses such as diabetes or surgery. Lack of development during the prenatal period, for a variety of causes, may result in a baby's being born without one or more limbs. Paralysis or motor loss in the muscles of the hips, lower trunk, legs feet and arms may be caused by accidents effecting lesions in the nerves at the brain or attached to the spinal cord. If a person has lost the use of both legs, he is said to be *paraplegic*; if all four limbs are affected, he is *quadriplegic*.

Congenital conditions causing physical disability include the following: *spina bifida*, a condition involving incomplete neurological development, which may cause loss of bowel and bladder control or paraplegia; *congenital hip dislocation*, a malpositioning of the hip that weakens the leg and hip muscles and occurs more commonly among girls than boys; and *talipes*, a congenital condition commonly known as club foot. Other orthopedic conditions that tend to affect boys in the pre-adolescent or early adolescent periods are *coxa plana* and *Osgood-Schlatter disease*, both of which cause limping and pain in the legs or hips and may affect locomotion.

Infectious diseases that affect limb function include *poliomyelitis*, which may result in paralysis of one or more parts of the body; *osteomyelitis*; and *tuberculosis of the bone*. These diseases have been reduced considerably in incidence by vacines and improved medical treatment, but they still affect many persons.

Despite greatly improved services for the physically disabled, severely orthopedic impairments have marked effects on the social, psychological and even economic lives of those with disability. Individuals who become disabled by accident or illness must often find new ways of earning a livelihood, adjust to the attitudes of family and friends and discover new social and recreational activities to replace those that may no longer be possible.

Attitudes of rejection toward the orthopedically disabled still persist widely in society. The high value placed on physical appearance means that persons with crippling disease or missing limbs are often ostracized—either openly or in subtle ways. Particularly when the impairment is sudden—as from an accident or severe illness—the problems of adjustment are extreme. Neser and Tillock write,

> A patient generally needs a period of time, which may range from nine to fifteen months, in order to translate his lack of physical improvement into the psychological acknowledgement that his disability is permanent. His attempt to integrate this knowledge often results in his entering a phase characterized by deep depression and mourning. . . .[3]

---

[3] William B. Neser and Eugene Tillock: "Special Problems Encountered in the Rehabilitation of Quadriplegic Patients." *Social Casework*, March, 1962.

Problems of the orthopedically handicapped are often accentuated by family attitudes. Financial difficulties resulting from the need for special care or equipment, as well as the need to devote considerable attention to the disabled child or youth, may cause family strain. Often parents or relatives of the disabled become overly cautious or overprotective, resulting in an attitude of excessive dependence. It is essential that the orthopedically disabled person come to grips with his or her disability and be encouraged to seek out activities that *can* be performed with success.

For patients in hospitals or rehabilitation centers who are recuperating from a serious accident or crippling illness, planned recreation programs may serve as a means of diverting attention from grief and providing constructive and rewarding ways of using time. It may lead to improvement in function and the development of *new* skills and interests that compensate for the disappearance of past abilities. Thus, it contributes to the physically disabled person's ability to accept his impairment and to his growing independence and acceptance of his new status in life.

With intelligent modification of activities and equipment, it is possible for the orthopedically disabled to participate in a variety of sports, such as archery, bowling, table tennis, horseshoes, fishing or even such team games—dependent on the exact nature of disability—as soccer, baseball, softball, basketball or football. In a game such as soccer, in which the use of hands and arms is normally not permitted, except for the goaltender, a player who has normal use of his legs can function well. A one-armed player has actually played major league professional baseball. Wheelchair basketball has become extremely popular, both in rehabilitation centers and community leagues, for players lacking the use of their limbs.

It must be recognized that the orthopedically disabled have an extremely wide range of capability, as well as limitation. A growing number of one-legged individuals have taken up downhill skiing, for example, with considerable success. At the first disabled Olympiad Games in Toronto, a one-legged Canadian, Arnie Boldt, soared over the high-jump crossbar at 6 feet, $1\frac{1}{4}$ inches, far better than many two-legged athletes can do. Claude Stevens, who won the silver medal in the discus at the Montreal Disabled Athletes Olympics, is 57 years old and totally disabled from the chest down—the result of a fall while he was in the merchant marine. Stevens had been hospitalized for nine years and, in his own words, was almost a "basket case," when two other wheelchair athletes persuaded him to take up sport:

> I was swathed in rugs. I couldn't hold my head up without a rest. I had no interest in life. . . . I was literally an old man dribbling. Then my whole life changed.[4]

Today, Stevens is fit and bronzed, youthful and strong in appearance. He maintains a vigorous daily training schedule, including two hours of weightlifting, an hour of push-ups, an hour of road work in his wheelchair and additional hours of warming up, throwing the discus and shot-put. He maintains that competitive sport and the training it entails has changed his whole life outlook:

---

[4] Ulick O'Connor: "Athletics: One Man's Path to a New Life." *New York Times*, January 2, 1977, p. 2-S.

It makes you mentally alert, aware of things in an almost psychedelic way. (It is)
the greatest cure for depression.[5]

Obviously, not all orthopedically disabled individuals have the will or physical potential for such a degree of involvement in physical recreation. Quadriplegics, in particular, who have usually suffered almost total bodily paralysis as the result of a severe accident, find themselves in a condition of extreme helplessness, often to be followed by serious psychological problems, withdrawal and depression. The general goal in active treatment centers is to facilitate the return of the quadriplegic to his or her home by maximizing the patient's potential for self-management. Over a period of a year or more, quadriplegics learn to accept their disability, pass through a period of mourning and develop certain physical capabilities, including bowel and bladder control, the ability to sit upright for a period of time and some degree of use of the upper extremities with the help of orthotic devices. Throughout this process, the recreation worker may work with patients at their bedside, in small groups on the ward and, ultimately, as they begin to move out into the community, gaining skills and competence that will aid them in independent community living after discharge.

For the orthopedically disabled as a group, in addition to modified sports activities (described later in this chapter), hunting, swimming and dancing may also be enjoyed. In the area of social activity, the orthopedically disabled are able to enjoy group games, parties, carnivals and similar activities and events. With sufficient motivation, *every* form of creative activity, such as art, crafts, music, drama or creative writing, may readily be enjoyed by the orthopedically disabled. Even when an individual is so severely disabled that he cannot grip a paint brush with his hands, it may be strapped to his arm, a foot or his chin.

Specific descriptions of varied recreational activities that may be carried on by the orthopedically disabled are provided in later sections of this book.

RECREATION FOR THE CEREBRAL PALSIED

Cerebral palsy is a condition affecting the motor control centers of the body and is a result of lesions in various parts of the brain arising from injury, infection or faulty development. The condition is not regarded as an orthopedic disability but is a neurological impairment.

More than 600,000 children and adults are victims of this condition. It may occur before or at birth or at any time later in life, although 90 per cent of all cases stem from natal or prenatal causes. These causes include maternal disease, severe maternal nutritional deficiencies, toxins, radiation therapy, incompatibility of Rh factors between parents or defective development of brain cells before birth and lack of oxygen to the developing brain (anoxia). Infectious diseases such as measles, mumps, whooping cough and encephalitis or accidents involving a severe head injury are responsible for the bulk of cerebral palsy cases that develop after birth.

The movement of the cerebral palsied is impaired and awkward and is often accompanied by postural malformations. Speech patterns are usually

---

[5] *Ibid.*

affected. The cerebral palsied may range from a complete inability to control muscular function to a very slight lack of muscular coordination. Several types of functional dysfunction have been identified. These include: (a) *spastic*, characterized by jerky and uncertain movements and tightly contracting muscles; (b) *athetotic*, typically showing uncontrolled, sprawling muscular functioning; (c) *rigid*, with extremely tight muscles and limited, resistant movement; and (d) *tremor*, characterized by uncontrollably shaking limbs. Eighty-five per cent of all cases are either spastic or athetotic.

Cerebral palsy is classified as *mild, moderate* or *severe* in its impact. It may affect one or more parts of the body and often includes a degree of impairment in verbal ability, vision, hearing or intelligence, although the cerebral palsied person may be perfectly normal in these respects. Unless it is a mild case, the cerebral palsy sufferer has considerable difficulty in functioning socially and in being accepted by others. Drooling and jerky physical movements, constant facial grimacing and the overall physical appearance, as well as the hard-to-understand speech of many palsied individuals, tend to make normal social relationships extremely difficult. As a result, withdrawal and fear of social contact are common among many children, youth and adults with this impairment.

Although the condition cannot at present be cured, research has shown that intensive treatment, using a variety of modalities, can markedly improve the social, physical and intellectual capabilities of the cerebral palsied. The primary function of recreation services for the child with cerebral palsy is to promote normal growth and development by providing the kinds of experiences and activities that other children receive. However, because of the limitations of the palsied, it is essential to design activities carefully to meet his needs.

The first step is to become familiar with his total history, including the details of his home-life, the attitudes of his family toward his impairment, his medical history, his present physical limitations, his psychological make-up, his present social involvement and interests and other accompanying symptoms or conditions he may have.

In planning programs for the cerebral palsied, it is necessary to select activities that do not produce tension and do not require quick response or performance. While programs should not be overstrenuous and frequent rest should be provided, it is important to provide physical activities to counteract the obesity and poorly developed motor skills characteristic of many cerebral palsied persons. Simple games, easy rhythmic activities and swimming are particularly desirable in working with this disability.

The United Cerebral Palsy Association of New York City is an example of a community-based voluntary agency that operates a day-care program for the cerebral palsied of all ages. Their recreation program, conducted under professional leadership, operates Monday through Friday in the evenings and during the day on Saturdays, serving teen-agers and adults.

Facilities operated by United Cerebral Palsy include two multipurpose rooms, an arts and crafts shop, a music room, a library and apartments used for training the cerebral palsied in self-care and other life skills. Activities include arts and crafts, music, drama, table games, social events and trips, homemaking projects, physical programs and discussion groups. They consist of approximately 40 per cent active programs and 60 per cent quiet and are varied, according to age and the physical, mental and social levels of participants.

The heart of the adult recreation program consists of social clubs that meet weekly, each with between 20 and 25 members of both sexes. They meet in all five boroughs of New York City and place emphasis on social events, bowling, creative writing and discussion groups and other common club activities. United Cerebral Palsy also operates a camping program to serve the cerebral palsied and conducts research, promotes legislation and disseminates publications in this field. Primary emphasis is given to helping clients with cerebral palsy realize maximal growth, achievement, recognition and success and to providing them with opportunities for developing skills and having experiences that have been neglected in their earlier lives. Strong emphasis is placed on self-help activities, playing a meaningful role in group decisions and program planning and especially on giving them the opportunity to mature and have meaningful relationships with members of the opposite sex. Nigro writes,

> One element of programming that has not so far been mentioned is the pairing off of people into romantic alliances and love affairs and sexual activity at many levels. Obviously, if we are going to bring adults together, stimulate growth, bombard them with social experiences, and increase self-esteem and promote self-awareness, we must be prepared to deal with this very adult kind of behavior. Perhaps it is not so obvious, however, for frequently staff members in adult programs panic at the first sign of such goings on. It is essential that anyone involved in the conduct of programs for severely disabled adults expect and perhaps even encourage such activity. . . . the program design will have to include an element of sex education and sex counseling, for both the disabled themselves and for the staff who work with them. It cannot be stated emphatically enough that the people we are concerned with are adults and have to be thought of in that context, regardless of how they might behave or how retarded or dependent they might be.[6]

In addition to clearly recreational activities then, United Cerebral Palsy offers many other kinds of educational and living experiences that promote the rounded development of its clients.

RECREATION AND MUSCULAR DYSTROPHY

Muscular dystrophy is the name given to a group of chronic diseases whose main characteristic is the progressive degeneration of the voluntary muscular system of the body. It is a noncontagious illness that weakens the victim, who is eventually confined to a wheelchair and ultimately to bed. Although its precise cause has not been determined, muscular dystrophy appears to result from an inborn metabolic defect—the lack of a specific enzyme essential for the conversion of food into tissues and energy.

There are four main types of muscular dystrophy: (a) *Duchenne*, which begins as a rule between the ages of three and 10, affects more males than females and is usually hereditary; (b) *juvenile*, which begins in adolescence and progresses slowly, sometimes reaching to middle age before it becomes severe; it is usually

---

[6] Giovanna Nigro: *Sexuality in the Handicapped*. Lecture at Institute of Rehabilitation Medicine, New York, November, 1973. See also Giovanna Nigro: "Recreation and Adult Education." *Rehabilitation Literature*, September, 1974, p. 270.

hereditary and affects both sexes equally; (c) *facioscapulohumeral*, which affects the facial muscles, shoulders and arms and makes very slow progress, rarely shortening the life of the person afflicted, although it may cause considerable disability; and (d) *limb-girdle*, which occurs from the first to the third decade of life and makes rapid progress, often causing death within from five to 10 years.

The disease is not usually fatal in itself, although there are instances where it may cause heart failure. However, since muscular dystrophy patients cannot combat infections well, even the most trifling cold may result in suffocation and respiratory failure. It is estimated that there are over 200,000 persons affected by muscular dystrophy in the United States. Almost two-thirds of these are children, a high proportion of whom die before reaching adulthood.

Recreation is extremely important for those afflicted with this disease. It helps to satisfy their basic human needs for recognition, creative expression, sense of accomplishment and group association. More specifically, it may be used to retard the progression of the illness by strengthening those muscles still functioning well. Prolonged bed rest or confinement to a wheelchair can lead to limb atrophy and weaken patients unnecessarily.

Activities that are frequently used with those suffering from muscular dystrophy include arts and crafts, card playing, table games, informal music, modified sports and camping. Since the disease results in marked physical deterioration in its later stages, it is often necessary to modify activities and use ingenious devices to permit participation.

For example, a game like checkers may be played with the use of an instrument held in the mouth to move the pieces across the board. Electric shufflers are used for card games, and racks have been constructed to hold the cards while they are played. Harmonica playing is often recommended because it is a good exercise for the lung muscles, and a device is available to hold the instrument in front of the player's mouth, so he need not use his hands. Arts and crafts may be simplified, and special devices may be used to hold tools or equipment. Sports activities are usually carried out with light, easily held equipment (whiffle bats and plastic balls) and with modified rules and court dimensions.

RECREATION AND MULTIPLE SCLEROSIS

Multiple sclerosis is an organic disease that affects the nervous system in a variety of ways. Most commonly, it attacks the spinal cord, resulting in partial or complete paralysis of the legs and, at times, the trunk and arms. It is often mistaken for other illnesses, since its symptoms are varied and unpredictable; sometimes there are periods of remission and even partial or complete recovery from the disease. Symptoms of multiple sclerosis include the following: partial or complete paralysis of parts of the body; numbness; double or otherwise defective vision; noticeable dragging of the feet; loss of control of bowels and bladder; poor balance; speech difficulties; extreme weakness or fatigue; a pricking sensation in parts of the body; loss of coordination; and tremors of the hands.

The disease is caused by a disintegration of the coating over the nerves and the formation of scar tissue that causes interference with nerve impulses and subsequent malfunctioning. It usually occurs between the ages of 20 and 35, rarely appearing after 45, and is slightly more frequent in women than men. Multiple sclerosis differs markedly from patient to patient. Some individuals are able to maintain occupational and family responsibilities and make an excellent adjustment to their illness. Others have severely crippling conditions followed by symptom-free periods. Still others are completely paralyzed and permanently incapacitated.

The National Multiple Sclerosis Society is an organization that serves persons afflicted with this illness in a variety of ways. It conducts research, provides medical and other referral services and offers recreational and social programs through local chapters. Through clubs and organized social programs, it provides companionship (including home visiting for the severely afflicted) and organizes picnics, parties, theater programs and visits to sports and other entertainment events. There are comparatively few special recreation programs operated by voluntary or public recreation agencies for those with multiple sclerosis alone. Instead, they are normally served by programs geared to meet the needs of adults with a variety of physical disabilities.

RECREATION AND CARDIAC MALFUNCTION

Over 50 per cent of all deaths in the United States today are the result of heart disease, a statistic that may be attributed both to the larger number of people who reach middle age today (owing to the elimination of other illnesses that attacked younger people in the past) and to changed styles of living. A second major factor is the high incidence of rheumatic fever among children, which causes cardiac damage in over two-thirds of those attacked.

Heart disease is generally classified under one of the following headings: (a) *rheumatic heart disease*, which usually occurs among children between the ages of six and 12 as a result of rheumatic fever that inflames and scars the heart valves; (b) *hypertensive heart disease*, which occurs as a result of high blood pressure or hypertension or in association with arteriosclerosis (hardening of the arteries); and (c) *coronary heart disease*, which occurs most often among middle-aged and older persons who suffer from one or a series of heart attacks. Other causative factors include congenital heart disease resulting from birth defects; anemia, which places a burden on the heart; and conditions brought on by such diseases or infections as diphtheria, myocarditis and endocarditis.

While the symptoms of heart disease are varied, their most significant impact on cardiac sufferers is that they impose an immense burden of fear. Heart disease carries the constant threat of death; although most individuals with cardiopathic conditions do not have the obvious impairments associated with other physical disabilities described in this chapter, they nonetheless are acutely aware of the danger of their condition. Thus, for both children and adults who are afflicted by heart disease, the normal urge to engage in physical recreation is frustrated.

Many children suffering from heart conditions are excessively restricted and become socially immature because they are shielded from any form of play and isolated from involvement with their peers. Fait writes,

> Such children need to be counseled into a better course of adjustment, one which recognizes the restrictions essential but points up the effective and enjoyable life which is possible within the limitations. . . .[7]

---

[7] Hollis F. Fait, *op. cit.*, p. 119.

Similarly, it is important that adult heart sufferers be helped to take part in a regimen of safe but enjoyable recreational and social activities in order to prevent inactivity and social withdrawal. If they do not, they tend to become so obsessed with their illness that they are isolated and lack normal outlets for energy, as well as other forms of release, which may result in a high degree of emotional tension and actually promote heart disease. However, certain safeguards should be kept in mind:

1. Competition in recreational activity should be avoided or kept to a minimum, since it may cause a high level of emotional stress that is dangerous to the cardiac condition.
2. Children should not be permitted to overexert themselves in physical play or in the duration of any sort of recreational activity and should therefore be carefully supervised.
3. Individuals with heart conditions should be given frequent rest periods to prevent strain or exhaustion.
4. Environmental conditions, such as bad weather, heat or cold, may have an effect on cardiac patients; attention must be given to such factors in planning recreation programs.

Associations serving heart disease sufferers have classified them in three categories, according to the degree of malfunction. Those in the *least serious* class are able to engage in active sports, such as swimming, softball, bowling, tetherball and similar pastimes, although care must be taken to avoid violent expenditures of energy or sustained periods of heavy activity. On the *middle levels of illness*, more moderate activity is required, and for the *most seriously* ill patient, only extremely quiet recreational activity, which can be carried on in bed or a sitting position, should be used. Since heart patients normally have full use of their vision, limbs and other body parts, they are readily capable of taking part in table games, cards, arts and crafts, music and similar sedentary activities. Recently, many individuals who have suffered serious heart attacks have taken up jogging as part of their rehabilitation program, and it is possible that physical recreation for heart disease sufferers may be expanded in the years ahead.

RECREATION FOR THE BLIND

An estimated 90 million Americans have some degree of ocular malfunction, with 3.5 million having a permanent noncorrectable eye defect. Approximately one million persons lacking the ability to read ordinary-sized newsprint are regarded as functionally blind. The legal definition of blindness is that an individual is blind if his vision is 20/200 or worse, meaning that, at 20 feet, he can see what a person with unimpaired vision can see at 200 feet. Based on this standard, there are an estimated 430,000 legally blind persons in the United States.

Thus, although blindness is commonly thought of as the total lack of vision, in reality it may mean possessing varying levels of sight. Statistics on blindness are often inconclusive owing to varying legal and medical definitions of it. Nonetheless, it is obvious that it represents a major physical deficiency for persons of all ages in the United States. It is particularly important for those concerned with therapeutic recreation service because those affected by blindness do not usually suffer from other limiting physical impairments and tend to live a normal life span; however, the effect of blindness is to severely limit the individual's social integration and other life functions.

There are several causes of blindness: (a) *infectious diseases*, such as measles, scarlet fever, typhoid fever and so on; (b) *accidents* causing injury to the eyes; (c) *functional disorders*, due to diabetes or vascular disease; and a number of miscellaneous causes, including cataracts, genetic defects or poisoning.

As indicated, most persons considered legally blind have some degree of residual vision and can distinguish light from darkness, see major forms or perceive movement. They are, however, extremely limited in mobility and in many aspects of daily living, since so many routine activities are heavily dependent on visual perception. Sometimes they develop motor disabilities, poor posture and other physical impairments. The degree to which blindness affects the individual depends to some extent on when it developed. Some studies have shown that a person who becomes blind during the course of his lifetime tends to have more difficulty in adjusting than those who are born without vision. Another study has shown that individuals with no useful vision at all are better adjusted, particularly in group situations, than those with *some* vision.

As a result of blindness, many persons tend to become withdrawn, lacking in initiative and deficient in social relationships, particularly when they are overprotected or when social opportunities are denied to them. Some blind persons develop anxiety and depression, while others become hostile; a variety of neurotic problems may develop as a consequence. That this is not the inevitable effect of blindness is demonstrated by the fact that many blind persons are able to lead full and happy lives, hold jobs, raise families and play meaningful roles in their communities.

Because services for the blind have frequently been inadequate, many blind persons are poorly developed physically. Often their locomotion, kinesthetic awareness and coordination are lacking. Approximately two-thirds of the visually impaired children in public schools are not given adequate physical education programs. Often, without adequate physical release, they develop a high level of tension. Many blind persons develop so-called blindisms, which are habits such as rocking, rubbing their eyes or waving their hands back and forth, that appear to stem from the repressed urge for physical movement.

All these factors reinforce the strong need of the blind for varied and interesting recreational outlets. Basically, such programs have three major purposes for the blind:

1. As an end in themselves—to satisfy the normal human needs and drives that the blind share with all persons.
2. As a diagnostic and evaluative tool—to determine the capabilities, weaknesses and needs of the blind individual.
3. As a specific tool in rehabilitation—to be used to develop physical, social or intellectual growth or to minimize overall disability.

Since many blind persons tend not to be employed and, therefore, possess great amounts of leisure, it is important that they be provided with the means of using this time productively and enjoyably. Thus, recreation can serve as a means of satisfying creative urges, releasing tensions, gaining self-esteem, promoting physical health and strengthening the socialization process. It is essential, in planning programs to meet the need of the blind, that this not be done *for* them but *with* them. Ireland writes,

> *A thorough understanding of the blind person is the only reliable basis upon which a recreation worker can set both a realistic and idealistic goal. What might be an ideal and yet realistic goal for one person might be wholly inadequate for the next person. The most important task of the recreation person is to assist the blind person to fulfill his desires and to be aware of his needs as fully as possible.*[8]

Blind persons today receive benefits in the form of education, rehabilitation services, Braille materials and income tax exemptions. Nearly all states have agencies that provide assistance with respect to homemaking, counseling for parents of blind children, vocational counseling, training and placement and varied kinds of information services. With respect to recreation, most blind individuals are served through special organizations concerned with this category of disability rather than through public or voluntary agencies for the public at large.

Programs Serving the Blind

An example of a special school for the blind may be found in the Ontario, Canada, School for the Blind, a residential school that offers a three-phase curriculum: (a) academic; (b) social development; and (c) extracurricular. Out-of-school hours are supervised by residence counselors, who conduct Brownie, Guide, Cub and Scout groups. Such groups operate just as they would with sighted boys and girls and in some cases share programs with similar groups in the community. The overall goals in the Ontario School for the Blind are

1. To provide healthy, vigorous, outdoor living activities related to the Canadian cultural milieu.
2. To give the children practical skills necessary to cope with independent living outside of the school.
3. To develop the child's personality to the fullest.
4. To integrate the visually handicapped with seeing children as much as possible and to guide them in handling themselves in such settings.

Trips and excursions are an important part of the program, and blind boys and girls in the school take part in track and field and wrestling meets, as well as in other clubs and associations in the community. Individuals are taught to travel, using the white cane for visibility, in order to facilitate independent mobility outside the school. Music in all forms, dramatics and other social and recreational activities are stressed for all residents.

A number of cities have special organizations that serve the blind. As an example, the New York Association for the Blind, also known as the Lighthouse, is a private, nonprofit, multiservice agency, serving approximately 3300 blind persons each year. It is funded through donations, grants, special funds and endowments and offers the following social and recreational services: (a) a nursery-school-age play program, meeting twice a week; (b) a recreation program

---

[8] Ralph R. Ireland: "Recreation's Role in Rehabilitating Blind People." *Journal of Health, Physical Education and Recreation.* January, 1958, p. 44.

for rehabilitation clients, meeting four times a week; (c) a youth recreation program, meeting all day on Saturdays; (d) an adult education program in leisure activities, meeting two evenings a week; and (e) an older adult recreation program, meeting two evenings a week.

The facilities of the Lighthouse include bowling alleys, a swimming pool, social hall, kitchen and dining room, auditorium and stage, arts and crafts room, ceramics room, recreation hall and two residential camping areas. Since it is necessary to provide transportation for many of the participants in the program, it operates four station wagons and also uses private cars for this purpose. The Lighthouse also operates residential accommodations for both men and women in its training program and has satellite programs elsewhere in the New York City area.

There are about 60 residential camps in the United States that are specifically designed to serve the visually impaired. One of these is Highbrook Lodge, a vacation camp for blind persons in northeastern Ohio, sponsored by the Cleveland Society for the Blind. It serves varied age groups, who attend four sessions of approximately one week each and who pay fees based on their financial capability. Program activities include hiking, swimming, boating and fishing, bowling, horseback riding, baseball, wrestling and similar physical and social pursuits—many of which are planned by the campers themselves.

In some cases, special community recreation programs are organized to serve the blind. These may involve the joint sponsorship of various private or governmental agencies; for example, in 1974, a special innovative program for the blind was established by the National Park Service at Glen Echo Park in Maryland. Begun at the request of the District of Columbia's school system, which felt that there was a strong need for programs in the creative arts for the blind, the Children's Experimental Workshop has featured quality instruction in dance, theater arts, pottery and design for hundreds of elementary and high school students with visual disability.[9] Specially designed parks, nature trails and other outdoor facilities that make use of rope trails, Braille markers and sometimes taped interpretative messages also serve the blind today with varied forms of outdoor recreation and education.

Special Methods and Equipment

Some forms of recreational activity, such as music listening or discussion groups, require no special adaptations or methods for the blind. Others need to be presented with special care or modification.

For example, in certain activities, such as playing a musical instrument or doing arts and crafts, it is helpful for the leader to perform the skill while allowing the hands of the blind to touch his throughout—thus "learning by feel." Similarly, the leader may move the hands or feet of the blind person through the skill. It is particularly important for the leader to give a full verbal description of what is happening. In a game like bowling, for example, the leader must indicate not only the number of pins knocked down but also the placement of the remaining pins.

---

[9] Wendy M. Ross: "The Children's Experimental Workshop, A Creative Arts Experience for the Visually Handicapped." *Parks and Recreation*, September, 1975, pp. 26–31.

Since blind people depend so heavily on auditory stimuli, special attention must be paid to sound and to hearing conditions. Whistles may be used to get attention or to give direction to runners in a game or running event. Since sound is often lost or distorted outdoors, the leader should always face the participants and project his or her voice loudly when giving verbal directions. In the play area, confusing noises in the background, such as a portable radio, may tend to distract blind players.

Stability of the play environment is also important to the blind. They must be allowed to familiarize themselves fully with the room or outside space, and equipment or play materials should not be moved without warning. This will enhance their security and ease of learning new activities. Some specific kinds of equipment often used for the blind in sports and games include the following: (a) guide wires that enable blind individuals to run at top speed without fear, holding a short rope attached to a ring that slides along the rope without interference; (b) audible goal detectors (consisting of a motor-driven noisemaker that makes clicking sounds at a constant rate), which are used in basketball goal-shooting, to locate bases or to indicate orientations in other play situations, such as swimming pools; (c) audible balls for modified ball games, such as kickball, that have either a battery-operated beeper or bell placed inside; and (d) a portable aluminum rail for use in bowling that is movable from lane to lane and provides the blind bowler with orientation.[10]

In other sports activities, sighted or partially sighted companions may assist the blind athlete. Indeed, hundreds of blind children and adults are learning to ski today as part of a nonprofit, volunteer instructional program called Blind Outdoor Leisure Development (BOLD).[11] Begun in Aspen, Colorado, in 1969, BOLD uses a method of having the instructor and blind pupil linked by a 12-foot long bamboo pole until the learner is ready to ski alone. At that point, the blind skier is accompanied on the downhill slopes by a sighted companion who calls out directions and warnings about the terrain ahead. In some cases, blind skiers have also worn special wireless headsets through which nearby instructors may broadcast turning directions. Given the speed and potential risk of skiing, the fact that many blind people are taking part in it successfully demonstrates that they, like other types of disabled persons, are capable of far more than they have been permitted to do in the past.

RECREATION FOR THE DEAF

The most commonly accepted definition of the deaf regards them as those whose sense of hearing is nonfunctional for the ordinary purposes of life. Complete loss of hearing is much less common than partial loss, in which sounds are garbled and unclear or high or low sounds are lost. There are several ways of classifying deafness. It may be done according to the time the loss of function occurred: (a) *congenital deafness*, meaning that an individual was born deaf as a result of prenatal or natal nerve destruction or injury, illness of the mother during pregnancy, incompatible Rh factors between parents or prolonged labor; or (b) *adventitious deafness*, referring to later loss of hearing caused by injury,

---

[10] Examples of modified equipment for the blind, taken from graduate paper by Steve Berman, Herbert Lehman College, New York, 1971.
[11] Linda Joseph: "Skiing. . . Is Believing." *WomenSports*, January, 1976, pp. 28–29.

infection or disease (measles, mumps, scarlet fever, diphtheria and meningitis are common causes) or psychogenic factors.

Deafness may also be classified as: (a) *nerve deafness*, usually congenital in origin but sometimes resulting from accidents, illness or senility and regarded as the more serious in its effects; and (b) *conduction deafness*, resulting from changes in the reception and conduction ear mechanisms. In many cases, both types of impairment may occur in the same individual. Finally, deafness may be seen more broadly as part of a concept of "auditory disorder," which is concerned with the total reception and interpretation of sound.

The effects of deafness are profound, since language and verbal communication are so important in all aspects of daily life. Since it is not a visible disability, people frequently show little understanding or sympathy toward the deaf and tend to regard them with hostile attitudes, epitomized by the label "deaf and dumb," which is often attached to them. In fact, many deaf persons learn to speak quite effectively, and deafness does not imply any mental subnormality. In some cases, since spoken language is such an important factor in development, the deaf may be weak in the capacity for abstract thinking, and in some children who are born deaf, this may be a contributing factor leading to mental retardation.

Deaf persons generally have good motor skills, although poor balance and dizziness may exist when the impairment is related to semicircular canal injury or cerebral palsy. In some cases, they may be slightly less skilled in touch perception; on the other hand, they frequently have faster reflexes than the person with normal hearing, probably because their level of tension is high, resulting from the understandable effort to compensate for the lack of hearing ability.

A primary objective of recreation and social programs for the deaf should be to integrate them with nondisabled peers. As in other areas of life, this poses a difficult problem because of the importance of verbal communication in most recreational activities. In many cases, deaf young adults who have spent 16 or 17 years in special schools for the deaf, with little social contact with the hearing population, continue to isolate themselves after graduation. Highly independent and proud, they often organize their own social clubs, sports groups, churches and state and national organizations. Although such groups provide valuable service for the deaf, they constitute a barrier of self-imposed isolation that must be overcome.

Teaching the deaf or leading them in recreational programs requires careful attention to the means of communication. Involving them in games, dancing or other group activities where directions must be heard should be done carefully. In special situations in which skilled leaders are working with the deaf exclusively, reliance may be placed on the manual method of spelling out words with "finger language." However, in mixed groups or with leaders not familiar with this method, lip reading is the more useful approach. Thus, the recreation leader should stand close to the persons he is working with, facing them directly, and should speak slowly and clearly, enunciating each word distinctly. He may also use hand gestures and other forms of direct demonstration, visual aids or diagrams or may rely on persons with normal hearing in the group to assist deaf participants in learning activities.

In leading the deaf in program activities such as sports and games, it is important to recognize that because of past exclusion from childhood play in neighborhood playgrounds or schools, they may not be familiar with the rules and strategies of games, as most normal children tend to be. In facilitating play, a variety of special devices may be used to improve understanding and to help the deaf participants overcome the effects of their impairment. For example, when they play flag football, they quickly learn that the best way to signal to have the ball "hiked" is to clap their hands—an unmistakable visual signal. In basketball, the official must not only blow a whistle but also simultaneously wave his hands to get deaf players' attention. Numerous other methods are used to compensate for the inability to hear verbal directions, signals or explanations.

Examples of Programs Serving the Deaf

Educational, vocational, social and recreational services for the deaf may be provided in a variety of settings, such as special schools or classes, voluntary organizations in the community or programs provided by public recreation departments. Special centers to serve deaf and blind children have been established in a number of cities with federal funding under Public Law 90-247. These assist local agencies with grants or contracts empowering them to provide diagnosis, evaluation, education, social services and consultants to parents and teachers.

An example of a special school for the deaf in New York City is the Lexington School for the Deaf, operated under the auspices of a board of trustees and the New York State Board of Education, with funding by the New York City Board of Education and private sources. This school serves some 400 students, almost half of whom are residents; all have auditory disability and some have multiple handicaps. Facilities operated by the Lexington School include a gymnasium, library, activity and game rooms, lounges, swimming pool, ballfields, playground, billiards room and arts and crafts shop.

The after-school recreation program includes a high proportion of physically active pursuits—all voluntarily participated in by students. It has been found that, once they have learned the basic rules, skills or strategy in a given activity, deaf children tend to participate extremely successfully. Particularly in sports or other activities in which hearing is not an important factor, such as wrestling or competitive swimming, they are able to compete with others on an equal footing; occasionally, deaf competitors have won N.C.A.A. or A.A.U. wrestling championships. However, the school has experienced continuing difficulty in integrating its students in programs with nondisabled peers, a problem facing other community recreation agencies that seek to accomplish this goal.

OTHER PHYSICALLY DISABLING CONDITIONS

In addition to the impairments described earlier, there are a number of other diseases or disabling conditions that may require specially designed therapeutic recreation service. These include, as examples, tuberculosis and diabetes.

TUBERCULOSIS

An infectious disease that affects the pulmonary system, tuberculosis may require long hospitalization in a sanitarium or rest home, together with sustained bed care and nutritious diet. Although it once was regarded as a major health problem and often resulted in progressive disability and death, today it has declined markedly in incidence, particularly among children. It continues to appear on all age levels, however, and there are a substantial number of persons who have arrested cases. For such individuals, activity must be limited and precautions taken to prevent reinfection.

Recreation plays a vital role in making the long period of hospitalization more bearable. It provides pleasure and interest, strengthens morale and helps the tubercular patient avoid depression and gain a sense of usefulness and involvement. It can also introduce new skills and interests to supplant those that must be given up by the patient. It may also contribute to the physical fitness level of the patient without unduly taxing his energies.

DIABETES MELLITUS

Diabetes mellitus is a disease in which the body is unable to properly ingest starches and sugars owing to an inadequate supply of naturally produced insulin. The highest incidence of diabetes is among middle-aged persons, although approximately 10 per cent of its cases occur among children. For the most part, diabetics can engage in a normal range of activities (some diabetics have actually been successful as professional athletes), and most can engage in the normal occupational, family and other community involvements of the non-disabled without danger. They tend to fatigue more easily than others, however, and care must be taken with respect to diet and regular medication. Therefore, camping or other residential programs serving the diabetic person must be specially designed to meet his health needs. When the condition is severe, it may require hospitalization and a sharply limited regimen of activity.

It has been estimated that there are approximately 4.5 million diabetics in the United States, with about 350,000 new cases being discovered each year. Thus it is extremely likely that recreation leaders, physical educators and coaches will come into contact with numbers of individuals with this disease and should be familiar with its causes and effects. For example, diabetics having insulin reactions may exhibit a wide variety of symptoms:

> The classic symptoms are increased "nervousness" or "shakiness," hunger, weakness, sweating, vision changes, irrational behavior, mental confusion and loss of coordination. A normally quiet, easygoing individual may become argumentative, irritable, and aggressive, and may exhibit uncharacteristic outbursts of temper. Occasionally diabetics in insulin shock are accused of being intoxicated or high on drugs.[12]

Since the onset of hypoglycemia may be quite rapid, requiring only hours or minutes to develop, it is important that the leader or coach be familiar with the symptoms and able to recognize them quickly. The normal treatment for insulin reaction is to compensate for low blood sugar by having the diabetic quickly eat or drink something sweet. Engebretson suggests that the participant should have a prearranged signal with the coach or adult leader so that if he needs to be taken out of an activity for this purpose, it can be done promptly, rather than try to "gut it out" by staying in the game. The leader should also be aware of the possible implications of diabetes for healing after an injury and the

---

[12] David L. Engebretson: "The Diabetic in Physical Education, Recreation and Athletics." *Journal of Physical Education and Recreation*, March, 1977, p. 19.

effects of exercise, although self-care is the diabetic's own responsibility. Finally, it is important to see this disability within a clear perspective. Many top college or professional athletes have been diabetics who learned to live with and control their disability successfully.

In addition to the examples given in this chapter, a number of other areas of activity particularly appropriate for the physically disabled are described in Chapter 10, along with guidelines for selecting and modifying them.

MODIFICATION OF FACILITIES FOR THE PHYSICALLY DISABLED

A final important area of concern in providing recreational opportunities for the physically disabled is the elimination of architectural barriers that prevent those with impairment from using parks, playgrounds, community centers or a variety of other special recreation facilities. This problem, which does not affect the mentally ill or retarded, *does* affect hundreds of thousands of individuals, young and old, who are in wheelchairs or on crutches or who have limited powers of locomotion. A 1967 report by the Bureau of Outdoor Recreation made this need clear:

> It is clearly evident . . . that great numbers of disabled persons are not receiving the benefits of our nation's recreation resources. The severity of their disabilities, architectural barriers, non-acceptance by society, and slowness of the recreation profession to adjust its programs and facilities to their needs all have contributed to a serious lack of opportunity.[13]

Similarly, in 1975, a lead editorial in *Parks and Recreation* identified "access" as the one most important issue of the modern park and recreation facility. The problem of making park and recreation facilities available to the blind, those using orthopedic aids such as wheelchairs and crutches and other severely disabled persons must be attacked vigorously and on all levels.[14]

A number of national and state-wide organizations concerned both with architectural design and engineering requirements and with recreation and parks have taken strong action in this field. Today, the Bureau of Outdoor Recreation requires that all comprehensive state outdoor recreation plans prepared as a prerequisite to participating in the Land and Water Conservation Fund program (federal subsidy for open space and recreation facility development) consider the needs of the disabled. In recent years, increasing numbers of federal or state agencies have developed guidelines, or laws have been passed, to insure that public facilities be designed and built along lines that will permit access and use by the disabled.

To promote this effort, a national hearing on the recreation needs of disabled persons was held in Boston, in October, 1976, by the Architectural and Transportation Barriers Compliance Board, in cooperation with the National Recreation and Park Association and the U.S. Department of the Interior.[15] It

---

[13] *Outdoor Recreation Planning for the Handicapped.* Washington, D.C., Bureau of Outdoor Recreation, April, 1967, p. 1.

[14] Editorial: "Sometimes You Can't Get There." *Parks and Recreation,* June, 1975, p. 17.

[15] *Newsletter of Architectural and Transportation Barriers Compliance Board.* Washington, D.C., October, 1976.

brought together recreation professionals, state and federal park officials, private recreation developers and representatives of various types of disabled persons. In addition to gathering information about the needs of the disabled and current trends in this field, the conference members formulated recommendations to the President and Congress to promote compliance with existing laws and standards to insure access to recreational facilities for the disabled.

The United States of America Standards Institute has published a pamphlet suggesting ways to adapt facilities so that they can be used readily by the physically disabled. Specific design details have also been established in a number of states for park and recreation facilities. For example, the New York State Council of Parks and Outdoor Recreation published a handbook of design standards for various types of facilities in order to make them accessible to the physically disabled. These standards must be followed by all municipalities that wish to qualify for state or federal assistance. Examples of such standards follow:

1. Parking facilities should have special parking stalls designed for wheelchair users. The parking area should be close to the recreation site and paved with a nonslip surface. An opening of 30 inches should be maintained between guardrails to permit a wheelchair to pass.
2. Walking trails should have a minimum width of 48 inches in order to be accessible to disabled persons. They should be smoothly graded without steep inclines and with sufficient area to turn around at various places on the way. Ramps should be used where necessary. Doors of buildings should have a minimum clear opening of 32 inches, with the threshold close to the floor.
3. Food service areas should have special service areas in at least one concession where wheelchair users may be served and seated. Public telephones mounted on poles at appropriate heights make it possible for wheelchair users to make calls unaided.
4. For toilets to be made accessible, ramps with sufficient width should be installed to reach stations that are above-grade. Urinals should be floor-mounted, no higher than 19 inches above the floor and equipped with horizontal handrails. Hand-driers, soap dispensers and mirrors should be at levels accessible to wheelchair users.

Many other detailed guidelines indicate the ways in which recreation and park agencies should plan specifically to provide access for the disabled. Swimming facilities can be made more useful by providing a paved walk leading to the swimming area. Sloping handrails or ropes mounted on posts make it easier to get into the swimming facility. Bathhouses should have enlarged dressing room facilities with a bench, guardrails and outward swinging doors for wheelchair users.

Spectator areas, picnicking, camping and boating sites should have similar modifications or design features. Fishing areas should have a paved surface at the water's edge, with a protective handrail to make the sport safe for the physically disabled. Auditoriums should have seats missing in some rows, with a level surface, so wheelchair users may sit there rather than in crowded aisles or at the back of the hall.[16]

A number of playgrounds, parks and other facilities have been designed for special use by the physically disabled. For example, a unique playground was developed for disabled preschool children at the New York University Medical Center's Institute of Rehabilitation Medicine. Planned by the well-known architect, Richard Dattner, it includes a ladder leading to a tree house

---

[16] *Outdoor Recreation for the Physically Handicapped.* Vollmer-Ostrower Associates and New York State Council of Parks and Recreation, August, 1967.

(which may also be reached by ramps), a waterfall, tabletop sandboxes and similar features that contribute to children's varied play opportunities and overall development. A special playground with large animal forms and modified equipment has been developed by the Child Study Center in Fort Worth, Texas.

A number of states have experimented in this field. Georgia, for example, has created a state park designed specifically for use by the disabled and their families. Located within the larger Fort Yargo State Park, this facility includes the following features:

> ... the park adjoins a lake whose sloping beach makes possible the construction of walks and ramps of moderate incline. Boat docks . . . serve small, flat-bottomed fishing boats that can be boarded safely, and pontoon boats . . . available for persons in wheelchairs. Planned recreation activities include organized resident camping, nature walks, swimming, picnicking, fishing and bicycling.[17]

Ideally, such specially designed facilities should not be for disabled persons alone, since this tends to reinforce their isolation from the rest of society. Instead, they should attract and serve their families, as well as other nondisabled individuals. Recently, the U.S. Department of Housing and Urban Development funded an architectural competition for the most innovative designs for special playgrounds that would integrate disabled and normal children. The competition, sponsored by the Eastern Paralyzed Veterans Association and the New York City Planning Commission, resulted in a number of prize-winning designs for a playground to be built in 1978 at Flushing Meadow Park.[18] Each design incorporated various forms of experimental play equipment leading to individual and group play on various levels of difficulty or complexity.

Travel has always imposed special problems for the physically disabled. Such states as Oregon, New Jersey and Michigan have constructed new rest areas along the highways with special aids for disabled persons or have stipulated that restaurant chains or lodging chains with concessions along major thruways must provide facilities to meet the needs of disabled persons. In addition, both voluntary agencies and commercial travel agencies are now making increased efforts to provide special travel facilities and arrangements for the disabled. Carr writes,

> ... thousands of severely handicapped persons are today making the tourist rounds, including those afflicted with muscular dystrophy, multiple sclerosis, myasthenia and polio. Paraplegics, even quadriplegics, as well as the blind, the deaf and the retarded are also taken on major trips by agents.[19]

In some cases, travel firms are specializing in foreign travel for the physically disabled. With a highly competitive market situation today, instead of discouraging tourists in wheelchairs who require special aisles and mechanical lifts in buses or ramps and large elevators, airlines and hotels are going out of their way to make necessary adjustments to serve such travelers. In varied ways, facilities and equipment are being modified to serve the disabled in many public

---

[17] Kent Ruth: "Pleasure Travel is Becoming Easier for the Handicapped." *New York Times*, May 26, 1968, p. 3.

[18] Paul Goldberger: "Playground for Disabled Designed." *New York Times*, December 9, 1976, p. 51.

[19] Stanley Carr: "The World From a Wheelchair: Travel for the Handicapped." *New York Times*, February 23, 1975, p. 10-1.

and commercial settings. The construction of all major federal and state buildings, including university structures and office buildings, is increasingly being geared to serve the physically disabled. Elevators are being designed with slow closing speeds, and with controls and alarm boxes set at appropriate heights on their walls. Nature trails have been developed in many national and state parks for the blind, with special guide ropes and Braille signs pointing out natural features.

In many other ways, attention is being given to meet the needs of the physically handicapped for varied recreational opportunities. Much progress needs to be made, however, particularly in terms of improving public attitudes toward accepting the physically disabled in recreation and park settings and having a larger number of recreation and park administrators accept this as a high-priority program concern.

**SUGGESTED TOPICS FOR CLASS
DISCUSSION, EXAMINATIONS OR
STUDENT PAPERS**

1. How does the problem of providing recreation for the physically disabled person differ sharply from that of planning for the mentally ill or retarded individual?

2. Select a specific area of physical disability. Based on the unique needs of this population, outline a set of goals and then a model program of recreational activities, including administrative guidelines.

3. We frequently underestimate the capability of such groups as the blind or orthopedically disabled. Discuss this point, using material from this chapter or other sources on the disabled. In your reply, deal with the psychological aspects of physical disability.

4. Discuss the need for specially designed or modified facilities to serve the physically disabled, showing how present facilities often limit their participation. What are some recent trends in travel for the disabled?

chapter 8

Recreation and the Aging

This chapter deals with the aging population in modern society. It discusses statistics of aging and retirement, the nature of the aging process and the special problems that face older persons in the world today, including the important area of leisure and its uses and values. It analyzes various types of settings in which recreation and related social services are provided for older persons. The bulk of statistics and illustrations provided are drawn from the United States; however, the pattern of service to the aging is quite similar in Canada.

THE AGING IN AMERICAN SOCIETY

Who are the aging in American society? There are approximately 23 million persons who are 65 years old or older, about twice the number from 20 years ago, who constitute over 10 per cent of the entire population. The percentage of Americans in the older age bracket is growing rapidly:

> When the first census was taken in 1790, half the people in the country were 16 years old or younger, and as recently as 1970 the median age was under 28. But as the nation moves into its third century, its people too, are getting older. The median age will . . . reach 35 by the year 2000 and approach 40 by 2030. Over the same span, the number of people over 65 will more than double to 52 million— one out of every six Americans.[1]

Within the over-65 population, the ratio of women to men is about four to three. This disparity increases with age. About 70 per cent of older Americans live in their homes or with relatives, while about 25 per cent live alone or with a nonrelative and about 5 per cent live in institutions.

Why is the aging population a matter of special concern for those involved with health and welfare services in the United States and Canada? This

---

[1] "The Graying of America." *Newsweek*, February 28, 1977, p. 50.

population's role in society has been rapidly shifting as a result of increased life span, changes in family structure and social attitudes, population shifts in our cities and other economic and psychological factors. Many older people today lead isolated, unhappy lives. They are often relegated to a position of inferiority within a youth-oriented culture. They are stereotyped and misunderstood and often shunted aside following retirement from business or family responsibility; they reach the point at which their lives become empty and meaningless, and they deteriorate both physically and psychologically.

This is not an inevitable part of aging. It happens only because society permits it to happen. In order to understand it, it is necessary to examine the following: (a) the process of human aging; (b) the social and psychological implications of aging; (c) the economics of retirement and aging; (d) needs and problems of older persons; and (e) the role of recreation and related services in programs for the aged.

THE PROCESS OF HUMAN AGING

First, it must be understood that aging is a universal process, although it varies greatly from person to person. It is generally regarded primarily as a physiological development, although it obviously has social and psychological components as well. *Gerontology* (study of the aging process and of aged persons in society) and *geriatrics* (the branch of medicine dealing with medical problems of the aged) have both contributed greatly to our understanding of this stage of life.

Although the age 65 is considered to be the beginning of old age, the process is not strictly age-correlated and can vary tremendously among individuals, with some persons beginning to show signs of aging in the 40s or 50s and others remaining extremely vital and alert well into the 80s. In general, the process of aging includes the following physiological changes:

1. Slowing of biological functions.
2. Breakdown in functioning of body systems.
3. Reduction in physiological reserve.
4. Altered structure of cells, tissues and organs.

These changes produce decreased efficiency in the functioning of the body systems and begin to bring about progressive disabilities related to the heart and nervous system, the five senses (especially vision and hearing) and the motor abilities of older persons. Geriatrists have concluded that such changes occur because of both internal and environmental causes. One of the obvious factors important in influencing the process of aging is the availability of competent medical care. Yet, a National Health Survey found that one in four persons age 65 and over had not been to see a physician for two years or more—a reflection of the inadequacy of our social concern and practical provision of services for the aged in society.

It is necessary to recognize that many persons have false stereotypes about the older people in American society that are usually detrimental to this segment of our population. In an effort to correct these stereotypes, the National

Council on Aging formulated 10 basic concepts of aging that may be summarized as follows:

> *Aging is a universal and normal process, which varies uniquely from person to person. Aging is not necessarily accompanied by illness, and one's life-style may greatly enhance one's chances for a healthy old age. Older people represent a span of three generations, each with its own characteristics. Despite stereotypes about them, older people can and do learn and change; old age is not inflexible. Older people wish to remain self-directing; they are vital human beings, who need only develop or maintain existing capacities to lead productive, rewarding lives.*[2]

Reinforcing these comments, it should be stressed that only 5 per cent of Americans over age 65 are confined to nursing homes or institutions, and over one-half of the nation's elderly live with their spouses in independent households, usually in communities where they have roots. Dr. George Maddox, director of the Duke University Center for the Study of Aging and Human Development in Durham, N.C., sums up the overall picture:

> *The old characterization of the elderly as impoverished, debilitated and depressed is badly wrong. That description fails to describe 85 per cent of older Americans.*[3]

Despite this statement, it must be recognized that the aged have been seriously affected by a variety of social changes and trends entirely apart from the biological process of aging. These changes relate chiefly to the problem of enforced retirement and exclusion from meaningful roles in community life and shifting patterns of family involvement. Although they are social in nature, they have a strong influence on the physical and psychological health of older persons.

PROBLEMS FACING OLDER PERSONS

COMPULSORY RETIREMENT

Early retirement, which has become widespread in American life as a result of pension and Social Security plans and Civil Service or personnel regulations in most businesses, has enormous implications for older persons. For many, retirement from work brings a loss of prestige and status. In a society that places great emphasis on work and productivity, being cut off from a job commitment means a drastic change in life style. Coupled with the general tendency in our society to value youth and denigrate age, it means that older persons who no longer play a meaningful role in society tend to have a feeling of uselessness and lack a sense of self-worth and dignity.

Linked with this is the problem of economic insecurity. The major sources of income for the elderly retired person are Social Security, employment pensions, welfare programs, savings and assistance by members of their family. Retirement almost always decreases income, however, and Social Security or pension benefits have no cost-of-living clauses to compensate for the inflationary trend in the economy.

---

[2] Adapted from statement of National Council on Aging. Reprinted in *Recreation*, February, 1963, p. 67.

[3] George Maddox, cited in "The Graying of America," p. 56.

Certain expenses, such as medical costs, tend to increase sharply for older persons, and, as a consequence, many face an economic nightmare, with their meagre incomes barely stretching to meet their basic needs of existence. Despite the reassuring overview presented earlier, it is clear that the elderly in society are disproportionately disadvantaged. In 1975, *Time Magazine* pointed out that, although far from all of the elderly were infirm,

> . . . 38 per cent do suffer from some kind of chronic condition that limits their activities. Of these, fully half have serious problems and five per cent, or one out of every 20, are homebound. About a third of all aged Americans are also plagued by poverty. Despite pensions, savings and Social Security, which will disburse $72 billion to 33.5 million recipients this year, fully 4.75 million of the nation's aged exist on less than $2,999 a year—well below the Federal Government's poverty line.[4]

In May, 1977, the U.S. Senate Special Committee on Aging issued its annual report showing that poverty among the elderly was rising steadily, particularly among older blacks, with over half of this population group living in poverty or near-poverty. Obviously, a large part of this problem is derived from the fact that older persons are customarily forced to retire from work and thus accept a sharply reduced standard of living, whether or not they are capable of continuing to do the job effectively. It has been pointed out that a substantial proportion of those over age 65 *would* be capable of continuing to do a full day's work; indeed, lawsuits have been initiated, with the support of the American Medical Association, challenging the Federal Government's retirement policies (see p. 257, for examples of other resistance to compulsory retirement.)

SHIFTING FAMILY ROLES

Traditionally in American society, several generations lived together, and older persons continued not only to receive the affection and support of their children or grandchildren but also to play meaningful roles in family life. With the shift toward urban and suburban living in apartments or one-family development houses, however, increasing numbers of older persons are living alone in small apartments or single-room units. This is particularly crucial for women who have lost their husbands; the life expectancy of women at birth is 74 years, 13 years greater than that of men.

Thus, many aged persons are faced with the problem of living alone, without family and with few friends, and are often unable to take care of themselves properly. Particularly in run-down areas of larger cities, where they are often victims of thieves or muggers, old people tend to be afraid to leave their homes, and thus they are deprived of the opportunity for social involvement. The need for companionship does not diminish for older persons, and with the breaking of other ties and the increased amount of leisure time at their disposal, their loneliness becomes all the more difficult to bear. In some cities, it is not at all uncommon to see older persons sitting on benches along malls in the middle of crowded traffic or spending their entire days in bus or train terminals—just to be near people.

---

[4] "New Outlook for the Aged." *Time,* June 2, 1975, p. 45.

STEREOTYPES OF AGING

Frequently, older people behave in ways that younger people find childish, or senile.

For example, many older people seem to live in the past and refuse to change or even be concerned with what is happening in the present. Although this is sometimes considered an evidence of senility, it is quite understandable. For many aged persons, the present is bleak and unpleasant, and they would *rather* live in the past. Childish behavior is also frequently considered to be a symptom of aging. However, this may be regarded in many cases as the result of a self-fulfilling prophecy; when older people are expected to be childish and when they are treated in this way, they naturally behave helplessly or petulantly.

Similarly, the tendency toward complaints about being ill, that often verge toward hypochondria, may readily be understood. Dr. Ewald Busse comments that when someone keeps criticizing the older person unjustly and

> . . . makes him feel unwanted, uncomfortable, he may retreat into an imaginary illness as a way of saying, "Don't make things harder for me. I'm sick and you should respect and take care of me." It is clear from our studies that if the older hypochrondriac's environment changes for the better, he will too. He will again become a reasonable, normal person.[5]

It is also important for the older person or those around him to recognize that certain forms of behavior, such as forgetfulness, typically tend to increase with aging but are not necessarily signs of senility. Altman points out that many conditions can produce symptoms that mimic senility, with the result that many older people are falsely labelled senile when their symptoms are due to depression, thyroid gland malfunction, pernicious anemia, effects of routine medication or other varied conditions that can be effectively treated or cured entirely by psychotherapy or drugs.[6] Dr. Eric Pfeiffer, a Duke psychiatrist, sums up the point:

> The most important stereotype regarding the elderly is that a certain amount of emotional instability, forgetfulness, depression and withdrawal is normal and therefore does not warrant medical intervention. On the contrary, early treatment might prevent deterioration or institutionalization, or both.[7]

It is also clear, however, that many older persons *do* find difficulty in adjusting to their changed status in life. One common problem is alcoholism. Although this is not commonly thought of as a disease of the aged, it was reported in the late 1960s that in the previous decade the death rate for alcohol-connected disorders had risen by over 52 per cent for white males between the ages of 60 and 69 and by 114 per cent for white females in the same age group. Similarly, suicide appears to be a special problem of aged persons. Studies of elderly persons have shown that an unusually high proportion of persons over the age of 60 commit suicide; in fact, almost 30 per cent of suicides in the United States are in this age group. The rate of self-inflicted death among white American males over age 65 is three times that at the ages of 20 to 24, and research suggests that many of the fatal "accidents" among the elderly are actually suicides in disguise.

---

[5] Ewald Busse, in "The Old in the Country of the Young." *Time*, August 3, 1970, p. 51.

[6] Lawrence K. Altman: "Senility Is Not Always What It Seems to Be." *New York Times*, May 8, 1977.

[7] Eric Pfeiffer, *cited in* "Can Aging Be Cured?" *Newsweek*, April 16, 1973, p. 57.

Researchers have concluded that many older persons, rather than directly injuring themselves, place themselves in vulnerable or life-threatening situations, which tend to increase the possibility of their demise. It suggests that a significant segment of the older population no longer *wishes* to live and in effect withdraws from previous active roles played in life.

This point of view has been expressed in a theory of adjustment in aging that was formulated in the early 1960s, known as "disengagement" theory.

Disengagement Theory

Cumming and Henry, who developed this theory, perceived aging as an inevitable mutual withdrawal or disengagement by older persons from others in the society. Withdrawal may be initiated on either side, and the aged person may withdraw dramatically from some groups of people while remaining relatively close to others. It

> . . . may be accompanied from the outset by an increased preoccupation with himself; certain institutions in society may make this withdrawal easy for him. When the aging process is complete, the equilibrium which existed in middle life between the individual and his society has given way to a new equilibrium characterized by a greater distance and an altered type of relationship.[8]

In essence, the theory suggests that society should accept the needs of older persons for a "dramatically reduced social life-space" and permit them, in effect, to disengage themselves from meaningful life relationships and move into roles of greater isolation. However, a number of leading sociologists and gerontologists have not been willing to accept this point of view. A Harvard sociologist, Chad Gordon, writes,

> Disengagement theory is a rationalization for the fact that old people haven't a damn thing to do, and nothing to do it with.[9]

The Activity Approach

In contrast, many authorities on aging favor an activity approach that sees successful adjustment as dependent on the ability to find substitutes for the life activities carried on in previous years or to maintain such activities for as long as possible.

Both the "disengagement" and the "activity" approaches to adjustment have been criticized because they fail to take into account the wide individual differences in mode of adjustment and deal with only one aspect of this process. Obviously, people differ in their response to the challenge of aging in terms of their family and marital status, their physical health, their economic status and their psychological well-being, in addition to such other important factors as the

---

[8] Elaine Cumming and William E. Henry: *Growing Old: The Process of Disengagement.* New York, Basic Books, 1961.
[9] Chad Gordon, *In* "The Old in the Country of the Young." p. 54.

availability of leisure opportunities, counseling services, travel, continuing education, political and citizenship activity and similar matters. Indeed, Reichard carried out a study of how retirement affected five different groups of men according to their personality types—the "mature," the "rocking chair," the "armored," the "angry" and the "self-haters."[10] In each category, there was a different response to retirement, with several of the groups adjusting to it with relative ease. It was concluded that an understanding of varied personality types is essential for those who work with the aged, since the method of successful adaptation and role alignment of one group would not necessarily be appropriate for another.

As one example of the falsity of certain stereotypes regarding the aged, one might point to the widely held belief that older persons normally no longer engage in sexual intercourse—and the dependent view that any older person who does is therefore "different." Research carried out at the Center for the Study of Aging and Human Development at Duke University indicated that between 40 and 60 per cent of different groups of subjects between the ages of 60 and 71 years reported that they still engaged in sexual intercourse with some frequency. Additional research has revealed that considerably older persons continue to have sexual relations successfully; such behavior seems to involve a continuation in modified form of earlier life patterns. Indeed, in some regions where large numbers of older retired persons settle, such as Southern Florida, observers have noted that growing numbers of elderly people are having emotionally close, long-term affairs—often to the dismay of their children and grandchildren:

> Rather than marry, many elderly men and women pair off in what one geriatric counselor calls "unmarriages of convenience"—relationships established for companionship and sex but never formalized because, as married couples, they would receive less income from Social Security and other retirement benefits than they do by remaining single.[11]

The basic point is that life does not *stop* when one reaches 65 or 75 years of age. The same needs and interests tend to continue; many of the weaknesses or problems demonstrated by older persons stem from their difficulty in adjusting to social, psychological, economic or physiological change. In order to help the elderly make such adjustments successfully, it is obviously necessary to develop programs and assistance within the following areas:

1. Provision of economic security, an element essential to all other aspects of aging.
2. Health assistance, including both community-based and hospital medical care—readily available and nondemeaning.
3. Practical assistance with housing and maintenance problems—living units for aged persons are today being included in larger, low- or middle-income housing projects, along with plans for assisting older persons who live by themselves in such developments.
4. A sense of importance and contribution to society, to supplant the loss of past work.
5. The opportunity for meaningful social relationships with others.

According to Duke University researchers, the key factor in long and successful aging is remaining active on all three major levels—psychological,

---

[10] Suzanne Reichard et al.: Cited in *Retirement Roles and Activities*. Washington, D.C., Report of 1971 White House Conference on Aging, 1971, pp. 20–21.
[11] "Romance and the Aged." *Time*, June 4, 1973, p. 48.

physical and social. Much depends on the attitudes the individual forms about the prospect of aging during his or her early years:

> Those who lived longest were the ones who refused to give in. If widowed, they usually remarried. If retired, they took up hobbies. They took long walks and watched what they ate. And they took old age in stride. "The decision to have an active mental, physical and social life is really the important decision," says Dr. Eric Pfeiffer. "It's a yea-saying to life."[12]

RECREATION'S ROLE WITH AGED PERSONS

Within this total context, it is obviously important for older people to have a range of interesting and appropriate recreational opportunities available to them, both to fill their long leisure hours and to meet, in a positive way, some of their important personal needs. What exactly are these needs, and what contribution does recreation make to them? They fall into six areas.

IMPROVES PHYSICAL HEALTH

A number of studies have established that recreation of a physical nature makes a significant contribution to the physical condition of the aged, particularly in terms of cardiac function. Moderate and enjoyable exercise frequently means that individuals need not take certain drugs for release of tension, and it helps to prevent unnecessary deterioration of the body and progressive breakdown of the body systems. There is evidence that the satisfaction derived from accomplishment and continued physical activity is linked to human longevity.[13]

Dr. Raymond Harris, a leading cardiologist, summed up the broad values of physical activity for older persons, suggesting that exercise programs should include four basic elements: (1) relaxation; (2) exercise of the endurance type to condition the heart, lungs and circulation; (3) muscle-strengthening exercise; and (4) stretching exercise to improve joint mobility and reduce the aches and pains accompanying the aging process. He writes,

> Proper exercise can delay or at least retard changes associated with age in the musculoskeletal, respiratory, cardiovascular and central nervous systems. Even when these systems have already deteriorated due to lack of physical conditioning or to disease, partial improvement of fitness and other functions may be obtained when properly prescribed and adequately supervised exercise is followed for an extended period of time.[14]

In addition to actual calisthenics or other therapeutic exercise programs, Harris points out that there is considerable value in older persons taking part in such recreational activities as horseshoes, croquet, pool, bowling, hiking, canoeing, fishing and gardening—all of which provide both pleasure and diversion as well as muscle toning, stretching and healthful relaxation and breathing benefits.

---

[12] Eric Pfeiffer: *In* "Can Aging Be Cured?" p. 66.
[13] "Physical, Mental, Social Predictors of Longevity." Report to International Congress of Gerontology, cited in *Geriatric Focus*, October, 1969, p. 1.
[14] Raymond Harris, M.D.: "Leisure Time and Exercise Activities for the Elderly." *In* Timothy Craig (ed.): *The Humanistic and Mental Health Aspects of Sports, Exercise and Recreation*. Chicago, American Medical Association, 1975, p. 100.

In addition to such games and leisure activities, a growing number of older persons today are taking part in more vigorous and active sports. In France, for example, elderly persons in *clubs d'animation* (vitality clubs) are encouraged to take part in a wide variety of physical activities, including exercise classes, hiking, swimming and cross-country skiing. Bowling, bike riding, tennis and jogging are becoming increasingly popular with the elderly. Despite the stereotype that generally assumes that people give up active sports once they reach their 30s, many people in their 60s, 70s and 80s today are playing strenuous games, competing in track and field events and even running the marathon!

In Florida, St. Petersburg's Three-Quarter Century Softball Club is composed of two teams, the Kids and the Kubs, who play each other in three seven-inning games a week from November through March. All players are at least 75 years old, with a number of star outfielders and catchers ranging up into the high 80s and 90s.[15] Another unusual program that has been of special interest to the University of Southern California's Andrus Gerontology Center is the Senior Olympics, in which elderly athletes compete under careful medical supervision in such sports as basketball, boxing, canoeing, the decathlon, diving, fencing, handball, karate, power-lifting, racquetball, rugby, squash, tennis, track and field, water polo and wrestling. Yasgur writes,

> *Men in their 60's who throw a discus well over 100 feet, 55 year old sprinters who crack the 24 second mark for 200 meters, 75 year old men who compete in 16 events over two weekends or win two tennis titles (in 100° heat), and women aged 60 and older who set records in swimming, sprinting, and field events can shame many persons 30 years their junior. Obviously, they must be doing something right.[16]*

Obviously, not all elderly people would be capable of such strenuous activity. Such examples, however, demonstrate that we are far too limited in our vision of what older people can accomplish—and of the benefits to be derived from regular, healthy exercise.

IMPROVES EMOTIONAL WELL-BEING

Meaningful involvement in social, physical and creative recreational activities tends to improve the state of mind of most aged participants. It takes their minds off the preoccupation with themselves, their illnesses and their problems and provides a sense of accomplishment in performance. Generally, it contributes to a positive outlook toward life.

RE-AWAKENS CREATIVE IMPULSES

For many older persons, the recreation programs found in a home for the aged or community-based senior center offer opportunities in the arts, music, theatre or literature that awaken or revive creative impulses not felt for many years. Again, these stimulate intellectual functioning and emotional well-being and encourage a sense of vitality and energy.

---

[15] Dan Levin: "Taking Part is Everything." *Sports Illustrated*, March 4, 1975.
[16] Stevan S. Yasgur: "The Senior Olympics: Games for Adults Who Won't Quit." *Geriatrics*, January, 1975, pp. 120–125.

ENCOURAGES SOCIAL INVOLVEMENT

Obviously, recreation can provide an atmosphere conducive to developing friendships and to overcoming isolation and resulting loneliness. For many older persons who have been widowed or divorced, such programs may even result in friendships between the sexes that develop into marriage. There is a surprisingly large number of such marriages among elderly persons who meet in recreational settings, although match-making is not, of course, their primary purpose.

In institutional as well as community settings, recreation has been shown to have positive value as far as socialization is concerned. In a series of experimental studies carried out in Pennsylvania state hospitals and nursing homes, it was demonstrated that such activities as swimming, arts and crafts, games and other social pastimes had a measurable positive effect on the social interaction patterns of aged mental patients or residents.[17]

PROVIDES MEANINGFUL ROLES

As described earlier, an important need of many older persons is for significant roles in society to supplant job or family responsibilities that have disappeared. For many aged persons, projects undertaken in recreation programs include giving assistance to the homebound or hospitalized, to children needing adult guidance or similar ventures. Sometimes projects involve political campaigning, working in ecology or providing advice to minority group members who are beginning a business and need help from experienced, retired businessmen. The opportunity to contribute to society and to feel of real value to other human beings is of great importance to aged persons.

There are numerous examples of such programs being initiated by public and voluntary agencies, often with federal or state financial assistance. For example, three such programs that have been highly successful in the United States are (a) the Foster Grandparent Program, which pays older people for working with dependent and neglected youngsters; (b) the Retired Senior Volunteer Program (RSVP), which pays expenses to a large number of retired individuals who provide volunteer services in such settings as libraries and hospitals; and (c) the Senior Corps of Retired Executives (SCORE), which reimburses thousands of retired businessmen who assist individuals and community groups in business management.

OFFERS THRESHOLD TO OTHER SERVICES

While recreation offers an important area of experience in itself for older persons, it is also valuable in that it often paves the way for their making use of other vital social services. Frequently, aged persons come initially to a center because of its recreational and social programs. As they become aware of other services, such as health care, legal aid, budget planning or other advisory assistance, they tend to make use of them.

---

[17] See Herbert M. Lundegren (ed.): *Penn State Studies on Recreation and the Aging.* State College, Pennsylvania, Pennsylvania State University, 1974, pp. 61–66, 75–79.

Concrete evidence of the increasing importance that is being given to recreation for the elderly is found in a summation of the application of federal funds under the Administration on Aging grants program for states and municipalities. Out of many millions of dollars spent to assist local programs in a recent typical year, 34 per cent was used to support recreation and leisure time activities, including hundreds of senior center programs—a higher percentage than that granted to any other form of service for older people living in communities.

PROGRAMS PROVIDED FOR AGING PERSONS

Recreation services are provided for aged persons in a variety of institutional and community settings, including the following:

1. Senior Citizen's centers and Golden Age clubs.
2. Special residential centers, such as "leisure villages" or "retirement communities," or special housing projects of residences for the "well aged."
3. Day care programs to serve aged persons who live at home but have serious disabilities that require special supportive services.
4. Programs for the homebound aged person.
5. Geriatric units in hospitals or nursing homes or skilled nursing care facilities that serve the dependent aged person.

The following section includes a description of programs offered in each of these categories. Since only 5 five per cent of aged persons in the United States live in institutions or nursing homes, the greatest number of those who are to be served are in community settings. Typically, such individuals are likely to find a range of leisure opportunities and social contacts in Senior Citizen's centers, Golden Age clubs or similar social programs designed for the elderly.

Senior Centers

These are described by Anderson, who carried out the first nationwide study of such programs, as

> . . . places where older persons come together for a variety of activities and programs, ranging from sitting and talking or playing cards to professionally directed hobby and group activities. Some centers also provide counseling services to help the individual make better use of personal and community resources; some assume responsibility for encouraging community agencies to provide more help to senior citizens.[18]

Senior centers are considered to be agencies that meet for substantial periods of time several days a week, have professional staff direction and offer more than one form of service. Usually, they operate in their own facilities and

---

[18] Nancy N. Anderson: *Senior Centers: Information from a National Survey.* Minneapolis, Minnesota, Institute for Interdisciplinary Studies, American Rehabilitation Foundation, 1969.

may be sponsored by a variety of types of agencies, such as municipal recreation and park departments, housing or welfare agencies or religious federations. In contrast, *Golden Age clubs* are usually thought of as social or recreational clubs for older persons operating under volunteer or nonprofessional leadership and meeting once or twice a week, or even less frequently.

In her study of 1002 senior centers, Anderson found that the average responding agency was reaching one-third of the estimated target population in its community. All agencies provided *recreational programs*; 73 per cent offered other *community services*; and 60 per cent offered *counseling services* as well. Slightly over one-third of all responding senior centers offered all three types of services.

FRANKLIN H. PIERCE CENTER

One example of a senior center may be found in Flint, Michigan, where the Franklin H. Pierce Center provides several hundred older persons with a wide variety of social activities, games, classes, musical activities, physical conditioning and weight-watching programs and special trips and outings. This center was built with funds from the city of Flint and is assisted by the city in its operation. It offers scheduled programs five days a week and also has special activities on weekends. The Flint municipal recreation department operates a Senior Citizens Services Division, which uses the Pierce Center as a headquarters, and other programs throughout the city, including the publication of a special newspaper for senior citizens.

Among the program activities offered in the Pierce Center for Senior Citizens are the following: card games and instruction, craft classes, men's and women's choruses, dancing, golf, shuffleboard, lectures, library services, supper club, bingo, a "Married 50 Years and Over" Club and a special program of recreation for stroke-afflicted persons that seeks to rehabilitate these individuals physically and socially. On a city-wide basis, the Flint Recreation and Park Board provides the following services to aged persons:

1. Publication of the *Senior Citizens News.*
2. Sponsorship of the Genesee County Senior Citizen Orchestra.
3. Publication of news releases for all news media regarding aging and senior citizens' programs.
4. Development of a discount card program, giving reduced rates and prices to older persons.
5. Sponsorship of a bicycle club, ecology club and over 80 club.
6. Planning of one-day bus trips and more extended vacation trips for older persons.
7. Sponsorship of other special events, including city-wide dances, parties, luncheons, tournaments and similar programs for senior citizens.

This center is fairly typical of programs operated by both public and voluntary agencies in communities around the United States.

ATWATER SENIOR CENTER

A second example, the Atwater Senior Center, operated by the New Haven, Connecticut, Department of Parks and Recreation, breaks its programs

Many communities provide recreation for the older citizen. Here, retired persons enjoy a band concert sponsored by the Los Angeles Department of Recreation and Parks, and in Flint, Michigan, Golden Agers belong to a city-sponsored bicycling club. Washington, D.C., senior clubs sponsor an annual hobby show at which members may sell their handicrafts, and the Chicago Park District serves homebound older persons with crafts and other individual activities.

down into several different categories. These include the following:

I. Organized Group Programs
   A. Groups with Definite Enrollments
      1. Interest groups, such as Christmas decorations, oil painting class, sewing, arts and crafts, singing, reading and discussion groups, knitting and cards.
      2. Committee meetings, including those responsible for birthday parties and socials, programs, membership, nominations, public relations, refreshments, telephone services, trip planning and similar functions.
   B. Organized Group Activities without Definite Enrollment
      1. Regularly Scheduled Activities
         a. Events at the Center, such as bingo parties, card parties, community singing, coffee hours, concerts, dancing, films and travelogues, lectures, luncheons, meetings and evening entertainments.
         b. Events away from the Center, such as annual Mass for deceased members of the club, entertainment by members at hospitals and homes in the vicinity or trips to resorts, New York City, Cape Cod, Senior Citizen's conventions, a glaucoma center, boat trips, country fairs, foliage festivals and similar outings.
   C. Special Events
      1. Fund raising, including raffles, rummage sales, food and cake sales and a Christmas bazaar.
      2. Fairs, special performances and holiday parties.

In addition to these services, the Atwater Center provides a substantial number of special services to individuals. These include consultation and referral services with senior citizens, which may include informational meetings or direct consultation, examination or assistance related to such concerns as health (glaucoma and diabetes checkups), visiting nurse services, Social Security advice, Housing Authority assistance and counseling on tax exemptions, food stamps and similar matters.

SEMINARS AND SERVICES

Senior centers *must* offer considerably more than bingo, cards or social dancing if they are to meet the realistic life needs of older persons. Such programs should help to support and improve the lives of older persons, particularly those in large cities who are isolated or dependent. For example, the Los Angeles Parks and Recreation Department sponsors a series of seminars directly related to the needs of older persons on such topics as "consumer protection," "dental care," "fraud schemes" and "housing." These are scheduled at 10 centers specifically designed to meet the needs of older residents and at more than 75 other facilities where programs for senior citizens are part of the overall departmental programs. In addition, Los Angeles sponsors a Senior Citizens' Federation that unites all older people in the metropolitan area in joint efforts to meet their needs in such areas as recreation, health and housing services, legal aid, Social Security, legislation and similar concerns. It sponsors major city-wide events for older persons, many of which attract thousands of aged participants.

Operating in cooperation with the Mayor's Departmental Council on Aging, the Detroit, Michigan, Department of Parks and Recreation provides an extensive program of services for senior citizens. In addition to its own centers, it sponsors several in cooperation with the United Auto Workers, a labor union that has traditionally taken a strong interest both in recreation and in the needs of its retired members. The Detroit Senior Citizens program places strong emphasis on developing leadership among older persons, having them serve as volunteers or paid leaders in programs and encouraging their involvement in public service.

Like Los Angeles, Detroit provides many informational and similar services to older persons; these are related to reduced rates for transportation, food, housing, library service, special resident camping for senior citizens, golf, fishing and other special programs available at limited cost.

In numerous other cities throughout the country, recreation and park departments are providing services for elderly and retired persons, operating chiefly through senior centers and Golden Age clubs. In many cases, as in New Haven, Cleveland and Milwaukee, the club members themselves assume a great deal of responsibility for planning and carrying on programs and for providing volunteer leadership to help homebound elderly persons.

An important element to program services provided by Senior Citizens Centers was added in the mid-1970s when the federal government began to provide funding of over $125 million a year to support nutrition programs. Offered under federal and state guidelines and the direct supervision of county or city agencies, this plan permitted centers of all types to provide low-cost or free meals daily to older persons who might otherwise have been able to meet their nutritional needs adequately.

How effective are such programs in meeting the needs of retired people in the community at large? It seems clear that they are providing a valuable service but that far too few older persons are being served by them. For example, in 1970, the Federal Administration on Aging assembled a directory of 1200 senior centers throughout the entire nation. If one were to estimate the average regular attendance of such centers, it would probably not be more than 100 or 150 members, although larger numbers of retired persons are registered and may attend special events. Thus, it seems probable that not more than 180,000 older persons (less than 1 per cent of all persons over 65 in the United States) are regularly served by senior centers.

In view of the extremely limited budgets of most senior centers and the fact that only about one-third of them have full-time directors, it seems clear that vigorous steps need to be taken to strengthen the Senior Center and Golden Age club movement. The very fact that there are many excellent centers, like those described in this chapter, supports the need to initiate many more such programs.

Special Residential Centers

Another important aspect of recreation service for the elderly may be found in special residential centers that serve older people in our society. They are of several different types: (a) "retirement communities" or "leisure villages"; (b) special apartments or units in housing projects that are set aside for the elderly; (c) adult homes or residential facilities that provide full care, including meals and activities for the well aged; and (d) new communal arrangements of older persons living in groups independently, with some supportive services.

RETIREMENT COMMUNITIES

In contrast to the typical image of older persons as individuals who are suffering from physical impairment or severe economic deprivation, many elderly persons are in relatively good health and are financially capable of independent living. Large numbers of such individuals have chosen in recent years to live in retirement villages or communities established specifically to attract older persons.

This concept, which began on the West Coast, has since gained popularity throughout the United States. Generally, it consists of homes or garden apartment developments that have been specially designed for maximum convenience and safety. Only persons beyond a certain age are normally eligible to enter such communities. They may do so by purchase of property, on a rental basis, through a condominium or cooperative arrangement or a variety of other financial procedures. Since they may be extremely expensive, they tend to appeal chiefly to elderly couples who are financially independent.

Although they vary considerably, in many leisure villages, medical and other services are made readily available as part of group plans. In some, meals are served in dining buildings as part of the overall plan; properties are maintained by central services, and housekeeping services may also be provided. Because of the convenience they offer, as well as the safety (most villages have elaborate security, and some are actually walled villages), retirement communities have become extremely attractive to many retired persons. Davies writes,

> By the tens of thousands they are flocking to new retirement homes, often leaving behind the clamor of cities, frequently moving to warmer climates for community living in villages and high-rise facilities tailored to their particular tastes. They are looking for people of similar ages and interests, for convenience, for peace and security and sometimes for a less expensive existence.[19]

Some of the best known retirement communities include Rossmoor-Walnut Creek in California, Heritage Village in Connecticut and Sun City, Arizona, probably the largest of its kind with over 28,000 residents in the late 1970s and the expectation of expanding to 50,000 homeowners within several years. Sun City has six shopping centers, nine golf courses and five recreation centers (one containing Arizona's largest indoor swimming pool), as well as an amphitheater, a stadium, two lakes and the country's first synthetic-surface lawn bowling green. Typically, all retirement communities place great stress on offering a wide variety of recreational facilities, hobbies, clubs and programs— both to attract new residents and to meet the needs of all interest groups and levels of capability. Rossmoor, for example, has over 160 different clubs, as well as service groups that carry out philanthropic activities, and professional associations of former teachers or engineers.

> These clubs help to integrate newcomers into the community. They also help structure people's time, giving them someplace to be or something to do at fixed hours and days. This can be particularly useful for men accustomed to going to an office, but it is also a boon for their wives. . . . Not only does it get the men out of their way, but it also helps preserve the distinction between male and female

---

[19] Lawrence E. Davies: "The Retirement Village—A New Life Style." *New York Times*, January 18, 1970, p. 1.

roles, which often gets blurred with retirement. A surprisingly large number of Rossmoor's clubs are designated as being for men only or for women only.[20]

Increasingly, retirement communities are employing social or recreation directors to conduct these programs, and usually a members' council serves in making policy and helping to carry out or schedule activities.

SPECIAL HOUSING UNITS FOR
THE ELDERLY

A somewhat different form of residential development for older persons is found in apartment buildings or other special housing units for the elderly. Unlike retirement villages, which are usually in suburban or rural areas with many separate housing units over a large tract of land, these developments may involve a single high-rise apartment building or converted hotel or possibly garden apartments that are specially designated for older persons. In some cases, they may involve a proportion of small apartments within a publicly assisted low-income or middle-income housing development that are set aside by pre-arrangement for senior citizens only. In such developments also, there are usually clubs and hobby activities and in some cases a senior center as part of the entire structure—although the recreation facilities are much less impressive than in retirement communities.

RESIDENTIAL FACILITIES FOR THE
SEMI-DEPENDENT AGED

In some cases, three or four different kinds of living arrangements may be provided within a large complex, including nursing home facilities for the ill and dependent aged, assisted but separate housing for the semi-dependent and relatively independent units for the well aged. In each case, recreation programs are likely to be provided at an appropriate level of skill and variety. As a later section will show, recreation activities in facilities serving residents with a serious degree of disability are necessarily more limited in content and more therapeutically designed than those serving the independent and capable individuals.

In some cases, special housing units for the elderly have been set up in which they live in a congregate, or "commune," environment and share skills and abilities to help maintain each other. Based on similar programs in England and Sweden, such living units require strong help from an outside agency. Typically, the Weinfeld Group Living Residence, a renovated townhouse complex in Evanston, Illinois, has 11 women residents, some of whom had formerly been in nursing homes or psychiatric hospitals. With each others' help and with services from a cook, caseworker, activities therapist and other aides provided by the Council for Jewish Elderly, these elderly women are able to carry on successfully in the community setting. It costs $500 a month to live at Weinfeld, considerably less than nursing home or hospital costs. Such arrangements provide a sensible and humane living environment for older people who would otherwise have to be institutionalized.

---

[20] Sheila K. Johnson: "Growing Old Alone Together." *New York Times Magazine*, November 11, 1973, p. 40.

Day Care Services for Disabled Aged in
the Community

As a variant of the above, a number of community centers or health complexes throughout the United States have established center programs providing vital medical, nutritional, social and activity programs that permit elderly disabled persons to live at home, rather than be forced to go into nursing homes or hospitals. For example, one such program, held at the Mosholu-Montefiore Community Center in New York, serves approximately 85 patients with a mixture of medical and social services, including transportation, meals, art, music and occupational therapy, physical examinations and health counseling, escorting patients to medical appointments and nursing care. Recreation is a significant part of the overall program, with a full-time recreation therapist serving as part of the interdisciplinary team. Beckerman describes the role of the recreational program:

> It consists of movies, current events discussion, trips, art, music and other activities. Participation in recreation is voluntary, with greatest involvement in arts and crafts. The overall purpose of the recreation therapy program is the opportunity for self-expression, physical exercise, and socializing. Through recreation, patients learn and sometimes relearn skills which they can utilize in their own home. Activities permit functioning at various levels of concentration, intensity and skill. Interaction between patients and group experiences create a familiar, safe environment. Over time, groups of patients begin to form their own communication network, encouraging dyad and triad for formally isolated patients.[21]

Like other programs described, such programs permit individuals to continue to live in the community at considerably lesser cost and with much greater life satisfaction than if they had to be placed in nursing home or hospital care geriatric units. In some cases, supplementary services such as podiatry, dentistry, ophthalmology and other specialist or rehabilitative services may be provided, along with social services and more intensive counseling. When linked with hospitals as a form of out-patient program, it is possible to move patients directly into short-term residential treatment and then back into independent living units again when they are able to function more independently.

Services for Homebound Elderly

A growing number of agencies have also developed outreach services that assist elderly persons who have severe impairments and cannot readily leave their homes. These include health-aide or nursing care, friendly visiting, shopping and cooking help, telephone reassurance and similar services. In many cases, elderly persons who are mobile themselves assist by visiting the homebound regularly, either on a volunteer basis or as part of a specially funded program under the Older Americans Act. Such assistance does much to overcome the physical and psychological isolation of homebound elderly persons and to make their lives more comfortable and happy. Recreation may be provided on a one-to-one basis, with outside visitors bringing in hobby activities, teaching skills or

---

[21] Sheba Beckerman: "Geriatric Day Care Center." Graduate paper at Herbert Lehman College, New York, 1975.

helping the homebound persons use their leisure more creatively and enjoyably than before.

Summing up such alternative kinds of community living arrangements for the elderly, *Newsweek* reported in 1977 that

> One of the most impressive community-service programs is the Older American Resources and Services program (OARS) at the Duke University Center. Aside from providing legal, medical and at-home nursing care, OARS arranges for "chore workers" who cook and do odd jobs in the house, "meals on wheels" to provide shut-ins with home-delivered meals, and a volunteer corps of drivers who take the disabled on trips. "We try to come up with a service package to allow each person to stay in the community," says director Dan G. Blazer. In Massachusetts, officials of the Department of Elderly Affairs are experimenting with a variety of alternative-living arrangements. Instead of purely social Golden Age Centers, they have established eight day-care centers and are experimenting with boarding houses and communes, where small groups of residents can care for each other, and an "adoption center," through which old people can live with young families.[22]

Although the overall number of such experimental arrangements is small, they offer much hope for preventing the avoidable institutionalization of hundreds of thousands of elderly persons. Today, however, the most widespread method of caring for elderly, disabled individuals who cannot, for physical or psychological reasons, care for themselves in the community is admission to nursing homes or geriatric units in hospitals.

Institutional Programs for the Elderly

Today, there are approximately 23,000 nursing homes in the United States, in addition to thousands of special geriatric or chronic care units in hospitals—some of them in state psychiatric hospitals for the disoriented or senile patient. Nursing homes are of all types, operated by public authorities, voluntary organizations and proprietary owners, many who rushed into this field when the federal government began to pay for nursing home care through Medicaid; by the mid-1970s, $4.4 billion of Medicaid's overall $12.7 budget was spent on the elderly. Monthly charges for elderly and chronically infirm patients ranged from $1200 to $1800 a month by the mid-1970s, with many unscrupulous operators providing seriously substandard services and facilities. Mary Adelaide Mendelson of Cleveland, a community-planning consultant who spent 10 years studying institutions for the aged, concluded that U.S. nursing homes were a national scandal and wrote a book titled *Tender Loving Greed*:

> There is a widespread neglect of patients in nursing homes across the country and evidence that owners are making excessive profits at the expenses of patients.[23]

To prevent such exploitation, a number of state departments of hospitals or health have developed strong nursing home codes and accreditation and inspection procedures. It is within such codes that the strongest support of

[22] "The Graying of America," p. 57.
[23] Mary Adelaide Mendelson, *In* "New Outlook for the Aged." p. 46.

recreation as a vital service for the institutionalized aged is found. For example, in the state of Connecticut, the State Department of Health has established the following code for approval of nursing homes:

Standards for Certification
of
Therapeutic Recreation Program
by
Connecticut State Department of Health

I. PHYSICAL REQUIREMENTS
   A. There shall be adequate space to accommodate recreation program in the form of recreation rooms and/or day spaces.
   B. There shall be separate facilities for administration of program, and for storage of supplies and equipment.
II. ADMINISTRATION
   A. There shall be a professional recreation director or a person having equivalent experience and training, who shall direct and supervise the recreation program in the institution. This program director shall be approved by the State Department of Health. Upon approval, two weeks' in-service training is required, and will be arranged by the State Department of Health.
   B. The program director will be other than a regular employee of the institutional staff, and will wear street dress.
   C. The program director will be required to work the number of hours per week as determined by the licensed capacity of the institution as follows:

5–14 beds	10 hours per week (at least 3 days)
15–29 beds	20 hours per week (5 days)
30–59 beds	30 hours per week (5 days)
60–120 beds	40 hours per week (5 days)

   For *each* additional 60 beds or fraction thereof, 40 hours per week is required.
   D. The program director shall generally work Monday through Friday, except for special program events on holidays and weekends or evenings. Work schedule shall be filed with the State Department of Health.
   E. The State Department of Health shall be notified immediately when any change in program director occurs.
III. RECORDS
   A. Monthly reports shall be submitted *by the 10th of each month* to the State Department of Health and shall include:
      1. Advanced Monthly Program Calendar
      2. Current month's Patient Participation Record
      3. Budget breakdown on program costs.
   B. Four additional records shall be kept on file at the facility:
      1. Patient Interest and Progress Record
      2. Volunteer Interview Record
      3. Volunteer Sign In Record
      4. Clergy Sign In Record
IV. PROGRAM REQUIREMENT
   A. The program shall be planned from *individual patient/resident needs and interests.*
   B. Activities shall be regularly scheduled and planned monthly in advance.
   C. There shall be diversified group and individual activities to include *per week*:
      1. *Art or Craft Program*
         a. Individual art or crafts for patient/resident at bedside where indicated.
      2. *Games* such as bingo, horse racing, bowling, and shuffleboard.
         a. Participation should be encouraged in special interest or small group games such as cards, checkers, chess and dominoes.
      3. *Cultural Activity*—music, literature, drama, adult education.
         a. Individual interest to be pursued and encouraged.

4. *Religious Assembly*—conducted by clergy and/or volunteers.
   a. Individual pastoral and lay visits should be encouraged.
5. *Personal Services*—to include letter writing, reading to, library service and patient/resident visitation.
D. At least two of the following activities shall be scheduled per month:
   1. Film
   2. Birthday Party
   3. Entertainment program
   4. Special event such as holiday party, picnic, bus trip, or carnival.
E. Special Interest or small hobby group activities shall be provided.
F. The program shall be evaluated and revitalized periodically with new ideas and/or adaptation of standard activities.
G. Work activity, community service, out trips, group discussions, current events, story telling, puppets, marionettes, skits, variety shows, and fashions, as well as hobbies should be incorporated in general programming when interest and capabilities so indicate.
H. Effort should be focused to secure volunteer assistance for all programs and especially for personal patient/resident contact as friend to friend.
   1. Interviewing, screening and orientation of volunteers is necessary.
   2. Supervision, evaluation, and coordination of volunteer efforts is required, with staff as well as with general program.
   3. Recognition of volunteer assistance should be encouraged by administrator and staff of facility.
V. GENERAL INFORMATION
A. Renewal of certification will occur yearly from date of initial accreditation.
B. Approval may be withdrawn by the State Department of Health at any time should the institution fail to meet the requirements outlined in the above specifications.
C. Approval will be automatically revoked within 30 days after the resignation of a program director. Re-certification must be made in the name of program director replacement.
D. Special seminars for program directors will be offered periodically by the State Department of Health, which program directors shall attend.
E. Program Directors should avail themselves of continuing training and educational opportunities through professional organizations and educational institutions.

Recreation Programs in Nursing Homes

Despite the negative publicity that has been disseminated about nursing homes, there are many excellent ones throughout the United States and Canada that live up to such guidelines for recreation and go far beyond them. On the other hand, there are also numerous states and localities that provide minimal services under unskilled direction.

As an example of the limited extent to which many extended-care facilities provide recreation, a study of nursing homes in the state of Kentucky was reported in 1970. One hundred and nine institutions licensed by the State Department of Health were surveyed. Of these, 47 replied and only 24 indicated that they had an organized recreation program for residents. In *no* case was a qualified recreation director or therapist responsible for programs, and in only four settings did respondents feel that the recreation activities provided for residents were adequate to meet their needs.[24]

What *are* the elements of effective recreation programming in nursing homes?

---

[24] Martha Peters and Peter J. Verhoven: "A Study of Therapeutic Recreation Services in Kentucky Nursing Homes." *Therapeutic Recreation Journal*, 4th Quarter, 1970, pp. 19–22.

SUITABLE ACTIVITIES

Since many residents are bedridden, confined to wheelchairs or otherwise limited physically, it is necessary to avoid physical activity of a strenuous nature. However, it certainly is possible to provide games that require a moderate amount of activity for those residents who are able to take part. Similarly, although many older persons in extended-care facilities may have limited mental capabilities, others are perfectly capable of enjoying activities that require verbal or intellectual participation.

In general, activities fall into the following classifications:

1. *Arts and crafts*—particularly activities such as knitting, needle-point, crocheting or similar crafts that do not require elaborate shops or complicated equipment.
2. *Music*—both as a participating activity (group singing, rhythm instruments or small ensembles) and as a form of entertainment.
3. *Dramatics*—in the form of skits, recitations, pantomimes or creative dramatic programs.
4. *Dance*—with social, folk and square dancing involving those residents who are physically able to take part, and with simple rhythmic movement involving even patients in beds or wheelchairs.
5. *Religious services*—including Bible readings, hymn singing, meditation or rosary programs or more formal worship services. Volunteer groups frequently come from the community to assist in such activities and then extend their involvement to include personal visiting and other recreational activities.
6. *Films*—may include travelogues or popular movies shown to all residents or home movies or slides of residents' families, which may be viewed individually in their bedrooms or dayrooms.
7. *Other activities*—include special interest groups such as *hobbies* (gardening, cooking, scrap book collections or photography), *social programs* (such as parties, bingo, birthday events or discussion groups), *games* (adapted bowling, golf, shuffleboard, horse racing and toss games) and *trips and outings*.

Programs should be geared to serve the needs of patients who are bedridden or limited in mobility as well as those who can get around easily. Services such as beauty parlor or other self-care or personal activities must be brought to those residents who are confined to their rooms. Even if a resident can benefit from no other activity than friendly visiting and conversation, it is important that this be provided. Often, patients who have few interests and who resist involvement at the outset, gradually begin to participate more fully.

Whenever possible, programs should give elderly patients the opportunity to take on meaningful responsibilities or provide needed services themselves. Residents of the A. Holly Patterson Home for the Aged in Uniondale, New York, for example, spend many hours stuffing envelopes for UNICEF, the March of Dimes and similar charitable or public service organizations and drives. Patients serve on a residents' council and on committees that help to greet new admissions and help to counsel them when they are having difficulty in making the transition. In many other ways, they assume meaningful responsibilities in the institution.

It must be recognized that recreation in the nursing home or skilled nursing care facility is more than simply an amenity or frill. Just as in the outside world, if stimulating and interesting activity is not provided for the patient who is confined to a bed, wheelchair or day room, boredom, lethargy and low morale will inevitably result. Thus, vital and absorbing recreation is essential to maintain alertness and interest and, indeed, to reverse a patient's isolation and withdrawal. In a study titled "Effects of an Individualized Activity Program on

Elderly Patients," Salter and Salter point out that elderly patients suffering from psychological disorders and long-term physical illness are often considered to be in an irreversible state of decline. On the other hand, they describe an individualized program of activity applied to 21 such patients and including reality orientation, activities of daily living and recreational activities, such as games, arts and crafts, singing, social programs and outdoor activity. The researchers reported that

> Those with the motivation to participate in the available activities increased from 14 per cent to 76 per cent in just four months. Many who had not cared for their daily necessities, walked, or talked in years came to do so once more, some to the extent that they could leave the hospital.[25]

They concluded that such approaches should be used much more widely in geriatric institutions. A leading nursing home administrator, Dulcy Miller has agreed that recreation in a nursing home implies far more than just spending leisure time enjoyably; instead, it is part of a total concept of patient care:

> Social rehabilitation of patients in a nursing home setting is effected through a treatment program that includes medicine, nursing, physical therapy, religion, occupational therapy, social work services and recreation. With optimal patient function the goal of the long-term care facility, recreation plays a particularly important part in the totality of professional disciplines. Consequently, the administration of a progressive nursing home is committed to the encouragement and development of the imaginative recreation service.[26]

Within such a setting, the recreation director must work closely with those in the other rehabilitative disciplines, as well as the director of volunteers. This policy is in keeping with the position of the American Hospital Association, which "encourages the active . . . use of volunteers in all long-term care facilities, provided that in proprietary institutions the volunteer's services are those that clearly benefit patients and do not serve to add to the institution's profits."[27]

Miller points out that therapeutic and diversional programs must be planned in terms of various levels of patient capability. Such activities as music, reading, gardening, crafts or games may be used individually or on a group basis, in order to help integrate individual patients into the overall community of patients. In addition, programs for the entire patient population, such as religious services or celebrations, music or dance performances or other entertainment events may provide colorful highlights for all residents.

Patients with organic brain damage may enjoy simple, rhythmical musical activities, simple crafts or repetitive exercises, parties or similar events. On the other hand, those patients who may have suffered physical impairment but whose brain function is sound will enjoy more sophisticated programming, including discussion groups, art and music appreciation, more complicated games and entertainment on a higher level.

Recreation personnel in nursing homes frequently complain that the service they provide is not understood, or supported, by other members of the

---

[25] Carlotta de Lerma Salter and Charles A. Salter: "Effects of an Individualized Activity Program on Elderly Patients." *The Gerontologist*, October, 1975.
[26] Dulcy B. Miller: "Nursing Home Setting." *Parks and Recreation*, January, 1967, p. 38.
[27] *Ibid.*, p. 39.

In Mt. Vernon, New York, senior citizens of all races enjoy varied social events; elderly residents of the A. Holly Patterson Home in Nassau County, New, York, take part in arts and crafts and community-service activities, such as volunteer mailing projects.

staff. Therefore, Miller suggests that the administrator should assist the recreation personnel in maintaining satisfactory intra-staff relationships:

> ... by interpreting the recreation program to other departments, seeking co-
> operation of the nursing and housekeeping departments as to scheduling to
> provide ample time for activity programs and by lending the weight of her position
> to experimental projects. The administrator also assists the staff in organization
> of written material of an administrative nature, e.g., development of manual and
> resources file.[28]

Activities must be scheduled at hours of greatest leisure and must avoid
conflict with nursing care or medical treatment. It is usually possible to provide
some individualized programs in the morning, but afternoons usually offer the
largest segment of completely free time; therefore, most group activities are
scheduled after lunch. In some homes, with supper over early, individual activities or special events may also be planned for the early evening hours. As much
as possible, patients should be involved in planning, both in terms of choosing
desirable activities for the program and in actually carrying out parties and other
special events. Many of the special techniques described in Chapter 4, such as
sensory training and remotivation, may also be provided as part of the activity
program. In some nursing homes, libraries operated by residents meet the leisure
needs of more alert patients and provide an area in which they can offer volunteer
help. Daily newspapers and current magazines, including publications in special
large print editions, help residents keep in touch with the outside world.
Speakers, films, slide showings, visits by outside groups and trips to places of
interest in the outside community, including shopping by residents who are able
to travel independently, all help to maintain contact with the outside.

Just as in other areas of disability, aged persons in institutions have
traditionally been given little voice in deciding issues affecting their own lives
and have often been treated as children. Today, there is a fuller effort to involve
them meaningfully in policy-making and to give them a greater degree of freedom
in determining their own behavior. It was pointed out earlier in this chapter
that aged persons often are capable of maintaining sexual relationships, contrary
to widespread stereotypic thinking. This has led to a serious policy question regarding the right of older persons in nursing homes to maintain sexual relationships. Recently a federally funded workshop for nursing home operators in
Arkansas, conducted by the National Association of Social Workers and funded
by the Department of Health, Education and Welfare, considered a proposal for
providing "privacy rooms" in which aged persons could hold hands, pet or engage
in sexual relations. The proposal was presented by a sociology professor at
Henderson State University, who contended that segregation of the sexes and
lack of privacy in institutions for older persons afford almost no opportunity
for physical or emotional contact:

> I am not advocating copies of Hustler magazine and a water bed, but these people
> are human beings. They enjoy petting, holding hands, kissing. All those things
> that make us feel good make them feel good, too. Age has nothing to do with the
> fact that you need nurture and comfort.[29]

---

[28] *Ibid.,* p. 54.
[29] "Sex for Aged Issue in Arkansas." *New York Times,* March 13, 1977, p. 26.

The proposal was almost universally opposed by the nursing home operators, arguing that patients might "abuse" privacy rooms. In the brochure of at least one home for the elderly, however, the policy is established that roommates of the opposite sex are not "frowned upon"; one's choice of a companion is the individual's decision, not the home's. Clearly, this is part of a larger trend toward treating the disabled as normal people, with normal desires and rights. As an earlier chapter showed, groups with physical disability today are also being given fuller rights and assistance in establishing appropriate sex roles and living patterns for themselves.

Given the tremendous variety in services for the aged in nursing homes, health-related facilities, proprietary homes and community-based services or centers, it would appear that there is a growing need for government to expand its role on all levels if the needs of aged persons in modern society are to be met more adequately. What *are* the major functions of government with respect to aging persons, at present?

ROLE OF THE FEDERAL GOVERNMENT IN AGING

The federal government has provided varied forms of help for older persons in the United States for several decades. Since 1935, when Social Security was established, it has provided retirement income for a large number of elderly persons. The Medicare and Medicaid programs greatly relieve the burden of medical costs for the aged by helping to pay hospital bills, bills for stays in extended-care facilities and medical bills for those who live at home. In addition, it has set standards for the care received in various types of facilities licensed to serve the aged. A second major contribution has been the passage of the Older Americans Act of 1965:

> The act is designed to develop needed services, opportunities and facilities for older persons by: 1) establishing an Administration on Aging in the Department of Health, Education and Welfare, to serve as the Federal focal point and clearing house of information on all matters of concern to older Americans; 2) providing grants to the States to develop services for older persons; and 3) providing grants to public and private agencies for demonstration, research, and training. Titles III, IV and V provide grants for planning, service and training programs. The Title III grants are made directly to State agencies on aging which, in turn, provide funds to public and private non-profit organizations to operate approved programs.[30]

As indicated earlier, many of the programs initiated by this program have had recreational elements. In some cases, they have given support to community services for aged persons, particularly senior centers and multiservice programs. In others, such as the Foster Grandparents Program, initiated by the Administration on Aging and supported at the outset by the Office of Economic Opportunity, older persons have been paid to work full- or part-time with disadvantaged children. In other programs, such as employment projects, funded

---

[30] *The Older Americans Act in New York State: A Progress Report.* Albany, New York, New York State Office for the Aging, 1967.

by the United States Department of Labor, older persons have been placed in jobs as community aides—many with recreation responsibilities.

Under Title IV of the Older Americans Act, many research programs and demonstration projects have been funded. These have tended to focus heavily on the process of successful aging and the kinds of community services required to promote healthy adjustment in later life. The goals of such projects have been described by the Social Rehabilitative Service of the Administration on Aging in the following terms:

> Each project focuses on the older American and a specific factor which contributes to his living a wholesome, meaningful and satisfying life—as free as possible from fear, loneliness, and undue disappointment. The need for differentiating the problems of various sub-groups of older persons and of tailoring solutions to the needs and resources of the community and of the particular persons to be served are also recognized in the projects funded under Title IV.[31]

It must be recognized, however, that the federal government in the United States has been far less active in helping the elderly than many European countries. In the Scandinavian countries, for example, city governments, with assistance from the national government, run housing developments where the aged can live close to transportation and recreational activities and provide a much fuller range of subsidized housing, transportation and day-help service. Beyond this, however, the federal government, alone or in cooperation with the states, should take stronger measures in such areas as nursing home care and (a) establish and enforce more meaningful standards; (b) apply higher qualifications for administrators and personnel on all levels; and (c) consolidate the present overlapping functions of different government agencies to provide more effective services for the aged, in and out of institutions.

STATE PROGRAMS FOR THE ELDERLY

An important section of the Older Americans Act was Title III, which authorized allotments to states for the purpose of supporting programs to serve the elderly. In order to receive grants, it was required that states organize statewide agencies and develop plans for serving the aged, which would be approved by the Secretary of Health, Education and Welfare.

Although this overall program has thus met the needs of only a small fraction of aged persons, it has obviously been a move in the right direction. With its assistance, a number of states have moved ahead aggressively to provide recreation programs and services for the elderly. Among these have been Michigan and Connecticut.

MICHIGAN

The state government of Michigan has organized a special Commission on Aging to coordinate the issuance of funds from Title III. This Commission has sponsored a Michigan White House Conference on Aging that has sought

---

[31] *Aging.* Washington, D.C., Social Rehabilitation Service of Administration on Aging, U.S. Department of Health, Education and Welfare, January, 1969, p. 6.

new solutions to the problems of the state's 762,000 elderly citizens and has also formulated recommendations for federal aid to the elderly. The state's attitude is reflected in the statement of Governor William Milliken, made to the 1971 Conference on Aging:

> *In this youth-oriented culture of ours, we have sent too many of our older citizens to a kind of early death—a quiet limbo where they will live out their remaining years without becoming a burden to our pocketbooks or our consciences.*[32]

Michigan provides aid to communities in establishing low-cost housing and developing community centers for the aged. Such centers customarily provide a wide range of services, including free community education at local schools (several Michigan school districts are leaders in the field of school-sponsored adult education and recreation); telephone calls, visitations and similar services for elderly shut-ins; counseling; trips; and other varied social activities. The state provides funding to the Institute of Gerontology at the University of Michigan and to Wayne State University to conduct research or hold workshops on problems of the aged.

Large numbers of senior citizens in Michigan have become actively organized in promoting services to meet their own needs. The level of participation in center-sponsored social and recreation programs, some of which are assisted by the Michigan Recreation and Parks Association, is high. A newspaper for the aged published in Flint, Michigan, boasts,

> *Not many communities in the United States can say they have senior citizens who are bowling, swimming, iceskating, hiking, golfing, and riding bicycles after they have reached their 75th birthdays. Flint can.*[33]

CONNECTICUT

For a number of years, this state has been a leader in recognizing the importance of recreation in programs for the aged. In 1960, with the support of funds from the Public Health Service of the United States, the Connecticut State Department of Health employed a recreational consultant to supervise the organization of recreation programs in institutions, hospitals and nursing homes. This consultant, Dorothy Mullen, has accomplished a number of major objectives, among them having the State Department of Health establish standards of physical, program and staffing requirements for institutions serving the chronically ill and aged.

Under Mullen's leadership, the state has also provided a variety of consultative services to improve patients' activities programs. Each year, several meetings of the Program Directors' Association are held, and training centers have been established at which recreation workers receive two weeks of intensive training in this field. Connecticut has also placed emphasis on the use of skilled volunteers and has established a yearly conference that serves both to recognize the important contribution made by volunteers and to provide them with needed skills training.

---

[32] "Report of 1971 Michigan Conference on Aging."
[33] Gertrude Cross: *Senior Citizens News.* Flint, Michigan, Department of Recreation and Parks, 1971.

In some states, considerable assistance is given to nursing homes, senior centers or other specialized programs through state departments of health and social services. Typically, the state of Wisconsin publishes a bimonthly newsletter, "The Oldster," for facilities caring for the aged and infirm that includes guidelines, reports of outstanding programs, research findings and similar helpful materials.

Such efforts on the part of the states are generally reflected in programs in major cities within them. For example, the New Haven Department of Parks and Recreation has assumed a major responsibility for providing programs for the elderly. Its programs include a number of senior centers and a "Mobile Workers Outreach Program" (which assists elderly persons in a number of low-income housing units), a "Meals on Wheels" program, a "friendly visiting" program, an Annual Senior Clubs Council Hobby Show and Fairs and many similar activities.

New Haven is the center of many statewide meetings on the aged and of special conferences of the Connecticut Council of Senior Citizens. Overall, it has tackled many aspects of the aging problem and has used a number of approaches, ranging from direct service to legislation and research in retirement preparation to improve programs for the aged.

Within its centers, New Haven offers religious services, crafts, health counseling and community services, lectures, trips and various other recreational activities to meet leisure needs. It publishes a periodical, *Senior Citizens News*, and has promoted the need for courses in gerontology, seminars, workshops and in-service training programs at nearby community colleges. Overall, its program represents one of the most comprehensive municipal efforts to serve the aged in the country.

In many other states and cities, innovative programming for the aged is being carried on. Two elements thus far have not been sufficiently developed to insure fully adequate services, however. These are: (a) a full understanding of the dynamics of aging and the kinds of services and pre-retirement preparation needed to insure the most healthy and happy kinds of adjustment to old age and (b) strong public concern that will support programs designed to meet the needs of aged persons and make it possible for them to find new roles in retirement.

RESEARCH ON AGING

A considerable portion of the research that has been carried on with respect to aging has dealt with the problems of geriatric patients in institutional settings—in part because hospitals and extended-care facilities provide subjects and controlled environments for scientific investigation and in part because funding has been made available for research on this level.

The trend of such research has been to show that much of the deterioration of older persons is not organic in nature but results from the circumstances under which they live.

Woodrow Morris, Director of the Institute of Gerontology and Dean of the College of Medicine at the University of Iowa, has concluded on the basis of a number of studies that senility is not inevitable but represents for many a "cultural artifact." Morris emphasizes the importance of economic, social and intrapersonal stresses that lead to insecurity, confusion and strong feelings of rejection and isolation. These, and not organic brain damage, are the real causes of the radical deterioration of many aged persons, in his view.[34]

It has been found, in a number of experimental projects, that "confused, deteriorated and withdrawn" geriatric patients have made dramatic improvements as a result of recreation programs geared to promoting social interaction. As simple a remedy as "beer and tender loving care," applied in a conscious program of recreation and social activity, has made remarkable changes in the life situation of badly deteriorated patients. Their self-awareness, general ability to function and cooperation with hospital staff have all been markedly improved in such programs. In many cases, the development of such programs has made it no longer necessary to prescribe drugs to geriatric patients.

Obviously, such research findings have important implications for the administrators of extended care facilities. Lissitz writes,

> The senile comprise about 60 percent of all residents and patients in nursing homes, homes for the aged, and geriatric hospitals. Requiring special supervision, care, stimulation and motivation, they represent a serious challenge to the capacity of extended care facilities.[35]

If, as these investigations suggest, social activities and carefully planned remotivation programs are able to improve the status and functioning of senile patients, they are worthy of much fuller use as part of the practical treatment of institutional geriatric mental patients.

There also is a significant need to examine systematically the role of recreation and leisure within the entire process of aging and to study its effects, as well as the motivations of the elderly for taking part in various leisure activities. McAvoy cites research by Neugarten, Havighurst and Tobin concerning life satisfaction and social interactions of the elderly, as well as other recent studies leading to the following findings:

> Individual studies . . . have concentrated on different aspects of successful aging and activities. These studies found that participation in social activities, and in leisure activities in general, is related to life satisfaction and the process of successfully aging. In a specific look at the motivations which prompted a sample of 540 elderly persons to engage in recreation activities, one study found that socializing was the most important motivation. This was followed by self-fulfillment, feeling close to nature, physical exercise, and learning, in that order.[36]

Preparation for Retirement

Some researchers have pointed out that the very fact of free time poses a major challenge of adjustment to retired older persons. Pfeiffer and Davis, of Duke University, have concluded that, because of the strong work orientation in American society, a great number of older persons find extreme difficulty in accustoming themselves to the constructive, creative and guiltless use of the

---

[34] Woodrow Morris: *In* "Senile Psychoses Termed 'Cultural Artifact.'" *Geriatric Focus,* May, 1967, pp. 1, 3, 5.

[35] Samuel Lissitz: In *Geriatric Focus,* February, 1967, pp. 1, 5.

[36] Leo A. McAvoy: "Needs of the Elderly: An Overview of the Research." *Parks and Recreation,* March, 1977, p. 33.

leisure that usually accompanies aging. They conclude,

In order to avoid serious dissatisfaction, our society must provide either more
training for leisure in middle age, or more opportunity for continued employment
in old age.[37]

Thompson found that among 1589 men more than 65 years old, those who
were employed had significantly higher morale than those who were retired. He
also concluded from the data that those who had accepted their retirement positively tended to regard leisure values as comparable to work values.[38]

Increasingly, universities and major industries are devoting themselves
to the problem of preparing older persons for retirement and for constructive
adjustment to aging. For example, Fordham University has a training program
for pre-retirement leaders supported by a grant under Title V of the Older
Americans Act. This curriculum deals with

1. Topics relating to retirement, including health care, financial planning, where to live,
   legal affairs and taxes and how to spend leisure time.
2. Basic conference and discussion skills and problem-solving techniques.
3. Practical training in leading pre-retirement education sessions and opportunity to
   evaluate ongoing programs.

Major business concerns, including utility companies, banks and oil
companies, as well as industrial unions and government agencies, have taken
part in this training program. In addition, a number of large companies have
become more fully involved in preparing their older employees for retirement.
IBM, for example, announced in April, 1977, a retirement assistance program
designed to prepare employees for an active and stimulating retirement. Through
it, IBM grants up to $2500 to assist employees who are within five years of retire-
ment to take courses that might equip them to go into a new career or simply to
gain new interests and skills.

Other universities and study centers are examining the probable effects
of having an increasingly older society and the possibility of extending the life
span markedly—based on new forms of medical care. If and when this occurs,
scientists agree that it will be necessary for us to develop entirely new approaches
in our social structure and economy and in personal and family attitudes toward
the elderly.

Morris has written,

The most significant problem for the future will be the evolution of new roles for
the older adults—roles that have a reasonable connection with the mainstream
of American society. . . . We must decide whether the elderly are to be encour-
aged to form a major subgroup with its own values and organizations, or to remain
part of our society.[39]

He suggests the following as an essential set of components in a program
for the elderly: (a) a mixture of work and nonwork activities; (b) improved pre-

---

[37] Eric Pfeiffer and Glenn C. Davis: "Free Time Poses Problems to Elderly in Our Society."
Geriatric Focus, February, 1971, p. 1.

[38] Gayle B. Thompson: "Work Versus Leisure Roles: An Investigation of Morale Among
Employed and Retired Men." *Journal of Gerontology*, Vol. 28, No. 3, 1973.

[39] Robert Morris: "Future of the Aged in a Changing Society—Testimony Before Senate
Sub-Committee on Aging." *Geriatric Focus*, March, 1968, pp. 1, 6.

retirement preparation; (c) extension of the opportunities for community service; and (d) new opportunities for retirement income. In addition to these elements, Walter McKain, Chairman of the Committee on Retirement Roles and Activities of the 1971 White House Conference on Aging, has stressed the need for more research on aging, more legislation to improve old-age benefits, improvement in long-term care facilities, expansion of senior centers, improved health care and preparation of more specialized personnel to serve the aged.

However, even if better programs to serve the aged are put in motion by government, this will only serve part of the problem. *Time Magazine* comments,

> *The ranker injustices of age-ism can be alleviated by governmental actions and familial concern, but the basic problem can be solved only by a fundamental and unlikely reordering of the values of society. Social obsolescence will probably be the chronic condition of the aged, like the other deficits and disabilities they learn to live with. But even in a society that has no role for them, aging individuals can try to carve out their own various niches. The noblest role of course, is an affirmative one—quite simply to demonstrate how to live and how to die.*[40]

This comment suggests a unique role that has begun to face more and more recreation workers in chronic-care and nursing home facilities—helping terminally ill patients accept the reality of dying and live to the fullest during their remaining months or years. In her pioneering work, *On Death and Dying*, Elisabeth Kubler-Ross suggests that the psychological process of dying has five stages: *denial and isolation, anger, bargaining, depression* and *acceptance*.[41] Donald Pelegrino, among others, argues that the recreation therapist is in a unique position to counsel the dying patient informally and to help him or her in the terminal phase of life. In at least one American hospital serving primarily terminal patients, Calvary Hospital in New York, the therapeutic recreation staff has played a major role in this effort.

THE MILITANT ELDERLY: GRAY PANTHERS

Aged persons themselves are beginning to mobilize to fight for improved benefits for the retired. Some six million elderly have joined politically oriented groups, such as the National Council of Senior Citizens and the American Association of Retired Persons, to lobby for improved legislation and better social services. As an estimated 17 per cent of all registered voters, the elderly have the strong potential for exerting considerable influence on government.

The American Association of Retired Persons has been active in fighting for increased Social Security and Supplemental Security checks and was successful in April, 1977, in a referendum in Los Angeles, the nation's second largest city, prohibiting mandatory retirement for the city's 45,000 municipal employees.[42] Consciousness-raising has now reached the elderly in full force, resulting in the establishment of a unique organization called the Gray Panthers. Their leader, a retired Philadelphia social worker in her 70s, Maggie Kuhn, says, "Most organizations tried to adjust old people to the system, and we want none

---

[40] "The Old in the Country of the Young." p. 54.
[41] Elisabeth Kubler-Ross: *On Death and Dying*. New York, Macmillan, 1969.
[42] *News Bulletin* of the American Association of Retired Persons, May, 1977, Washington, D.C., p. 1.

of that. The system is what needs changing." To do this, the Gray Panthers have agitated for better housing and medical care, along with improved employment opportunities for the elderly.

It seems clear that, within an increasingly mechanized society and with more and more stringent union and Civil Service regulations, the amount of available work is not going to expand, and the work life of a great number of people will not be lengthened. Therefore, the fact of retirement is a reality that must be faced. Clearly, the task of providing a meaningful set of involvements in life that will hold the interest and provide the potential for creative and rewarding involvement for older persons is going to be the responsibility of those providing senior center, institutional and other programs of special care. Recreation will continue to be a major element in such programs. Broadly conceived, it will not be "thumb-twiddling" or bingo alone but a full range of cultural, social, creative and similar activities—including structured opportunities for older persons to provide meaningful volunteer services to society.

The real challenge will be for recreation professionals to establish their expertise in this area and to do so by *action* rather than words. The trend toward providing professional education for administrators of multiservice programs for aged persons in college and university recreation departments is a healthy one. However, the recreation and park profession itself must develop a fuller sense of responsibility in this field and must expand its programs markedly in the years ahead. Many millions of older persons are still unserved and provide a clear challenge in terms of the need for leisure programs and allied social service.

In concluding this chapter, it should be stressed that we have tended to be pessimistic in our appraisal of the effects of aging in modern life. An extensive recent study by Louis Harris and Associates, *The Myth and Reality of Aging in America*,[43] indicates that the problems of older people are very much like those of younger people—except for health and fear of crime, which affect them inordinately. Substantial numbers of older people see themselves as useful to the community or are already involved in varied forms of community service. Despite the real hardships that they face, older persons tend to be only slightly less satisfied with their lives than those less than 65 years old, and the stereotype of aged people as a totally deprived population, economically and socially, is not justified.

David Gray points out that the final issue of old age is that of integrity and courage against despair. Integrity, he says, is acceptance of one's life and a sense of comradeship with others—a determination to make the best of one's circumstances. He urges us to discard the damaging stereotype of elderly people and to embrace the concept of a life cycle with a rising curve of growth throughout most of life. For therapeutic recreation specialists, the challenge is clear— we must help the elderly make the most of their human potential. He concludes,

> *Our nation is in need of the awareness, intellect, perspective, time and power of our senior citizens . . . . The role of the social agency is to work with them to release the enormous reservoir of energy and competence our elderly citizens represent. In the end we will all benefit and not the least among the beneficiaries will be the senior citizen himself.*[44]

---

[43] Louis Harris and Associates: *The Myth and Reality of Aging.* Washington, D.C., National Council on the Aging, 1975.
[44] David E. Gray: "To Illuminate the Way." *Parks and Recreation*, October, 1976, p. 33.

The message is clear. For the aged, as for the other kinds of individuals discussed in this text, it is essential that we think of them not as handicapped or even disabled but rather as special populations with unique potential and resources. The task of the therapeutic recreation specialist is to use the unique medium of recreation and leisure, along with certain allied forms of service, to help release these human resources, so that the aged, as well as other special populations, can maximize their own lives for themselves.

SUGGESTED TOPICS FOR CLASS DISCUSSION, EXAMINATIONS OR STUDENT PAPERS

1. What are the unique problems of the aged in modern society that differ from those of the past? How can recreation and related services play a significant role in meeting the needs of older persons?

2. To what extent *are* the needs of aged persons being met today, with respect to recreation and leisure? What social or governmental policies would help to improve this situation?

3. Outline a model program of recreation or activity therapy for a specific type of setting, such as a nursing home or senior center.

4. Within the last several years we have begun to realize that aged people can continue to be active in areas such as sports or sexual relationships. What are the implications of this growing awareness for recreation specialists serving the aged?

chapter 9
Programs for Socially Deviant or Dependent Youth

This chapter is primarily concerned with the role of recreation in institutional programs designed to serve socially deviant children, youth and adults. It deals with such settings as homes and special schools for children who have come from broken homes or have a degree of personal disturbance that makes it difficult for them to function adequately in the community or in regular schools. It also considers correctional or penal institutions for those who have broken the law and special programs designed for drug-addicted or alcohol-dependent youth and adults.

The concept of social deviance includes such special problems as juvenile delinquency, drug addiction, alcoholism, aggressive and hostile behavior, truancy, sexual promiscuity and similar problems. Recognizing that deviation may take a variety of such forms, this chapter deals primarily with those groups in society that are regarded as requiring special care or rehabilitation because they are socially maladjusted and unable or unwilling to conform to the demands of society.

Delinquency is the most common cause of such commitment. This has been defined in many ways. One state police manual describes the juvenile delinquent as "... a child of more than seven and less than sixteen years of age, who does any act which would be a crime if done by an adult, is deemed guilty of juvenile delinquency."[1] Other codes list a variety of minor offenses as the basis for a charge of delinquency. Commonly, children below the age of 16 or 18 who are "incorrigible, ungovernable, or habitually disobedient and beyond the lawful control of parents or other authorities," are subject to juvenile court action and may be committed to institutions for care of deviant youth.

The problem of juvenile delinquency was described by the President's Commission on Law Enforcement and Administration of Justice in 1967 as the "single most pressing and threatening aspect of the crime problem in the United States." It found that one out of every nine children is referred to juvenile courts

---

[1] *New York State Police Manual*, 1971, p. 109.

for an act of delinquency before his 18th birthday. To illustrate the seriousness of this problem, 52 per cent of those charged with burglary, 45 per cent of those charged with larceny and 61 per cent of those charged with auto theft are juveniles.

The overall problem of crime has also been increasing steadily; it was reported in 1977 that the prison population had risen by 13 per cent in the previous year, to a new high of more than 283,000 persons in federal and state prisons.[2] In addition, there are about 160,000 inmates in local jails at any given time, with up to four million persons being held in such institutions during the course of a year. Clearly, this represents a major concern for modern society. Since it is in childhood and youth that socially deviant behavior and delinquency are established, it is in this early period of life that strong programs of prevention must be developed.

THE CAUSES OF SOCIAL DEVIANCE

The causes of delinquency have been widely debated. There are basically two schools of thought—one that sees it as a psychological or psychogenic problem and another that sees it primarily from a sociological or cultural viewpoint.

The psychological view regards habitual antisocial or criminal activity as an outcome of defective personality structure, stemming from feelings of inferiority, poorly developed control mechanisms or inadequate or disturbed family relationships. The typical delinquent has a relatively weak ego, is highly insecure and has a strong tendency toward aggressive and hostile behavior.

The sociological view of delinquency sees it primarily as the result of cultural and environmental factors. This view is supported by evidence that there is a much higher percentage of delinquent behavior in low-income areas— marked by slum housing, poor schools, broken or unstable families and the lack of desirable adult models—than in middle- or upper-class neighborhoods. It rejects the notion that juvenile delinquency indicates a disturbed or disorganized personality and suggests instead that the youthful lawbreaker may be a member of a cultural group that deliberately rejects "establishment" values and regulations and determines its own code of peer behavior.

Talcott Parsons suggests that the problem is chiefly one of masculine identification. In this view, delinquents are protesting against female domination and affirming their own masculine self-image through antisocial behavior.[3] Block and Neiderhoffer regard delinquency as the result of inadequate societal processes for helping adolescents become adults; in their view, gangs engage in criminal activity as a way of stating their independence and adult identity.[4]

Merton explains socially deviant behavior as a form of protest by disadvantaged and racial minority youth. He writes,

When a system of cultural values extols . . . certain common *success goals* for the population at large, *while the social structure rigorously restricts or closes*

---

[2] Farnsworth Fowle: "Study Shows Prison Population Rose 13% in 1976 to Set a Record." *New York Times*, February 18, 1977, p. A-16.
[3] Talcott Parsons: *Essays in Sociological Theory.* Glencoe, Illinois, Free Press, 1954, pp. 304–306.
[4] Herbert Bloch and Arthur Neiderhoffer: *The Gang: A Study in Adolescent Behavior.* New York, Philosophical Library, 1958, p. 17.

access to . . . these goals for a considerable part of the population . . . deviant behavior then results on a large scale.[5]

The theory that the baffled aspirations of lower-class youth are responsible for delinquent gang behavior was most fully developed by Cloward and Ohlin. They established a set of categories of urban youth gangs, including *fighting* gangs who derived their status chiefly from making war on the community and on other gangs, *criminal* gangs concerned mainly with financial gain through theft, racketeering and similar activities and *retreatist* gangs, who are involved chiefly with drugs, sex and alcohol as forms of escape.[6]

Recently, writers on juvenile delinquency have tended to minimize the role of play and recreation in the prevention of antisocial behavior. There has been considerable evidence, however, that there is a meaningful relationship between the leisure and recreational patterns of many youth gang members and their criminal activities. This relationship takes two forms.

1. Play itself frequently is used in antisocial ways; leisure becomes the time in which early delinquent patterns are established. Tannenbaum writes,

> *In the beginning, the definition of the situation by the delinquent may be in the form of play, adventure, excitement, interest, mischief, fun. Breaking windows, annoying people . . . playing truant—all are forms of play. . . . To the community, however, these activities may and often do take on the form of nuisance, evil, delinquency, with the demand for control . . . punishment, police court.*[7]

It seems probable that the relationship between the play impulse and delinquent activity is particularly high among middle-class and wealthy youth:

> *In the case of the low-income teen-age thief, often the drive represents a craving for possessions that the parents can't afford or simply won't consider buying. . . . But for the youth from a better and even high-income background, the stimulus is curiosity, a desire for "kicks," and escape from boredom . . . they want a thrill.*[8]

Often, what begins as random or occasional behavior related to minor theft, gang fighting, drug experimentation or sexual exploitation gradually becomes more consistent and serious. When a child is arrested and brought before a juvenile court, and particularly when he is sent to a youth house, the pattern of behavior becomes fixed. The behavior traits of the young offender become more firmly established. Ultimately, what began as casual, impulsive play becomes serious criminal behavior.

Based on this understanding of the roots of juvenile delinquency, thousands of communities throughout the years have initiated recreation programs for youth. These programs have been seen as a valuable means of preventing juvenile delinquency for the following reasons: (a) successful youth recreation programs take teen-agers "off the streets" and involve them in positive and attractive leisure programs; (b) they help youth burn up their exuberant energy and express hostile, aggressive or competitive drives in constructive and useful ways; (c) the

---

[5] Robert K. Merton: *Social Theory and Social Structure.* Glencoe, Illinois, Free Press, 1957, p. 105.
[6] Richard A. Cloward and Lloyd E. Ohlin: *Delinquency and Opportunity: A Theory of Delinquent Gangs.* New York, Free Press, 1960, pp. 20–30, 161–186.
[7] Frank Tannenbaum: *Crime and the Community.* New York, Columbia University Press, 1938, pp. 17–20.
[8] *New York Times.* December 1, 1968, p. F-1.

programs meet many of their needs for group affiliation and approval by others, which might otherwise be the basis for gang activity; (d) they expose them to the influence of helpful adults who provide desirable models and help to promote favorable social values; and (e) they help to attract young people into organized programs where they may then become involved in other needed tutorial, vocational or counseling programs.

Many civic leaders, police officials, judges and probational authorities have attested to the value of recreation in minimizing youth crime. In a study of the effects of a Boy's Club in Louisville, Kentucky, it was concluded that this youth organization had helped to reduce juvenile delinquency. In 1976, after the program had been in operation for over two decades, the chief of police of Louisville stated,

> Reported crimes in the areas served by this agency in 1975 were below the total in other parts of Louisville. When young people are actively involved in constructively supervised activities, their opportunity to participate in crime is greatly reduced.

> Boys' Clubs in Louisville not only prevent juvenile delinquency, but also are a prime positive influence on the lives of many boys in underprivileged areas. The care and concern offered by effective youth workers helps develop a strong character and values which are carried by the young into adult life.[9]

2. A second important element of the relationship between recreation and juvenile delinquency lies in the fact that youthful offenders typically have not learned to use their leisure in constructive and creative ways. It has been found that their family life usually lacks shared recreational pastimes and that they usually avoid taking part in organized community recreation programs.

As a consequence, many socially deviant youth have extremely narrow recreational interests. A former reformatory warden has written,

> Among the inmates of correctional institutions there are many who have no knowledge or skills which will enable them to make acceptable use of their leisure. Most of them lack the avocational interests of the well adjusted. They cannot play, they do not read, they have no hobbies. In many instances, improper use of leisure is a factor in their criminality. Others lack the ability to engage in any cooperative activity with their fellows; teamwork is something foreign to their experience. Still others lack self-control or a sense of fair play; they cannot engage in competitive activity without losing their heads. If these men are to leave the institutions as stable, well-adjusted individuals, these needs must be filled; the missing interests, knowledge, and skills must be provided.[10]

TYPES OF INSTITUTIONS

There are many different types of institutions serving socially deviant or dependent children and youth. These include the following:

1. State youth camps, frequently set in rural surroundings, with an emphasis on conservation work and outdoor living.

---

[9] John H. Nevin, *cited in* "Officials Still Claim It's 'Critically Valid' . . . Boys' Clubs Reduce Delinquency Rates." Brochure of National Boys' Clubs of America, 1976.
[10] Garrett Heyns: "Penal Institutions." In *Annals of the American Academy of Political Science.* September, 1951, pp. 71–75.

2. Cottage schools or homes operated by public, religious or voluntary agencies that tend to serve youth from broken homes or with a degree of emotional disturbance or problems of social adjustment who may or may not have been involved in delinquent activity.
3. Youth houses or "remand" centers that hold young people until their cases are brought before the courts.
4. Other penal institutions, ranging from jails to state and federal prisons, for older individuals who have been convicted of crimes.
5. Narcotics addiction treatment centers or rehabilitation centers for alcoholics.

As a rule, those who are sent to correctional or penal institutions do not come to the attention of the authorities until their behavior has become seriously antisocial. Society's solution to the problem has been to place such offenders in treatment centers—ostensibly for rehabilitation rather than for punishment. The Children's Bureau has described, in cooperation with the National Association of Training Schools and Juvenile Agencies, their goals in the following terms:

> The word "treatment", as used in training schools today, means help given to the child—the total effort made by the school to rehabilitate the child and the after-care services in his home community. It denotes helping a child by providing a new and more satisfying experience in community living, together with any special services that he may need. It includes a proper diagnosis of the child's problems and a plan of care based on that diagnosis. It implies providing an environment in which all activities are directed to getting the child ready for a successful return to community living.[11]

In general, it is believed that institutions serving those convicted of juvenile delinquency have high recidivism rates. Almost 75 per cent of those discharged from youth training schools or other correctional institutions are rearrested within five years. What this suggests is that, in many cases, treatment centers for the socially deviant are defeating their own purpose. Many young people who enter such institutions leave after a year or two far more hardened to society and knowledgeable in crime techniques than when they entered. Amos writes,

> The ineffectiveness of our institutional programs is partly to blame . . . because many of the youngsters who return to their neighborhoods carry with them the added sophistication of a one-year course in delinquency, manipulation, conning, utilization of the sub-cultural codes, and assume roles of leadership and influence among other youngsters in their areas.[12]

Young people who enter such institutions often have immature expectations regarding authority figures stemming from earlier parent-child conflicts. They have confused self-images regarding their own worth, vocational goals, personal skills and sexual identification. Usually, they are listless and tend toward the passive use of free time; yet they have a great deal of pent-up energy and hostility. They tend to have a low level of tolerance for failure or frustration and desperately need to acquire skills, training and a sense of accomplishment. Although they come to the institution to be rehabilitated, the bulk of their time is often spent in learning about better ways to commit crimes and establishing

---

[11] Ruth Cavan (ed.): *Juvenile Delinquency*, Philadelphia, Lippincott, 1969, p. 26.
[12] William E. Amos: "The Future of Juvenile Institutions." *In* Ruth Cavan (ed.): *op. cit.*, p. 26.

relationships with their peers on the basis of their own toughness and resistance to societal values. Barker and Adams write,

> *They often react against the dominant value structure and develop the feeling that anything that is valuable and acceptable for the dominant culture is wrong for them and vice-versa.*[13]

This sense of alienation and resistance is understandable. The mere fact of the institutional setting is one that militates against the resident's responding to even the most intelligent and constructive treatment. MacIver writes,

> *Technically, the institution is a place where the youth is sent for friendly guidance and training, but for the youth himself, it is a prison, a punishment. He is cut off from all familiar associations. He is under restraints that he bitterly resents.*[14]

Within this context, then, it is essential that the program be one that provides a variety of needed kinds of experiences and human relationships. These should include counseling services, group discussions and therapy, academic education, vocational classes, work experience and recreation.

GOALS OF RECREATION IN TREATMENT CENTERS FOR THE SOCIALLY DEVIANT

The goals of recreation in youth camps and other correctional or treatment facilities include certain unique elements:

1. Recognizing that institutional life represents an unnatural and limiting kind of living arrangement, a primary purpose of recreation is to improve morale and to help make the setting more bearable and enjoyable. The lack of freedom and a high level of anxiety, tension and boredom can all be alleviated by a well-organized program of enjoyable activities.
2. A second purpose of recreation in the institutional setting is to help individuals learn new recreational skills, discover talents and interests and generally learn to use their leisure in socially acceptable and constructive ways.
3. Recreation provides a means of improving the social adjustment of participants; through it, they are helped to develop constructive social relationships with adults or with their peers, to learn to become cooperative group members and to accept social rules and values of sportsmanship and responsibility.
4. Generally, recreation may help the individual participant gain a more favorable self-concept and a sense of accomplishment and personal worth, as well as the knowledge that he is using his free time in a productive and acceptable way.
5. By providing a release for energies and drives that are pent up in the prison situation, recreation may help to reduce the danger of friction and hostility; sports and creative and social activities are particularly useful in this respect.

While recreation—like other rehabilitative services—is an important part of the institutional program, it is clear that it can accomplish little by itself.

---

[13] Gordon Barker and W. Thomas Adams: *In* Ruth Cavan (ed.): *op. cit.*, p. 435.
[14] Robert M. MacIver: *The Prevention and Control of Delinquency.* New York, Atherton Press, 1966, p. 163.

Decker writes,

> *Recreation is not a cure-all. It does not prevent, control or cure unacceptable behavior. But it does have an important role in the total rehabilitation process. . . . If a program is well-planned and adapted to the participants, they can be guided and assisted in learning self-control and self-discipline, engaging in cooperative enterprises, building more constructive social relationships, and acquiring interests that replace undesirable past interests.*[15]

RECREATION IN CORRECTIONAL INSTITUTIONS

Despite the growing awareness of these purposes for recreation in correctional institutions, in many youth camps, training schools or prisons, the provision of recreation services is extremely limited. In part, this stems from a concept of such institutions as places meant for the *punishment* rather than the *rehabilitation* of inmates. Although this viewpoint is gradually being replaced by more constructive views, the fact is that a brutal and harsh attitude toward offenders has characterized American penal institutions until comparatively recently.

Among the more brutal measures employed in the recent past were the following:

In North Carolina, a decade or so ago, men were thrown naked into solitary confinement cells, where guards used high-pressure water hoses from time to time to "knock them up against the wall."

In Maryland, inmates were disciplined until recently by receiving a meal only once every 72 hours.

In Pennsylvania, until the mid-1950s, recalcitrant prisoners were placed for long periods in dark, damp underground holes.

In Arkansas, until the late 1960s, men were whipped on the bare buttocks with rawhide straps (flogging was practiced in 26 prisons as recently as 1963), and some were tortured by having needles pushed under their fingernails.[16]

Given this record of extreme harshness, it is understandable that meaningful educational, vocational, counseling and recreational services have been slow to enter many youth correctional institutions or adult prisons. Even where there is a desire to provide such services, staff limitations and overcrowded facilities have made it difficult to do so. The former Attorney General of the United States, Ramsey Clark, has pointed out that 95 cents out of every dollar spent in prisons is for custodial care, and only 5 cents is spent for rehabilitation services.

Many youth houses and prisons throughout the United States are extremely overcrowded and lack badly needed programs to carry out rehabilitation goals. Examples may be drawn from institutions in New York City—probably no better and no worse than those in other large cities.

---

[15] Larry E. Decker: "Recreation in Correctional Institutions." *Parks and Recreation*, April, 1969, p. 32.

[16] "Prisons Curb Brutal Discipline; Find Relaxed Controls Effective." *New York Times*, May 15, 1971, p. 14.

Typically, a world of "fear, violence, filth and degradation" was described by prisoners who answered an uncensored questionnaire about conditions in the Tombs, a municipal house of detention for men. The use of force by guards and the lack of adequate medical care, schooling or other services, plus extreme overcrowding, made this facility a "dungeon of fear," in the words of one prisoner. In other centers, the shortage of caseworkers, teachers and recreation personnel limits programs markedly. Rikers Island, a reformatory jammed with almost twice the number of inmates originally planned for it, is marked by beatings, sexual abuse and suicides; observers have described it as an "island of idleness." There, writes one reporter,

> . . . teenagers can associate with accused felons and spend the day talking about the best kind of drugs to take, the most lucrative crimes, their real or imagined sexual experiences and the people they've beaten up. There is time, lots of time, for them to plan great crimes because their days are not disrupted by such unpleasantries as education, work, or sports. They get three meals a day and a place to sleep.[17]

Unfortunately, the national pattern is much the same. Flynn pointed out in the mid-1970s that a study of all jails and penitentiaries built in the United States during the preceding decade revealed that the majority of institutions seemed to have been built to perform but one function—"to warehouse men at the lowest possible per capita cost." Some buildings were constructed with no dayrooms, no auditorium, no gymnasiums and almost no facilities for outside recreation. This study concluded, based on the much higher level of inmate morale in the institutions that did provide adequate recreation, that such facilities and programs should no longer be viewed as luxuries but rather as essential elements in correctional programs, critical to the physical and mental health of all inmates.[18]

Even when facilities are provided, the lack of skilled staff members with training in recreation and appropriate attitudes often makes it difficult to provide adequate programs. Decker comments that within the corrections field there has been comparatively limited acceptance of the need for professionally staffed recreation personnel. He summarizes the findings of a recently completed Recreation Planning Study for the Oregon State Division of Corrections that indicate some of the reasons why recreation programs in correctional institutions are inadequate:

1. The role and values of recreation are not emphasized.
2. There is no professional staff member trained in recreation.
3. The emphasis is on custodial care and security.
4. Professional guidance and assistance in recreational services are not readily available to the staff.
5. Where recreation programs do exist, they often are instituted with little planning and few long-range objectives in mind.
6. The administrative climate is not conducive to evaluation and change.

---

[17] Joseph Feurey: "Idle Rikers Teens Get Crime 'Tutoring'." *New York Post*, February 20, 1970, p. 22.
[18] Edith E. Flynn: "Recreation—A Privilege or a Necessity?" *Parks and Recreation*, September, 1974, p. 35.

7. *The professional recreator's efforts have not been directed toward explaining and increasing the role of recreation in the institutional setting.*[19]

Despite this generally negative picture, there are a number of good programs of recreation in youth institutions throughout the United States. Among the leading states to have moved vigorously into the improvement and reform of their correctional institutions are Ohio, Illinois, Georgia and California.

EFFECTIVE STATE PROGRAMS

Probably the leading example of a state that has taken action to reform and vitalize its correctional program is Illinois. There, in 1968, Governor Richard Ogilvie moved to merge separate state departments or boards dealing with youth offenders, adult correction facilities and penal institutions into a single state department with cabinet-level representation.

As part of this effort, Illinois took the following actions in the years immediately following 1968: (a) it raised its correctional budget sharply; (b) it established a strong central administrative staff to provide research, long-range planning, program analysis, policy evaluation, public information and medical and professional services; (c) it established a larger, full-time Parole and Pardon Board; (d) it developed a variety of new community-based programs, including four halfway house community centers for parolees, six new work-release centers, ten group homes for youth parolees, a special services unit in Chicago to provide counseling and job placement for youth parolees and a new pre-release program to aid adults about to be discharged; (e) it developed several new minimum security facilities with emphasis on vocational and educational treatment programs; and (f) it expanded professional counseling and vocational and educational services in all facilities.

Within two years, the recidivism rate dropped sharply for youth and adults who had access to the new programs and procedures. Among juveniles, the rate dropped from 51.4 per cent in 1969 to 35.3 per cent in 1970—a decline of almost one-third.

Illinois State Training School for Boys, St. Charles

This medium security facility, serving an average daily resident population of approximately 500 to 600 boys, provides extensive academic and prevocational programs, as well as medical, dental, religious, recreational, psychiatric, psychological and social services. It is the largest facility for delinquent youth in the state. In an effort to overcome this disadvantage, it has been divided into smaller operational units with separate staffs and program identities, housed in clusters cottages. Each such unit develops its own statement of rehabilitation goals and methods of achieving them. Intensive use is made of group living experiences, student council programs and planning and advisory roles in policy-making, along with more traditional forms of individual and group therapy.

---

[19] Larry E. Decker, *op. cit.*, p. 31.

Overall, the school's physical education and recreation program is operated under the direction of the Recreation Division, staffed by a director of recreation, an assistant director, an occupational therapist and a staff of physical education instructors. Facilities include a gymnasium and indoor swimming pool, 12 combination basketball, badminton and volleyball all-weather courts located near the cottages, 13 softball diamonds with backstops, a football field, a running track, a baseball field and four tennis courts that double as ice skating rinks during the winter months.

In addition to formal physical education, health and first aid instruction, the Illinois State Training School at St. Charles sponsors the following recreational activities:

1. Varsity sports competition with other schools or boys' clubs for highly skilled participants.
2. Intramural competition, including leagues and tournaments in all seasonal sports, carried on among the cottages.
3. Weekly swimming participation and instruction in small groups for nonswimmers.
4. Weekly movies of 35 mm first-run features and talent shows by service organizations, colleges or other entertainment groups.
5. Ice skating during the winter and roller skating during the summer, using outdoor facilities.
6. Monthly birthday parties, special holiday parties (including trips to neighboring communities or special activities) and special events for Halloween, Labor Day, Thanksgiving and other holidays.
7. A hobby shop program, including lanyard, leather, clay, raffia and other craft activities.
8. Individual units may also sponsor special interest clubs; among the activities provided have been swimming, chess, Spanish, guitar lessons, physical fitness, tailoring and horseback riding.
9. Drum and Bugle Corps and other musical activities.

Although each of the units provides somewhat different approaches to treatment, the following statement is typical of the overall institution's philosophy and the framework in which recreational activities are carried on:

> The Rehabilitative Environment. *It is the intended purpose of this Unit to create an accepting, warm, non-threatening, humane, and enriched environment in which the delinquent youth can learn that the world is not overwhelmingly hostile and alien. However, unlike the therapeutic setting in which the neurotic child or adult would likely be placed, this environment is not to be permissive. It is to be highly structured. A sense of authority is to be consistently maintained. The consequences of the delinquent youth's behavior, whether positive or negative, are to be clearly defined. An integral part of this environment is the creation of learning situations in which the delinquent youth can:*
>
> *1. Ventilate his anger constructively.*
> *2. Modify undesirable behavior and learn age-appropriate means to satisfy his desires and wants.*
> *3. Learn the rewards of socially desirable behavior and deferred gratification of needs.*
> *4. Experience the rewards of close, non-delinquent interpersonal relationships.*
> *5. Correct distorted perceptions so that he can deal more effectively with the demands and stresses of life.*[20]

---

[20] *Statement of Rehabilitative Objectives and Approaches, Unit III.* Departmental Manual, Illinois State Training School for Boys, St. Charles, Illinois, 1971, p. 2.

At other institutions operated by the Illinois Department of Corrections, there are similar approaches and programs. In one center, the Reception and Diagnostic Center for Girls, and in the Illinois State Training School for Girls, at Geneva, Illinois, cottages engage in similar activities—with the difference that a variety of coeducational activities are provided. At the Geneva school, at least four such social events co-sponsored with all-male juvenile facilities are held each month, two on the Geneva campus and two away. In addition, varied cultural programs, such as a campus choir, drama club, gardening program and similar activities, have been introduced—some carried on with the assistance of community groups.

Ohio Department of Mental Hygiene and Correction

Another state that has taken vigorous action to improve its correctional institutions is Ohio. Here, until 1954, there were three separate departments with related responsibilities: the Division of Mental Hygiene, responsible for all mental institutions; the Division of Correction, responsible for all penal institutions; and the Division of Juvenile Research, Classification and Training, responsible for juvenile institutions. At present, these functions are combined within a single Department of Mental Hygiene and Correction.

This administrative structure has facilitated the development of programs concerned with psychiatric criminology. A special division operating under this title is responsible for providing care for the criminally insane, sociopaths and sex offenders.

Both in experimental new facilities operating under this division and in institutions run by the Division of Correction, recreation is offered along with academic and vocational programs and religious, psychological and other social services. As an example, in 1970, a new treatment center for psychosocially handicapped young offenders was opened at Junction City, Ohio. This psychiatrically oriented 135-bed center operates a large multipurpose gym-auditorium, classrooms, vocational shops, appliance repair shops and hobby rooms, along with a library and conference room. The center is divided into four living units consisting of either individual rooms or six-man dormitories. Each unit has a day-room for recreation, group therapy and other activities.

The Junction City Treatment Center has the advantage of small size, a treatment-oriented staff (with a high patient-staff ratio of approximately one to one) and a relaxed, flexible atmostphere. An individualized treatment program is tailored to each man's needs; it normally includes academic and vocational training, recreation, work assignment, development of an avocation or hobby, group therapy and similar forms of rehabilitation. Recreation is provided by activity therapists who offer a variety of sports, hobbies, social activities, music, art and similar programs. The institution's size and approach allow the inmate-patients and staff to get to know each other on a very personalized basis. In fact, staff and inmate-patients eat their meals together and mingle freely and informally throughout the institution.

In general, recreation programs in most penal or correctional institutions around the country are extremely limited. In one survey of women's penal institutions in the United States, Canada and Puerto Rico, it was found, for example, that a number of prisons or reformatories had no organized programs at all. Of 17 responding institutions, only six had formal educational requirements for the director of recreation; in others, degrees were not required and staffing responsibilities were heavily assumed by male guards or female supervisors. In this survey, the most frequently found activities tended to be *active games*, such as softball, volleyball, badminton, croquet, basketball, tennis, horseshoes and tumbling, and *quiet activities*, such as cards, bingo and shuffleboard. It was concluded that the women's penal institutions with the most clearly defined purposes and with leadership assigned to specific recreation directors tended to have the most extensive and well-organized programs.[21]

RECREATION IN CALIFORNIA YOUTH AUTHORITY INSTITUTIONS

Traditionally, the California Youth Authority has used recreation in varying degrees as a rehabilitative tool, with primary responsibility for planning and organizing physical education and recreation programs assigned to instructors in recreation and physical education. Additional recreation programs within living units in state youth institutions have been provided by group supervisors or youth counselors assigned to living units. Programs have varied considerably in different institutions, depending on group workers' interest and talent in the recreation field; the absence of any stipulation requiring group workers to have formal training in recreation has led to inadequate and unimaginative programs in many Youth Authority centers.

In 1966, the Youth Authority initiated a new treatment team approach that has since been adopted as a standard program method in all of its institutions. It was decided to carry out an in-depth recreation demonstration project at two recently opened schools in Stockton—the O. H. Close and Karl Holton Schools for Boys. With funding by the van Loben Sels Foundation, an 18-month project was conducted at these two schools, from January, 1968, to June, 1969.

Under the direction of the Institute for the Study of Crime and Delinquency in Sacramento, California, the overall objective of this project was

> To demonstrate whether a dynamic total recreation program, implemented by professionally trained recreation consultants, would have a significant impact as a rehabilitative technique for institutionalized delinquent youth. These related questions were also explored: How much recreation is desirable in a juvenile institution? How much time can an institution afford to spend on recreation in view of all of the other elements of treatment?[22]

It had the following specific aims:

1. To organize and implement an inservice training program in recreation leadership for Youth Counselors.
2. To experiment in the use of Youth Authority wards as "Recreation Staff Aides."

---

[21] Diane Peoples and Russ Walkup: *Survey of Women's Penal Facilities.* Unpublished report, Ohio Reformatory for Women, Maryville, Ohio, 1970.

[22] Robert E. Meyers, Jr. and Cleveland Williams: *Operation Recreation: A Demonstration Project at Two California Youth Authority Institutions.* Sacramento, California, California Youth Authority, 1970, p. 2.

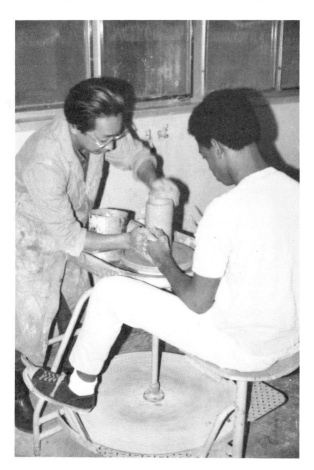

Institutionalized youth at the O.H. Close School for Boys, of the California Youth Authority, take part in ceramics, informal dramatics and discussion groups and outdoor sports including, as shown here, rough-and tumble team stunts.

3. To develop a community "Recreation Volunteer" program.
4. To evaluate the desirability of employing a professionally trained recreation specialist in all Youth Authority institutions.
5. To develop a recreation intern program by providing recreation field work placements in Youth Authority institutions for undergraduate majors.
6. To test and evaluate various recreation equipment and supplies.
7. To produce a recreation handbook for use primarily by the institution line worker and to develop a standardized recreation budget.

The demonstration project that was put into effect had a number of major components. Initially, it placed two trained recreation specialists in the Close and Holton Schools as consultants. They devoted six months to preparing for the program and the training and orientation of staff members, including inmate Ward Aides. Ward recreation committees were set up that involved the boys in the planning of their own recreation programs.

Volunteer programs were coordinated by the recreation consultant, with a considerable number of volunteers being recruited from nearby high schools, a college, churches, civic clubs, labor unions and similar organizations. A recreation internship program was established, with student interns from San Jose State College assuming responsibility for volunteers and other special phases of the program. In addition, recreation activity specialists were employed to conduct activities requiring specialized skills.

New Approaches to Recreation Programming

In the past, programs had been nondirective in nature, and often dependent on spontaneous participation:

> *A typical occurrence would find youth counselors, upon seeing a group of boys milling about, attempting to direct them into activities such as table tennis or shooting baskets. This approach used recreation as a management rather than a rehabilitation tool. There was little recreation planning of a systematic nature. . . .*[23]

In developing a more carefully planned program, a survey was carried out to determine how many leisure hours were available to the boys in the two schools. The survey indicated that wards had about 30 hours per week, the bulk of this coming on Saturdays and Sundays. It was therefore decided to concentrate schoolwide recreation activities on these days. Recreation consultants conducted training sessions for staff, wards and volunteers. Hall recreation committees were formed that developed monthly recreation program calendars. Typically, they developed such projects as

Coeducational Events. Coed swim parties, including a swim, a barbecue and a dance, were held, inviting girls who were on parole in the Sacramento area. Coed sports nights were held, including activities such as table tennis, checkers, cards, volleyball, billiards and dancing; girls from nearby schools in Stockton were invited to these events.

Other Parties. These included carnivals, shows, holiday events, playdays and picnics and barbecues spaced throughout the demonstration project.

Schoolwide activities included the establishment of music and dance, arts and crafts and talent shows. Social dancing classes were held; the school's glee clubs and "rock" bands and outside groups put on performances.

Extensive intramural sports leagues in basketball, tackle football, flag football, and other instructional or competitive events in boxing, golf, gymnastics, handball, soccer, kickball, wrestling and volleyball attracted large numbers of participants. Other developmental activities, such as physical fitness and weightlifting, were introduced successfully. In addition, hobby activities, such as a camera club and a slot-car program, were carried on.

The demonstration project in recreation service in the two Youth Authority schools was subjected to a careful evaluation in three major areas: (a) the degree of staff and ward participation in recreational activities both in the institution and the community; (b) the effect of recreation on relationships among the boys and between the boys and staff members; and (c) staff and ward attitude toward the value of recreation. Evaluative questionnaires were filled out by wards and staff members on all levels, and records were kept on the various elements in the project.

Findings of the Project

1. The project had a significant impact on the attitudes of the wards in residence at both the O. H. Close and Karl Holton Schools. Analysis of questionnaire responses showed that most of the wards' commitment offenses had occurred during their "free time." Many boys indicated that active recreation programs in the community would have

---

[23] *Ibid.*, p. 9.

provided positive outlets for their leisure needs and that the project had helped them become more aware of organized recreation and its advantages.

2. It was found that the shifting of program emphasis to weekends, which had formerly been unscheduled, meant that many hours of "dead time" were now being filled with meaningful activity. A realignment of staff schedules was recommended by the project staff in order to provide additional coverage in the living units during weekends and holidays.
3. The report concluded that trained leadership was essential to the planning of successful recreation activities and that staff members primarily concerned with security or casework responsibilities had neither the time nor the ability to consistently plan and carry out dynamic and imaginative programs.
4. It concluded that recreation programs are most successful when community resources and volunteers are used. The contributions of skilled and interested volunteers from the community provided an element of vitality and assured the wards that others cared about them—an important therapeutic message.
5. The interest of wards in institutional recreation programs was stimulated when they had a chance to plan them and select equipment and supplies; this supplanted an attitude of apathy or even defiance when programs were imposed by authority.
6. Facilities were shown to be markedly inadequate for a well-rounded recreation program and were primarily geared to housing and security needs; thus, much improvisation had to be done to insure the use of facilities.

In general, it was concluded that the best programs were those that were carefully planned, structured and carried out. The project showed that Ward Aides and college recreation interns could be extremely valuable in carrying out a total recreation program. A final interesting finding was that white youth felt that recreation would be more useful to them when they were discharged than black or Mexican-American youth. It was concluded that this was because minority group youth felt that their home communities offered extremely limited recreation facilities or programs, and thus, what they had learned in the program could not readily be carried over into community life.

NEED FOR IMPROVEMENT OF CORRECTIONAL PROGRAMS

Despite these examples, it should be stressed that the majority of correctional institutions do *not* provide adequate recreational programs or, for that matter, adequate rehabilitation services overall. This is particularly true of prisons for adult offenders. One authority has characterized the nation's prison systems as a "total failure." He describes the criminal justice program as a "perpetual-motion machine" in which police arrest felons and send them into the courts, that send them into prisons, that in turn send them out into the streets to be re-arrested:

> We do no more for the criminal in jail than we do for animals in the zoo. We cage them and feed them. The average citizen has seen prison purely and simply as retribution. The uglier and grimier and older the prison, the more it has seemed to the average citizen to be a fine and splendid prison.[24]

What is needed is a widespread revolution in public attitudes and the infusion of large sums of money to replace vengeance with rehabilitation in the

---

[24] "Murphy Attacks Nation's Prisons as 'Total Failure'." *New York Times*, January 29, 1972, p. 33.

Many prisons, like the Chillicothe, Ohio, Correctional Institute, have excellent sports and other recreational facilities, as shown here.

Too often, however, the recreation program itself is sadly lacking. For example, in the federal prison shown here, weight-lifting equipment lies in disarray, and prisoners who wish to play cards must do so through the bars of their cells (see next page).

correctional system. If this does not happen, jails will continue to be nothing more than "warehouses for contaminated goods," and prison riots, crime and the rate of recidivism will continue unabated.

This point of view is strongly supported by Ramsey Clark, who stresses that it is necessary to develop entirely different approaches to law enforcement and corrections. He urges the following priorities:

1. *A philosophy of avoiding detention wherever possible through prevention efforts, community treatment, and probation supervision.*
2. *Recognition that the needs of each individual are different. Corrections programs should be carefully tailored to individual needs.*
3. *The creation of new substantive rights of persons convicted of crime that would require government to fulfill basic human needs in the following areas:*
   (a) *health and social services;*
   (b) *safety from assault, forced homosexuality, corporal punishment or solitary confinement;*
   (c) *communications, including the free access to family, friends, advisors and attorneys, and the right to write and read freely;*
   (d) *improved educational and vocational training programs; and*
   (e) *job placement services.*
4. *The creation of new procedural rights for prisoners.*
5. *An intensive effort to move offenders to the community where they will live, making use of the following:*
   (a) *improved probation and parole programs; and*

(b) a network of work-release, pre-release guidance, and halfway houses, with small, unmarked community facilities that will assist discharged or paroled prisoners in making the transition to responsible and law-abiding community life.[25]

Only if such programs are developed will it be possible to overcome the present weaknesses of our corrective and penal system that are so destructive to human life and dignity. Within such programs, recreation must play an increasingly strong role in contributing to the rehabilitation process and in helping offenders return successfully to their communities. What steps need to be taken in this direction? Obviously, the fundamental basis for any meaningful redirection or improvement of recreation in the correctional setting would have to be an administrative philosophy that accepts the primary goal of helping to prepare inmates to return successfully to the community, rather than simply punishing them for past crimes. Within this context, recreation would have to receive adequate support in terms of needed facilities and equipment, qualified leadership and scheduling of groups of prisoners to permit participation in a variety of activities. Unlike many institutions today, where most prisoners are limited to reading, listening to the radio, playing cards, a daily session in an exercise yard and an occasional movie or other form of mass entertainment, the opportunity would have to be provided to engage in varied forms of challenging individual and group activities. Such activities might include the following:

OUTDOOR RECREATION

The California Youth Authority has successfully experimented with small groups of youthful offenders who take extended wilderness trips in the Mojave Desert high country of the Lassen National Forest.[26] Hiking more than 100 miles, using rock climbing and rappelling, the young wards gained greatly in self-confidence and the ability to deal with others in a meaningful and responsible way. These trips have included three-day "solo" survival experiences, encounter sessions using transactional analysis and other experiences that helped bring maturity and self-confidence to the participants. Obviously, not all prisoners could be trusted in such a situation; however, with careful selection of participants, programs of this type have an immense potential.

THEATER ARTS

A number of prisons have encouraged dramatics as an activity that is rewarding in its own right as well as serving as a means of entertaining the entire prison population. Recently, some theater groups have been formed that present not popular Broadway plays or other standard works from the theatrical literature but rather works written by convicts themselves out of their own experience. One such group has been "The Family" a group that began with eight inmates at the Bedford, New York, Correctional Facility who became involved in group therapy experiences such as theater games, exercises, role-playing and psychodrama, in which inmates acted out traumatic scenes from their own life.[27] The

---

[25] "A Nickel for Rehabilitation." *New York Times*, September 30, 1971, p. 46.
[26] Allen F. Breed: "Mojave Desert Diary." *Parks and Recreation*, September, 1974, pp. 40–42.
[27] Luisa Kreisberg: "Bedford Inmates' Theater as Therapy." *New York Times*, June 19, 1977, p. WC-13.

prison theater workshops gave rise to a dozen new plays that were acted out, as the company grew, in such places as homes for unwed mothers, drug rehabilitation centers and even leading professional theaters in the East. Ultimately, it became a touring professional company of 150 actors and stage technicians in the outside community. A number of successful playwrights and actors on the professional stage today had their first experience in prison theater programs like this one. Other prisons have experimented successfully in fine arts, music and creative writing.

COEDUCATIONAL PRISONS

The typical prison or correctional institution is established on a one-sex basis—all men or all women. This single sex environment tends to create an atmosphere of extreme tension; often homosexuality is widespread, with many younger or weaker inmates being forcibly seduced or violently gang-raped. Correctional institutions or state youth camps have often scheduled coeducational recreation activities in an effort to overcome some of the effects of such segregation, and a number of prisons have experimented with conjugal visits, in which small apartments are set aside and prisoners live for brief periods of time with their visiting families. Recently, several state and federal prisons have been restructured on a coeducational basis. For example, Framingham State Prison in Massachusetts now accepts both male and female minimum-security prisoners, who may transfer from other state prisons. Although it is far from a country club, inmates at Framingham can dine together, go for strolls in the prison courtyard, enjoy dinner dances, grooming classes, fashion shows, a pool paid for by the inmates and other recreation opportunities. Prisoners agree that this experimental arrangement has helped to reduce much of the tension that is normally found in penal institutions. The superintendent comments that, although the public accepts this approach chiefly as a means of reducing prison homosexuality, in her view the coed approach is simply more realistic:

> She reasons that the residents are going to have to cope with a man-woman world when they get out, and that learning to get along with the opposite sex inside the four walls will help with their adjustment to society once they are released.[28]

PRE-VOCATIONAL EXPERIENCE

Another important aspect of recreation programs in prisons and correctional institutions is that they may be structured to provide useful experience in recreation leadership, so that inmates, when they have been discharged, are able to move into recreation aide positions in community or therapeutic agencies. Obviously, there are numerous opportunities for them to take on direct leadership responsibilities; Cipriano urges that these be combined with short-term training programs in job competencies in the institution itself, along with a coordinated effort to identify appropriate job opportunities in the outside community and to help place qualified individuals in these positions.[29] Many normal job opportu-

---

[28] Judy Klemesrud: "Men and Women in One Prison: 'Realistic' Idea Is Given a Try." *New York Times*, June 20, 1974, p. 44.

[29] Robert Cipriano: "Training of Former Inmates as Therapeutic Recreation Assistants." *Therapeutic Recreation Journal*, 2nd Quarter, 1975, pp. 60–62.

nities are virtually closed to ex-convicts because of their record; on the other hand, their background can be invaluable in helping them work with problem youth, with drug addicts or in other socially oriented programs.

LEISURE COUNSELING

A final important aspect of recreation service for youth and adults who have been committed to correctional or penal institutions is leisure counseling. In a recent study of 50 male clients of the Pennsylvania Board of Probation and Parole, Panik and Mobley found that the most popular leisure activities of these individuals, prior to their conviction, were watching television, drinking and other tavern-related activities.[30] Ninety-eight per cent of the clients committed the act for which they were convicted (including such crimes as murder, arson, robbery and sex offenses) during nonwork or leisure time. It was concluded that a program of group leisure counseling for probationers and parolees should be instituted, both to give the parole agent a better understanding of the leisure patterns of these clients and to help guide them in appropriate directions. Excellent rapport was established in these counseling sessions, with a high level of attendance, and planning was initiated to develop a more complex counseling project, with experimental controls to measure its actual impact in terms of recidivism.

RECREATION AND THE TREATMENT OF DRUG ADDICTS

The problem of drug addiction has increased tremendously in the Western world over the past two decades. There has been an explosion of drug experimentation and abuse, particularly among the young. Although estimates vary greatly, there was evidence in the early 1970s that a majority of the students in many schools and colleges in the United States were at least occasional users of marijuana. Government surveys reported in 1976 that there was a continued rise in the use of marijuana, with one-third of all high school seniors reporting themselves as current users.[31] The use of other, "harder" drugs, such as heroin, cocaine and LSD, was reported to have remained unchanged over the previous two years.

It is evident that the use of drugs has become a major problem of American youth on all levels of society. Heroin, once used chiefly by blacks in urban ghettos, has now made inroads in fashionable suburban communities. It is being used at an increasingly early age. At the California-based Synanon self-help centers for addicts, the teen-age population rose from zero in the mid-1960s to 400 by 1970. After the end of the Viet Nam war, it appeared for a time as if heroin use was declining in the United States; however, during the mid- and late 1970s, it was reported on the upswing again. On all levels, the drug problem poses a challenge to educational, medical and social authorities in modern society.

---

[30] Martin A. Panik and Tony A. Mobley: "The Bottle and the Tube: Leisure for the Convicted." *Parks and Recreation*, March, 1977, pp. 28–30, 54–55.
[31] "U.S. Survey Finds Rise in High School in Use of Marijuana." Associated Press Dispatch, November 23, 1976.

Although most adults tend to be shocked by the growing statistics of drug use among children and youth, the fact is that adults themselves are extremely heavy users of tranquilizers and other legal, or prescribed, stimulants. Many millions of adults are "hooked" on cigarettes or alcohol, and teen-agers frequently comment that for them "pot" is no different from their parents' martini cocktails. Indeed, it seems clear that for many, drug-taking represents a form of leisure activity, a way of having fun, of avoiding boredom. One mental health authority suggests that "for people who are chronically unhappy, drugs bring some relief from a world without purpose." Corry writes,

> Students themselves are not particularly articulate about why they take drugs. For kicks, they say, or because they are bored, or because drugs are easy to get or because drugs offer them deep personal insights. . . . They offer an illicit pleasure that is almost entirely without sanction in the adult world and they open an immense gap between parent and child.[32]

Hechinger suggests that among middle-class youth, drug experimentation is the "chain reaction of a combination of permissive homes with the speed-up of youth's experiences in an affluent society." The early onrush of adolescence encourages youth to experiment with partying, dating, sex, smoking, drinking and before long, glue-sniffing and marijuana. "As old thrills wear off, the search is on for new ones."[33] In the armed forces, it has been concluded that alcoholism among senior noncomissioned officers and drug abuse among young draftees stem from boredom.

Resistance to constructive, organized programs and the choice of escape through drugs frequently stem from social attitudes that "put down" the "establishment" and prefer instead the illicit lure of narcotics or alcohol. Realistically, the sensation gained from drug use provides pleasure that is far more overwhelming than that other activities might yield.

Goode concludes,

> The simple fact is, marijuana is fun to smoke. . . . In my own study of marijuana users, pleasure emerged as the dominant motive for continued use. Almost 70 per cent said that sex was more enjoyable high. Almost 90 per cent said that the simple act of eating became more fun. Almost 90 per cent said that listening to music was a richer, more exciting adventure. . . . Marijuana has become, and will continue to be, increasingly, a recreational drug, and for larger and larger numbers of young (and not so young) people. This will not disappear, and it will not abate; drug "education" campaigns are doomed to failure. . . . Outlawing fun has always been a tough job.[34]

There continues to be considerable controversy about the actual effects of marijuana. A growing body of experts have concluded that this form of drug use is nonaddictive and actually less dangerous than many other stimulants, including alcohol. A comprehensive report, issued by the National Governors Conference and prepared under a grant from the Federal Law Enforcement Assistance Administration, concluded that moderate or infrequent marijuana

---

[32] John Corry: "Drugs a Growing Campus Problem." *New York Times*, March 21, 1966, p. 26.
[33] Fred Hechinger: "Drugs: Threat on Campus." *New York Times*, April 10, 1966, p. E-7.
[34] Erich Goode: "Turning on for Fun." *New York Times*, January 9, 1971, p. 27.

use did not appear to pose a significant health hazard and urged that harsh laws penalizing the possession of "pot" be repealed. On the other hand, evidence has been gathered of numerous psychotic reactions stemming from marijuana use. There appear to be marked behavioral changes associated with the use of marijuana among some subjects. Wikler writes of a group of subjects involved in a pharmacological experiment that

> *During the first few days, they exhibited euphoria, bursts of spontaneous laughter, silly behavior, and difficulty in concentrating. Later, they showed loss of interest in work, decreased activity, indolence, non-productivity, and neglect of personal hygiene. . . .*[35]

Similarly, a number of medical authorities have documented the damaging effects of marijuana, particularly with adolescents, the age group most open to experimentation with drugs, with the highest rate of usage and most vulnerable to its effects. One doctor urges that legal sanction *not* be given to marijuana, writing of its

> *. . . adverse psychological effects: hallucinations, paranoid reactions, depressive reactions, acute psychotic reactions, spontaneous flashbacks and chronic withdrawn reactions (i.e., the so-called amotivational syndrome). All of these adverse responses have been noted and recorded in scientific journals, but receive little or no recognition in the lay media. . . . Since we cannot, ethically, use adolescent subjects for deliberate experimentation, we must rely on clinical observation and on reports from foreign countries, where cannabis has been widely used, and for countless generations. A review of the world literature is replete with confirmation of our admitted limited American clinical experience.*[36]

There is also considerable evidence that many young people move from experimentation with marijuana, glue-sniffing, pills and other soft drugs to involvement with harder and more dangerous narcotics. Without question, it is essential that every effort be made to stem the tide of drug use in American society.

Recreation in Drug Treatment Centers

Obviously, there are a number of different forms of care for drug addicts. One method is the so-called British system, based on the premise that heroin addiction is a sickness, not a crime. This approach makes drugs available, by prescription, to formally registered addicts and is intended to meet the needs of those who are unwilling to undergo a cure or enter an institution—thus minimizing the commercial exploitation of the drug addict's needs.

A second approach to the problem of heroin addiction is the methadone maintenance program. This involves switching an addict from heroin to methadone, a synthetic substitute that costs relatively little for a day's dosage. Methadone eases heroin withdrawal and blocks heroin's euphoric effects. It is addictive in itself, however, and many legal and medical authorities resist substituting

---

[35] Abraham Wikler: "Marijuana *Is* Dangerous." *New York Times*, April 3, 1971, p. 29.
[36] Doris H. Milman: "Of Marijuana, Health and the Law." *New York Times*, June 2, 1977.

one form of addiction for another. On the other hand, methadone is much less dangerous than heroin and permits the addict to lead a relatively normal life.

The most popular approach to working with drug addicts has become the small, controlled therapeutic community, like Synanon, begun in California and extended throughout the country, or New York's city-run Phoenix and Horizon House. Such residential centers are run largely by former addicts; they first detoxify and then attempt to rehabilitate the drug user by restructuring his ego and life pattern. They accept only those who have proved their determination to kick the habit, and they strive to increase the addict's self-understanding and self-regard through frequently brutal group-encounter sessions.

The traditional method of institutional care has been the special hospital, or hospital unit, such as the two federal narcotics hospitals at Lexington, Kentucky, and Fort Worth, Texas. Most of these programs are more conservatively run. Having been ordered there by the courts, their patients are less highly motivated for change, and records indicate that over 90 per cent of those discharged from such institutions eventually return to heroin.

Finally, there are a variety of treatment centers connected to mental health hospitals or outpatient programs, part of state mental health systems or municipal or voluntary hospitals. Many of these are residential, while others provide a variety of "crisis" or continuing treatment services for addicts living in the community. In almost all cases, they use a variety of treatment approaches, including individual and group therapy, remedial education, vocational training and placement and other social services—including recreation.

The nature of recreation service in drug addiction centers is heavily influenced by the typical personality patterns of drug users. Characteristically, they tend to have extremely low self-esteem, be overly dependent on others and have a very weak capacity for frustration. Their defense and adjustment mechanisms are often juvenile; they demand immediate gratification, have little sense of time and are unable to plan effectively for the future.

Like other social deviants, drug users typically engage in few organized, constructive recreational activities. Although they may have been involved in sports or social programs at an earlier point, they usually relinquish such interests when they become heavily addicted. Their lives revolve about the drug culture. They associate with other addicts; getting and using drugs becomes their chief preoccupation. Those who work with addicts in drug treatment programs comment that they tend to be extremely passive in their use of free time and usually resist structured programs.

The goals of recreation in treatment centers for drug users should therefore be:

1. To contribute to the overall rehabilitation of the addict in terms of his developing more varied interests and talents for the constructive use of leisure time that may lessen the need for him to turn to drugs for pleasure or release.
2. To encourage personality changes that will strengthen his self-concept and ego controls and give him a sense of personal worth and accomplishment.
3. To contribute to the overall therapeutic environment by providing a relaxed, tension-free atmosphere and by encouraging enjoyable group activities, which can break down barriers among participants, and between participants and staff members.

Young and Hutchison suggest that a key factor in such programs is the need for the recreation specialist to establish a relationship of mutual trust and respect with the addict under treatment. It may take days or weeks for this to develop, and it is essential that he become accepted as a trustworthy person who is not going to "put down" the addict in any verbal or nonverbal way. Gradually, he must come to be seen—not as a representative of the establishment—simply as a friend and helper. They write,

> *The therapeutic recreation program revolves around a "core" of planned group activities. Enough variety is provided in group programming to give each individual patient a chance to find his sphere of interest and to function at his particular level of comfortable interaction with others. Because the attention and interest span of the post-addict tends to be limited, specific recreative activities are provided in periods of from thirty minutes to one hour in length. The number of activities per day, and the number of times an individual patient is involved in a given activity per day or per week depend on the center's population at a given time. Activities that allow for various combinations of patient-staff ratio are scheduled according to the individual patient's current level of dependency.* [37]

Young and Hutchison stress that it is important not to place too much pressure on the addict during the initial stages of his treatment. Although he has passed through the physiological trauma of withdrawal, he is still fighting a psychological battle to remain off drugs. The specific rules related to attendance and behavior many addicts find difficult to accept. Until they can comfortably handle these basic responsibilities, it is useless—and can be damaging—to exert additional pressures.

Gradually, patients are encouraged to develop sustained interest in specific forms of recreative activity. Among the special interest activities suggested by Young and Hutchison as appropriate for such groups are instrumental "combos," listening to music, vocal groups, weightlifting, dramatics, newspaper work, social dancing, cooking and such hobbies as stamp clubs and model railroading. Other program activities found in addict rehabilitation programs include bingo, table tennis, billiards, table games like chess and checkers, crafts like ceramics and weaving, movies, gardening, work parties and discussion groups.

At this phase of involvement, there is usually a shift in the addict's level of participation. When this is observed, leadership approaches are changed:

> *. . . a gradual increase of pressure from the staff, and involvement in situations where the post-addict takes more responsibility—and risks greater chance of failure—are introduced into the individual program plan. At this point, the recreation specialist becomes primarily a supportive figure. He spares no effort to ease the transition from a dependent attitude and existence to a semi-independent or independent level of functioning.* [38]

LEADERSHIP RESPONSIBILITIES

Throughout this process, the recreation leader working with addict groups must operate much less as a direct, authoritarian leader of activities and much more as a nondirective counselor and friend, a catalyst who gently encourages and makes changes in behavior and attitudes possible.

---

[37] Elliott G. Young and Ira Hutchison: "Prescription Recreation: A Bridge to Community Living for the Narcotics Addict." *Recreation in Treatment Centers*, September, 1964, p. 60.
[38] *Ibid.*, p. 61.

The recreation specialist must function as a professional member of the treatment team. He should be fully involved in interdisciplinary staff meetings and should work closely with psychiatrists, psychologists, unit counselors, vocational rehabilitation specialists and other personnel to exchange information and share in planning to meet the needs of each patient. Furthermore, he should be active in promoting community programs designed to serve addicts and discharged patients.

RECREATION AND THE TREATMENT OF ALCOHOLISM

Although the public has been greatly disturbed by the growth of drug abuse in recent years, alcoholism represents a much greater threat to society. There are an estimated 10 million alcoholics in the United States today who cannot control their drinking and have serious personal, social or vocational problems stemming from it. It was reported in 1975 that

> According to the National Institute on Alcohol Abuse and Alcoholism, 1.3 million Americans between 12 and 17 have serious drinking problems. About one-third of our high school students get drunk at least once a month. Arrests of teenagers for drunken driving have tripled since 1960; 60 per cent of the people killed in drunken driving accidents are now in their teens.[39]

Overall, according to the American Medical Association, an average of 35,000 Americans are killed each year in automobile accidents in which alcohol is involved. Alcohol now ranks as the third major cause of death in the United States, and it has been estimated that the life span of the alcoholic is 12 years shorter than that of the nonalcoholic. Not only is excessive drinking a major health risk but it also is often linked to the loss of jobs, marital breakdown and total personality disintegration.

Nature of Alcoholism

Alcoholism is the subject of numerous misconceptions and stereotypes in our society. The popular way of thinking of alcoholism is that it represents a form of immoral behavior or weak character and that the typical alcoholic is a "skid row" type—a disheveled, helpless vagrant or bum. In reality, the American Medical Association has identified alcoholism as a complex disease "with biological, psychological, and sociological components" that takes numerous forms.

Alcoholism affects all levels of society, including many extremely successful and hard-working men and women. Studies have shown that, in some populations, the incidence of alcoholism is actually higher among more economically successful individuals. It is peculiarly linked to the work world; heavy drinking is encouraged by the very nature of many jobs that require the enter-

---

[39] "School Study Calls 28% of Teen-Agers 'Problem' Drinkers." Associated Press Dispatch, November 20, 1975.

taining of business contacts and heavy travel and carry a high degree of tension. We are extremely ambivalent in society as a whole about drinking. On the one hand, we decry and discourage it, particularly in excess; yet on the other hand, it is a built-in part of most adult social occasions, and it is a mark of maturity to be "able to hold one's liquor" or "drink like a man." Drinking is important throughout culture. When people pledge loyalty and friendship, a drink is often shared. Alcohol represents an accepted ritual at such occasions as betrothals, marriage, christenings, banquets and receptions. It is taken for granted as a way to relax, a social lubricant, a way to relieve self-consciousness and loosen the tongue. Most people drink chiefly to produce the kind of pleasant relaxation and glow that comes from a mild concentration of alcohol in the bloodstream. Indeed, in some therapeutic settings, such as nursing homes, the practice has developed of having modest cocktail parties or beer sessions, when residents may have a drink or two under controlled circumstances.

Although it is popularly thought of as a stimulant, alcohol is a depressant of the central nervous system and particularly its inhibitory mechanisms. It tends to reduce tension and anxiety and often results in exaggerated behavior, such as aggression toward others, loud joking, crying or extremely extroverted behavior. It may be considered a psychoactive, or mind-altering drug, as well as an addictive substance. Sessoms writes of the "alcoholic personality" as one who suffers from extreme feelings of inadequacy and anxiety, excessively dependent upon others for support and direction.[40] For such individuals, drinking becomes a quick and effective method to find an "escape from reality," a temporary and destructive mechanism that brings an artificial sense of pleasure and satisfaction.

Navar and Nordoff agree, pointing out that

> For the alcoholic, drinking has become a means of coping with stress. As stress builds, an individual must take some action to obtain relief in order to achieve a state of balance. The alcoholic has learned that consuming alcohol brings a sense of relief. However, that sensation is short-lived, as drinking produces more problems and thus more stress. A state of balance or well-being is not reached. The alcoholic has attempted to use alcohol as a change agent. The person must find another change agent of a healthier nature to reach a state of balance or well-being.[41]

There have been numerous approaches to curing people of alcoholism in the past; these have included imprisoning them (alcoholism is a crime in many states and is typically linked to the commission of many other crimes), psychoanalysis, use of antiabuse or aversion therapy, group therapy and behavior modification. Alcoholics Anonymous, a nonprofessional, self-help organization, along with its companion organizations, Al-Anon and Al-a-Teen, has been extremely helpful with many thousands of alcoholics. It is a fundamental tenet of alcoholic rehabilitation that people who have this disease simply cannot drink at all, even in minor amounts (although some recent findings suggest that many former alcoholics have become social drinkers, imbibing in moderation).

---

[40] H. Douglas Sessoms: "Recreation and the Alcoholic and Drug Addict." *In* Thomas A. Stein and H. Douglas Sessoms: *Recreation and Special Populations.* Boston, Holbrook, 1977, p. 180.

[41] Nancy Navar and Jacquelyn A. Nordoff: "Recreation as a Change Agent for the Alcoholic." *Journal of Physical Education and Recreation,* May, 1975, pp. 36–37.

Recreation and Alcohol Rehabilitation

A landmark research study in this field by Sessoms and Oakley found that patients in a state alcoholic rehabilitation center in North Carolina differed sharply in their leisure involvements from the general population.[42] Typically, they engaged most in those activities that required a minimum of skill and equipment and demanded little personal commitment. A heavy stress on work and spectator activities and a generally passive attitude toward leisure and recreation, particularly outdoor recreation, characterized those studied. Much of the recreation of the typical alcoholic is built around drinking—and he tends to stay away from places where drinking is not possible.

Any approach to helping in the rehabilitation of the alcoholic through recreation must accept the nature of his or her personality—often dependent, compulsive, lacking in confidence and self-esteem. The recreation program must seek to build self-understanding and self-acceptance, as well as important group skills. The alcoholic's life style must be modified by providing new and different satisfactions that give the individual a different kind of "high," without liquor. Sheridan suggests that an effective recreation program for alcoholics, while obviously not a panacea by itself, should have the following values (in effect, these supplant the "payoffs" formerly derived from alcohol):

1. *Socialization with a minimum of tension and anxiety.*
2. *Alternative methods of dealing with feelings of frustration, anxiety, anger, depression, etc.*
3. *Fun or escape from life situations which cause tension.*
4. *Relaxation.*
5. *Adventure and the opportunity to express oneself creatively.*[43]

To accomplish these ends, recreation should be used as a significant tool to fill the patient's leisure with constructive, enjoyable and nonthreatening activity. Emphasis should be placed on helping each individual overcome his feelings of inhibitions and guilt and relax, behaving spontaneously and freely in a socially accepted and nondestructive manner. Leisure counseling is also a much needed part of this program, both on an individualized and small-group basis, so that clients may understand the role of leisure in their lives and develop values, attitudes and resources to use it most constructively. Finally, Navar and Nordoff point out that the family ties of many alcoholics have deteriorated because of drinking and the therapeutic recreation program should attempt to involve the family and reintegrate clients under treatment with their close relatives.

RESIDENTIAL PROGRAMS FOR DEPENDENT YOUTH

A final category of therapeutic recreation programming may be found in residential programs serving neglected, emotionally disturbed or socially

---

[42] H. Douglas Sessoms and Sidney R. Oakley: "Recreation, Leisure and the Alcoholic." *Journal of Leisure Research*, Winter, 1969, pp. 21–31.

[43] Paul M. Sheridan: "Therapeutic Recreation and the Alcoholic." *Therapeutic Recreation Journal*, 1st Quarter, 1976, pp. 14–17.

maladjusted children and youth whose families are unable to provide adequate care for them, or who do not have functioning family units. Typically, although such children and youth have not been adjudged delinquent, many of them have been unsuccessful in school, have emotional difficulties and are likely to move into an antisocial gang or other criminal affiliations unless they are cared for in a stable, nurturing environment.

In such residential settings, recreation supplies the means for normalizing the daily living routine by providing the opportunity for the full range of recreational, cultural and social activities that children living in the community at large have—or should have. Youth-care institutions of this type may be sponsored by a variety of agencies. Typically, they are often operated by voluntary or religious organizations funded by both charitable donations and government grants. An excellent illustration of such facilities is the Dobbs Ferry Children's Village, in Dobbs Ferry, New York.

Children's Village, founded in 1851, has been a pioneer in the field of child care since its inception. It was among the first institutions serving indigent and homeless children to establish a mental health clinic on campus; to employ a staff psychiatrist; to develop a therapeutic environment that integrated casework, child care, education and recreation; and to prescribe individual treatment programs for all young residents.

It has an extensive program of sports, musical and dramatic activities, hobbies, trips and special events. In addition to these regularly provided activities, it has experimented with a number of unique programs that have been extremely successful in involving children with limited recreational backgrounds and interests.

One of these programs has involved nature activities. Children's Village operates an extensive nature study and hobby program, including 32 different organized activities, such as the study and observation of mammals, reptiles and amphibians, plants, birds, insects and other arthropods. While studying mammals, for example, the children collected nearly 30 assorted skulls and portions of skeletons, usually of skunks, raccoons, opossums and birds, found in the woods adjacent to the Village. They restored and mounted these artifacts and became involved in field trips and in a variety of other experiences related to natural science and animal life.

The institution also maintains an extensive winterized zoo, with a variety of birds and domestic and small wild animals. Many of the children are involved in the care of these animals; this experience has been found to be of great value in working with emotionally disturbed children, who often have difficulty in relating to their peers and in accepting other types of responsibility.[44]

A second major project of the Children's Village has been the development of unique outdoor recreation areas. Working under the direction of professional staff members, children have built an elaborate Indian village, with tepees, totem poles, archery ranges and similar facilities. Materials were bought from government surplus stocks or donated. The Indian village has become the site of many interesting activities related to Indian lore, including arts and crafts, tests of courage, music, dance and other programs based on Indian rituals. In addition to this project, children have also built a space center, an Army camp

---

[44] Howard Romack: "Children's Village Experiments." *Parks and Recreation*, April, 1969, p. 39.

center, a pioneer fort and a Western town. Each of these facilities is used for varied forms of outdoor recreation activity, including camping out, pageants and similar program features.

At Children's Village, recreation is fully accepted as an important aspect of the institution's overall program in terms of status on the treatment team, qualifications and salaries of recreation staff members and similar criteria. For this situation to be maintained, the director of recreation services must be certain that every effort is made to identify new and more meaningful potential services, that the help of other disciplines is brought into planning programs and developing treatment plans, that needed research is carried on and that all programs are carefully evaluated. Among the unique features of Children's Village is its continuing effort not simply to deal with the child in the institution but to work with families through counseling, group therapy sessions and other supportive services, to re-establish an environment to which children can return successfully.[45] Recreation plays an important role in this, both in terms of helping to familiarize parents with the community resources available to them and counseling residents at the Village about community opportunities and helping them establish favorable affiliations when they return to their families or foster homes.

COMMUNITY RECREATION PROGRAMS AND DELINQUENCY

As indicated previously, since its inception in the early decades of this century, the recreation movement has had as a major purpose the prevention and "cure" of juvenile delinquency. The slogans of "keep kids off the streets" or "give them something useful to do" have been the basis for funding many public recreation agencies, particularly in large cities, where youth problems have been severe. Few recreation departments have been successful in this area of concern, however. There are several reasons for this failure:

1. Most obviously, delinquency is the result of a variety of factors, such as family instability, slum housing, poor education, limited vocational opportunity or the lack of other vitally needed social services. Within this context, it is unrealistic to believe that recreation, by itself, can significantly deter delinquent activity. However, it can and should be an important part of total community efforts to serve the socially deviant.
2. Most recreation departments and agencies do *not* make a special attempt to serve delinquent or pre-delinquent youths. Often they view this as a difficult task that they are not equipped to handle. In many cases they bar disruptive and antisocial youth from their facilities, thus making it impossible to serve them meaningfully.
3. Usually, antisocial and gang youth reject organized activities and are unwilling to become part of the formal structure of community agencies. In part, this is because they do not wish to be controlled or because their high-impulse, hedonistic values are unwilling to conform to the rules and limitations inherent in youth programs, team sports and the like.

In some cities, gangs may use community centers as hangouts—often discouraging other participants from entering. However, it is rare for them to

---

[45] J. Kent Davis: "Continued Care: A Vital Part of the Treatment Process." *Children's Village Bulletin*, January, 1977, p. 17.

be meaningfully involved in such programs. Instead, in most communities, special youth boards or commissions or antipoverty organizations—where these exist—have been the only formal agencies to work with delinquent youth.

Guidelines for Working with Problem Youth

How *can* the public recreation department or voluntary agency that is concerned about working with delinquent or pre-delinquent youth gangs do so effectively?

1. It is essential to view recreation, at the outset, as a positive and meaningful form of community service. Unless it is seen and supported in this light, it cannot be successful in any form of significant social programming.

2. In working with problem youth, it is not possible to plan programs at a high level of authority and simply present them with the results. Instead, it is essential to involve youth *fully* in the planning and development of programs. This may be done by having representatives from various gangs or neighborhoods join together in a recreation center council to plan programs and formulate agency policies.

3. Gangs generally are thought of negatively—and it is true that they often are responsible for various forms of crime in urban slums. However, gangs also represent an understandable need for group affiliation, for status and even for self-protection in ghetto areas. In some cases, minority-group gangs have taken on the task of driving drug pushers out of their neighborhoods or similar desirable goals. It is essential to recognize their existence and attempt to work with them positively rather than simply to try to wipe them out.

4. Recreation programs designed to serve antisocial youth often fail to attract them because they are not interesting or challenging enough. Therefore, such programs *must* be well planned and staffed and should involve exciting goals and experiences. They may include trips, cultural programs, activities that have career-development potential, and—when possible—activities that have a degree of risk or danger about them. Activities like skiing or tobogganing, horseback riding or underwater exploration, which are in a sense a "testing" of manhood, have been used successfully with such youth. Their particular value is that they may sublimate the urge to take part in dangerous, unlawful activities by providing an equally challenging, but socially acceptable, leisure outlet.

5. Community center programs designed to meet the needs of delinquent youth *must* provide more than recreation. They should also include educational or remedial educational programs, vocational training and placement, psychological counseling services, drug abuse programs and similar activities. All this can be woven into the overall program of an agency that is primarily geared to offer recreation services.

6. In any long-range program intended to reduce delinquency, it is essential to reach children in the elementary school age range, between the ages of six and 12. Often, the patterns of antisocial behavior are set at the age of as low as six or seven, and children, by eight or nine, are involved regularly in criminal activity and antisocial gang affiliation. Therefore, every effort must be made to work regularly with children at this age, to reduce antisocial group

involvement and to recognize and refer to appropriate agencies those children who have severe individual problems of adjustment. As much as possible, parents should be drawn into this effort.

7. Programs in centers need to be more carefully organized and structured. In many community centers in low-income areas, there is a constant flow—in and out—of unregistered participants. Often activities are carried on in a completely casual way, with informal games and music being the heart of the program. Instead, it is desirable to have a registration system so that only center members may enter, with rules set by the youth council itself as to the basis for membership. Programs should be scheduled and carefully directed to encourage the maximum participation in organized activities.

8. A final guideline applies to those youth who are *not* willing to enter community centers at all and who have no regular contact with adult leaders or youth workers. These are unaffiliated gang youth who hang out in the neighborhoods, are frequently school dropouts and are often responsible for incidents of gang violence or sporadic criminal activity. For such youth, a special "outreach" approach is required.

The Roving Leader Approach

A number of cities have adopted an approach under which special youth workers—usually individuals who have themselves grown up in slum neighborhoods and may have been involved in gangs—are assigned the task of making contact with unaffiliated youth. They are usually detached from organized programs and go out into the street, neighborhood hangouts or other places where problem youth may be found.

Typically, in Washington, D.C., roving leaders work directly with several hundred gang youth, as well as others who are sporadically associated with gangs. They receive on-the-job training in group-work techniques, street-corner contact methods, community resources and psychological counseling. The goals of these workers are both short-range and long-range.

Their short-range objectives are to (a) reduce the severity and frequency of offenses, such as gang warfare, murder and theft; (b) redirect behavior into more desirable channels; and (c) help adolescents make use of available community resources. Their long-range goals are to help gang youth become more fully integrated in the "major culture" and to change their social values and life patterns in more constructive directions, in terms of becoming responsible law-abiding and gainfully employed citizens.

Since they are often attempting to reach extremely hostile and alienated individuals who come from broken homes, have arrest records or have been confined to correctional institutions and are wary of adult contact, leaders must often work for months and years to establish favorable rapport with target gangs. They seek to get to know them, gain their confidence, counsel and assist them and ultimately guide them in the constructive directions previously described.

Although this may be seen primarily as a social-work function, it has been assigned to the Recreation Department in Washington and other cities, simply because the recreation program has the broadest capability for reaching and involving the large mass of youth in the community. In addition, recreation *is* an important aspect of the Roving Leader program. For example, programs offered by Washington's detached workers have included trips to such places as amusement parks, theatres and art galleries and soccer, football, baseball and basketball games; picnics, fishing, nursing aide and census-taking projects, bowling, skating, talent shows, camping and boat and airplane rides are also offered.

The roving leader approach is being used in an increasing number of large cities. It has been encouraged by the U.S. Office of Education's Division of Manpower Development and Training, which has funded the Office of Recreation and Park Resources at the University of Illinois, in cooperation with the National Recreation and Park Association, to promote and research the roving leader concept.

Over a three-year period, between 1968 and 1971, project personnel researched examples of roving leader programs throughout the country, developed guidelines for the training of roving leaders and conducted—with assistance from the Office of Education—a series of workshops in large cities throughout the country for Roving Leader trainers. Efforts were later made to promote programs of Roving Leader training in two-year community colleges throughout the country as part of manpower leadership development to meet social needs.[46]

Such programs are examples of how recreation may serve preventative as well as treatment needs—in community settings as well as in institutions. Obviously, the problem of working with deviant groups is much less costly, both in human and financial terms, if it can be done before patterns of serious antisocial behavior are clearly established. The treatment process in institutions is too often ineffective when antisocial attitudes and deviant behavior patterns have become deeply ingrained, and youth often leave correctional institutions more fully committed to a life of crime than they were when first committed. The cost of residential programs for deviant or dependent youth is extremely high, ranging up to $20,000 to $25,000 per child per year in some states, with one publicly funded addiction treatment facility costing $45,000 a year per patient. Clearly, then, a major thrust of all community youth agencies, including therapeutic recreation service, must be to prevent antisocial behavior at its outset.

In many cities, police departments join forces with other voluntary or public organizations, either through Police Athletic Leagues or police youth bureaus, to provide recreation activities and youth centers. In some instances, special projects have been mounted with funding from the Federal Law Enforcement Assistance Administration to combat juvenile delinquency. One such recent program, carried out by the Youth Services Program of the Dallas, Texas, Police Department, appears to have been strikingly successful in reducing the rearrest rate among juvenile offenders who were involved in a police-sponsored sports and physical fitness program.[47]

The long-range trend in youth services appears to be away from institutional care and toward community-based programs, either in foster-care or small-group homes or intensive services provided for youth living with their families on a semi-probationary status. Typically, the New York State Division

---

[46] Joseph J. Bannon: "The Roving Leader: A New Look." *Parks and Recreation*, February, 1972, pp. 23–24.
[47] T. R. Collingwood and Mike Engelsgjerd: "Physical Fitness, Physical Activity, and Juvenile Delinquency." *Journal of Physical Education and Recreation*, June, 1977, p. 23.

for Youth's Cooperative Placement Program has made intensive efforts to involve local voluntary agencies in youth care programs and has moved assertively to end the practice of caring for dependent children and youth (known as PINS, or Persons in Need of Supervision) in state training schools. It seems likely that this trend will continue to grow throughout the United States, imposing a need to provide much richer and more effective programs of youth recreation in the communities themselves to serve problem youth.

SUGGESTED TOPICS FOR CLASS DISCUSSION, EXAMINATIONS OR STUDENT PAPERS

1. What are some of the basic factors underlying juvenile delinquency, as a form of social deviance, that make constructive and well-planned recreation programs an essential in correctional institutions?

2. What are the major obstacles to improving recreation in correctional and penal institutions today? How might these be overcome?

3. Describe the roving leader approach as a technique used by recreation departments to combat socially deviant gang behavior. What are its strengths and limitations as a form of community service?

4. How can recreation serve both as a preventative and a form of treatment in community and institutional programs for alcoholics and drug addicts? In your reply, deal with the nature of the addictive personality and the substitution of recreation for drugs or alcohol as a means of meeting psychosocial needs, or getting a "high."

chapter **10**

Selection and Modification of Program Activities

Although therapeutic recreation specialists have varied roles, such as supervisors, educators, community organizers and consultants, many of them still have as a primary responsibility the presentation of activity programs for special populations. Even the head of recreation or activity therapy in a large hospital typically must direct other leaders, aides or volunteers in the planning and presentation of activities. It is essential, therefore, that therapeutic recreation personnel on all levels be familiar with methods of selecting and modifying activities that will be appropriate for different types of disabled populations.

Earlier chapters listed the types of activities that are normally presented in therapeutic recreation programs or guidelines for modifying activities for specific populations. In addition, Chapter 4 presented suggestions for planning programs and gave examples of special techniques, such as *sensory training*, *remotivation* and *behavior modification*. This chapter explores the basic areas of activity in greater depth, describing their values and methods of selection and presentation and giving useful techniques for their modification. Specific examples of activity, such as games, songs, and arts and crafts projects, are not presented here but may be found readily in other general texts on recreation leadership.

SELECTION OF APPROPRIATE ACTIVITIES

The selection of appropriate program activities for individuals or groups of participants is influenced by such factors as (a) the overall philosophy of the sponsoring institution or agency; (b) the specific goals established for the program itself; (c) the available leadership, equipment and facilities; and (d) the interests, needs and capabilities of those being served.

Activity Analysis

Obviously, activities that can provide satisfaction and success to the participant should be chosen. If they are to meet specific needs, the activities themselves should be carefully analyzed to determine their essential qualities. Too often, recreation activities are chosen almost at random, with little consideration for their group structure, cognitive demands or the values they impose. For example, games may be analyzed under the following headings:

Level of Physical Demand. Does the game require little, moderate or strenuous output? Is the physical activity that is demanded momentary or sustained? What level of motor skill development (coordination, balance and so on) is required? What degree of strength is required? What portions of the body must function to carry out the activity?

Psychological Aspects of Activity. Is the game one that requires individuals to act autonomously or as part of a group or team? Does it enforce a positive self-image, or might it threaten or undercut a participant's self-concept? Does it foster personal creativity and self-expressiveness and offer release for tension or hostility?

Cognitive Demands. Is the game appropriate for the participants as far as level of complexity is concerned? Specifically, does it require an understanding of numbers, strategies, directions or facts that is reasonably within their grasp? Can it be used to teach desired concepts, information or intellectual skills?

Patterns of Social Interaction. Does the game stress cooperation or competition and to what degree? Does it promote favorable group interaction, or does it encourage participants to win at all costs? What is the precise nature of the group structure?

In analyzing activities, it is necessary to be as precise and detailed as possible. For example, the exact physical skills or levels of cognitive understanding needed to play a game may be readily identified in detail. Behavioral objectives for any activity may be outlined, in terms of both specific actions and overall effects on participants' personalities. In relation to behavioral change, desired goals of activity may be stated in positive terms, such as "what we want a patient or client to do," and negative terms, such as "what we want a patient or client *not* to do." Through analysis of this type, each activity must be selected not only because it represents an enjoyable form of activity but also because it is a useful tool in the overall process of rehabilitation. Peterson has suggested that activity analysis can lead to the following:

1. A better comprehension of the expected outcome of participation.
2. A greater understanding of the activity itself, to be useful in determining appropriate leadership methods or ways of introducing it and providing opportunities for participation.
3. Fuller understanding of how the activity can be related to the functional level of participants, to determine its potential value, as well as how it might be modified or adapted, to be more suitable.
4. Linkage of program activities with specific therapeutic goals and objectives.[1]

When appropriate activities have been selected, they may then be blended into a total program suited to the varied needs of participants. The following areas of activity are generally the key elements in most programs of therapeutic recreation service; obviously, whether they apply to specific individuals or groups would depend on their levels of function, past experience, personal needs and wishes and the goals established for them. In a number of cases,

---

[1] Adapted from Carol A. Peterson: "Activity Analysis and Prescriptive Programming: State of the Art." *In* Gerald S. O'Morrow: *Therapeutic Recreation: A Helping Profession.* Reston, Virginia, Reston, 1976, p. 196.

suggestions are provided for modifying and adapting them, with special emphasis on their use with the physically disabled.

MODIFICATION OF ACTIVITIES FOR THE PHYSICALLY DISABLED

A previous chapter described the major areas of physical disability and the needs and types of programs provided for each. A number of categories of activity are now described, with specific illustrations of how each one is modified to meet the needs of physically disabled persons.

Physical Activities: Aquatics, Games and Sports

As indicated earlier, almost all the games and sports played by non-disabled persons can also be enjoyed by those with impairment. It is necessary in many cases to modify them with respect to playing conditions, rules and equipment, however, so that the disabled player can be successful rather than frustrated. Often, since such participants have had limited experience in physical activities, it is necessary to stress slow, careful, sequential teaching of basic skills.

SWIMMING

This is one of the most useful activities, because it can be adapted to the needs and capabilities of almost every type of disabled person. It is particularly suitable for those who have serious physical impairments. Grove writes,

> *Regardless of a person's mental or physical condition, buoyancy of the water allows him to move his most useless muscles. Water activities include movements, patterns and skills almost anyone can perform—if they are adapted to the individual.*[2]

Swimming provides the disabled child in particular with a kind of exercise and freedom of movement he cannot enjoy out of water. He is free of wheelchairs, special appliances or the support of his parents' arms and is able to join his family or nondisabled friends in an enjoyable pastime that brings new confidence and pleasure. It offers the opportunity for the disabled to socialize with their peers in many programs.

For most categories of disability, water should be heated to a warm temperature to avoid tension or chilling that may discourage the disabled child or youth from entering the water or have an adverse effect on his impairment. There should be a fairly large area with shallow water to permit casual water play for children who have not yet gained confidence in the water. The pool should have a wide surrounding deck with a slip-proof surface. Steps with hand-rails leading into the water should be built with short risers and a wide step to

---

[2] Frances Grove: "Aquatic Therapy: A First Real Step to Rehabilitation." *Journal of Health, Physical Education and Recreation*, October, 1970, p. 65.

permit easy entrance or exit. In some cases, rails are fixed across the pool to permit participants to hold on and gain a feeling of security.

Daniels has suggested a number of guidelines for teaching swimming to the disabled:

1. *The group method of instruction should be used whenever possible, supplemented by individual instruction when necessary.*
2. *All available teaching aids and equipment should be used to gain the participant's interest and encourage his attempting to learn to swim.*
3. *Instruction should be informal, with short teaching periods and frequent rest or opportunity for free play in the water.*
4. *Participants should be grouped according to their level of accomplishment or readiness for swimming, rather than by type of disability.*
5. *Each session should involve some progress or feeling of achievement, for all participants.*[3]

Since fear of the water may be present in all nonswimmers, and especially so for the physically disabled, it is important for the swimming instructor to gain the trust of the participants and to help them relax in the water. Working in small groups, with aides personally helping those children who need special support, the first step is to accustom participants to being in the water and help them lose their fear of it. The fun aspect of swimming should be emphasized, and simple ball play, like water dodge ball, may be used to bring this about. In a manual on swimming for the disabled, the Canadian Red Cross outlines the following steps for helping fearful children become used to the water:

1. *Talk with the child. Explain to him the pool or beach rules.*
2. *Take him on tour of the swimming area and if possible show him children his own age swimming in deep water.*
3. *Getting wet and water entry—initially any way the child wants to, e.g., washing himself, splashing, drowning the instructor. Don't be impatient if a child won't get in the water completely the first day—once he trusts you he will.*
4. *Different ways of entering the water, e.g., walking, jumping, hopping, slipping, cannon-ball, downstairs, etc.*
5. *Walking out into deeper water holding hands.*
6. *Walking out into deeper water unassisted beside instructor.*
7. *Ducking to shoulders, neck, eyes, hair, completely under, holding breath as long as he can.*
8. *Jumping into water and submerging holding breath.*
9. *Blow bubbles on top of water; with face in water; completely submerged.*
10. *Tow the child on his front and back, head out, and then head in the water.*
11. *Bobbing holding breath, then blowing bubbles.*[4]

Artificial floats should be used for beginners; this is generally considered preferable to having them held by other persons. Children using foam or inflated floats should be closely watched at all times, however, to prevent the accident that might occur if they slip from the supporting surface.

The selection of strokes depends on the specific disability of each participant. For persons with loss of arm function, an asymmetrical stroke, such as the side stroke or trudgeon stroke, is often used. Learners who have had a loss of

[3] Arthur S. Daniels: *Adapted Physical Education.* New York, Harper and Brothers 1954, pp. 227–229.

[4] *Swimming for the Handicapped: Instructor's Guide.* Toronto, Canadian Red Cross, 1974.

leg function, either full or partial, usually prefer symmetrical strokes, such as the elementary backstroke, breast stroke or dog paddle. For those individuals who cannot put their heads in the water, the body should be held at approximately a 70 degree angle, with the face lifted enough to be out of the water. If learners do not have use of their arms, a glide and flutter kick action may be used; swim fins help to give them added propulsion and build up leg strength.

For more severely disabled persons, the emphasis at the outset may simply be on teaching breathing rhythms and beginning to learn to float. Even if they cannot learn to swim, just being in the water is likely to bring pleasure.

Swimming is particularly useful in working with blind children and adults since it provides a degree of freedom that they do not normally experience on land. A slight elevation around the pool provides safety against blind persons accidentally falling in while walking around the deck. Swimming areas should be carefully roped off for those of different swimming ability, and ropes may be used to guard the blind participant from deep areas or to help him find his way to the ladder. No particular stroke is to be preferred for the blind. Since many of them fear to wet their eyes, however, they may prefer to learn a slow backstroke or breast stroke, with the head above the water. A safety precaution that is often helpful is the use of the buddy system. If diving is permitted, the diving area should be carefully roped off from swimming areas in the pool to prevent accidents.

ACTIVE GAMES AND SPORTS

Many different types of ball games may be used with the physically disabled. In order to permit such groups as the orthopedically disabled to take part in these activities, Pomeroy suggests a number of ways to simplify ball games:

1. *Walking or wheeling may be substituted for skipping or running, when necessary.*
2. *A bounced throw or underhand toss may be used to replace a regular throw.*
3. *Positions such as sitting, kneeling or lying down may be substituted for standing positions.*
4. *The distances of bases or boundary lines, or of the dimensions of playing areas such as horseshoe courts, volleyball fields or baseball diamonds, may be reduced.*
5. *Lighter or more easily controlled equipment may be substituted for regular equipment.*
6. *Players may be restricted to a definite position or area on the playing field.*
7. *Players may be allowed to hit a ball any number of times, or to hold the ball longer in games like volleyball or basketball.*
8. *In games like baseball, if a child is unable to run, a runner may be used for him.*[5]

Other devices may be used, such as increasing the number of players, permitting an extra number of strikes or modifying the rules. Those children who are not able to play, even under these circumstances, may act as umpires or referees or scorekeepers.

---

[5] Janet Pomeroy: *Recreation for the Physically Handicapped.* New York, Macmillan, 1964, pp. 306–307.

Even with such modifications, it is usually desirable to build up the readiness of disabled children through low-organized games in which they learn the fundamentals of throwing or catching, kicking, running or dodging—before attempting to play more complex sports. All sports activities should be designed to emphasize the *abilities* rather than the *disabilities* of those taking part. They should stress maximum physical development, consonant with medical safeguards, and should emphasize the cooperative aspects of play. When competition is carried on, the pressure to win should be very low-keyed, and care should be taken to equalize teams according to ability.

For youth and adults with paraplegic conditions or amputations, but who are otherwise physically capable, one of the best organized sports programs is the wheelchair sports movement. A number of games and sports have been carried on by players in wheelchairs since World War II. In 1957, Benjamin H. Lipton, director of the Joseph Bulova School of Watchmaking, launched the first National Wheelchair Games in the United States. A year later, the National Wheelchair Athletic Association was organized "for the prime function of establishing rules and regulations-governing all wheelchair sports in the United States, except basketball, which had its own national association."[6]

Today, over 10,000 athletes engage in organized wheelchair sports competition throughout the United States. In addition, 56 other nations sponsor similar programs. There is a "Paralympics" that takes place around the time of the regular Olympics at which teams and disabled individuals from various nations compete in wheelchair sports. Some of the specific events include archery, bowling, track and field (including javelin, shotput and racing), swimming, weight-lifting and basketball. Participants are placed in one of five classes, according to their degree of disability, and competition in each of the sports is classed according to different levels of ability. In each event, modifications or devices may be used to adapt the rules to the needs of wheelchair competitors. Thus, in throwing events such as the shotput, an official shotput circle is used, but a stop-board or attendant may be used to hold back the contestant's chair from going outside the circle.

In the 1976 Olympiad for the Physically Disabled, held in Toronto, Canada, just after the Montreal Olympics, 50 countries were represented by about 1600 competitors, including, for the first time, amputee and blind, as well as wheelchair, athletes.

An obvious benefit of wheelchair sports is that participants are helped to develop self-confidence. Furthermore, wheelchair sports events tend to improve society's attitude toward the physically disabled. Stein writes,

> *Their accomplishments and feats through sports and athletics can do much to inform the public, to educate it, and to attack those rigid attitudinal barriers which promote the continuation of hardened categories. The ideology of sports rests in what one does, and upon ability, not disability.*[7]

Realistically, many physically disabled persons, particularly those with such conditions as cerebral palsy, muscular dystrophy or severe orthopedic im-

---

[6] Benjamin H. Lipton: "Wheelchair Sports: Its Role in the Rehabilitation of the Physically Disabled." *Therapeutic Recreation Journal*, 4th Quarter, 1970, p. 9.

[7] Julian R. Stein: "Why Sports?" *Performance.* Washington, D.C. President's Committee on Employment of the Handicapped, October–November, 1971, p. 5.

pairments, are *not* able to compete on this level. However, many different sports and games can be modified still further to permit enjoyment for even the most limited players.

For example, *archery* may be carried on with lighter bows and at shorter distances. When shooting, a person on crutches should lean forward on one crutch and a person in a wheelchair should turn his wheelchair sideways and shoot from that angle. Even a person with only one hand or arm may take part in archery by having the bow fixed to a post anchored in the ground.

Bowling. Bowling is enjoyed by many disabled persons. Again, lighter balls and pins and shortened alleys may be used. Individuals in wheelchairs may be permitted to swing the ball back and forth more than once, to give it extra momentum, or they may use a specially constructed metal rack to release the ball. Players on crutches may stand at the foul line. Bowling is also carried on with blind players, who use a guide rail in approaching the foul line. A sighted person assists by telling the blind player what pins he must shoot for and by keeping score. A Blind Bowlers' Association assists in the formation of leagues and conducts tournaments through the mail.

Dual Games. These games, such as badminton, billiards, table tennis, tennis or shuffleboard, which are usually played with two players, may all be carried on successfully with the disabled. In tennis, for example, the court may be smaller and several players may be put on the court at a time to make up for their limited mobility. When advisable, players may use shortened rackets or hold the racket further up the handle; players with one arm begin the serve with the ball on the racket. In this or other racket games, like badminton, even double arm amputees may take part by having the racket strapped to their arm stump.

Table tennis has been adapted in several ways for the physically disabled. Special paddles have been made that permit poorly coordinated players, such as those with cerebral palsy, to play the game. Patients with scoliosis and in a body cast or children with Legg-Perthes disease or with dislocated hips can all take part in table tennis using high stretchers that support them. Those in wheelchairs can play, provided that there is enough room around the table for them to maneuver. Similar adaptations are made for other dual games.

Golf. This sport has also been used successfully with physically disabled players. A small and less demanding course can be developed, with players using an electric golf cart to get around. In some cases, miniature or "putt-putt" courses are used for the disabled. Depending on the disability, players may use lighter or shorter clubs and vary the stance or grip in order to be able to stroke successfully.

In addition to such sports, many other forms of physical activity are useful with the disabled, including dancing, roller-skating, fishing, quiet games and camping and nature activities.

QUIET GAMES

Quiet games and hobby activities are extremely useful with the physically disabled, partly because they may be carried on with extremely limited skills and partly because they lend themselves either to individual or small-group participation.

Table games, including cards, chess and checkers, dominoes, Parcheesi or equipment games like Nok Hockey or Skittles, are extremely useful. Special equipment may be designed for those with manual limitations, particularly with cerebral palsy and similar conditions. This may include holding racks for cards, electric shufflers or devices with which to move chessmen or checkers; as crude an instrument as a stick held in the mouth may be used to move pieces. Braille playing cards have been designed for the blind, and board games with raised squares that can be felt are also helpful. Other quiet games include social games and mixers, usually played while sitting in a circle.

Hobby activities may be carried out in a variety of settings, such as social clubs, hospital wards in rehabilitation centers and even as individual activities for those confined to their homes. These usually involve special interests like collecting (stamps, coins, records, dolls, postcards and so on) or the development of a particular skill or craft. Hobbies may be pursued as group projects and often lend themselves to hobby shows or demonstrations at which the disabled can show what they have accomplished.

Dance and Movement Therapy

Dancing and movement therapy represent other forms of physical activity that place stress on creative expression, socialization or exploration of one's movement potential—rather than on competition, which is the focus of most sports and games. Dance in particular is used in many hospitals for the mentally ill but may also be adapted to the needs of the physically disabled. Essentially, three forms may be presented: (a) *creative dance* in any of its forms, such as modern dance, ballet or children's rhythmics; (b) *social dancing*, also known as ballroom dancing; and (c) *folk* or *square dancing*, which is usually conducted as a group activity. It is an extremely useful form of activity because it combines physical exercise with an emotionally or artistically expressive quality.

Creative dance may be readily adapted for the physically disabled, depending on the nature of the impairment. Deaf men and women students at Gallaudet College in Washington, D.C., have formed an outstanding modern dance club that gives many performances throughout the year; despite their not being able to hear music, deaf people are able to "feel" the rhythm through floor vibrations and use visual cues to coordinate their movement. Dance is uniquely important for the deaf, as Peter Wisher, professor of physical education at Gallaudet College, points out,

> Because of the reduced influence of sound in the lives of the deaf, perception of visual images increases in importance in all phases of education and daily living. This dependence on the visual serves to emphasize the importance of movement, which is an important aspect of communication. . . . Consequently, the area of the dance may have relatively more importance in the lives of the deaf than of the hearing.[8]

Children with varied disabilities also enjoy creative dance, particularly when it is presented in an unstructured way, with free and spontaneous movement of the body to music or other rhythmic accompaniment. Blind children,

---

[8] Peter R. Wisher: "Dance and the Deaf." *Journal of Health, Physical Education and Recreation*, March, 1969, p. 81.

in particular, profit from this form of activity since it encourages them to learn space relationships and to move about freely and expressively—as opposed to their usual cautious and restrained movement.

Simple folk and square dances, in lines, circles or squares, can also be mastered by the physically disabled. Obviously, dances at a high tempo or with complicated foot movements should be avoided. However, the blind, the deaf and other disabled individuals can do a wide range of such traditional dances and find pleasure in their lively rhythm and social involvement. When a group with mixed disabilities is taking part in folk and square dancing, it is helpful to pair them off so their abilities complement each other. In other words, if a deaf teen-ager is partnered with a blind teen-ager, as a *couple* they have both *vision* and *hearing* and can help each other master the dance.

Wheelchair square dancing has become a popular activity for many orthopedically disabled persons. They are able to do many of the same dances that are done by the nondisabled, but certain modifications need to be made. Since a wheelchair is considerably wider than a person and cannot revolve or turn in as narrow a course, it is necessary to enlarge the dance area and to slow down, or allow longer musical sections, in order to perform each part of the dance. Since wheelchairs cannot move sideways, forward-and-back movements should be substituted where appropriate. Other actions, such as the swing, do-si-do and promenade, can all be done in modified form by wheelchair square dancers.

MOVEMENT THERAPY

Movement or dance therapy (often the terms are used interchangeably) is used primarily with mentally ill patients. It incorporates psychoanalytic principles that see a close relationship between one's bodily carriage and one's psychological makeup. Jung explored artistic experience as a nonliteral means of expressing deep feelings that defied verbal communication but presented symbolic movement images that could be seen and dealt with. Reich spoke of chronic muscular tensions as being deeply entrenched defense mechanisms that confined the body as a "defensive armor." The movement or dance therapist deals directly with releasing these muscles and thus exposing repressed feelings. Thus dance becomes a medium through which the psychiatric patient can express and communicate his feelings, release his inner tensions and find a sense of security.

Dance therapy was initially used as a diagnostic tool and then as a therapeutic modality. Espenak, for example, described typical postures of patients that displayed their inner feelings:

1. *The dejected attitude—slumped shoulders, fallen chest, head on chest, flumbling steps.*
2. *The retiring attitude—shy, inwardly drawn, regressive, shoulders turned in, head between shoulders.*
3. *The heightened tension—with restricted and ineffectual movement in states of anxiety; shoulders lifted up to ears, head in the neck, elbows tense, hands nervous.*
4. *The aggressive attitude—strutting chest, swagger of shoulders, accent on heels.*[9]

---

[9] Lilian Espenak, *cited in* E. Thayer Gaston: *Music in Therapy.* New York, Macmillan, 1968.

Typically, the therapist would adapt his or her approach to the needs and characteristic movement of the patient. Marian Chace, for example, a leading pioneer in dance therapy, would move lightly back and forth, touching palms lightly with a passive, fearful schizophrenic, with these initial contacts gradually increasing in velocity and impact as the patient gained confidence. With an aggressive, psychotic patient, she might present a passive, submissive pose or perhaps, with hands placed on the patient's shoulders, begin a swinging motion to draw her into a common rhythm.[10] Other physical manifestations of tension in psychotic patients, such as hyperactivity, tics, grimaces, rigidity or postural distortions, might all be dealt with through movement.

At the same time that the patient develops movement expression, verbalization of feelings and group interactions are encouraged, with movement sessions taking on a decidedly social character. Dance movements as such are not taught, although the leader may express themes, suggest directions, provide music or lead discussions that help to stimulate creative expression on an individual or small-group basis. Ultimately, patients are helped to come to grips with their bodies more fully, to have a clearer image of themselves and to discover a new medium through which they can communicate their feelings and release their inner tensions. In some cases, images of childhood experiences may be evoked as a way of helping patients recognize and express repressed feelings and memories—thus contributing to other psychotherapeutic processes. Although primary emphasis is given to the use of movement therapy with psychiatric patients, it has also been used with the physically disabled, the elderly and even the deaf and blind as a way of helping them come to grips with their own body images and become more fully integrated emotionally and physically through nonverbal experience.

Movement has also been used with the mentally retarded or other developmentally disabled children and youth to promote overall growth. Sometimes titled "adapted physical education" and sometimes "perceptual-motor" learning, a variety of tests of motor skills may be used at the outset to assess each individual's status, and then a plan may be developed for remedying gross motor deficits.[11] Emphasis is usually placed on essential movement patterns and on enhancing such elements as strength, balance and agility in an effort to help children avoid being labelled "awkward" or "clumsy." Basic skills, such as standing, hopping, walking, crawling, jumping, climbing, sliding and hitting, are emphasized, as well as concepts of level, direction, tempo, intensity, repetition and movement quality.

On another level, modified dance and movement techniques may be used with older residents in a nursing home, both as a pleasurable form of recreation and as a moderate form of conditioning exercise. Even patients who are in wheelchairs or in bed may perform upper-body and arm movements as a small-group activity to music.

---

[10] Marian Chace: "Dance As an Adjunctive Therapy with Hospitalized Mental Patients." *Bulletin of the Menninger Clinic*, November, 1953, p. 222.

[11] Robert E. Grace and Linda S. Dye: "Adapted Physical Education Practicum." *Journal of Physical Education and Recreation*, June, 1976, pp. 39–40. See also Newell Kephart: *Slow Learner in the Classroom.* Columbus, Ohio, Merrill, 1960; and Bryant J. Cratty: *Perceptual-Motor Behavior and Education Processes.* Springfield, Illinois, Charles C Thomas, 1969, for a fuller discussion of the influence of motor learning on overall development.

Dramatics

This represents another extremely useful and enjoyable kind of recreational experience in which the disabled may take part. It is easily adapted so that people with different levels of ability and almost every type of impairment may take part with great satisfaction. In part, this is because it can take so many forms and be approached on so many different levels. It provides, more than any other medium, the opportunity to play roles, express emotions, ventilate fears and hostilities and find release from tensions. Individuals who normally stammer severely are often able to speak with fluency and ease when playing a dramatic role.

The rehabilitation therapies manual of a large state mental hospital comments on the role of drama in working with psychiatric patients:

> It is a method of diagnosis as well as a method of treatment. One of its characteristic features is that role-acting is organically included in the treatment process. It can be adapted to every type of problem, personal or group, of children or adults. . . . The psychodrama is human society in miniature, the simplest possible set-up for a methodical study of its psychological structure. Through techniques such as the auxiliary ego, spontaneous improvisation, self-presentation, soliloquy, the interpolation of resistance, new dimensions of the mind are opened up, and what is most important, they can be explored under experimental conditions.[12]

Although emotional catharsis is not as significant a part of the need of physically disabled persons, it is obvious that many of them have psychological problems stemming from their disability. The blind, deaf, paraplegic or otherwise severely impaired person frequently is withdrawn, isolated, lacking in confidence and unable to relate easily to others. Dramatics—because it is *make-believe*—provides a vehicle through which he can *safely* express himself, making his feelings and needs known to others, and temporarily leave his *own* identity to play other roles.

Dramatics have been especially successful in senior centers and residential care settings serving elderly persons. Their particular value is that they help reinforce the self-confidence of the actors, particularly when they succeed in memorizing lines, a task that many of them feel is impossible. Based on a survey of dramatics with the elderly, Gray writes,

> Participants in dramatics stressed that their participation kept them mentally active at a time of life when opportunities for mental activity were greatly reduced through loss of work roles and physical decrements such as deteriorating eyesight. Another source of great satisfaction to members of dramatics groups was the fact that they succeeded in acting for the first time in their lives. They were delighted to disprove the old adage that "you can't teach an old dog new tricks."[13]

Other benefits are that elderly participants are helped to work together as a group, thus overcoming withdrawal and isolation, and are provided with a rich means of emotional release—often keeping elderly patients in nursing

---

[12] *Program Media.* Manual of Rehabilitation Therapies Department, Spring Grove State Hospital, Catonsville, Maryland, September, 1970, p. 6.

[13] Paula Gross Gray: *Dramatics for the Elderly.* New York, Teachers College Press, Columbia University, 1974, p. 4.

homes so involved that they forget their aches and pains. Even the audience benefits from dramatic performances, in that they show vividly what the elderly are capable of, and other residents proudly identify with the performers. As in any form of recreation or activity therapy with the disabled, there are obviously problems to overcome. Gray reported a number of the most common problems encountered in working with the elderly in dramatics, as well as the methods used by recreation leaders in working with them (Fig. 10–1).

Figure 10–1. Physical and psychological limitations of participants as perceived by recreation personnel. (From Paula Gross Gray: *Dramatics for the Elderly*. New York, Columbia University, Teachers College Press, 1974, p. 7.)

Problem	Most Common Solution
Inability to memorize, or fear of memorization	Use of improvisation
Hearing disability	Helped by fellow actor
Visual impairment (blindness)	Large print scripts, and individual coaching
Physical disability (confinement to wheelchair)	Limited action; used ramps to move about
Lack of interest	Individual contact and encouragement
Senility	Gave no lines
Limited reading skill	Individual coaching
Lack of self-confidence	Constant reassurance

Other expressive activities related to dramatics have proved extremely useful in working with the elderly. One technique recently explored among patients in nursing homes, hospitals and prisons is poetry therapy. Like drama, poetry may serve as a means of expressing one's chaotic or hostile emotions or even helping to explore one's own feelings and past experiences. A Yale psychiatrist, Albert Rothenberg, comments that a patient who suddenly discovers the message of a great poet may experience a flash of understanding similar to the dramatic insight that may also come through intensive psychotherapy.[14] Similarly, by writing an original poem, an inhibited, repressed person may tell his or her therapist much that was secret previously. A leading modern poet, Kenneth Koch, has worked closely with patients in nursing homes and achieved remarkable success in involving them enthusiastically and creatively.[15]

Musical Activities

Music is one of the most varied and useful activities in meeting the needs of every type of disability. It can be conducted on every level from the simplest to the most complex and has value both as a "listening" and as a "doing" activity. It may involve single individuals or large groups in choral or instrumental programs. It engenders a feeling of companionship and group solidarity and at the same time is an expressive art that brings emotional pleasure and

---

[14] "Poetry Therapy." *Time*, March 13, 1972, p. 45.
[15] Kenneth Koch: *I Never Told Anybody: Teaching Poetry Writing in a Nursing Home.* New York, Random House, 1977.

release. In one state hospital manual, the following description of the values of music is provided:

> In general, music can elevate the depressed patient, calm the hyperactive one, create a desired mood, dispel unpleasant sensations, unite a disparate body of people. By appealing to the senses, the mind is released from inhibitions and out of the environment both physical and mental, into a more appealing world. . . . The interrelationship of the members of the group to each other and to the therapist develops a special aura of its own quite different from other more structured therapies in atmosphere and affect.[16]

Essentially, there are three phases to the program of music as it may be provided for the physically disabled: (a) listening; (b) singing; and (c) instrumental music.

1. *Music listening.* This can range from listening to recorded or taped popular or classical music to having visiting performers entertain in large hospital situations. Sometimes listening may involve music appreciation sessions, with discussion of the background of the music—whether it be classical, jazz or folk.

2. *Singing.* This may involve informal folk singing or community songfests, as well as choruses, madrigal groups or other forms of performing units. Young children are likely to enjoy action songs, while older persons will prefer songs that were popular years ago. Singing for disabled persons may simply be a casual recreational activity—preferably with an accompanist at a piano or accordion—or it may become an important area of personal growth and emotional release. In general, all those with physical disability, except the deaf, may take part, although some individuals with major speech defects (such as the severely cerebral palsied) may have some difficulty in singing. It may actually be used to *improve* voice production.

3. *Instrumental music.* Obviously, this requires skilled leadership. Often, if the recreation leader is not able to direct instrumental music programs and there is no skilled music therapist available, it is possible to get volunteers from the community who have a high degree of skill in instrumental music. This may range from rhythmic sessions with children or beginners, using simple percussion or other rhythm instruments, to instruction on beginning, intermediate or advanced levels for players of all ages. Since the key factor in playing music is the use of hands and arms, and particularly finger dexterity, individuals with other types of disability are usually able to play wind, string or percussion instruments.

Arts and Crafts

Probably more than any other major category of recreation, arts and crafts lend themselves to adaptation for individuals at all levels of ability. Like hobbies, they may be carried on individually or in group settings and may range from the most simple projects to extremely advanced activities. They offer an

---

[16] *Program Media.* Manual of Rehabilitation Therapies Department, Spring Grove State Hospital, Catonsville, Maryland, September, 1970, p. 6.

excellent outlet for creative expression and the constructive use of energy. In addition, since the work produced may be used as decorations in a home or hospital ward, as gifts to friends or family or as exhibits in shows, they help to bring about a strong sense of personal accomplishment.

One major area of activity is the graphic arts: sketching, water-color and oil painting or print-making. For those with adequate vision and manipulative skills, these activities may be approached just as with nondisabled persons. For those with more limited dexterity, it may be necessary to devise special holders for crayons, charcoal or brushes.

Clay modeling, soap carving and papier-mâché work also are useful for the physically disabled. These may be approached on an extremely rudimentary level or may involve advanced projects. They may include carving or modeling animals, dolls, puppets and similar projects. Ceramics represents a more advanced medium that may be carried on using the mold process or, for those capable of using hands effectively, with the potter's wheel or by building slabs or pinch-pots. There are many other craft activities that can be suited to the physically disabled, many of which improve manual dexterity and coordination.

The emphasis in using arts and crafts should be on creative expression rather than on developing useful or impressive products. Participants should be allowed considerable choice in selecting their products and should be able to move at their own rate. Although it may be convenient for the leader to use prestructured craft materials, such as "paint-by-the-numbers" kits, these reduce the value of the activity for participants. As much as possible, they should be creating their *own* works.

Art may also be used as a basic therapeutic technique, particularly with disturbed or psychotic patients. Like other creative or expressive forms, it has the potential for promoting healing psychological processes through essentially nonverbal forms of communication. Edith Kramer, who has worked with delinquents, the blind and the mentally ill, points out that art should be regarded as a distinct form of therapy in its own right rather than a tool of psychotherapy. The art therapist, she writes, functions as an artist and educator who is capable of modifying his methods according to the patient's pathology and needs:

> He is trained to appraise the patient's behavior and production and to interpret his observations to the therapeutic team. He implements the team's therapeutic goals, but he does not ordinarily use his clinical insight for uncovering or interpreting to the patient deep unconscious material, nor does he encourage the development of a transference relationship.[17]

As patients create art, Kramer suggests that the art therapist's response must be geared to their needs and developmental level. In some cases, they should be helped to relate what they have done to reality or to apply aesthetic criteria to their work. In others, the mere fact that they have been able to make a creative effort is sufficient, and it would be a mistake to apply external standards that might inhibit or discourage them or to force them into a recognition of why they have created the kinds of images they have. Although technique is never an end in itself, the art therapist helps patients explore the elements of art and learn how to use its tools most fully and expressively.

---

[17] Edith Kramer: *Art as Therapy With Children.* New York, Schocken, 1971, p. 25.

Special Events

These represent an important aspect of recreation programs for the physically disabled in all kinds of settings. They provide an opportunity for working together with others to plan events or simply to enjoy the entertainment offered. Special events may be informal last-minute activities or elaborately planned parties, carnivals, concerts, shows, dances, sports programs, celebrations or trips.

In addition to providing recreation for physically disabled persons in a rehabilitation center or community-sponsored program, special events may be used to educate the public about programs serving disabled people. By holding an open house or inviting outsiders to come to a party, carnival or other event, it is possible to show them what disabled persons are like, dispel their misconceptions and build more positive links with community groups.

Hooper, Mullen and Kennedy suggest varied special events that may be offered in nursing homes:

> A monthly birthday party, celebrating for each birthday in that month; holiday parties such as Hallowe'en or St. Valentine's Day. . . . Talent and fashion shows, teas, bazaars, open houses, hobby shows and entertainment programs can be scheduled throughout the year. Trips and outings can be arranged in many instances, in small groups by car or by bus when proper permission is granted.[18]

Although these suggestions apply specially to the elderly, they also are useful for other types of residential situations.

In Veterans Administration hospitals, special programs frequently include visits by performing groups from the community who will put on musical, dramatic or dance programs or provide other special entertainment for large numbers of patients. In hospitals in large cities, professional performing companies will often appear on their nights off, and professional athletes may also give talks, demonstrations or clinics. When physically disabled persons plan their own programs, such as carnivals, festivals, large-scale picnics or barbecues or talent shows, these events should be carefully organized. As much as possible, the disabled persons themselves should form committees (such as program, publicity, finance, clean-up or special arrangements committees) and do the actual work of running the event.

An actual example of a special event may be found in a skilled nursing home that sponsors an annual bazaar to raise money for a charity selected by members of the Residents' Council.[19] This event had the following steps or tasks:

1. Reviewing literature and film material about potential agencies to be aided and making a decision as to which one should receive a charitable gift.
2. Establishing a planning committee and setting up sub-committees to handle each aspect of the bazaar: refreshments, publicity, selling raffle tickets and other functions.
3. Preparing products to be sold at the raffle, in crafts groups, sewing, jewelry-making and other sessions conducted by the home's recreation staff.
4. Holding the bazaar itself, as a full day event, on a Sunday before Thanksgiving.

---

[18] Langdon Hooper, Dorothy Mullen and Irene J. Kennedy: *Recreation Service in Connecticut Nursing Homes for the Aged.* Hartford, Connecticut, State Department of Health, 1968, p. 17.

[19] Rhonda Schuval, Graduate Paper at Herbert Lehman College, New York, 1976.

5. Post-event activities, such as an evening of home movies of the bazaar or a special day when the check was presented in a ceremonial award to the recipient agency.

This event, which was well attended by members of the home's staff, volunteers, guests from the community and members of residents' families, raised an impressive sum and was regarded as a major success. One of its positive values was to increase the residents' sense of self-worth by having them participate in a service to people outside the institutional setting. The award was given to a small nonprofit agency in the nearby neighborhood, so that the home's residents had a sense of helping their immediate community. By working over a period of time toward a distinct and achievable goal, many of the recreation activities carried on during the preceding weeks and months were given a sense of purpose and high morale. Cooperative relationships were developed among the staff and residents of the home itself, along with a sense of group awareness and improved communication. Finally, family members were drawn into the process in a variety of ways, with the home's residents having the opportunity to feel pride in themselves and to welcome their relatives to a positive and significant experience.

Many agencies and institutions sponsor such events to raise money, improve morale, strengthen ties to family members and community groups and as a desirable form of public relations. For example, the New Lisbon State School in New Lisbon, New Jersey, sponsors a series of large-scale events throughout the year, including a Memorial Day Program, an Annual Picnic and Governor's Day (attended by the state governor), an Independence Day Celebration, a Circus Day, Labor Day Carnival, annual Parents' Bazaars and other shows, sports events or holiday programs that succeed in attracting thousands of relatives, families and friends to the school. Such programs help to break down the barrier that too often exists between large state institutions for the retarded and the outside world and provide positive and productive ways of involving families and friends of the school's residents in its program. Seen in this light, recreation becomes an absolutely vital service within the overall administration of the institution.

Camping and Nature Activities

Day camping, resident camping and nature activities in general are among the most successful and valuable programs provided for the disabled. Usually, such activities provide an opportunity to live, play and work with others in an environment that promotes good fellowship and understanding of the outdoors. Group interaction is a strong benefit of camping programs, and participants learn new skills and recreational interests that may serve them in good stead. Particularly for individuals who may be restricted to a hospital or other residential setting with crowded wards, hospital beds and bleak surroundings, the opportunity to experience the out-of-doors can be an enriching and morale-building experience.

There are special camps in the United States today that serve epileptics, diabetics, cardiac patients, the blind, deaf, mentally retarded, convalescent patients and other persons with physical disability. Such programs usually require a high staff-to-patient ratio and often make considerable use of volunteers. Day camping programs are usually easier to operate; the extensive care that many disabled persons require makes overnight or residential camping much more demanding. Frequently in such settings, campers who are given responsibilities for self-care or for helping to do chores for their bunks or in the dining area gain a new degree of independence and social functioning and make dramatic gains in personal adjustment.

Camping programs may be scheduled in a variety of ways:

1. Day camping, in which a group of physically disabled children or youth attend a program near their home regularly. To be considered a "day camp" program, as opposed to an ordinary vacation playground program, it should be a full-day activity, including lunch, have some involvement with nature and the outdoors and be organized in groups. As opposed to an ordinary summer playground program, day camping involves formal registration and regular attendance and usually has a carefully organized program with trips and outings to places of special interest.
2. Resident camping for the physically disabled is usually sponsored by organizations concerned with a specific disability, such as cerebral palsy, blindness or orthopedic impairment. Frequently such camps have one- or two-week sessions; in some instances they are sponsored by public recreation departments, in which case they usually serve children or youth with different types of disabilities.
3. Nature activities, either in a camping program or as part of any recreation program, might include any of the following: hiking and exploring natural settings; camping and camp-craft, such as putting up tents, sleeping in the outdoors, knot-tying or camp cookery; campfires and related activities; nature-related crafts, such as shell and rock painting, building bird feeders or flower and leaf pressing; or the study of nature: vegetation and wildlife, effects of erosion, conservation projects and gardening activities.

In addition, water activities, such as boating, fishing, swimming or water games, are usually extremely popular. If a lake or beach area is being used, extreme caution must be taken with the physically disabled, since such areas are not as easily supervised as a swimming pool (because of the rapidly changing depth of the water or surf or the difficulty in seeing beneath the surface). Safe swimming areas should be clearly marked off with ropes and closely watched, with a high ratio of staff to participants.

Other special factors involved in selecting a camping area include the desirability of having nearby natural settings suitable for outdoor education or nature-oriented activities or for more advanced hiking, boating or other survival-related programs, when appropriate. If numbers of the campers are in wheelchairs, it should be recognized that it is difficult to move these through low, muddy areas or along sandy beaches without walkways. Camps provided for older persons in particular may require an additional level of warmth, confort and access to toilet areas.

The ideal camp situation is one in which the physically disabled are integrated with the nondisabled. For many, however, their limitations are such that they cannot keep up with the full range of activities enjoyed by the nondisabled and are not yet ready for the degree of independent self-care required in such a setting. For them, a segregated camp setting is preferable, in order to build the necessary skills and help them gain confidence. For some physically disabled children, there may be a progression through the following stages: (a) day camp, in which they begin to gain skills and confidence; (b) resident or overnight camp for the disabled alone; and (c) resident or overnight camp for both disabled and nondisabled children.

A number of examples of special camps for disabled children and youth are described elsewhere in this text, particularly in Chapters 5 and 6. Wilderness camping with a survival element has been particularly successful with psychiatric patients, who often show remarkable progress in terms of relating to reality and meaningful social interaction in the camp setting. It is also possible to define different goals for separate groups of patients, within an overall camp situation, and thus to focus on the unique needs of each of the separate groups.[20] Information about established camps for the disabled may be gained from major voluntary organizations serving special populations, which have chapters in large metropolitan areas.

TRIPS AND OUTINGS

When any sort of trip or special outing is planned for the disabled, careful arrangements need to be made with respect to (a) arranging transportation; (b) getting permission for those who will be traveling (either from parents or, when necessary, medical approval); (c) screening all participants to determine whether the trip will be appropriate for them; and (d) making arrangements at the place that will be visited, to be certain that they are prepared to accept and have suitable accommodations for a group of physically disabled persons.

The value of such programs is that they provide novelty and special interest to the lives of the physically disabled and help to keep their morale high. They tend to maintain constructive ties with the community and promote socialization and group involvement. For patients in a rehabilitation center, trips and outings have the very special value of helping them learn to get around in the outside world and to develop the kinds of practical skills they will need when they are discharged.

FISHING

Fishing is an extremely popular recreational activity for all age levels in the general population and may be used successfully with disabled groups. It depends on the availability of fishing waters, although it is always possible to provide transportation to nearby lakes or fishing piers at the seashore. The activity may be more or less vigorous, depending on the capability of the participants, ranging from sitting by a stream or pier holding a handline to actual bait-casting, surf-casting or more difficult forms of fishing.

Numerous other outdoor activities, such as hiking or nature walks, aquatics, skiing, and similar pastimes, are described elsewhere in this text. Apart from such activities, one of the primary values of camping is that it is an intensely social kind of experience. Particularly in the case of elderly, retired persons, who are often isolated from others in their day-by-day living, camping has extremely important emotional benefits.

PLAYROOM ACTIVITIES IN PEDIATRIC HOSPITAL UNITS

As a final example of the selection and modification of activities in therapeutic settings, one might use playroom activities in pediatric hospitals.

---

[20] Thomas E. Arthur, George M. Phillips and Susan B. Thomas: "Camping by Objectives." *Therapeutic Recreation Journal*, 4th Quarter, 1976, pp. 132–137.

Unlike a number of the other kinds of treatment settings described in this text, such units serve a wide diversity of patients of different ages and levels of need. In general, recreation is seen as a way of helping children who are removed from their everyday world and placed in a stressful situation maintain a link with their normal daily routine. Narwold suggests that the goals of recreation in such a situation are

> . . . aimed at helping children adjust emotionally to the hospital situation, come to terms with their physical handicaps, and accept themselves as worthwhile individuals. . . . Spontaneity and a warm, trusting, nonthreatening atmosphere are stressed.[21]

Within the playroom itself, children who are tense and apprehensive are able to become more comfortable. Parents and the playroom supervisor may become involved with the child's play or craft activity if they wish; normally, a wide range of simple toys, puzzles or craft projects are available. If children cannot come to the room itself, recreation therapists often make use of a movable cart, brightly decorated and filled with various play and game materials, that can be taken to the patient's bedside. A unique value of recreation in the pediatric setting is that it can be used to help children accept, understand and adjust to the hospital situation. Using projective dolls and toys, children may act out their fears, play the role of doctors and nurses and become familiar with many of the instruments and procedures found in the hospital in a positive, rather than passive, way.

Children in the hospital, because of fear of being deserted, often become more dependent, clinging to their parents and sometimes showing regressive behavior symptoms. They tend to have virtually no control over what will happen to them and are subjected to painful and frightening procedures. Since play is a normal part of the child's life pattern and allows him to take charge of a "make-believe" world, expressing and communicating feelings about his or her environment, it can be an extremely helpful therapeutic agent. Dramatic play, water play and activities that channel the child's aggressive feelings (such as the punching doll that pops back up, pegs that are hammered into the board or blocks that can be built up and then crashed to the floor) are all helpful forms of expression. Particularly for children confined to their beds or in heavy casts, who tend to become extremely restless and hyperactive, play can provide an extremely important release. Beside games, music, stories told by hospital volunteers and arts and crafts are particularly useful in such situations.

For children who have undergone surgery and are on the road to recovery, play can be provided in close cooperation with physical and occupational therapy. The patient is encouraged to take part in activities that increase strength, maintain or improve motion in a joint or otherwise aid in rehabilitation. Swimming or even such active games as wheelchair basketball or other modified sports are extremely helpful, under the direction of medical staff. Narwold writes,

> In this way, children are encourged to be active, aggressive and noisy. Competition, a normal healthy aspect of growing up, is not lost when the child is hospitalized.[22]

---

[21] Sally J. Narwold: "Coping with Hospitalization through Play." *In* Larry Neal (ed.): *Leisure Today: Selected Readings.* Washington, D.C., American Association for Leisure and Recreation, 1975, p. 35.

[22] *Ibid.*

When the problem is more severe and the patient is undergoing a series of difficult operations and treatments, along with a high level of impairment, disfigurement or pain, recreation in the pediatric setting becomes all the more important. Observers note that many children who have been in treatment over a period of time lose vitality and initiative and become sad, depressed and withdrawn. For such patients, it is critical that recreation serve as a vital tool in maintaining morale, interest in life and a positive self-image and outlook toward others.

This chapter has given examples of several of the major areas of recreation activity provided in programs for the disabled, along with illustrations of how they may be designed to meet specific therapeutic needs. Taken in combination with the techniques described in Chapter 4 and the other sections dealing with the major categories of disability, it gives a useful overview of the content of therapeutic recreation service.

SUGGESTED TOPICS FOR CLASS DISCUSSION, EXAMINATION OR STUDENT PAPERS

1. What are the key elements that must be considered in selecting program activities for a specific patient/client population?

2. Select a specific form of activity and analyze it in terms of physical, social, psychological and other elements and its demands and potential outcomes or benefits.

3. What are the unique values to be derived from creative forms of activity, such as dance, music or art? How may they be used for those with either physical or mental disability?

4. Special events, as described in this chapter, have a unique set of social values and objectives. Discuss these.

chapter 11

Community Services
for the Disabled

This chapter focuses on the role of community organizations in providing special programs to serve the needs of the disabled in noninstitutional settings. It describes the scope and focus of such agencies—both public and voluntary— and presents guidelines for expanding their efforts.

FOCUS OF COMMUNITY-BASED THERAPEUTIC RECREATION

Obviously, it is the purpose of community-based recreation or social service agencies to serve disabled persons who are not housed in institutions but live with their families or in other settings in which they have a degree of social independence. The great majority of aged or mentally retarded persons, for example, are not institutionalized. They may, however, require modified or specially designed programs or environments to meet their recreational needs.

It should be stressed that, although integration of the disabled with the nondisabled is a highly desirable goal, it is not always a feasible one. In the field of education, for example, the passage in the mid-1970s of the Education of All Handicapped Children Act, which required that all states receiving federal aid provide "free and appropriate" education for the handicapped, gave a tremendous stimulus to those who sought to end educational isolation of the disabled. Yet, as Hechinger points out, some disabilities are far more receptive to "mainstreaming" than others. Many children with physical disabilities such as blindness, deafness or limited mobility

> . . . are endowed with high intellectual and motivational qualities that enable them to overcome their handicaps. . . . Children with varying degrees of retardation pose substantially different problems. Some may benefit from being integrated into nonintellectual activities, such as sports, shop and other nonverbal subjects. But their sense of defeat and frustration might be heightened rather than diminished in intellectual competition with their non-handicapped peers.

Children with serious emotional problems may not only disrupt ordinary educational procedures but also arouse anger and antagonism in their classmates. Here too, however, the degree of the emotional disturbance should be seriously considered.[1]

Similar considerations prevail in planning recreation services for the disabled in the community setting. Essentially, the disabled may be divided into three categories, whatever the nature of their impairment:

1. Those whose limitations are so severe that they require completely separate and segregated programs and social groupings. This may be because they are unable to participate successfully in activities carried on by the nondisabled or because they are rejected by the nondisabled or excluded by sponsoring authorities.
2. Those whose disabilities prevent them from taking part in integrated programs in some areas of activity but who can readily share in other programs. To illustrate, children with severe physical impairments might not be able to engage in sports leagues with nondisabled children, as part of a summer playground program, but might engage successfully in arts and crafts or dramatic activities on an integrated basis.
3. Those who are able to take part with a considerable degree of success in varied activities with the nondisabled. Efforts should be made to integrate such individuals as fully as possible with the overall population.

For many individuals, it is possible to go through a process of gaining social and physical skills and self-confidence and thus move from segregated programs into integrated group membership. As an example, disabled children may become involved first in a day camp serving those with impairment on a segregated basis. Gradually, they may be able to attend a sleep-away camp and, ultimately, to take part in camping programs that serve both the disabled and the nondisabled.

In the case of illness involving a process of recovery and rehabilitation, the issue of segregated versus integrated grouping should be seen as a continuum of service.

According to the degree of integration possible, various types of programs may be provided. Usually, their sponsors fall into the following categories.

Sponsors of Community Services for the Disabled

PUBLIC RECREATION AGENCIES

These include public recreation or recreation and park departments, school districts, youth service agencies, community service departments in housing projects, publicly sponsored libraries, museums and other agencies that provide recreation for the public at large. Included may be programs the disabled persons enter or facilities they use without any special planning, identification or modification of activities or equipment, provided they are able to achieve a degree of success and satisfaction on this informal basis. Specially designed programs intended to serve the disabled and established for this purpose are also

---

[1] Fred M. Hechinger: "Bringing the Handicapped Into the Mainstream." *New York Times*, April 25, 1976, p. ES-15.

included. More and more, such special recreation programs are becoming collaborative efforts, involving the joint sponsorship of two or more public agencies or the cooperation of public and private or voluntary groups.

ORGANIZATIONS CONCERNED WITH DISABILITY

As described earlier, a considerable number of national organizations with local or regional chapters promote programs designed to meet the needs of individuals with special disability. If they do not provide such services directly, they often cooperate with other agencies that do by providing funding, technical advisement, volunteers or other forms of support.

SERVICE ORGANIZATIONS

In most American communities, there are a variety of service organizations or civic clubs that are committed to providing or assisting programs that meet social needs. Fraternal or service organizations such as the Elks, Moose, Kiwanis and Oddfellows and veterans' organizations, such as the Veterans of Foreign Wars and the American Legion are frequently involved in sponsoring programs serving disabled children and youth. In addition to such organizations, other voluntary organizations in the recreation field, such as the Y.M.C.A. or Y.W.C.A. and Boys' Clubs or Girl Scouts, frequently mount special programs for the disabled.

SPECIAL AGENCIES

In a few cities, special agencies have been established that have as their primary purpose the provision of recreation to varied groups of disabled persons. One such agency, the San Francisco Recreation Center for the Handicapped, is described later in this chapter.

COMMUNITY COUNCILS OR BOARDS

In order to develop systematic recreation services to meet the leisure needs of disabled persons, special community councils or boards have been formed in a number of major cities. Such councils usually serve to promote public awareness of the needs of the disabled, to identify existing programs and to make recommendations, develop support and coordinate new services.

The range of services offered is extremely wide. It may include any or all of the following:

Social clubs for mentally retarded or physically disabled youth and adults.

Day camps or special residential vacation camps for those with varied disabilities, including the aged.

The sponsorship of special facilities, such as playgrounds, parks or community centers, designed to be suitable for those with physical handicaps.

After-care programs for discharged mental patients, former drug addicts or other persons who require sheltered social settings in their transition to community life.

Volunteer services for homebound individuals with severe disability.

PUBLIC RECREATION PROGRAMS FOR
THE DISABLED

In a number of major cities, as well as in many smaller communities, public recreation or recreation and park departments offer comprehensive programs to serve the leisure needs of the physically and mentally disabled.

In Seattle, Washington, an extensive program of service is offered under the direction of a full-time therapeutic recreation specialist employed by the Recreation Division of the municipal Park Department. The schedule of special programs in Seattle includes such elements as:

1. Monthly meetings for disabled children in various recreation centers around the city, usually on Friday or Saturday afternoons. These are continued throughout the year and involve varied club and recreational activities.
2. Special swimming lessons for disabled children, given in 10-week series during the fall. These are specially designed so that there is at least one instructor for every two or three children. Beginners, or those who cannot support themselves in the water, are taught individually.
3. A summer day camp for disabled children six years of age or older. These are held in three three-week sessions at several camp and park locations in Seattle and King County. Activities include nature crafts, music, games, singing, creative dramatics, sports, cookouts and hiking.

Other programs in Seattle include special groups organized by the Cerebral Palsy Workshop and the Washington Association for the Retarded. There is a special bowling league for the retarded and wheelchair basketball for the orthopedically disabled, as well as a basketball league for adult deaf participants. A major portion of the leadership is provided through the use of volunteers, with the assistance of a central volunteer bureau and a number of service agencies in the community.

Many other cities offer comparable programs. For example, the Los Angeles Park and Recreation Department provides programs for blind adults, multiply disabled youth, the physically disabled and the mentally retarded.

The Chicago Park District has special programs for the disabled in 15 of its major centers, providing assistance to Alcoholics Anonymous, the mentally retarded or perceptually handicapped, the deaf and blind and discharged mental patients and their families.

The Ill and Handicapped Division of the Greensboro, North Carolina Parks and Recreation Commission provides 18 different programs for the mentally retarded, cerebral palsied, blind, orthopedically handicapped, emotionally disturbed and other disabled individuals. Special programs are provided for nursing homes, and a six-week summer day camp serves a substantial number of disabled children with music, nature activities, games, sports and crafts.

The Memphis, Tennessee, Park Commission, in cooperation with a nonprofit Memphis organization called Handicapped, Inc., has established a year-round comprehensive recreation program for the disabled, with an outstanding, specially redesigned center building equipped to serve the mentally retarded, blind, deaf and other special groups. The program serves all age levels with a wide range of activities, trips and camping programs and is assisted by over 2000 volunteers yearly.

Similarly, the Washington, D.C., Recreation Department has built an excellent, new, multimillion dollar facility to serve district-wide recreation needs of the disabled. Over the past two decades, Washington has pioneered in the field of community recreation service for the disabled. One of its unique contributions during the early 1970s was to employ a substantial number of disabled youth and adults, including those with such conditions as retardation, visual disability and orthopedic impairment, as recreation leaders and bussing aides in its own summer programs.

Community Recreation for the Disabled in Canada

In recent years, both local municipalities and provincial governments in Canada have also assumed a growing responsibility for providing community recreation opportunities for special populations. In Vancouver, British Columbia, for example, the number of elderly persons served in municipal recreation programs during a recent seven-year period rose from 21,414 to 108,269 annually; participation figures for disabled children in summer programs increased from 781 to 2519 during the same span. The city park and recreation department offers "meals on wheels" services to shut-ins, serves disabled elderly persons in community center day-care programs and offers weekly recreational activities to mental health patients living in city-licensed boarding houses. In Winnipeg, Manitoba, and in the city of Montreal, similar programs have been initiated to serve mentally retarded children, the physically disabled and aged persons.

In 1975, Haist reported the findings of a survey of municipal recreation services for special groups in the Province of Ontario.[2] Based on an analysis of all Ontario communities with a population of 5000 or more, it was found that

Eighty-seven of the 169 municipalities surveyed (51.5 per cent) indicated that they were providing recreation services for at least one of the four special groups: the mentally retarded, the physically handicapped, the emotionally disturbed, and the learning disabled.

Forty-five per cent of the municipalities surveyed provided recreation services for the mentally retarded, compared with 29 per cent for the physically handicapped, 13 per cent for the learning disabled, and 8.3 per cent for the emotionally disturbed.[3]

Obviously, such figures do not provide an in-depth picture of the range or qualities of the services provided; in addition, the survey's finding that only 8 (4.7 per cent) of the municipalities surveyed had special staff members who were responsible for working with the disabled suggests that many such programs are of a limited or superficial nature. In general, Haist found that recreation programs for special populations tended to be offered more fully in larger cities having a population of 50,000 and more.

A number of Canadian provinces have begun to move vigorously into the promotion of leisure services for the ill and disabled. In Alberta, for example, the provincial government has established a Recreation Services to Special

---

[2] Doris Haist: "A Survey of Municipal Recreation Services for Special Groups in Ontario." *Recreation Review*, August, 1975, pp. 29–50.
[3] *Ibid.*, pp. 36–37.

Groups Branch that

> ... *provides consultative services, information, Provincial, Area and Regional Workshops, and financial assistance to various clientele to facilitate greater recreational opportunities for the mentally and physically disabled, pre-school and school-age children, senior citizens and those in correctional systems, while making the public aware of the existence and needs of these individuals and groups.*[4]

As part of its overall effort, the Branch has supported a planning and research program, as well as the production of public relations materials (such as films, slides and tapes) designed to promote outdoor recreation for senior citizens, sports for the physically disabled, hospital recreation and, most of all, favorable public attitudes toward the entire matter of the disabled individual's place in community life.

Based on a study of recreation services for the ill and disabled in selected public recreation departments, Miller has presented a number of basic recommendations for community organization in this field.

It is her view that, although voluntary organizations or inter-agency councils may be extremely effective in arousing public awareness of needs or providing advice or technical assistance, it is the public recreation department that should carry the major responsibility in this area. She recommends that

1. Local public recreation systems recognize and assume responsibility for making recreation opportunities available to the ill and disabled in their communities.
2. Public recreation administrators assume the initiative and leadership in developing such programs.
3. Established principles for community recreation be used, in carrying on non-institutional recreation programs for the ill and disabled.
4. The resources of those agencies familiar with working with the ill and disabled be used in planning, cooperating, and evaluating such programs.
5. Such programs represent "community efforts," from their initial planning, to the developmental phase and finally the execution of the program.
6. Primary responsibility for administering the program be centered in the local, public recreation managing authority.
7. Financial support be established on a continuing basis, through the contributions of both public and private agencies.
8. An advisory committee be established, representing various community groups, with definite duties and responsibilities outlined in a written charter, and consistent with the administrative policies of the local public recreation system.
9. Appropriate professional consultation be utilized, especially in the initial stages of planning and development of community recreation services for the ill and disabled.[5]

Although this approach is generally sound, today it would have to include a much stronger element of consultation with disabled persons themselves and, when possible, have them play key roles in the planning and organization. Increasingly, the fact that disabled persons have been discriminated against in

---

[4] *Recreation Services to Special Groups Branch.* Manual, Provincial Department of Parks, Recreation and Wildlife, Edmonton, Alberta, April, 1975, p. 5.1.
[5] Betty Miller: "Re-Count for Recreators." *American Recreation Journal*, November–December, 1963, p. 19.

employment, health, social services and education has led them to take a strong line in demanding equal rights and more involvement on all levels. As a single example, in April, 1977, a coalition of groups representing 36 million disabled persons in the United States staged sit-in demonstrations in national and regional offices of the Department of Health, Education and Welfare, demanding stronger regulations against discrimination.[6] It is no longer appropriate to plan programs *for* the disabled as passive recipients; instead, whenever possible, planning must be done *with* and *by* them.

ORGANIZATIONS CONCERNED WITH SPECIFIC FORMS OF DISABILITY

Many voluntary community organizations concerned with specific disabilities, such as blindness, mental retardation, cerebral palsy or orthopedic disability, provide recreation service as a part of their total program of rehabilitation and social assistance. In many cases, the national organization carries on research, develops guidelines or materials in this area or provides other forms of funding assistance. Usually, when direct programs of recreation sponsorship are offered, it is by local chapters or organizations in the cities themselves.

Although it is not possible to provide examples drawn from each of these organizations, an excellent illustration may be found in the work of the Lighthouse, a service center operated by the New York Association for the Blind. This voluntary, nonsectarian, nonprofit agency serves legally blind, visually impaired persons (many of whom are multiply disabled) with a year-round program. Its clientele consists of approximately 3300 persons ranging in age from six months to 90 years and of all races, creeds and socioeconomic backgrounds.

Its overall services include the following:

1. Medical, including a Low Vision Clinic.
2. Rehabilitation, including evaluation of needs, orientation and individual training in mobility.
3. Social services: admission, referral consultation and case work, with respect to personal and economic problems, welfare status and similar problems.
4. Music school.
5. Library service.
6. Recreation and camping.
7. Transportation.
8. Men's and women's residences.
9. Lighthouse Industries, including a sheltered workshop.
10. Craft shop.
11. Child development center.
12. Nursery school.
13. Reader's service.
14. Food service.

The objectives of the Recreation and Camping Division include the following: (a) providing recreational counseling in order to help clients develop a personal philosophy of recreation that meets their needs and skills for participation; (b) providing information as to available community opportunities for

---

[6] Nancy Hicks: "Handicapped Use Protests to Push H.E.W. to Implement '73 Bias Law." *New York Times*, April 11, 1977, p. 12.

recreation; (c) using recreation to assist in the personal development, social adjustment, health and appearance of participants; and (d) promoting participation in independent, self-directed programs.

Activities are offered for five different age groups or categories of visually disabled persons, ranging from children of nursery school age to a recreation program for older adults. They include a wide variety of both active and passive activities, such as arts and crafts, bowling, trips, table games, dancing, dramatics, swimming, newspaper work and such special events as parties, festivals, carnivals, fairs and similar programs. The Lighthouse operates its own 14-story building, with such recreation facilities as bowling alleys, a swimming pool, social hall, auditorium, lounges, crafts shops, a play roof for younger children and two summer camps for residential camping.[7]

Similar programs for the blind are offered by voluntary agencies in such cities as San Francisco, California; Duluth, Minnesota; Jackson, Mississippi; Newark, New Jersey; Raleigh, North Carolina; and Cleveland, Ohio. A number of these organizations sponsor excellent summer camping programs, using their own camps and lodges, specially adapted for those with visual disability.

Mental retardation is another field in which specialized voluntary community organizations make a strong contribution. For example, in Toronto, Canada, the mental retardation movement has been the fastest growing area of social service of its type since the late 1940s. Today, the gross operating budget of the Metropolitan Toronto Association for the Mentally Retarded is close to $2 million, with funds gathered from public sources, the United Appeal and parents' fees. There are four full-time recreation staff members who supervise 50 different recreation programs throughout the Metropolitan Toronto area with volunteer assistance. Elsewhere in this text, the work of numerous other voluntary agencies serving specific types of disabled populations is described. Without question, such groups make a tremendous contribution to meeting the needs of the disabled in community life.

Service Organizations

Fraternal, civic and service organizations like the Elks, Moose, Lions, Oddfellows and Kiwanis have traditionally taken a strong responsibility for providing special programs for the disabled. In the past, with comparatively few services offered by public recreation departments, these organizations cooperated closely with health and welfare agencies to co-sponsor recreation programs of this type. As a single illustration, the Lions of North Carolina have joined together with the North Carolina Association for the Blind to develop Camp Dogwood, a camp and vacation facility for visually handicapped residents of that state, at a cost of approximately a half million dollars.

There are numerous other examples of such organizations, along with civic groups and youth associations, such as the Scouts or Y's, that assist or sponsor programs for the disabled. In Ottawa, Canada, the Y.M.-Y.W.C.A. operates physical recreation programs for the disabled, including weekly swim sessions for children with asthma, learning disabilities or other physical impair-

---

[7] *Program Report of Recreation and Camping Department.* New York Association for the Blind, 1975.

ments. Other special programs are operated for blind adults, those with psychiatric disabilities and similar special groups. Many other Y's operate similar programs. One particularly innovative example of "out-reach" programming is found in Westchester County, New York, where the Y.W.C.A. has conducted an in-facility activities program (including crafts, creative writing, music, cooking, grooming and exercise) and an after-care program for women in the Women's Correctional Facility, Valhalla, New York.

In both the United States and Canada, Boy and Girl Scouts have made a strong effort over the past decade to serve physically and mentally disabled children and youth. In the United States, it has been estimated that there are 59,000 disabled Scouts, including "blind, deaf, crippled, spastic, and even lepers." New York City alone has 150 "special handicapped" scouting units, involving about 2000 boys out of a total of 80,000 Boy Scouts in the city. An equal number of regular units include some disabled boys in their programs. In one troop, the volunteer scoutmaster is learning sign language to communicate with the boys who cannot talk:

> *Only two of the 10 Boy Scouts in Troop 198 can talk, but they have learned personal fitness, know how to tie knots and have studied firemanship. They have earned their family skill award by helping to clean up communities, and they will soon attain the Tenderfoot Badge. Next they will start on the Community Merit Badge.*[8]

Special Agencies for Therapeutic Recreation

In a limited number of cities, special centers have been established under private sponsorship to provide recreation for the mentally and physically disabled.

A leading example is the Recreation Center for the Handicapped, Inc., in San Francisco, California.[9] This nonprofit corporation has pioneered in providing therapeutic recreation service in the San Francisco Bay Area since 1952, when it was founded as a demonstration project to meet the needs of the disabled. It provides year-round recreation and camping programs for children, youth and adults. Most are severely handicapped—many in wheelchairs, on crutches or even bedfast. Others have severe speech impediments, visual handicaps or hearing loss. This program, directed by Janet Pomeroy, a noted authority in the field of therapeutic recreation service, began with six severely handicapped adults; today it has an enrollment of approximately 1100 participants of all ages and every level and type of disability.

For years, the bulk of the Center's programs were carried on in the Fleishhacker Pool Building, a previously unused, publicly owned structure on the Great Highway in San Francisco that was converted to include two large social halls, a craft room, music room, library, multipurpose rooms, stage, offices, kitchen, gymnasium, indoor swimming pool and four activity rooms. This building, which was made available by the San Francisco Recreation and Park Department, has now been replaced by an impressive large new facility specially built

---

[8] "Boy Scouts Reaching Out for Handicapped Members." *New York Times*, February 9, 1976, p. 31.
[9] "San Francisco Has 'Model Recreation Program.'" *Information Center, Recreation For the Handicapped, Newsletter*, Southern Illinois University, June, 1970, pp. 1, 4.

in the mid 1970s to serve the disabled. Outdoor activities are also provided on a day camp site adjacent to the Center and at Lake Merced—a nearby zoo, playground and beach. Resident camping is provided at La Honda, approximately 60 miles from San Francisco.

FUNDING

The Center began with completely private funding and still relies heavily on contributions. Its Board of Directors raises a major portion of the budget through solicitations from individuals, civic and fraternal organizations, fundraising campaigns, shows, benefits and rummage sales. However, the San Francisco Recreation and Park Department, the Community Mental Health Service and the Department of Social Services subsidize a portion of the Center's budget on a contractual basis. It has also received as many as five federal grants at a time to provide care for previously institutionalized, mentally retarded participants and children receiving day care services and to support a physical fitness program serving all participants. The San Francisco Recreation and Park Department donates the use of the Fleishhacker Pool Building, and fees are paid by the families of participants who are able to afford them.

TRANSPORTATION

Participants of all ages are transported from their homes to the Center and back each day, including those in wheelchairs, on crutches and on portable cots. Nine specially equipped buses are in operation six days a week, from 8 A.M. to 11:30 P.M., with transportation planned by a full-time coordinator, and 14 bus drivers—specially selected for their skill in working with severely retarded and disabled participants—working on day and evening shifts.

Whenever possible, parents of disabled children provide transportation for their children; furthermore, volunteer aides assist in accompanying children on the daily bus trips. In addition to traveling to and from the Center, many special trips are scheduled throughout the year to nearby sites of interest.

With the growth of enrollment, it has become necessary to expand the services of the Center in other locations. Today, it has reduced the need for additional facilities and transportation and made it possible to serve large numbers of disabled persons at low cost by conducting programs in neighborhood social halls, housing project meeting rooms, Y's and youth clubs and other recreation and park facilities. Special services are provided for severely disabled persons in their homes—including withdrawn elderly individuals or severely retarded children and youth who are unable to interact within the Center program.

PROGRAM SPONSORSHIP

The immense effort required to plan and carry out this program would not be possible without the help of an active Board of Directors, composed of both lay and professional persons representing public and private institutions and such fields as recreation, education, medicine, welfare and business. The Board works through committees that deal with finance and budget, program, personnel, publicity, speakers' bureau, transportation, parent auxiliary, building construction, equipment and supplies and by-laws.

STAFF

The paid staff includes three recreation program supervisors, a coordinator of volunteer services, a social worker and a number of recreation leaders and specialists in varied activity areas—along with a business manager, clerical staff and other dietary and housekeeping personnel. This staff is assisted by approximately 225 volunteers throughout the year. Each year, a number of graduate and undergraduate college students serve full-semester internships at the Recreation Center for the Handicapped, along with a number of classes from various California colleges whose students carry out field work assignments there.

Program participants are separated into small groups, according to such factors as age, degree of retardation or physical impairment, social independence and mobility. A substantial proportion of the participants are multidisabled children and youth who have not been accepted in any school. During a recent five-year period, almost half of these participants improved so markedly that they were able to be accepted in city schools for the retarded or in special classes in regular schools. In addition to this group, many previously institutionalized teen-agers and adults have gained sufficient confidence and leisure skills to be able to "graduate" into community-sponsored recreation and park programs.

The activities provided cover a broad range of recreation services, including arts and crafts, music, dance, games, sports, drama, trips and a variety of special events and trip programs. Increasingly, camping and nature-oriented activities have been introduced. Special programs for integrating even the most severely disabled with nondisabled children, teens and adults are offered regularly at the Center. In addition, integrated programs are conducted at other community recreation and camping facilities under the direction of the Center's staff.

The Recreation Center for the Handicapped has based its program on recognition of a critical need that was not being met. Janet Pomeroy writes,

> *For the handicapped who attend the Center, recreation has been found to be the only activity experience available to most of them. Some children and teens attend school but many do not. A few adults attend workshops, but the vast majority have been judged to lack the ability for work training or job experience. . . . their days are filled with emptiness and recreation has been seen as the only possible outlet for their energies.[10]*

As a consequence, parents, social agencies and the disabled themselves have turned to the Center's programs, in part as a point of entry into the community service system and in part simply to fulfil their full range of social, emotional, physical and intellectual needs. In addition to purely recreational services, a day-care program and nutritional, referral and educational services have all been provided to clients, and close relationships are maintained with other social and rehabilitative agencies in the community. Recreation is seen both as an end and a means and is presented as an important developmental experience for all clients.

The Recreation Center for the Handicapped is unique, in terms of its variety and scope, in the United States. Despite the fact that it owes much of

---

[10] Janet Pomeroy: "Recreation Unlimited: An Approach to Community Recreation for the Handicapped." *Journal of Physical Education and Recreation*, May, 1975, p. 30.

its success to the energy and interest of its founder, Janet Pomeroy, it should be possible for other cities throughout the nation to develop similar centers through large-scale citizen support and the development of the kinds of recreation opportunities for the disabled that are now available in San Francisco.

Community Councils or Boards

A final type of administrative structure for programs serving the disabled is the formation of a special council or board with representation from a variety of agencies and professional disciplines and with a primary concern for providing programs for the disabled. The author has described in another text the unique work of the Greater Kansas City Council on Recreation for the Handicapped.[11] He repeats that description here because it provides an excellent model for other communities to follow.

The Recreation Division of the Welfare Department of the Kansas City municipal government has for a number of years conducted special summer programs for the orthopedically disabled, diabetic, cardiac and cerebral palsied children. In the early 1950s, it established day camp programs for the deaf and hard of hearing and the orthopedically disabled.

In 1955, a Supervisor of Special Recreation was appointed with the purpose of establishing a year-round comprehensive program of recreation service—initially for the orthopedically disabled, of whom there were estimated to be about 14,000 within the Kansas City metropolitan area. Before developing the program, the following agencies were approached for consultation and advice: the United Cerebral Palsy Association, the National Foundation for Infantile Paralysis, the Jackson County Society for Crippled Children, the Kansas City Board of Education, Goodwill Industries, the Muscular Dystrophy Association, the Arthritis and Rheumatism Foundation, the Multiple Sclerosis Association and others.

It was found that 11 different day and overnight camping, Scouting, club and swimming programs were already being sponsored for the disabled by various organizations in the metropolitan area. However, the following important needs were revealed:

1. The majority of orthopedically disabled youth and adults in the city were not being served by the programs offered.
2. There were many adults who were able to leave their homes but who felt they were too disabled to join regular social groups, as well as teen-agers who had gone as far as they could in school but could not find work and therefore had lost all meaningful social involvement.
3. Many homebound children and adults were completely left to their own resources in terms of recreational pursuits.
4. Existing programs were so limited in terms of budget and staff that they could not satisfactorily meet the needs of those they attempted to serve.

In an effort to meet these needs, a Greater Kansas City Council of Recreation for the Handicapped was formed—to serve not only the physically disabled but also those with emotional or social limitations. Encouragement and

---

[11] See description of Kansas City plan in Richard Kraus: *Recreation Today: Program Planning and Leadership*. Santa Monica, California, Goodyear, 1977, pp. 216–218.

support came from a nearby Veterans Administration hospital that sought to improve opportunities in the community for its discharged patients. Other organizations that joined the Council—in addition to those first involved—included the Y.W.C.A., American Red Cross, the Junior League, the Boys' Clubs, the Visiting Nurses' Association and others. This Council worked closely with the Recreation Division in establishing policies and procedures, planning programs, helping to recruit and train volunteers, stimulating interest and participation in the program by referring disabled persons to appropriate groups and providing clerical and office assistance. Among its first steps was the establishment of a comprehensive insurance plan to protect program participants and sponsors.

Through the years that followed, the Greater Kansas City Council on Recreation for the Handicapped developed a program that included the following elements:

1. A visiting program for homebound children and adults, to help them discover new interests and abilities in such areas as games, crafts, puppetry, collections, instrument playing and other hobbies. This was based heavily on the use of volunteers.
2. A club program for orthopedically disabled adults, with stress on their taking over leadership responsibility themselves. Activities included weekly meetings, parties for holidays and special occasions, square dancing, group singing, movies, hobbies, dramatics and games.
3. A similar program for orthopedically disabled teen-agers, with activities suited to their interests.
4. A training program in home recreation activities for orthopedically disabled children, which was given to parents of such children or to other interested adults. In a series of 10 sessions, workshops and discussions were held, dealing with ways of minimizing disability, modifications of recreational activities and other forms of assistance.
5. Television programs directed to the orthopedically disabled. These served both to encourage them by presenting "write-in" tournaments and contests, interviews with disabled persons who had special hobbies and the teaching of craft projects and games and to educate the public in general with respect to the needs and capabilities of the disabled.

In addition, special outdoor programs were initiated during the summer months, including overnight camping for children with cardiac conditions, diabetes, cerebral palsy or blindness and day camping for children who were deaf or hard of hearing, orthopedically disabled or mentally retarded.

Overall, the Kansas City Council on Recreation for the Handicapped serves a valuable coordinating function by (a) making surveys of community needs for therapeutic recreation and carrying on other research projects; (b) acting as a referral agency for disabled individuals; (c) stimulating public interest; (d) enlisting the help of community groups and the public at large; and (e) recruiting and training professional and volunteer workers in this field.

Jointly Operated Programs

A final type of community-based therapeutic recreation service that may have elements of all the preceding is the jointly operated program. This may involve two or more public agencies cooperating to provide recreation for the disabled, two or more voluntary or service organizations or other combinations.

As an example of the first type, the Nor-West Regional Special Services Program in northern Westchester County, New York, was among the first joint efforts by several adjacent units of government to provide varied services for the disabled, which they could not do independently. The towns of Cortlandt and Yorktown, the city of Peekskill and the village of Ossining initially planned and then set in motion a therapeutic recreation program, with matching funds from the County Mental Health Board. Under this joint sponsorship, Nor-West has sponsored varied activities, such as swimming, bowling, crafts and movement education, a canteen and special events, trips, Scouting and similar programs for the physically disabled, mentally retarded, learning-disabled and emotionally disturbed (including discharged mental patients). The program is directed by a professional who serves in this role on a full-time basis under a supervising board composed of the superintendents of each of the communities involved, who, in turn, act as liaison with their own governing boards.

Another type of structure is one in which colleges or universities with recreation curricula sponsor programs for the disabled in cooperation with community groups. Temple University, in Philadelphia, has conducted a special project titled, "A Coordinated Approach to Community Recreation Services for Multiply Handicapped Adults," under a grant designed in part to help disabled individuals develop favorable leisure attitudes and involvements. The University's Developmental Disabilities Office and Recreation and Leisure Studies Department, in cooperation with several community agencies (Woodhaven Center, Haverford State Hospital, Elwyn Institute, Interact Group Home, Programs for Exceptional Children and the Frankford Y.W.C.A.), have conducted leisure awareness sessions, workshops, social programs and other activities to serve the mentally retarded, as well as those with other disabilities.

GUIDELINES FOR AGENCIES PROVIDING THERAPEUTIC RECREATION SERVICE

Community agencies that seek to provide recreation services for the disabled must function within several areas of administrative concern. These include the following: (a) determining needs, priorities and capabilities; (b) developing programs; (c) providing trained leadership; (d) maintaining an effective public relations and community relations program; (e) financing programs; (f) operating needed transportation services; and (g) planning and developing facilities to serve the disabled.

Each of these is described in the following section of this chapter.

Surveying Needs, Priorities and Capabilities

It is essential to get a clear picture of the existing need for therapeutic recreation service within a given community before attempting to plan programs. In general, this is done by determining the number of persons with disability and then assessing the current ability of existing programs to serve these individuals.

There are three possible ways of determining the extent of disability in a given area. Allan writes,

The first is the abstract method of applying a formula based on the estimated or known national figures for specific types of disabilities, or the composite figures

and percentages for broad classes of disability from national or regional surveys, applied to the local population. The second is the pooling of available data from local agencies and services to form the basis for an "educated guess" on the total disability picture. The third method is the house-to-house survey or canvass type of personal contact, carried out on either a broad or limited segment of the community.[12]

The community survey is generally regarded as the most useful of these approaches, because it provides a fuller and more accurate picture of actual needs than the other methods and also because it may serve as an important first step in developing community interest and a nucleus of individuals and agencies that will be prepared to carry the work further. As described by Warren, here are the major steps to be followed in carrying out a community survey:

1. Determine Scope and Size of Survey. *It is important to determine in advance the size of the service area, the number of people to participate in the study, the amount of time available, and the degree of detail required in the survey.*
2. Sponsorship of the Survey. *Appropriate sponsorship not only lends prestige to the survey but also provides effective guidance, funding and authority. If no single sponsoring organization is suitable, it may be desirable to form a special sponsoring group or council.*
3. Cost of Survey. *It is necessary to estimate, in advance, the costs of the survey, including personnel needs, supplies, equipment, transportation and printing costs. This estimate should be realistic, and if different co-sponsoring groups agree to share the costs, this arrangement should be clearly spelled out.*
4. Organization. *A typical pattern is to develop an overall survey committee, which selects its own chairman, and a number of sub-committees. The survey committee should represent the major interests of the community, as well as those with special interest in therapeutic recreation, and with appropriate technical skills. In a large-scale survey, it may be necessary to hire a professional researcher, or team of experts, to head up the study.*
5. Volunteers. *In any survey which involves large-scale interviewing or canvassing, it is helpful to be able to count on volunteers. These may be drawn from interested parents, representatives of service organizations, college students, or similar groups.*
6. Survey Instruments. *Forms for the collection of data should be carefully developed, or adapted from previously used instruments. If they have not been used before, they should be pilot-tested to determine their validity, ease of administration, and general usefulness. Complete accuracy in the collection, tabulation and presentation of all data is imperative.*
7. The Survey Report. *The survey report should cover the work of the entire survey team, integrating the findings of various sub-committees. It should outline the need for therapeutic recreation service, the target populations, the existing programs, and both short and long-range recommendations both for policies and specific projects in this area.*[13]

In addition to surveys of this type, it is also advisable to consult with individuals or agencies serving the disabled. Public school administrators, special educational services for the disabled, visiting nurse services, hospital-based recreation and social work personnel, doctors, public health departments and organizations working with the disabled can all provide much information.

---

[12] W. Scott Allan: In *Community Planning for the Rehabilitation of Persons with Communication Disorders.* Washington, D.C.: National Association of Hearing and Speech Agencies, 1967, p. 45.

[13] R. I. Warren: *Studying Your Community.* New York, Russell Sage Foundation, 1955.

If the plan is to develop program services for a specific population, inquiries may be directed at that population. Mitchell, for example, describes the planning process followed in Washington, D.C., in developing a comprehensive community-based recreation program for the mentally retarded. After an initial survey had disclosed some 7000 retardates in the District, she writes,

> *In order to assess the availability of persons in this group for program, 500 of the 7,000 were sent a brief questionnaire. The 500 names were selected at random and represented a cross-section of the retarded population. Other factors considered were the families' economic conditions, place of residence, and ages of the retarded children. The results of this sample indicated that the bulk of those questioned would be interested in programs in the morning and early afternoon, and those currently enrolled in other programs would be available for Saturday programs. It was evident that many of the retarded were concentrated in certain geographic regions of the District. The original 500 names, plus an additional 1,000 names were located by address on an overlay of the District. . . . the resulting map showing both postal zones and recreation regions enabled us to locate the children in terms of their accessibility to the playgrounds and community centers which could provide special programs.*[14]

If information is gathered about specific individuals, Pomeroy suggests that it should include the following:

> *1. Name, address, age, sex, and type of disability.*
> *2. Type of services already being received: i.e., recreational, educational, vocational, etc.*
> *3. Formal education, past and present; social experiences.*
> *4. Current or past membership in or association with organizations, agencies, or clubs.*
> *5. Individual interests, hobbies, and skills.*
> *6. Transportation needs and resources.*
> *7. Economic status of family.*[15]

In addition to such information, community surveys should examine all recreation agencies in the community—whether or not they are currently serving the disabled. This might include the numbers, ages and types of those served, the types of recreation programs offered, available facilities and leadership, financial resources and funding potential, transportation capability and similar information.

Program Development

In planning a recreation program to serve the disabled, whether it is to be for a broad range of impairments or for a single, clearly defined group, several steps need to be taken:

1. A careful survey of need, as indicated in the preceding section, carried out with both the number and type of disabled persons and the potential sponsors of programs clearly identified.

---

[14] Helene Jo Mitchell: "A Community Recreation Program for the Mentally Retarded." *Therapeutic Recreation Journal*, 1st Quarter, 1971, p. 4.

[15] Janet Pomeroy: *Recreation for the Physically Handicapped.* New York, Macmillan, 1964, p. 41.

2. In order to indicate the possible directions the program might take, programs serving similar populations in other communities should be observed and the professional literature explored for specific guidelines and examples. In addition, consultants and authorities on therapeutic service, or on the disability itself, might be asked to make recommendations.

3. At this point, it might be advisable to call a meeting of interested parents or relatives to answer such questions as: "What are the recreational needs of their children?" "What types of activities would be most desirable?" "Would the parents themselves be willing to assist in terms of volunteering as program aides, or providing transportation?"

The purpose and scope of the program would have to be defined. Decisions would be made with respect to (a) whether the program would be separate from programs for the nondisabled or linked fully or in part; (b) whether it would be open to all types of disabled persons or designed for one or more specific disabilities; (c) whether the program would use regular community recreation facilities or specially designed facilities for the disabled; and (d) the time schedule that would be most suitable for the program.

When these basic guidelines are determined, it becomes necessary to plan program activities. The most suitable ones are chosen and fitted into a schedule, based on the following factors:

1. Appeal of activity: whether it would be enjoyed by participants as any group of nondisabled persons might enjoy it.
2. Suitability for age level: the activity should be one appropriate for the chronological age of participants.
3. Within range of capability: the activity should be one that can be carried on by disabled persons with a reasonable degree of success and accomplishment.
4. Therapeutic benefits: where possible, activities should be chosen that are valuable in terms of the particular disability or disabilities of the participants.
5. Suitability in terms of other factors: number of participants in group, needed facilities and equipment, staff numbers and leadership skills available.

In general, it is desirable to provide certain regular activities that are familiar and require little new instruction. At the same time, each session should involve some opportunity for new creative development or learning. There should be a reasonable balance between physical, mental, creative, social and other activities. As much as possible, disabled children should be treated like those with no physical or mental impairments and encouraged to help themselves, rather than rely on adult leaders or volunteers for assistance. Older participants should be drawn into planning and leadership whenever possible.

Providing Trained Leadership

Whenever possible, it is desirable to have professionally educated leaders with a background in therapeutic recreation service in key supervisory and leadership position. Pomeroy, for example, provides a detailed statement of the duties, training and experience requirements for three levels of leadership personnel (Center Director, Program Director and Senior Leader) as they have been developed at the San Francisco Recreation Center for the Handicapped.[16]

---

[16] Janet Pomeroy: *Personnel Handbook, Recreation Center for the Handicapped.* San Francisco, California, 1970, pp. 5–22.

These include such elements as graduation from a recognized college or university with a degree in recreation, group work or a related field and a minimum number of years of experience in responsible leadership or supervisory positions in recreation.

Although she points out that, as a general rule, recreation leaders successful in working with the nondisabled are also able to work effectively with the disabled, it seems clear that those who have had basic courses in therapeutic recreation concepts and methods, are familiar with medical terminology and practices in the field of rehabilitation and have had previous clinical experience with the disabled are likely to be most effective in such situations. Based on the recent growth of college and university departments with special curricula in therapeutic recreation, it would appear appropriate today to employ graduates of such programs for all professional-level positions in community recreation for special populations. The same expectations that are applied in employing personnel in institutions (such as registration with the National Therapeutic Recreation Society on an appropriate professional level) should apply in community situations. When workers are employed on sub-professional levels, it is particularly important to have them supervised by qualified specialists and to provide needed orientation and in-service training by experts in the field.

Apart from formal qualifications, the traits expected of leaders in therapeutic recreation are similar to those expected of all leaders in this field. They are expected to be emotionally stable, secure, patient, imaginative, enthusiastic, fair and responsible. Pomeroy also outlines several other important qualifications for therapeutic recreation leaders:

1. *They must accept disabled persons fully as individuals who have the same basic needs, desires and problems as all other people.*
2. *They must be sympathetic to each participant's disability, but must not permit themselves to indulge in pity.*
3. *They must be patient and ingenious in helping adapt activities so that the severely disabled can take part in them, and must be able to inspire and encourage them to persevere.*
4. *They must recognize and be able to meet the specific, immediate social and recreational needs of participants, setting goals that allow a reasonable degree of achievement and pleasure.*
5. *They must be willing to help the disabled participants help themselves, rather than do everything for them.*
6. *They must be willing to do menial tasks such as feeding and lifting the disabled, assisting with toileting, and handling wheel chairs and portable beds. Pomeroy indicates that in many settings, "matrons" or "orderlies" are used for such tasks, but that when it is necessary to carry them out in community recreation programs, they are best handled by recreation staff members, with the help of additional staff and volunteers.*[17]

As indicated elsewhere, the ratio of staff to participants must necessarily be much higher in community programs for the disabled than in programs for the general population. It is therefore essential that, in addition to trained professional leadership, substantial numbers of nonprofessional aides or volunteers be involved in such programs.

---

[17] *Ibid.*, pp. 14–16; see also Pomeroy: *Recreation for the Physically Handicapped.* pp. 52–59.

Public Relations and Community Relations

This is one of the key areas of responsibility in planning and carrying out community recreation programs for the disabled. The goals of public relations include the following:

1. To arouse concern and public awareness of the need for recreation for disabled persons in the community.
2. To encourage volunteers to provide service in existing and new programs and to stimulate financial support for programs.
3. To create a climate in which municipal government and other voluntary agencies will support programs of therapeutic recreation.
4. To inform disabled persons and their families of recreation opportunities in order to encourage their registration and participation.
5. To report program accomplishments and development to the community at large.
6. To share information regarding therapeutic recreation with other health, welfare and social agencies that provide services to the disabled.

Depending on the specific public that must be reached, the following types of public relations media are useful:

Printed materials: newspaper stories and special features; magazine articles; newsletters and brochures; annual reports and other printed reports.

Visual and other outlets: television and radio programs; special exhibits and displays; bulletin boards; speeches, motion pictures and slide talks.

Special events: open houses, tours, special programs to which the press and public are invited.

A well-designed public relations program makes use of each of these methods.

Newspaper stories are obviously most useful in reaching the public at large with timely information, particularly publicity designed to encourage attendance at events or to provide information about special functions, fund-raising drives or other newsworthy matters. It is important to develop favorable contacts with newspaper editors and feature writers and to prepare professionally designed releases and articles for their use. Such releases should be simple, clear and factual and should emphasize the human relations aspect of programs and special projects.

Newsletters and brochures are useful in reaching more specific audiences of parents, disabled youth and adults, other professionals and municipal officials. Usually, they describe the total range of therapeutic recreation services in the community and encourage participation in specific activities, day camps, clubs or other programs. They may range from inexpensive and brief mimeographed one- or two-page leaflets to carefully printed and attractive full-color brochures.

Annual reports are important in summing up the total accomplishments of a therapeutic recreation program. They usually include full details of those served, budgets, facilities and staffing arrangements, cooperating organizations, special projects and similar information.

Visual media, such as television, motion pictures, slide talks or radio programs, are more difficult to arrange than printed publicity but can provide effective public relations results. Therapeutic recreation program directors should constantly be alert to the possibility of getting television or radio news coverage of interesting events or of scheduling panel programs or other informational "spots" on the mass media. As in the case of newspaper and magazine editors, it is important to cultivate the interest and support of radio station or television program directors. They will best be able to judge the newsworthy quality of events or possible features that are brought to their attention.

Speeches, slide talks or similar presentations are useful in reaching audiences of high school or college students, Parent-Teacher Associations, service and civic clubs and similar groups.

It is not enough to publicize the existing program in the hope that it will receive adequate coverage in the media. The program director who is alert to public relations possibilities will deliberately *plan* events of an unusual nature, which lend themselves to promotion. These may include displays, exhibits, performances, open houses, tours, field days and similar ventures that are particularly newsworthy and of interest to the public.

Since the preparation of releases, radio or television scripts, brochures or films involves highly specialized expertise, it is important to get competent staff assistance on such efforts. Frequently, volunteer assistance may be obtained from skilled members of the community who are willing to contribute their services. A professional writer or film-maker who is not able to contribute in other ways may be willing to assist in preparing releases or articles, radio or television features or even in the making of informational films about the program. College and university departments of film-making or television may also include such projects as class assignments.

Community relations are obviously associated with the need for developing community support for therapeutic recreation programs. They involve, however, developing community relationships, in the form of advisory councils and planning groups, neighborhood teams, task forces and similar efforts. It is essential to get citizen input in planning and to obtain the cooperation of all interested individuals and organizations if a community-based therapeutic recreation program is to receive the fullest possible support.

Financial Support

The process of fiscal management is a complicated one and is handled in detail in books on recreation and park administration. It includes the process of budget planning and approval, maintaining fiscal controls and auditing procedures and similar functions and is not dealt with here in detail.

It is important, however, to recognize the unique problem of community-based recreation programs in obtaining adequate financial support. Such programs are inevitably much more expensive than programs that serve the non-disabled. They require a more intensive level of staffing, specialized equipment, transportation facilities and other costly services if they are to be effective. How can the needed funds be raised? Pomeroy suggests the following sources.[18]

VOLUNTARY GROUPS

Service clubs, parent auxiliaries, Parent-Teacher Associations, United Chest or United Crusade and similar organizations may all contribute funds to programs serving the disabled.

---

[18] *Ibid.*, pp. 97–108.

FOUNDATIONS

National or local foundations often are willing to provide funds for developing facilities or for establishing demonstration projects. Usually, they will support an ongoing program for a limited period of time—such as two or three years—and will then expect other sources of funding to be found. In some cases, they may be willing to provide a portion of continued funding year after year for a special program.

INDIVIDUAL GIVING

Many organizations conduct their own funding drives annually. These may include mail solicitations of individuals, companies or organizations, door-to-door campaigns or fund-raising solicitation through churches or similar organizations. They may be carried on for a limited period of weeks at Christmas time or another appropriate season or may include a variety of fund-raising events, such as carnivals, cake sales, bazaars, charity balls, dinners or theatre parties spaced throughout the year. In addition, some organizations make a concentrated effort to encourage large-scale individual gifts, legacies, and bequests among wealthy donors or families.

GOVERNMENT CONTRACTS AND GRANTS

Some agencies, like the San Francisco Center for the Handicapped, have been successful in negotiating contracts with municipal government to provide needed services for the disabled. Such contracts may be with recreation and park departments (which in effect subcontract this particular function to a voluntary agency) or may be provided by a department of welfare, youth services or aging. Other grants may be obtained from county or state welfare departments, social rehabilitation agencies for the blind or mentally ill and similar sources. Federal funding, as in the case of day care programs, may be obtained on a matching basis through the Department of Health, Education and Welfare, (Title IV of the Social Security Act) or other sections of recent federal legislation supporting special education programs.[19]

FEES AND CHARGES

A final important source of funding may be through fees charged to the families of participants. Reasonable fees may be established for day-camping, residential camping and similar services. It is essential, however, that scholarships be provided for those unable to pay such fees, to avoid excluding participants from low-income families.

Whether the sponsoring department is a public or voluntary agency, it is essential that fund-raising be recognized as a high-priority concern and that every possible avenue of obtaining grants and needed subsidies be explored. This function also represents a responsibility in which volunteer assistance may be obtained. A financial or fund-raising subcommittee may be established, which systematically develops a financial plan, does research on possible grants and subsidies, develops proposals and sponsors fund-raising events. Businessmen, bankers and other financial experts are useful on such committees, partly because of their personal expertise and partly because they have the contacts in the business and government world that are essential in fund-raising.

Transportation Services

This area of concern often represents the chief stumbling block that prevents large numbers of individuals from taking part in community-based

---

[19] *Ibid.*, pp. 127–129.

programs. Thompson describes a number of major problems encountered in transporting homebound adults to a special recreation demonstration project:

1. *Untrained or uncooperative drivers.*
2. *Uncomfortable vehicles (with unpadded seats, for example).*
3. *Vehicles late for pick-ups.*
4. *Jostling of patients.*
5. *Lack of portable steps.*
6. *Overcrowding of vehicles.*
7. *Poor planning by transportation management.*
8. *Lack of ramp for wheelchairs.*
9. *Unheated vehicle (winter).*
10. *Improper handling of wheelchairs.*[20]

Private vehicles can be used in transporting the mentally retarded, mentally ill or aged persons who do not have serious physical disabilities. In some cases, volunteers are used to man such programs through car-pool arrangements. This approach tends to be somewhat unreliable, however. Proper insurance coverage is essential, and it is necessary to have additional volunteers to go along with the disabled persons being transported. Buses and taxicabs may also be used on a contract basis to provide transportation, and, although expensive, this may offer a more reliable solution to the problem.

In some communities, service organizations, such as the Kiwanis, Lions and Elks, provide transportation services; in others, the American Red Cross Motor Corps provides cars and trained drivers. Whenever commercial services are used, drivers must have appropriate licenses and should be fully aware of the responsibilities involved in carrying the disabled. Drivers must understand the special needs of the disabled, and it is important for them to know first aid procedures and be able to handle emergencies that may occur.

The task of transporting those who are severely physically impaired and wear heavy braces and are on crutches or in wheelchairs or portable cots is obviously much more difficult. Special vehicles must be provided, with fuller space, special steps to assist the ambulatory, ramps for wheelchairs or lifting devices to assist loading and unloading. A number of car manufacturing companies have designed special vehicles for this purpose.

Whatever form of special transportation is provided, the role of the driver is extremely important. Pomeroy describes the responsibilities and needed qualities of such drivers, as outlined in the job description code of the Recreation Center for the Handicapped. Drivers must have

1. Knowledge of:
   The California State Motor Vehicle Code and the Education Code, particularly
      as they relate to the operation of vehicles in transporting children.
   Geography of the local area.
   Safe driving practices.
   Basic preventive maintenance of automotive equipment.
2. Ability to:
   Operate a large and small bus with patience and skill.
   Make minor mechanical adjustments of automotive equipment.

---

[20] Morton Thompson: *Meeting Some Social-Psychological Needs of Homebound Persons Through Recreative Experience: Project Report.* New York, National Recreation Association, 1962.

Understand and carry out oral directions.
Get along well with children.
Maintain a calm, even disposition.
Exercise mature judgment in relation to driving and child care.
Maintain a semblance of order on the bus.
Handle large children and adults with heavy braces.

3. License:
   A valid Class "B" chauffeur's license.
   Red Cross first aid certificate.

4. Experience:
   Two years of successful full-time paid experience in driving commercial or heavy-duty vehicles. Experience with children. Safe driving record and current driver's license.[21]

Precise policies should be established for all aspects of the transportation program, and schedules for pickup and delivery should be worked out in full detail and maintained as accurately as possible. Generally, this is easier to do in small towns or suburban areas than in large cities where congested traffic conditions and parking difficulties make the transportation problem even more difficult to solve.

Planning Facilities for the Disabled

In general, the facilities used by recreation programs for the disabled are of the same type as those used for the population at large. Parks, playgrounds, community centers, day camps and similar facilities are widely available and, in most cases, are able to accommodate the disabled with comparatively little modification being required. As a general policy, it is desirable for programs serving the disabled to use such facilities, since they enable disabled participants to mingle with the nondisabled.

When programs involve severely disabled persons, it is obviously necessary to make sure that halls, rest rooms, entrances and similar locations are constructed so that they can readily be used by those in wheelchairs, on crutches and in braces. A number of recommended standards for outdoor recreation facilities and community centers are described in Chapter 7. In some communities, elaborate playgrounds and day-camp sites have been constructed for special use by the disabled. Some authorities have questioned this practice, particularly when it leads to a segregated pattern of use by the disabled—thus defeating attempts at mainstreaming them within the nondisabled population. In some cases (see p. 220), special facilities have been built to serve both the disabled and their families or other nondisabled individuals, which makes much greater sense.

A number of innovative designers have developed facilities that go beyond a routine concept of recreation use to provide a much fuller range of developmental and growth experiences. For example, the town of Hempstead, New York, has constructed an Environmental Resource Center on the Atlantic Ocean at Lido Beach Town Park. This facility provides year-round recreational opportunities for those with varied disabilities, both children and adults, as well as the nondisabled population. It was constructed to serve the town's ANCHOR

---

[21] Janet Pomeroy: *Recreation for the Physically Handicapped.* p. 140.

Program (Answering the Needs of Children with Handicaps through Organized Recreation), with a volume of about 750 participants. McGrath describes the planning emphasis given to environmental activities in the Center's program:

> ... *(in addition to) music, arts and crafts, physical exercise, field and court games, aquatics, special events such as Christmas shows and family picnics, field trips, home economics and hygiene, and cultural activities ... it is expected that environment-related activities will be substantially increased (such as):*
>
> *Interpretation of the economy of Long Island and New York in terms of animal life, erosion, plant life, etc.*
>
> *Horticulture, including gardening*
>
> *Animal husbandry—care, feeding, and raising of animals*
>
> *Outdoor recreation skills—bait and fly casting, fly tying, resource management, camping skills, riflery, and laboratory techniques*
>
> *Special events—nature projects (building bird houses, conservation programs), hikes, fishing, trips, flower shows, pet shows, fishing contests, and hobby shows and activities*[22]

The actual physical elements of the Environmental Resource Center include large garden plots worked by the participants, nature trails related to the ecological systems of the seashore, three camping units for platform tent camping, a large Center building, outdoor shelter areas, beach access at three locations, special curbing and sitting walls to guide the blind, hard-topped game areas and pathways and a playground designed to reflect the concept of a progressive obstacle course. McGrath describes the original thinking underlying this design:

> *The playground ... will function as an obstacle course or can be utilized for separate play activities or units. The handicapped will be directed around the playground to the various activity areas that require specific motor skills or combinations of motor movements. Appropriate by-passes will be provided for the severely handicapped and those in wheelchairs. However, the by-passes will contain obstacles or challenges so that the youngsters will experience the satisfaction of success and learn to cope with obstacles they will face every day in their "normal" environment.*[23]

It is essential that increasing numbers of such facilities be built to provide enriched play and learning experiences for the disabled in a specially designed setting at the same time that *all* community recreation facilities be remodeled, where necessary, to provide reasonable opportunity for the disabled. It goes without saying that, today, all *new* facilities being constructed to serve the general public must be made accessible for the disabled.

LEISURE COUNSELING

There are basically two kinds of populations that must be considered in planning community recreation services for the disabled. One is the population

---

[22] Ray McGrath: "Environmental Resource Center—Making the Outdoors Available to the Handicapped. *In* Larry Neal (ed.): *Leisure Today: Selected Readings.* Washington, D.C., American Association for Leisure and Recreation 1975, p. 92.

[23] *Ibid.*

living at home, with either physical or mental disability, that has some form of impairment as a continuing condition of life and that requires appropriate opportunity for leisure involvement either as a supplement to other family or work involvements or as a primary form of commitment. The other population consists of those who have been hospitalized or are in a special school, rehabilitation center or other residential facility and who are in the process of returning to the community. Often, this group must relearn old skills, make new contacts and develop both confidence and "know-how" in re-establishing a healthy, full leisure life.

For both groups, leisure counseling is a key element in achieving successful involvement in community-based recreation programs. For all groups, as McDowell points out, such counseling is essential to remove blocks or difficulties that may interfere with the individual's capability for creative use of leisure. Through observation, testing and counseling that analyzes the source of difficulty, a better understanding of such maladaptive factors as the following is achieved:

> ... guilt, obligation, anxiety, fear, social isolation, procrastination, boredom, uncertainty, flightiness, or obsessive compulsiveness, to name a few. This approach attempts to promote awareness, understanding, and clarification of the individual's self (attitudes, beliefs, values, personal resources) so that alienation from leisure is minimized.[24]

Having established a more positive outlook and constructive attitudes toward participation, the leisure counseling process must clarify leisure goals for the individual, identify potential community resources and follow through with a sequence of referral, building contacts, helping with transportation if necessary and assisting in establishing a solid base of recreational participation. In some cases, as indicated in an earlier chapter, this may involve first participation in a protected or "special" environment and then satisfying and successful involvement in an integrated program. It should be stressed that leisure counseling is not designed only for the disabled. For example, Overs, Taylor and Adkins describe an experimental project designed to help individuals in later middle age (55 years and older) prepare constructively for oncoming retirement and growing leisure opportunity through a process of avocational counseling.[25]

Similarly, Magulski, Faull and Rutkowski describe a computer-based approach to leisure counseling developed by Milwaukee, Wisconsin, Public Schools Division of Municipal Recreation and Community Education. In addition to serving large numbers of disabled persons in sheltered environments (such as prison inmates, hospital patients and alcholics) or in the community at large (such as the aged or mentally retarded), the service has also been made available to people already in the mainstream of life who wanted to raise the quality of their lives through leisure participation.[26] It would appear, then, that

---

[24] Chester F. McDowell, Jr.: "Leisure Counseling: Professional Considerations for Therapeutic Recreation." *Journal of Physical Education and Recreation*, January, 1976, p. 27.
[25] Robert P. Overs, Sharon Taylor and Catherine Adkins: "Avocational Counseling for the Elderly." *Journal of Physical Education and Recreation, Leisure Today*, April, 1977, pp. 20–21.
[26] Michael Magulski, Virginia Hirsch Faull and Barbara Rutkowski: "The Milwaukee Leisure Counseling Model." *Journal of Physical Education and Recreation, Leisure Today*, April, 1977, pp. 25–26.

leisure counseling must continue to develop as a key service to facilitate participation by all groups—and particularly the disabled—in community recreation programs.

In conclusion, this chapter has outlined a number of examples of community-based recreation programs and approaches for the disabled, which supplement other examples provided throughout this text. The final chapter deals with the important role of research and evaluation in programming for the disabled.

SUGGESTED TOPICS FOR CLASS DISCUSSION, EXAMINATIONS OR STUDENT PAPERS

1. Develop a model program of therapeutic recreation service for a municipal recreation and park department. Show how this program might be linked to institutions or voluntary agencies serving the disabled.

2. Carry out a direct analysis of a community agency providing comprehensive services for a specific form of disability—such as the mentally retarded or cerebral-palsied. Show how recreation is provided or assisted by this agency; make recommendations for its improvement.

3. What is the rationale for having a nonpublic agency, such as the San Francisco Recreation Center for the Handicapped, assume major community responsibility in this area? What are the advantages and disadvantages of such an administrative approach?

4. Mainstreaming of the disabled has become a major thrust in many community agencies. Develop a set of policies designed to bring about this objective, including circumstances when it is not a realistic goal.

chapter **12**

Evaluation and Research in Therapeutic Recreation

Within any field of social service or professional practice, it is essential that efforts be made to determine the effectiveness of programs and to develop a foundation of knowledge that will buttress both the ongoing performance and the general image of the field. The two terms that are generally applied to such efforts are *evaluation* and *research*.

These processes are quite similar, in that both rely on the use of standardized instruments or investigative procedures to gather information that will be useful in improving professional practice. They differ, however, in the following respects.

MEANING OF EVALUATION

Evaluation is usually regarded as the process of determining the effectiveness of programs, leadership or other elements of professional service in terms of achieving predetermined goals. It is generally concerned with the examination of specific agencies or situations, and it makes use of a number of research techniques, both of a quantitative and qualitative nature.

Patient or Client Evaluation. In the field of therapeutic recreation, a second specific use of the term evaluation applies to the examination of patients or clients. They are systematically and regularly examined through interviews, observations or check-lists and rating scales to determine their interests, needs, disabilities and capabilities. Information gathered in this way leads to the planning of therapeutic programs and the prescription of appropriate areas of participation for patients and clients.

MEANING OF RESEARCH

Research is usually thought of as an organized search for knowledge. Its objective is to discover answers to questions through the application of scientific procedures of measurement. It may simply involve examining what *is*—that is to say, a given phenomenon or institution as it exists—or may involve establishing certain artificial conditions or circumstances, which are then systematically observed. Research generally falls into two major categories: (a) so-called *pure* research, which is concerned with conceptual or theoretical questions that do not have immediate practical value and (b) *applied* research, which is pragmatic and purposeful in nature, intended to provide useful information. *Statistics Canada* has developed definitions of these two categories, based on a formulation by the Organization for Economic Cooperation and Development:

> Basic Research. *Original investigation undertaken in order to gain new scientific knowledge with the primary purpose of contributing to the conceptual development of science. Basic research yields hypotheses, theories and general laws. . . .*

> Applied Research. *Original investigation undertaken in order to gain new scientific knowledge with the primary purpose of applying such knowledge to the solution of practical or technical problems. It is required either to determine possible uses for the findings of basic research or to select the appropriate method of achieving some predetermined objective. It develops ideas into operational forms.*[1]

Like evaluation, research may gather both quantitative and qualitative information. Although it may involve a wide variety of measurement procedures or patterns of design, customarily it includes the following steps: (a) a concise formulation of a problem or hypothesis; (b) the development of an investigative procedure (usually referred to as a study design) appropriate to this problem; (c) the carrying out of the study, including the gathering of data; (d) scoring, analyzing and interpreting the data; and (e) presentation of conclusions and possible recommendations for action or further study.

IMPORTANCE OF EVALUATION AND RESEARCH

Why are these two processes of importance to the field of therapeutic recreation service? The most obvious reason is that they provide information that can be directly useful in developing recreation programs and services.

Beyond this practical need, however, it is obvious that any field of professional service *must* rely on more than the judgment or common sense of its practitioners as a basis for operation. The entire field of recreation service demands a fuller understanding of the dynamics of play, the meaning of leisure in society, the attitudes and expectations that underlie participation and the significance of recreation as a form of social service or government responsibility. Specifically, within the more specialized area of therapeutic recreation service, the role of recreation *as* therapy, and its relationship to other rehabilitative functions, is an issue that demands thoughtful and intelligent analysis.

During the early decades of the development of the recreation profession, it was commonplace to comment that no significant research was being carried on in recreation and that its evaluative procedures were lacking in validity or meaning. Today, this is not the case. With the assistance of government and foundation grants, the growth of recreation curricula in colleges and universities and increased efforts being made by professional organizations in this field,

---

[1] "Research Definitions." *Recreation Review*, March, 1973, p. 12.

remarkable strides have been made in developing meaningful programs of research.

EVALUATION IN THERAPEUTIC RECREATION

Evaluation in therapeutic recreation may be carried on in the following areas: (a) evaluation of an entire department, including all relevant elements; (b) evaluation of program effectiveness, in terms of meeting specific goals and objectives; (c) evaluation of patients' or clients' needs and interests or progress within given program areas; (d) evaluation of staff performance; (e) evaluation of facilities; and (f) evaluation of entire institutions or agencies.

The Evaluation Process

Too often, people or programs are evaluated in sketchy, informal or subjective ways. Based simply on an "impression" or on attendance figures, judgments are made on rating sheets or other evaluation forms. The best kind of evaluation is based on careful, systematic observation carried out regularly and keyed to clearly stated goals, objectives or other criteria. Evaluation should seek to be quantitative as much as possible—that is, stated in terms of ratings that can be scored, to give a meaningful final index of quality or a profile that demonstrates strengths and weaknesses.

Normally, ratings should avoid "yes or no" scoring and such questions as "is a program successful?" or "is it a failure?" Instead, evaluation seeks to measure gradations of quality or performance. Thus, ratings might include such possible choices as "always, often, sometimes, never" or "excellent, very good, good, fair, poor," with each response given an appropriate number value. On the other hand, they might be couched in descriptive phrases like "Places heavy emphasis on acquiring new skills," "Gives moderate emphasis on acquiring new skills" or "Seldom encourages children to learn new skills." In general, each institution or program must develop its own evaluative instruments, since no standardized tests of this kind have been widely developed to cover the broad range of programs in therapeutic recreation.

A key element in such evaluative procedures is the ability of the observer to make intelligent judgments. There are four possible types of raters:

SELF-EVALUATION BY PRACTITIONER

Although it is certainly valuable to encourage self-evaluation, usually the person who is responsible for a program is not able to examine his program in a completely objective light. In any case, it is usually desirable to get other viewpoints and critical reactions.

EVALUATION BY PARTICIPANTS

Those who take part in a program may be asked to judge whether in their view its goals are being met. Often, such reactions may be extremely helpful in an evaluation process. Certain groups, such as the mentally retarded or the mentally ill, may not be able to make effective judgments in their area, although their opinions or wishes may be helpful in other ways.

EVALUATION BY OTHER
PROFESSIONAL PERSONNEL

Other staff members in the same institution, who are thoroughly familiar with the work of the recreation department, may be asked to evaluate its effectiveness in reaching goals. This might include nurses, doctors, social workers or other personnel.

EVALUATION BY OUTSIDE EXPERTS

Outsiders, such as leading therapeutic recreation specialists from other institutions, college teachers, professional consultants in this field or state department officials, might carry out this type of evaluation. In some cases, a thorough evaluation process might include each of these elements.

Evaluation of Program or Department

An evaluation may be made of a therapeutic recreation program or department that has been either in action over a period of time or set up a short while before on an experimental or demonstration basis. Customarily, when this is done, the program is evaluated in terms of several major areas of concern. Most important of these is the extent to which it is meeting its stated goals and objectives. A useful set of standards for the evaluation of recreation services in residential institutions was developed by Berryman and associates as part of a three-year study of therapeutic recreation service supported by a grant from the Children's Bureau of the U.S. Department of Health, Education and Welfare.[2] This document provides a systematic means of looking at a total program, based on 55 different standards grouped under several major categories, and supported by illustrative criteria. Examples of several standards and illustrative criteria follow:

PHILOSOPHY AND GOALS
Standard 1. *The therapeutic recreation services offered are based on a written philosophy of recreation as it applies to the residential treatment center.*
Criteria
a) *The statement is in accord with the philosophy, purpose, and policies of the agency and has been approved by its administrative authority.*
b) *Within the department, provisions are made to acquaint all recreation staff members and volunteers with this statement.*
ADMINISTRATION
Standard 5. *Structure. Recreation services are administered by a professional department as an integral part of the institution's overall functional structure.*
Criteria
a) *Administrative authority and responsibilities are clearly delineated in writing.*
b) *Responsibility for recreation services is assigned to professionally qualified staff.*
c) *The department administrator participates in interdepartmental meetings.*
PERSONNEL
Standard 13. *Personnel Practices. The institution has written personnel policies and practices which are periodically reviewed by its governing body and revised as necessary.*

[2] Doris L. Berryman, Project Director: *Recommended Standards with Evaluative Criteria for Recreation Services in Residential Institutions.* New York, New York University School of Education, 1971.

Criteria

a) *There is a written statement of personnel policies and practices.*

b) *A copy of the statement is given to each employee as well as kept on file in the department.*

PROGRAMMING

Standard 37. *Needs and Interests of Residents. Recreation Services are designed to meet the needs, competencies, capabilities and interests of individuals and groups and take into account individual treatment objectives.*

Criteria

a) *There is an established method for assessing the needs, interests, competencies and capabilities of residents which includes:*

1) *an interview with each resident; and/or*

2) *access to pertinent medical, psychiatric and other information concerning each resident.*

b) *Resident committees are utilized in planning the activities program where feasible.*

AREAS, FACILITIES, AND EQUIPMENT

Standard 45. *Design and Layout. Recreation areas and facilities are designed and constructed or modified to permit all recreation services to be carried out to the fullest possible extent in pleasant and functional surroundings accessible to all residents regardless of their disabilities.*

Criteria

a) *Recreation staff and appropriate outside consultants are consulted in the designing or modification of all recreation areas and facilities.*

b) *Recreation areas and facilities meet local legal requirements concerning safety, fire, health, sanitation, etc., codes.*

EVALUATION AND RESEARCH

Standard 54. *Evaluation of Recreation Services. The recreation department has established procedures for evaluating recreation services in relation to stated purposes, goals and objectives.*

Criteria

a) *The recreation department maintains adequate records concerning the residents. These records include:*

1) *periodic surveys of their interests;*

2) *periodic surveys of their attitudes and opinions of the recreation services;*

3) *extent and level of each individual's participation in the activities program;*

4) *where appropriate, progress reports are maintained*

b) *An appropriate time schedule is established for each type of evaluation. (Some aspects of recreation services will be evaluated annually, some periodically, some after each event, etc.)*[3]

It should be noted that this is only a partial list of the standards and criteria developed by Berryman and a panel of experts. For example, the separate standards under the heading of Personnel include the following: personnel practices; job descriptions and classification system; salary ranges; hours of work; fringe benefits; hiring, assignment and promotion of employees; recruitment; evaluation of performance; workload; staffing; supporting services; orientation program; staff development; responsibilities of director; supervision; contribution to the profession; consultation; use of volunteers; and statements of suggested qualifications on several job levels.

Another example of program or department evaluation may be found in the accreditation process initiated in 1975 by the Council on Accreditation of the National Recreation and Park Association. The overall purpose of this process is to (a) serve the public by promoting and maintaining high standards

---

[3] *Ibid.*, pp. 11, 12, 17, 33, 37, 43.

of professional education; (b) assist college and university officials in attaining defensible goals of recreation education within the framework of their own institutional purpose and policies; (c) foster continual self-study and improvement of professional preparation programs; and (d) encourage experimentation to improve professional education and services in Recreation, Leisure Services and Resources.

In order to carry out accreditation procedures in a standardized and thorough way, a set of standards and evaluative criteria have been developed covering the following major areas of concern: *Philosophy and Purposes; Faculty; Students; Research; Public Service; Organization and Administration; Areas, Facilities, Equipment and Instruction Resources.*[4] In addition, detailed standards and evaluative criteria are provided for both undergraduate and graduate curricula. Procedural guidelines outline the sequence through which a given institution may apply to the Council for accreditation, complete a Self-Study Evaluation Report, be visited by an Accreditation Visitation Team of qualified professionals and so on.

This process has been made more specifically meaningful by the publication of a set of competencies needed for both undergraduate and graduate professional emphasis in therapeutic recreation. The undergraduate emphasis, for example, includes the following competencies, which serve as a useful means of evaluating a college or university's curriculum and overall operation:

Knowledge of illness and disability with implications for recreation programming, i.e., physically handicapped, mentally ill, emotionally disturbed, developmentally disabled, penally incarcerated, and aging.

Knowledge of specific service delivery systems related to treatment and rehabilitation, i.e., medical models, leisure education models, etc.

Knowledge of administrative policies and procedures associated with treatment and rehabilitation settings.

Understanding of specific facilitation and counseling techniques predominantly used with special populations.

Knowledge of specific needs of special populations, and activity modification techniques needed to adapt activities to individual needs.

Knowledge of procedures used in formulating individual and group assessment, prescription, and evaluation plans with special populations.

Understanding of principles used for recording and reporting client information in treatment and rehabilitation settings.

Understanding of administrative principles related to community recreation programs for special populations.

Knowledge of facility design and equipment modification related to accessibility and mainstreaming concepts.

Knowledge of institution to community service continuum designs.

---

[4] *Standards and Evaluative Criteria for Recreation, Leisure Services and Resources Curricula: Baccalaureate and Master's Degree Programs.* Arlington, Virginia, National Recreation and Park Association Council on Accreditation, October, 1975.

Knowledge of both normal and abnormal growth and development as traditionally taught in related fields, including: special education, psychology, sociology, anatomy/physiology/kinesiology.

Ability to apply the unique practices and principles of therapeutic recreation in authorized practicum experiences commensurate with the approved NTRS guidelines for field placement.[5]

On the graduate level, competencies suggested in the Accreditation Standards and Evaluative Criteria include (a) the ability to conceptualize and articulate major professional issues related to therapeutic recreation; (b) demonstrated involvement in professional growth experiences other than academic, such as professional memberships, workshops or conferences; (c) in-depth knowledge in a minimum of two disability groupings; (d) the ability to conceptualize, design, implement and evaluate therapeutic recreation programs; and (e) an in-depth knowledge of activity analysis and its application for assessment and prescription of programs for special populations.

Such specific standards and criteria are extremely useful in evaluating a college or university therapeutic recreation curriculum, in terms of whether it is providing undergraduate or graduate majors with essential competencies in their chosen area of specialization. It should be pointed out that such evaluative tools cannot be developed by a single individual—no matter how competent or authoritative. Instead, they must be the product of teams of qualified practitioners and educators who share their varied viewpoints and professional expertise.

Evaluation of Program Effectiveness

A somewhat more limited type of evaluative procedure involves the assessment of a single type of program service. Here, any given area of program, such as sports and games, arts and crafts, social activities, or other events, may be evaluated by asking such questions as the following:

"Does it contribute to overall program goals of the institution?"
"Does it attract participation and regular attendance; is it popular with patients?"
"Is it administratively feasible—that is, can it easily be provided in terms of schedule, staff and facility demands?"
"Does it contribute to specific treatment needs of individual patients?"

In addition, evaluation may focus on the programs provided for a specific *population*, in a particular *unit* or other *special setting* or using a unique or *experimental method*. If it is being carried out as a routine procedure designed to measure and improve the effectiveness of an ongoing program, then it should legitimately be considered evaluation. If, on the other hand, it is concerned with measuring a program that has been set up specifically to test the effectiveness of certain techniques or program methods, then it should be regarded as a form of research.

Evaluation of specific programs tends to be carried out on two levels: (a) by gathering statistics of attendance or participation, staffing arrangements,

---

[5] *Addendum to Accreditation Standards and Evaluative Criteria: Competencies Needed for Undergraduate Professional Emphasis in Therapeutic Recreation.* Arlington, Virginia, National Recreation and Park Association Council on Accreditation, October, 1976.

Figure 12–1. Questionnaire on night, week-end and holiday therapeutic recreation programs. (Modified from State Department of Public Welfare, Office of Mental Health and Mental Retardation, Harrisburg, Pennsylvania, 1970.)

---

1. What is the average number of week-nights per week that activities are conducted? _____

2. What is the average number of activities per night? _____

3. Where are activities conducted? Wards _____, Rec Building _____, Gym _____, Off-grounds _____, Other _____

4. What is the average number of staff working per evening? _____

5. What is the average number of volunteers working per evening? _____

6. Is evening duty rotated among staff? Yes _____, No _____

   If "Yes," are activities provided Sat. morning _____, afternoon _____, evening _____ ; Sun. morning _____, afternoon _____, evening _____.
   If "No," do you regularly provide activities weekends? Yes _____ ; No _____
      If "Yes," what is the average number of evenings each staff member works per week?

7. Do you regularly provide activities weekends? Yes _____ ; No _____
   If "Yes," are activities provided Sat. morning _____, afternoon _____, evening _____ ; Sun. morning _____, afternoon _____, evening _____

---

costs and similar data and making judgements based on them; and (b) by attempting to assess, in a more analytical way, the actual quality of the program or its demonstrable outcomes in terms of patient or client service and outcomes. As an example of the first approach, Figure 12–1 indicates questions on a report form used in the Pennsylvania State Department of Public Welfare intended to assess practices with respect to night, week-end and holiday programming in state mental hospitals and schools.

A second report form used by the same department seeks information as to therapeutic recreation participation by patients within six categories of involvement: (a) mass activities; (b) off-grounds activities; (c) ward activities; (d) interest group activities; (e) individual activities; and (f) recreation therapy groups. Frequency of participation, as well as total and average hours of involvement, and similar kinds of information are gathered through such instruments to assist in overall review of the program.

Evaluation and Patients' or Clients' Needs, Interests and Participation

The second major method of evaluating program effectiveness would be to assess the extent to which goals are being met—rather than simply gathering facts and figures about services provided and amounts of participation. Evaluation of outcome is most reliable when based on careful observation of patients' or clients' involvement and behavioral change. There are several steps in this process: (a) assessment of their needs and interests; (b) developing prescriptions or recommendations for program involvement; (c) implementing recommended plan; and (d) evaluation, based on systematic observation and feedback.

ASSESSMENT OF PATIENT'S OR
CLIENT'S NEEDS AND INTERESTS

This may be done in a variety of ways. The therapist may use forms such as those shown in Chapter 5 (see p. 152–156) to gain a comprehensive picture of the individual's past leisure interests and hobbies, as well as those he or she might like to carry on within the institution or special program. Many community agencies use an "intake" form that gathers information regarding the patient's or client's degree and type of disability, in addition to his or her skills, life circumstances and other relevant information (Fig. 12–2).

Figure 12–2. Participant application form. (Adapted from *Participant Intake Form*, San Francisco Recreation Center for the Handicapped, 1974.)

Date _____

Name _____
　　　Last　　First　　Middle

Birthdate	Age	Race	Sex	Religion

Address _____
City _____
Telephone _____

Emergency Information: _____
Name _____
Address _____
City _____
Telephone _____ Relationship _____

Marital Status of Applicant (Circle One)
1. Never Married　　　4. Divorced
2. Married　　　　　　5. Separated
3. Widowed

Other children in the home
Number of Boys _____ Ages _____
　　　　　　Girls _____ Ages _____
Name of Guardian _____

Lives with Parents [　] Guardian [　]

Parents	Occupation	Business Address	Telephone Number
Father			
Mother			

Diagnosis: _____　Cause _____

Special Handicaps (Check Degree)	None	Mild	Moderate	Severe	Comments
Emotional Disturbance					
Speech Impairment					
Impairment of Mobility					
Impairment of Hearing					
Impairment of Vision					
Epilepsy					
Suffers Motion Sickness					

Name of Doctor _____ Address _____ Telephone _____

Please Check Correct Box:	Yes	No		Yes	No
Needs toilet assistance			Can read		
Uses public transportation with assistance			Can write		
Uses public transportation with no assistance			Can dress self		
Can make self understood with words			Can feed self		
Can make self understood with motions					
Can understand simple word commands					
Can understand motion commands only					

Note: In addition to above sections, the form also asks for detailed information regarding the applicant's educational background, transportation needs, social worker (if any), available financial assistance, and family income. It concludes with parental consent and photographic release forms and a space for general comments regarding the applicant's needs and admissions decision. Accompanying it is a separate medical report form to be filled out by a doctor.

In addition to such information, the therapeutic recreation specialist might make use of an observation form, which is helpful in assessing the individual's social behavior. One example of a range of possible behaviors is shown in Figure 12–3. A much more systematic form has been developed by Parker, Ellison, Kirby and Short for use in short-term, acute-care psychiatric settings.[6] This instrument, called the Comprehensive Evaluation in Recreational Therapy Scale (CERT Scale) requires careful observation over a period of time. It measures varied aspects of appearance, physical performance and group behavior, including such specific elements as the ability to take part in structured or unstructured group activities, to relate meaningfully to others, to play appropriate sexual roles, to handle conflict situations, to tolerate frustration, to apply judgment and to make decisions. Although these might appear to be difficult abilities to judge or measure objectively, the percentage of agreement between therapists who rated a large number of patients was extremely high, averaging over 90 per

Figure 12–3. Chart for recording patient participation in group sessions. (Adapted from *Patient Behavior Assessment Form,* Bellevue Hospital, New York, 1975.)

Date: _____ Weekly Session No.: _____ Participant's Name: _____

Topic: _____ Group Leader: _____

Categories of observable participation	LEVEL OF PERFORMANCE				COMMENTS
	Never	Occasionally	Often	Most of the time	Give illustrations of behavior, including both positive and negative examples.
Appears isolated and uninvolved in midst of group					
Listens passively		✓			
Shows interest but responds only when called on					
Speaks voluntarily on occasion but only to group leader					
Speaks to others but without reference to self					
Reports personal experiences with some insight					
Seeks information					
Speaks with support of others' feelings					
Establishes relationships with others					
Clearly expresses feelings and personal ambitions					
Other behavior (explain)					

[6] Robert A. Parker, Curtis H. Ellison, Thomas F. Kirby and M. J. Short: "The Comprehensive Evaluation in Recreational Therapy Scale: A Tool for Patient Evaluation." *Therapeutic Recreation Journal,* 4th Quarter, 1975, pp. 143–152.

cent. In most cases, staff members of different institutions or agencies tend to make up their own assessment instruments, but the CERT Scale has been used successfully in a number of different settings.

In some cases, institutional recreation staffs have employed a variety of different techniques to gain a rounded picture of patients' or clients' needs, interests and capabilities. For example, in the Penetanguishene, Ontario, Mental Health Centre in Canada, the patient evaluation process includes a series of sessions, with (a) anonymous observation of the individual taking part in evening group activities; (b) videotaped interview between the assessor and the client dealing with his or her attitudes about recreation and pre-hospital interests and social involvement; (c) administration of a psychological projective test, the Guilford-Zimmerman Temperament Survey, and a printed Interest Survey; (d) a second interview between the assessor and the patient, including use of a game or other activity in which the subject may be involved; (e) observation of the individual taking part in regular group activities, with the client and assessor interacting around the framework of a game; and (f) other sessions involving observation, group interaction and a final interview in which the assessment program is discussed and the client indicates his or her reactions to it.[7]

In addition to information gathered through such procedures, the entire treatment team, including medical and nursing staff and other therapists or social service personnel, may contribute their views of the patient's or client's needs, interests and capabilities. Specific psychological or physical needs, which serve as the basis for prescribing, recommending or contracting for activity may also be indicated.

PRESCRIBING ACTIVITY INVOLVEMENT

This may take a number of forms. In some cases, particularly under the *medical model* of therapeutic recreation service, there may be a direct prescription of activity to achieve treatment objectives. For example, if a patient or client is extremely withdrawn, shy or lacking in self-confidence, the prescription may be for group involvement in social activities. If the individual is extremely aggressive or hostile, competitive sports or other vigorous forms of activity may be indicated. Specific movement exercises or crafts may be used to minimize impairment or restore function to those with physical disability.

In other situations, instead of directly prescribing activity, the treatment team may help the patient or client come to an accurate realization of his or her own needs and select a program of activities to achieve certain mutually accepted goals. In some cases, specific behavioral goals may be designated and agreed upon by the therapist and patient or client. For example, in some behavior modification programs for disturbed or socially deviant individuals, the *contingency contracting* approach is used.[8] Simply described, this means that, based

---

[7] For a fuller description, see: Richard G. Kraus and Barbara J. Bates: *Recreation Leadership and Supervision: Guidelines for Professional Development.* Philadelphia, W. B. Saunders Co., 1975. pp. 291–292.

[8] For descriptions of behavior modification and contingency contracting methods see: R. D. Jodrell and R. S. Fisher: Basic Concepts of Behavior Therapy: An Experiment Involving Disturbed Adolescent Girls. *American Journal of Occupational Therapy*, November–December, 1975; and R. R. Parlour: Some Behavioral Techniques in Community Psychiatry. *American Journal of Psychology, 29*:79–91, 1975.

Figure 12–4A. Group interaction tasks excerpted from Fairview Hospital and Training Center Manual. (Adapted from Barbara Mumford, Coordinator: *Therapeutic Recreation Curriculum Manual*. Salem, Oregon, Fairview Hospital and Training Center, 1973, pp. 3–4.)

Levels	I	II	III	IV	V
1.	Joins group and participates in all Level I activities upon request of instructor	Knows his own position within in group formation and takes his turn	Recognizes other peoples' turns and positions within group	Knows his position within more complicated activities (e.g., *when to speak* in a play or *position* in a team sport)	Organizes and directs group game involving peers during *free time* on own initiative
2.	*Waits to take turn*	Communicates *ideas* and *needs* to instructor and peers in a *polite* and considerate manner	Listens to and accepts ideas of others within group	Gives appropriate encouragement to peers in activities	Participates actively and appropriately in group *discussions*
3.	Communicates ideas and needs to instructor	Shares play area and materials on his own initiative	Develops concept of *sportsmanship*; being good *winner* and *loser*	Displays good *sportsmanship* in all activities	Participates actively and appropriately in group *decision making*
4.	*Shares* play area and materials upon request of instructor	Accepts and *follows* rules of Level I and Level II activities	Understands and follows rules of Level I, II, and III activities	Understands and follows rules of Level I, II, III, and IV activities	Exhibits socially acceptable behavior when participating in community recreation programs

Note: Levels I through V represent increasingly advanced levels of performance. Some tasks or skills begin at a low level and continue up through the higher levels. Others begin initially at higher level.

Figure 12–4*B.*   Therapeutic recreation progress report form. (From Barbara Mumford, Coordinator: *Therapeutic Recreation Curriculum Manual.* Salem, Oregon, Fairview Hospital and Training Center, 1973, pp. 3–4.)

Name: _____   Cottage: _____   Level: _____

Score

Music and Dramatic Activities:
  a. Music expression   _____
  b. Rhythmic movement   _____
  c. Creative dramatics   _____
  d. Care and use of equipment   _____
  e. Receptive and expressive language   _____
                              Sub-total _____

Physical Activities:
  a. Locomotor activities   _____
  b. Nonlocomotor activities   _____
  c. Group activities and individual-team sports   _____
  d. Care and use of equipment   _____
  e. Receptive and expressive language   _____
                              Sub-total _____

Arts and Crafts:
  a. Eye-hand coordination and finger dexterity   _____
  b. Identification and discrimination   _____
  c. Expressive art   _____
  d. Care and use of equipment   _____
  e. Receptive and expressive language   _____
                              Sub-total _____

Social Activities:
  a. Group interaction   _____
  b. Leadership and followership   _____
  c. Spectator skills   _____
  d. Care and use of equipment   _____
  e. Receptive and expressive language   _____
                              Sub-total _____

General Skills and Concepts:
  a. Self-help skills   _____
  b. Number and time concepts   _____
  c. Travel   _____
  d. Care and use of equipment   _____
  e. Receptive and expressive language   _____
                              Sub-total _____

                           Total Score _____

There are four points possible for each item; the highest score possible is 100%.
  Rating Code: 4 = does correctly   2 = attempts incorrectly
                    3 = attempts correctly   1 = does not attempt

Comments: _____
_____
_____

on the analysis of the treatment team, certain behavioral objectives are identified—either in terms of strengths to be built or deficits to be overcome. These might include such behaviors as (a) cursing or attacking others; (b) coming to sessions regularly and on time; (c) carrying out group responsibilities; (d) not coming to sessions "high" on liquor or drugs; or (e) carrying out work tasks effectively. Both the client and the therapist sign an agreement to the effect that, if the objectives are attained, certain rewards or reinforcers will be granted; if not, certain negative reinforcers will be applied. Thus, as an ongoing part of the process, evaluation is carried on with immediate feedback.

In other situations, evaluation is more of a one-way process. In working with the mentally retarded or the brain-injured, for example, specific exercises, or activity-related tasks may be prescribed, with a sequence of skills to be mastered. For example, physical activities may be outlined in a step-by-step process, with each skill, its purpose, and a criterion for measuring its performance, listed in sequential order. In a Therapeutic Recreation Curriculum Manual developed at the Fairview Hospital and Training Center in Salem, Oregon, for example, goals and graded tasks are presented under five major headings: (a) Music and Dramatic Activities; (b) Physical Activities; (c) Arts and Crafts; (d) Social Activities; and (e) General Skills and Concepts. These in turn are broken down in the manual with a variety of sub-tasks presented under five levels of difficulty. For example, sequential tasks are identified under the heading of Group Interaction in the Social Activities area (Fig. 12–4A). In the manual, a rating system for assigning points to each sub-task, and each overall activity area, is presented. This approach provides a means of identifying desired tracks for improving performance of participants, monitoring performance, and arriving at scores through which to appraise their progress over a period of time. The Progress Report Form used to sum up a client's total effort, as evaluated by the therapeutic recreation team, is shown in Figure 12–4B.

EVALUATION OF PERFORMANCE

It is essential that there be regular observation and evaluation of the participation and performance of the patient or client in recreation and activity therapy. Only in this way can there be an accurate judgment of the progress a patient is making and of the value of the prescription of activity. By keeping accurate records, this information may then be shared with the treatment team and may be used as the basis for continuing or changing the therapeutic plan, for modifying activity or for gaining new insights about a patient's or client's needs.

Certain specific methods may use standardized evaluation forms. For example, a form has been developed for the evaluation of patient or client performance in *sensory training programs* (see Chapter 4). A number of examples of rating categories are shown in Figure 12–5. This selection of items (other items include response to such stimuli as sound, taste, sight, touch and hearing) demonstrates how major categories of response or behavior may be evaluated. The fact that suggested scores are given for each item makes it possible to rate a patient's or client's overall performance or to develop a profile sheet that will graphically show all areas of strength and weakness.

It should be pointed out that not all departments or institutions make use of such forms in the evaluation process. Touchstone points out that in many

Figure 12–5. Sensory training analysis report. (From Leona Richman, Patricia Nolan and Mathew Gold: *Sensory Training Analysis Report.* Bronx, New York, Psychiatric Center, 1974.)

	Comments
Interest	
Refused to come to meeting. 0	
Attended, but showed minimal interest 1	
Showed some interest 2	
Interested 3	
Interested and appreciative. 4	
Awareness	
Unaware of what went on. 0	
Distracted by "voices" 1	
At times was unaware of what went on 2	
Generally aware of proceedings 3	
Extremely aware of proceedings 4	
Participation	
Did not talk 0	
Answered some direct questions 1	
Would echo answers of others 1	
Answered most direct questions 2	
Volunteered some answers and comments 3	
Volunteered many answers and comments 4	
Talked too much 3	
Speech	
Difficult to understand 1	
At times difficult to understand 2	
Fair speech 3	
Good speech. 4	
Awareness	
Can neither name nor locate body parts 0	
Can name, but can't locate body parts 1	
Can locate, but can't name body parts 2	
Can name and locate some body parts 3	
Can name and locate all body parts 4	
Physical Exercise	
Refused to do exercises 0	
Imitated gestures. 1	
Needed assistance 2	
Tried, but physically unable 3	
Did all exercises independently 4	
Physical Contact	
Hostile withdrawal 0	
Withdraws 1	
Non-committed 2	
Reacts positively 3	
Initiates contact 4	

cases considerable reliance is placed on methods like psychodrama or role-playing, which do not lend themselves to quantitative evaluation, and that in general, standardized instruments are not used widely in this field. This would suggest that the evaluation process must be designed for a particular institution or agency or set of patients or clients, along with the unique objectives that have been established for a given situation. In some cases, a deliberate policy has been to *resist* elaborate or complicated evaluation report forms as unnecessary paper work and simply to require brief, written, anecdotal statements appraising a patient's or client's behavior and progress within a program.

OTHER AREAS OF EVALUATION

In addition to the overall evaluation of an agency or department or of specific program elements, patients or clients, evaluation is customarily carried out in two other areas: staff and facilities.

Evaluation of Staff Performance

Customarily, in large institutions, it is the practice to carry out regular evaluation of staff personnel by their supervisors. These evaluations are normally based on formal records that rate the employee on such elements as attendance, appearance, leadership qualities, organizing ability, control and discipline, initiative, judgment and responsibility.

This tends to be a fairly mechanical procedure, although it is a useful way of getting a numerical picture of staff performance. Another method is to rely on anecdotal records, in which a supervisor will observe a leader or therapist at work over a period of time and will write a descriptive account of his performance, including both strengths and weaknesses. This case record becomes the basis for supervisory conferences. Thus, the evaluation leads to improvement of performance, which should be the main justification for carrying it out.

Evaluation of Facilities

This may be carried out with a pre-established list of desirable facilities for a particular type of rehabilitative or therapeutic recreation setting, such as gymnasium, swimming pool, outdoor sports facilities, lounges, arts and crafts rooms and meeting rooms. Despite the fact that institutions vary widely, certainly it would be feasible to develop a *minimal list* as a standard for institutions.

Another way to evaluate facilities might be to establish questions that relate to their quality and usefulness. A checklist could be developed applying to various types of facilities, such as the playground: Does it offer varied pieces of equipment for creative and active physical play? Is it aesthetically designed? Are health and safety guidelines followed? Does it permit participation by children on crutches, in wheelchairs or in braces? Does it meet the needs of various age groups? Has it been effectively maintained and is maximum use being made of it?

Summing up this section of the text, evaluation must be regarded as an important tool in appraising the quality and effectiveness of overall therapeutic recreation programs or their component parts or in assessing patient or client needs and interests, as a basis for program involvement.

RESEARCH IN THERAPEUTIC RECREATION

In general, research tends to be much broader than evaluation, both in its possible focus and in the methods employed. For example, evaluation generally deals in the here and now and is concerned with directly observable phenomena, such as patient behavior, staff strategies or program outcomes. Research, however, may deal with the past as well as the present, may ask conceptual questions and may structure arbitrary or artificial environments and situations to impose a degree of control over elements in the situation, which would not be possible in a natural setting. At a fairly early point in the development of therapeutic recreation as a professional service field, a number of key questions for research in this area were identified and stimulated research efforts. These included the following:

"What are the relative contributions of recreation activity, the relationship of the therapist to the patient and patient activity per se?"
"What is the comparative effectiveness of free versus forced choice of recreation activities?"
"Does the personality profile of an individual determine the type of career he chooses and the recreation activity he selects?"
"How can recreation further a patient's ability to meet reality?"
"Does recreation encourage fantasy?"
"How do patients' recreational needs compare with those of the average person outside of the hospital?"
"Do psychotic patients in mental hospitals tend to have had impoverished recreational lives before their illness?"

The problems suggested fell into four major categories: (1) What is the intrinsic value in a specific recreational activity? (2) What types of leadership are helpful in working with patients? (3) What should be the basis and values of "prescribed" over "voluntary" selected activity? (4) Is there a relationship, not necessarily cause and effect, between the recreational experiences of people and mental illness?

During the late 1960s and 1970s, with the establishment of the National Therapeutic Recreation Society and the *Therapeutic Recreation Journal* and the stimulus provided by other publications, such as the *Research Quarterly* and *Journal of Leisure Research* in the United States and *Recreation Review* in Canada, the range of research subjects expanded considerably. Several broad areas of concern have emerged; a number of illustrations of studies carried out within each of these areas within the past 10 years are presented in the following section.

EXAMPLES OF PUBLISHED RESEARCH IN
THERAPEUTIC RECREATION

The following brief summaries of research studies fall under major headings: (a) examinations of organized programs and surveys of professional practices; (b) studies of professional development in therapeutic recreation; and

(c) analyses of special populations in relationship to recreation and leisure. The examples chosen are only a few of dozens of such studies carried out and reported in the literature in recent years; however, they are a fairly representative selection and give a picture of the research thrust in this field.

Examinations of Organized Programs and Surveys of Practices

THERAPEUTIC PLAY SERVICES IN CHILDREN'S HOSPITALS IN THE U.S. (1969)

This study examined a sampling of children's general hospitals in the United States in an effort to determine the following: which hospitals provided supervised play; under what kinds of leadership; using what kinds of activities, materials and equipment; and with what degree of program evaluation and interpretation.[9]

RECREATION SERVICES FOR THE MENTALLY RETARDED IN THE STATE OF KANSAS (1969)

This study involved a large-scale survey intended to determine the scope and nature of recreation programs for mentally retarded children and youth in the state of Kansas and to develop a set of recommendations designed to improve programs and services.[10]

A STUDY OF THERAPEUTIC RECREATION SERVICES IN KENTUCKY NURSING HOMES (1970)

This study examined the extent, nature and administrative arrangements of recreation programs provided for older persons in extended care facilities in the state of Kentucky. As in similar reports, in addition to providing a statistical picture of existing services, the study concluded with recommendations for improved and expanded services.[11]

AVAILABILITY AND UTILIZATION OF RECREATION RESOURCES FOR CHRONICALLY ILL AND DISABLED CHILDREN AND YOUTH IN THE UNITED STATES (1970)

This survey sought to determine the extent of recreation services offered to disabled children in a cluster sampling of nine Standard Metropolitan Statistical Areas and one Consolidated Metropolitan Statistical Area in the United

---

[9] Yvonne Barnthouse Williams: "Therapeutic Play Services in Children's General Hospitals in the U.S." *Therapeutic Recreation Journal,* 2nd Quarter, 1970, pp. 17–21, 46.
[10] Gene A. Hayes: "Recreation Services for the Mentally Retarded in the State of Kansas." *Therapeutic Recreation Journal,* 3rd Quarter, 1969, p. 13.
[11] Martha Peters and Peter J. Verhoven, Jr.: "A Study of Therapeutic Recreation Services in Kentucky Nursing Homes." *Therapeutic Recreation Journal,* 4th Quarter, 1970, pp. 19–22.

States. It identified a variety of existing and potential recreation resources for children and youth, as well as major needs for development in this field.[12]

RECREATION AND RELATED THERAPIES IN PSYCHIATRIC REHABILITATION (1973)

This study examined practices and trends in varied types of psychiatric treatment centers in the New York-New Jersey-Connecticut region, with emphasis on objectives, administrative structure, staffing, programming and leisure counseling in recreation and activity therapy. It sought also to determine the effect of "unitization" or psychiatric treatment centers and the influence of milieu therapy and therapeutic community approaches upon programming and leadership.[13]

AN EXAMINATION OF WEEKEND RECREATIONAL PATTERNS AT THE MENTAL HEALTH CENTRE, PENETANGUISHENE, ONTARIO (1973)

This study sought to examine (a) the provision made for organized recreation programs on weekends in the institution under study; and (b) the actual use of weekends by patients, including town or home-visiting privileges. The basic question was whether the recreation staff was responding creatively to the real leisure needs of patients.[14]

RECREATION SERVICES FOR THE HANDICAPPED IN CANADA (1974)

This was a large-scale survey of recreation services for the disabled in agencies, institutions and municipalities with populations over 1000 persons throughout Canada. It sought to determine the populations served, the nature of sponsorship, programming elements and particularly the degree of concern for the disabled in the communities studied.[15]

SURVEY OF MUNICIPAL RECREATION SERVICES FOR SPECIAL GROUPS IN ONTARIO (1975)

Somewhat similar to the preceding study, this survey examined programs provided by municipal recreation authorities in communities of 5000 or more residents, for four special populations: the mentally retarded, physically disabled, emotionally disturbed and learning-disabled. It examined the nature of special

---

[12] John E. Silson et al.: "Availability and Utilization of Recreation Resources for Chronically Ill and Disabled Children and Youth in the U.S." *Therapeutic Recreation Journal*, 4th Quarter, 1970, pp. 1, 36.

[13] Richard G. Kraus: "Recreation and Related Therapies in Psychiatric Rehabilitation: A Research Study." *Therapeutic Recreation Journal.*

[14] D. C. Green, P. N. Byrne and J. M. Montagnes: "An Examination of Weekend Recreational Patterns at the Mental Health Centre, Penetanguishene, Ontario." *Recreation Review*, March, 1973, pp. 13–23.

[15] Peter A. Witt: *Status of Recreation Services for the Handicapped.* Ottawa, Department of National Health and Welfare, 1974.

services, the role of recreation authorities, administrative problems and solutions and the degree of integration or segregation of the disabled in the programs reported.[16]

CAMPING FOR THE HANDICAPPED IN
SELECTED CAMPS IN CALIFORNIA
(1975)

This survey examined the status of camping for disabled children and youth in 305 California camps and agencies accredited by the American Camping Association and the Western Association of Independent Camps. It studied the extent of such provision, the reasons why camps did not serve the disabled (if they did not), the nature of integration or segregation in camp life, special administrative or leadership adaptations in serving the disabled and, finally, the potential for increasing camping opportunities for the disabled in California.[17]

STUDY OF FIVE LAND AND WATER
CONSERVATION FUND PROJECTS FOR
ACCESSIBILITY FOR THE PHYSICALLY
DISABLED (1976)

Using a 13-section checklist of items to determine the degree of accessibility and usability of recreation facilities and buildings for the physically disabled, this study examined five selected projects in Georgia that had received funding under the Land and Water Conservation Fund Act by the Bureau of Outdoor Recreation. Its primary purpose was to determine whether the minimum standards established by the American National Standards and Specifications in this area and required according to the Outdoor Recreation Grants-in-Aid Manual were actually being met.[18]

Studies of Professional Development in
Therapeutic Recreation

Typically, many research studies have been concerned with professional development in the field of therapeutic recreation service. The following are a few illustrations.

THERAPEUTIC RECREATION
EDUCATION: 1969 SURVEY

This report gave findings of a major curriculum study carried out by the Society of Park and Recreation Educators. It identified specialized curricula in therapeutic recreation service in colleges and universities in eight regions of the

---

[16] Doris Haist: "A Survey of Municipal Recreation Services for Special Groups in Ontario." *Recreation Review*, August, 1975, pp. 29–50.
[17] Susan C. Buchan: "Camping for the Handicapped in Selected Camps in California." *Therapeutic Recreation Journal*, 1st Quarter, 1975, pp. 38–41.
[18] Charlene D. Farmer: "A study of Five Land and Water Conservation Fund Projects in Regard to Accessibility and Usability for the Physically Handicapped." *Therapeutic Recreation Journal*, 1st Quarter, 1976, pp. 27–30.

United States and examined such elements as faculty, number of student majors, degrees offered and similar aspects of these programs.[19]

RELATIVE IMPORTANCE OF COLLEGE COURSES IN THERAPEUTIC RECREATION (1970)

This study examined the degree of importance assigned to undergraduate and graduate college courses in nine major categories by a panel of 15 national leaders and 15 educators in therapeutic recreation service. Courses were placed in rank order, and conclusions were drawn that would lead to the improvement of such curricula.[20]

THE CENTRAL LIFE INTERESTS OF ACTIVITY THERAPY LEADERS IN THERAPEUTIC RECREATION (1970)

This study was concerned with the basic interest patterns of individuals working in activity therapy programs in medically oriented settings. It contrasts their interests and values with those of professionals and nonprofessionals in other areas of service and represents an example of critical examination of the membership of a professional group.[21]

ATTITUDE CHANGES TOWARD THE DISABLED (1975)

This study explored the different changes in attitude toward disabled children, as measured by the Minnesota Teacher Attitude Inventory, of two groups of students at the University of Texas at Austin. One group consisted of physical education majors required to do student teaching; the other was composed of student volunteers working at the physical development clinic for disabled children. The purpose of the study was to assess the initial attitudes and attitude changes of the student groups after different intervening experiences in order to determine how favorable attitudes toward the disabled may best be developed.[22]

PRACTITIONERS' EVALUATION OF COLLEGE CURRICULA IN THERAPEUTIC RECREATION (1976)

Given the lack of uniformity or common agreement about appropriate content in undergraduate therapeutic recreation preparation, this study sought to use bachelor level practitioners to evaluate professional undergraduate

---

[19] Thomas A. Stein: "Therapeutic Recreation Education: 1969 Survey." *Therapeutic Recreation Journal*, 2nd Quarter, 1970, pp. 4–7, 25.

[20] Donald Lindley: "Relative Importance of College Courses in Therapeutic Recreation." *Therapeutic Recreation Journal*, 2nd Quarter, 1970, pp. 8–12.

[21] Gus Zaso: "The Central Life Interests of Activity Therapy Leaders in Therapeutic Recreation." *Therapeutic Recreation Journal*, 4th Quarter, 1970, pp. 15–18.

[22] William C. Chasey, John D. Swartz, Carol C. Chasey, Ruth Brogman and Howard Sandler: "Attitude Changes Following Exposure to Handicapped Children in Clinical Physical Education." *Therapeutic Recreation Journal*, 2nd Quarter, 1975, pp. 68–73.

courses, required competencies for practice in the field and appropriate functions of professionals on the job. Sixty-five professional undergraduate courses in nine areas, 40 competencies and 27 functions were evaluated and rated in terms of their importance and value.[23]

ANALYSIS OF THERAPEUTIC
RECREATION AS A SERVICE (1976)

Therapeutic recreation as a service, as conceptualized by a paradigm appearing in the professional literature, was analyzed using the content analysis method. Fifty-three citations drawn from 300 randomly selected references were content analyzed, using the delivery-of-service paradigm, with sub-categories based on specialized knowledge and personnel, primary knowledge base and general and specific target populations.[24]

Studies of Special Groups

Many recent studies have been concerned with the leisure characteristics or recreational needs of specific population groups.

RECREATION, LEISURE AND THE
ALCOHOLIC (1969)

This study examined the alcoholic's use of leisure time prior to commitment to an alcoholic rehabilitation center and its relationship to his drinking problem. A sample of 129 patients was compared to study data on the use of leisure time by the general population that had been gathered by the Outdoor Recreation Resources Review Commission.[25]

A COMPUTERIZED ANALYSIS OF
CHARACTERISTICS OF DOWN'S
SYNDROME AND NORMAL CHILDREN'S
FREE PLAY PATTERNS (1971)

This study examined the free play patterns of a group of four- to eight-year-old Down's syndrome (mongoloid) children and four groups of normal children of preschool chronological age. The range in play and the use of special pieces of apparatus were recorded by a ceiling-mounted camera, and the data gathered in this way were carefully analyzed by computer.[26]

---

[23] S. Harold Smith: "Practitioners' Evaluation of College Courses, Competencies and Functions in Therapeutic Recreation." *Therapeutic Recreation Journal*, 4th Quarter, 1976, pp. 152–156.

[24] John H. Lewko: "An Analysis of Therapeutic Recreation as a Service." *Therapeutic Recreation Journal*, 1st Quarter, 1976, pp. 35–48.

[25] H. Douglas Sessoms and Sidney R. Oakley: "Recreation, Leisure, and the Alcoholic." *Journal of Leisure Research*, Winter, 1969, pp. 21–31.

[26] A. G. Linford et al.: "A Computerized Analysis of Down's Syndrome and Normal Children's Free Play Patterns." *Journal of Leisure Research*, Winter, 1971, pp. 44–52.

A COMPARISON OF ACTIVE AND PASSIVE RECREATIONAL ACTIVITIES FOR PSYCHOTIC PATIENTS (1971)

This study examined the effects of a program of active and passive recreation on two groups of long-term schizophrenic patients in a state mental hospital, as measured by pulse rate and a 16-item Behavioral Adjustment Scale. Information was gathered in areas of mood, cooperation, communication and social contact over a six-month period of involvement and at a later stage.[27]

THE LEISURE ACTIVITIES AND SOCIAL PARTICIPATION OF MENTAL PATIENTS PRIOR TO HOSPITALIZATION (1971)

This study used data gathered from interviews of a sample of psychiatric patients at a state mental hospital to determine what the leisure activities and social participation of these patients were before hospitalization, as a basis for policy-making in the area of hospital and community recreation programs and to initiate conceptualization in certain areas of rehabilitation practice.[28]

ANALYSIS OF RECREATIONAL INVOLVEMENT OF PAROLEES FROM STATE CORRECTIONAL INSTITUTION (1972)

This study examined the recreation pursuits of 20 parolees from a Pennsylvania State prison at three points: prior to entering prison, while in prison and after release. Its purpose was to ascertain what relationships might exist between patterns of involvement during these three periods and to draw implications either for recreation programming in correctional institutions or community-based services that might be linked to prison programs.[29]

OTHER SOURCES

Approximately 50 entries in a bibliography of theses and dissertations dealing with recreation, parks, camping and outdoor education apply specifically to therapeutic recreation and the leisure needs of special groups.[30] These research studies, carried out at colleges and universities, usually to meet Master's or Doctoral requirements, cover such topics as the following:

"The Determination of the Course Areas for a Graduate Curriculum in Hospital Recreation."

---

[27] Grant W. Bigelow: "A Comparison of Active and Passive Recreational Activities for Psychotic Patients." *Therapeutic Recreation Journal*, 4th Quarter, 1971, pp. 145–151.

[28] Irvin Babow and Sol Simkin: "The Leisure Activities and Social Participation of Mental Patients Prior to Hospitalization." *Therapeutic Recreation Journal*, 4th Quarter, 1971, pp. 161–167.

[29] Larry W. Williams: "An Analysis of the Recreational Pursuits of Selected Parolees from a State Correctional Institution in Pennsylvania." *Therapeutic Recreation Journal*, 3rd Quarter, 1972.

[30] Betty van der Smissen and Donald V. Joyce: *Bibliography of Theses and Dissertations in Recreation, Parks, Camping and Outdoor Education.* Washington, D.C., National Recreation and Park Association, 1970.

"Integrative Aspects of Therapeutic Recreation."

"A Study of Adapted Equipment for the Use of the Orthopedically Handicapped in Sports and Games."

"The Effect of an Active Recreation Program on Selected Mentally Ill Female Patients at Cambridge State Hospital."

"Developmental Dance in the Education of the Educable Mentally Handicapped Child."

"The Effects of a Program of Balance Activities on Cerebral Palsied Children."

"The Effects of a Selected Recreation Activity on the I.Q. Scores, Social Adjustment, and Physical Coordination of the Educable Mentally Retarded Child."

Two other recent publications of Pennsylvania State University deal with the effect of therapeutic recreation and adapted physical education in working with two special population groups, the mentally retarded and the institutionalized aged.[31] Experimental studies indicated that appropriately designed activity programs were effective in improving sensory-motor skills, stimulating verbalization and positive socialization, curbing disruptive behavior and expanding the range of play involvements of the mentally retarded. Similarly, special programs of arts and crafts, games and water activities were shown to have a positive effect in improving socialization and reducing withdrawal among the institutionalized aged population.

TYPES OF RESEARCH STUDY DESIGNS

Research in therapeutic recreation service tends to make use of the following types of research design.

CASE STUDY

This is generally used to examine a single program, institution or culture and involves intensive study utilizing a variety of data-gathering techniques. It may be of a comparative or cross-sectional type, in which two or more cases or subjects are compared.

EVALUATIVE DESIGN

This involves the analysis or appraisal of an existing program, process or service in an effort to determine how effective it is in meeting goals.

EXPERIMENTAL DESIGN

This usually involves the testing of a new type of program or service or establishing new environmental conditions and determining their effect. It requires careful sampling procedures or the establishment of experimental and control groups, although, when carried on as a demonstration project, the conditions of testing need not be as rigorous.

---

[31] Herberta M. Lundegren (ed.): *Physical Education and Recreation for the Mentally Retarded* (1975); and *Penn State Studies on Recreation and the Aging* (1974). State College, Pennsylvania, Penn State HPER Series.

HISTORICAL-PHILOSOPHICAL DESIGN

This approach is usually employed in studying events that occurred in the past or in analyzing theoretical concepts or systems.

LONGITUDINAL DESIGN

This usually involves the study of quantifiable data over a period of time and differs from historical research in that it is not as concerned with the context and interpretation of change as in the analysis and interpretation of evidence.

The specific techniques that are employed in therapeutic recreation research tend to fall into the following categories:

SURVEY ANALYSIS

This is the most common form of research tool used in this field, as in the broad field of social research. It represents an attempt to determine current conditions with respect to such elements as practices, participation, recreational choices and attitudes, employment, program content or a host of other subjects. Generally, it is concerned with examining a number of programs, communities or organizations or with information about a class of people, a region or even the entire country. It may make use of such tools as the mailed questionnaire, structured interview, check lists, rating scales, opinion polls or similar data-gathering procedures.

EXPERIMENTAL ANALYSIS

This involves the application of new services, treatment procedures, equipment or other types of environmental changes and the careful measurement of the outcomes of such changes. Usually, it is carried on in an attempt to determine whether certain pre-existing hypotheses are correct and whether they can be supported by statistically treated data. Experimental analysis may be carried on in an actual service situation, in a community or in a carefully controlled laboratory situation. It may involve the comparison of two or more groups that have been subjected to different treatment or program procedures, or it may involve the examination of a single group of subjects over a period of time.

In the field of recreation service, comparatively little research of an experimental nature has been carried on, chiefly because of the difficulty in controlling the environmental conditions and excluding other factors or influences that make for change.

Other research techniques may involve *documentary analysis*, which consists of the careful study of documents, reports or other written information; *critical-incident method*, which is based on the in-depth study of one or more significant episodes or incidents: *field study*, a technique widely used in both sociology and anthropology, in which the researcher immerses himself in an ongoing situation or environment and gathers information about it, using a variety of methods; *judge's appraisal*, a method of utilizing the expert judgment of a group of authorities; and *tests of behavior or performance*, which are normally used in experimental research.

As indicated earlier, research may gather quantitative or qualitative data, or both. When it gathers the former—that is to say, information that can be measured and put in terms of numbers—it normally must be analyzed statistically. This might consist of simply grouping and reporting responses by percentages or simple frequencies or may involve the use of more sophisticated statistical procedures and formulas, including computer analysis.

Customarily, research may be carried on by a number of different types of sponsors or investigators. These include the following:

Institutions and agencies. Many hospitals, rehabilitation centers or other agencies or departments conduct research studies more or less frequently to determine their own effectiveness, establish needs and outcomes or provide a basis for program development.

Colleges and universities. A substantial amount of research is carried out by graduate students working on theses or dissertations or by faculty members with student assistants.

Governmental agencies. Government, on its various levels, is a major sponsor of research. In the field of therapeutic recreation service, this may be carried out in government hospitals or treatment centers or, more commonly, by government funding of research projects that are then carried on by research teams in universities or other settings.

Professional organizations. National or state organizations may carry on research, usually directed toward determining needs and trends in the field rather than toward the development or evaluation of existing programs.

Increasingly, research of an interdisciplinary nature is being carried on with the collaboration of two or more such sponsors. For example, in some recent studies, collaboration consists of the government approving and funding a research project that is manned and carried on by researchers drawn from a university faculty and is actually carried out in an institutional setting. Thus all three sponsors have a part in the research effort. Similarly, although the initiative for such research may come from therapeutic recreation educators, other faculty personnel or research specialists, such as psychologists, sociologists, physicians or statisticians, might be drawn into the research process.

In developing proposals for research in therapeutic recreation, the following kinds of questions should be asked:

"Am I—as the researcher—genuinely interested in the problem and free from strong biases that might imperil my objectivity?"

"Is the problem an important one, in the sense that research related to it is likely to be helpful to my institution or program, advance knowledge in the field or be of value to other professionals?"

"Has similar research already been carried on or will the proposed investigation yield substantially new information?"

"Can the needed administrative support and cooperation be obtained in order to carry out the study successfully?"

"Do I have, as an individual, or does my department or agency have the needed expertise to carry on the study? If not, can assistance be obtained?"

"Will access to the needed subjects, informants or other resources necessary to carry out the study be available?"

"Will it be possible to gather accurate data in sufficient scope required to validate findings?"

Encouragement Given to Research

Within any major department or large-scale institutional program, both evaluation and research should be consistently encouraged and supported. Obviously, it must not represent a diversion from the primary objective of providing service. The most meaningful programs, however, are those that are intelligently evaluated, and the most successful professions are likely to be those that have a solid basis of scientifically gained knowledge underlying their practices. Therefore, therapeutic recreation specialists should be encouraged to

1. Use a scientific and systematic approach at all times in gathering information on program needs and services or solving on-the-spot recreation programs.
2. Attempt to gain skill in the application of research instruments and the use of research results.
3. Cooperate with personnel in colleges and universities or in other organizations or departments to carry on jointly sponsored research projects.
4. Be alert to the possibilities for foundation or government-sponsored grants for research or demonstration projects.
5. Assist in identifying problems in the field that require research that might be carried on by professional colleagues or experts in a better position to follow up on them.
6. Press for the allocation of both funds and staff time to carry out research and evaluation studies.

As an example of an agency that gives a high priority to generating research, Children's Village, in Dobbs Ferry, New York (see p. 289), had eight different research studies under way during a recent year.[32] Approved by the institution's Research Council and a Technical Research Consultation Committee, the projects included the following: (a) a study of *remediation of language difficulties*, with emphasis on testing remedial procedures; (b) *decision-making in child welfare*, focusing on the placement policies of the child welfare system; (c) *behavior rating reliability study*, an analysis of the usefulness of the agency's behavior rating scales; (d) *Revere Unit follow-up study*, a study of the community adjustment of discharged boys; (e) *after-care team to facilitate community adjustment of discharged boys*, a proposed expanded team approach to assist in this process; (f) *community volunteer continued care program*, a grant proposal to use community volunteers to assist in the community adjustment process; (g) *learning correlates of behavior problems*, a study clarifying the relationship between boys' behavior and learning disabilities; and (h) *teaching young aggressive boys to cooperate through play*, a grant proposal to develop materials and techniques useful in teaching cooperative behavior.

Obviously, several of these research studies either are directly concerned with recreation and its outcomes or use recreation as a medium to improve other processes or gather research data. Similarly, Children's Village carries out extensive evaluation procedures closely linked to its overall research effort. Behavior assessment, studies of the effectiveness of peer tutoring and special reading programs and evaluations of such special recreation activities as African drumming and dance training, the Annual Children's Circus and a new teen-ager center are all examples of services undergoing systematic evaluation in a recent year. Evaluation, in turn, is closely linked to staff orientation and training at a number of key points. Its essential purpose is to improve *accountability*—to make sure that the agency is accomplishing its stated goals as fully as possible. Elias writes,

Institutions are generally hesitant to look closely at themselves. Self-examination often seems threatening and seems likely to disrupt the familiar, secure routines. In recent years new programs at Children's Village have been required to be

---

[32] Howard L. Millman: "Research at C.V." *Children's Village Bulletin,* June, 1976, p. 7.

evaluated to see if they meet their goals. This is an advance many children's facilities have not yet undertaken. But Children's Village must still face difficult questions: how effective is its structure in helping children and their families cope with their lives in the community; what within-institution programs lead to strengths that children maintain; which children are more likely to be helped; and how can effectiveness in preparing boys for a less structured environment be improved?.... The idea of evaluating the community effectiveness of Children's Village treatment programs so closely fits in with the concepts of continued care and feedback from the community that such evaluation seems attainable in the very near future.[33]

Within its own set of goals, each institution or agency that provides special care or rehabilitative service—including therapeutic recreation or activity therapy—must make use of research and evaluation to strengthen its own effectiveness.

RESEARCH AND EVALUATION: CONCLUDING STATEMENT

It should be made clear that research does not automatically provide the solution to all problems of professional development or program enrichment in therapeutic recreation service. Although rehabilitation authorities may be convinced of the value of activity therapies in general and although medical practitioners may strongly support therapeutic recreation programs, it may not be possible to derive statistical evidence as to its value in many cases.

It should be clearly understood, however, that this limitation is not peculiar to the field of therapeutic recreation. The author has pointed out elsewhere how major educational programs or experiments in social innovation have yielded disappointing results when carefully evaluated. The value of Head Start, for example, a major federally sponsored educational program designed to counteract the effects of poverty and cultural deprivation for pre-school children, which was highly praised in its early stages, has been shown to be only temporary and to have no lasting benefits.[34] Intensive group work therapy programs for teen-agers or casework services for families with multiple problems have shown no measurable benefits. Indeed, in the latter case, it was indicated that the more often a problem family saw its caseworker, the less progress was shown.[35] A heavily financed program of performance contracting by educational firms that were funded to provide specially designed educational programs in both rural areas and large cities has been shown to be no more effective than traditional classroom instruction.[36]

Therefore, it should not be expected that research will automatically yield supportive evidence that will assist therapeutic recreation personnel in developing their programs and that will consistently support their professional status and importance.

It is essential nonetheless that every effort be made to explore, as systematically as possible, both the theoretical and practical questions under-

---

[33] Maurice J. Elias: "From Children's Village to Community—How Effective is Treatment?" *Children's Village Bulletin*, January, 1977, p. 18.

[34] Robert B. Semple, Jr.: "Head Start Value Found Temporary." *New York Times*, October 23, 1966, p. 1.

[35] "Casework Found No Poverty Cure." *New York Times*, September 19, 1968, p. 55.

[36] "Result of a Test: F." *Time*, February 4, 1972, p. 42.

lying this field. One major conference on physical education and recreation for disabled children identified the need to carry out meaningful research within the following areas:

1. The contributions, values and effects of participation.
2. The design of programs and their underlying rationale.
3. The extent and nature of current services on a geographical or demographic basis or in terms of the needs of specific disabled groups in the population.
4. The development of effective instruments and tools to assess performance or measure program outcomes.
5. The development and application of meaningful program standards for evaluation.

Finally, it is essential that new and more effective means of storing, disseminating and using research findings be developed. Often there is a marked gulf between college or university researchers and the practitioner in the field who might be able to use their findings.

Linford and Kennedy comment that the researcher is often wrongly accused of failing to communicate his results to workers in the field. In their view, this criticism is unjustified:

> . . . the role of the researcher is to solve problems. The transmission of informa-tion to others is the role of the teacher and communications expert—not the researcher. While they are perhaps not too well qualified as researchers them-selves, any college lecturer should be at least able to read research literature and interpret it for students. The communication and dissemination problem is a major one. . . .[37]

The author agrees and is convinced that college and university educators who write textbooks in the field of professional recreation service have a further responsibility for acting as intermediaries between the technical or highly specialized professional journals that report research and the faculty member in programs of professional preparation. In this and other texts, the author has documented any major content area with significant research and literature references; such references are extremely helpful in pointing the way to college teachers as they carry out their own continued reading to maintain profes-sional literature and in lecture preparation. They also encourage students to do additional bibliographic research in appropriate sources.

The problem of dissemination has been materially aided by national "data banks" or other comprehensive collections of research reports, which can systematically organize findings and make them available to the field. A begin-ning step was made in this direction by the establishment of TRIC (Therapeutic Recreation Information Center), a literature and document storage and retrieval center for the field of therapeutic recreation service. Founded at Teachers College, Columbia University, in 1970, this valuable project was later moved to the University of Waterloo, in Ontario, Canada.

Coordinated by Fred W. Martin, TRIC acquired published and unpub-lished articles, books, conference proceedings and reports. It abstracted and indexed them for storage in a computer-based information retrieval system. In-formation requests were accepted from educators, professionals, students and others seeking information concerning therapeutic recreation service. TRIC

---

[37] Anthony G. Linford and Dan W. Kennedy: "Research—the State of the Art in Therapeutic Recreation." *Therapeutic Recreation Journal*, 4th Quarter, 1971, p. 169.

included references gained from such primary sources as *Parks and Recreation; Journal of Health, Physical Education and Recreation; Research Quarterly; Journal of Leisure Research; Recreation for the Ill and Handicapped;* and *Therapeutic Recreation Journal.* Secondary sources, such as *Psychological Abstracts; Sociological Abstracts; Mental Retardation Abstracts; Hospital Abstracts; Education Index; Rehabilitation Literature;* and *Educational Resources Information Center* (ERIC), were also used, along with other information systems, particularly the *Medical Literature Analysis and Retrieval System (MED-LARS),* in gathering data and developing abstracts key-punched within computer formats for convenient and economical storage.

Martin has written,

> *TRIC can be used to assist the preparation of course bibliographies by educators offering these courses, students engaged in term projects, as well as for surveys of the literature for master's theses and doctoral dissertations. Researchers both within our field and in other fields and disciplines can save valuable research time and avoid wasteful duplication of effort. Research gaps may become more clearly defined with systematically stored and retrievable data available. Reducing the effort of the practitioner in obtaining research results and other information may increase the utilization of such material in programs removed from the academic sphere and ultimately improve on the delivery of service to clients.*[38]

With Martin's return to the United States, where he is presently on the faculty of the University of California at Sacramento, the TRIC service has been curtailed, although efforts are being made to restore it to full function. A somewhat similar service has also been provided over the last several years by the Information and Research Utilization Center (IRUC) of the AAHPER Unit on Programs for the Handicapped (see p. 74). IRUC has assisted faculty members and practitioners with reprint services of hard to find materials, updated resource lists, a mailing list and other customized services such as special searches of titles, library and other sources. It has not thus far, however, developed TRIC's computerized retrieval capability.

Programs of this type, which encourage the dissemination of research findings, make a strong contribution to the scientific development of the field of therapeutic recreation service and to the quality of college programs of professional preparation in it. In the years ahead, improved and expanded efforts in both evaluation and research will support and strengthen this field. They deserve major priority by all therapeutic agencies and institutions in terms of university curriculum development, government funding and allocation of staff energies and time.

SUGGESTED TOPICS FOR CLASS DISCUSSION, EXAMINATIONS OR STUDENT PAPERS

1. Define and compare the two related processes of evaluation and research and show how they are vital to upgrading professional practice in therapeutic recreation service.

---

[38] Fred W. Martin: "TRIC—A Computer-Based Information Storage and Retrieval Center for the Field of Therapeutic Recreation Service." *Therapeutic Recreation Journal,* 4th Quarter, 1971, p. 173.

2. Increasing emphasis is being given today to patient evaluation, needs assessment, and so forth in therapeutic recreation programming. Describe some of the methods used in this process.

3. Develop a statement of a specific problem area in therapeutic recreation service. Then prepare a preliminary research proposal intended to investigate this problem, including each of the elements mentioned in the text.

4. Why is the interdisciplinary cooperation of government, institutions of higher education and agencies serving the disabled necessary to promote effective research in this field? Give an example of how such cooperation might be developed.

Appendix A
Personnel Standards
Developed by the
National Therapeutic
Recreation Society

The National Therapeutic Recreation Society, a branch of the National Recreation and Park Association, has adopted the following set of minimum standards for six levels of practice in therapeutic recreation service. Based on these standards, individuals may apply for voluntary registration with the society as a means of establishing their professional qualifications at a given job classification level. Increasing numbers of public and voluntary therapeutic agencies are now requiring NTRS registration at an appropriate level as a requirement for employment. By 1977, over 2000 individuals were registered under this plan.

1. **Therapeutic Recreation Assistant**

   a. Two years of successful, full-time, paid experience in the therapeutic recreation field or
   b. Two hundred clock hours in-service training in the therapeutic recreation field or
   c. A combination of "a" and "b" may be substituted.

2. **Therapeutic Recreation Technician I**

   a. (Provisional-Nonrenewable). Certificate of enrollment in National Therapeutic Recreation Society–approved Training-Program for Therapeutic Recreation Technician I or;
   b. (Provisional-Nonrenewable). Two years of successful full-time experience in the therapeutic recreation field with both physically and mentally handicapped individuals plus completion of a minimum of 80 hours of NTRS-approved training or;
   c. (Registered). Successful completion of NTRS-approved Training Program for Therapeutic Recreation Technician I or;
   d. (Registered). Four years of successful full-time paid experience in the therapeutic recreation field with both physically and mentally handicapped individuals plus completion of a minimum of 140 hours of NTRS-approved training.

3. **Therapeutic Recreation Technician II**

   a. Associate of Arts degree from an accredited college or university or satisfactory completion of two years of college with major work in recreation or other field related to therapeutic recreation (physical education, music, drama, dance, psychology and sociology) or;

b. Diploma, certificate, or other proof of satisfactory completion of two academic years of study in an art or technical field related to therapeutic recreation from an approved or recognized school.

4. Therapeutic Recreation Leader

a. (Provisional). Baccalaureate degree from an accredited college or university with a major in recreation or field related to therapeutic recreation or;

b. (Registered). Baccalaureate degree from an accredited college or university with an option or emphasis in therapeutic recreation or;

c. (Registered). Baccalaureate degree from an accredited college or university with a major in recreation and one year of experience in the therapeutic recreation field or;

d. (Registered). Baccalaureate degree from an accredited college or university with a degree in a field related to therapeutic recreation and two years of experience in the therapeutic recreation field or;

e. (Registered). Master's degree from an accredited college or university with a major in recreation or other field related to therapeutic recreation.

5. Therapeutic Recreation Specialist

a. Master's degree from an accredited college or university with an option or emphasis in therapeutic recreation or;

b. Master's degree from an accredited college or university with a major in recreation and one year of experience in the therapeutic recreation field or;

c. Master's degree from an accredited college or university with a major in a field related to therapeutic recreation and two years of experience in the therapeutic recreation field or;

d. Baccalaureate degree from an accredited college or university with an option or emphasis in therapeutic recreation and three years of experience in the therapeutic recreation field or;

e. Baccalaureate degree from an accredited college or university with a major in recreation and four years of experience in the therapeutic recreation field or;

f. Baccalaureate degree from an accredited college or university with a major in a field related to therapeutic recreation and five years of experience in the therapeutic recreation field.

6. Master Therapeutic Recreation Specialist

a. Master's degree from an accredited college or university with an option or emphasis in therapeutic recreation and two years of experience in the therapeutic recreation field or;

b. Master's degree from an accredited college or university with a major in recreation and three years of experience in the therapeutic recreation field or;

c. Master's degree from an accredited college or university with a major in a field related to therapeutic recreation and four years of experience in the therapeutic recreation field or;

d. Baccalaureate degree from an accredited college or university with an option or emphasis in therapeutic recreation, five years of experience in the therapeutic recreation field and six credits of work at the graduate level or;

e. Baccalaureate degree from an accredited college or university with a major in recreation, six years of experience in the therapeutic recreation field and twelve credits of work at the graduate level or;

f. Baccalaureate degree from an accredited college or university with a major in a field related to therapeutic recreation, seven years of experience in the therapeutic recreation field and eighteen credits or work at the graduate level.

Appendix B
Competency-Based Curriculum Development in Therapeutic Recreation

The most recent trend in therapeutic recreation curriculum development has been based on the development of essential competencies or skills related to professional practice that serve as objectives for undergraduate and graduate programs of professional preparation. On the undergraduate level, for example, the National Recreation and Park Council on Accreditation approved the following competencies in October, 1976, as a section of its Accreditation Standards and Evaluative Criteria.

Competencies Needed for Undergraduate Professional Emphasis in Therapeutic Recreation

8.35 Knowledge of illness and disability with implications for recreation programming, i.e., physically handicapped, mentally ill, emotionally disturbed, developmentally disabled, penally incarcerated, and aging.

8.36 Knowledge of specific service delivery systems related to treatment and rehabilitation, i.e. medical models, leisure education models, etc.

8.37 Knowledge of administrative policies and procedures associated with treatment and rehabilitation settings.

8.38 Knowledge of specific facilitation and counseling techniques predominantly used with special populations.

8.39 Knowledge of specific needs of special populations, and activity modification techniques needed to adapt activities to individual needs.

8.40 Understanding of procedures used in formulating individual and group assessment, prescription, and evaluation plans with special populations.

8.41 Understanding of principles used for recording and reporting client information in treatment and rehabilitation settings.

8.42 Understanding of administrative principles related to community recreation programs for special populations.

8.43 Knowledge of facility design and equipment modification related to accessibility and mainstreaming concepts.

8.44 Knowledge of institution to community service continuum designs.

8.45 Knowledge of both normal and abnormal growth and development as traditionally taught in related fields, including: Special Education; Psychology; Sociology; Anatomy/Physiology/Kinesiology.

8.46   Ability to apply the unique practices and principles of therapeutic recreation in authorized practicum experiences commensurate with the approved NTRS guidelines for field placement.

Competency-Based Graduate Curricula in Therapeutic Recreation

On the graduate level, Temple University in Philadelphia has been funded by the Bureau of Education for the Handicapped of the United States Office of Education, to carry out a three-year project to develop and design a competency-based curriculum in therapeutic recreation at the master's degree level. Under the direction of Prof. Jerry Jordan, of Temple's Department of Recreation and Leisure Studies, a progress report was issued in 1977, identifying 30 essential competencies for master's level preparation, grouped under five major headings of therapeutic recreation service responsibilities.

I.   Management

1. Ability to formulate a department philosophy of therapeutic recreation which is consistent with the philosophies of agencies providing a therapeutic recreation program.
2. Ability to develop departmental policies and procedures which incorporate the department's philosophy, and which detail how the department will function in providing its recreation service within the structure of an agency.
3. Ability to hire staff through proper utilization of personnel practices and procedures.
4. Ability to prepare, present, and defend an adequate budget for a therapeutic recreation program.
5. Ability to organize and prepare routine reports required by agencies.
6. Ability to participate appropriately and effectively in administrative meetings.
7. Ability to identify funding sources and to develop, write, and submit proposals for grants.
8. Ability to utilize public relations to enhance therapeutic recreation programs.
9. Ability to facilitate and promote inter-agency coordination.
10. Ability to provide consultation services.

II.   Supervision

11. Ability to effectively supervise staff.
12. Ability to effectively supervise practicum fieldwork students.
13. Ability to effectively utilize and supervise volunteers.

III.   Staff Training

14. Ability to identify individual and group training needs of staff and volunteers.
15. Ability to develop learning objectives from identified training needs.
16. Ability to identify and develop training activities to meet specified learning objectives.
17. Ability to evaluate the cost and effectiveness of training programs.

IV. Programming

18. Ability to develop and implement a basic recreation program that incorporates currently accepted recreation principles and goals.

19. Ability to retrieve, interpret, and apply current research to recreation program development.

20. Ability to plan and conduct program evaluation.

21. Ability to organize, service, and maintain equipment and supplies.

22. Ability to function effectively as a member of a treatment team.

23. Ability to assess a client's functional level as a basis for his/her involvement in therapeutic recreation services.

24. Ability to develop treatment plans for clients.

25. Ability to analyze activities to determine their functional elements and potential therapeutic value for clients.

26. Ability to plan and conduct therapeutic recreation activities to meet individual client needs and treatment objectives.

27. Ability to write clinical reports and records concerning clients and their involvement in therapeutic recreation services.

28. Ability to provide leisure counseling services for clients.

29. Ability to implement and maximize integration of clients into the community.

V. Research

30. Ability to plan, conduct, and report research.

Appendix C
Films

Selected Films on Recreation and Related Services for the Disabled

And So They Move. (16 mm, Black and White, Sound, 19 minutes). Use of creative play in specially designed environment with physically disabled children. Audio-Visual Center, Michigan State University, East Lansing, Michigan 48824.

Basic Skills for Independent Living. (16 mm, Color, Sound, 10 minutes). Depicts a special college program for adults with varied physical and mental disabilities; emphasis on recreational and social activities. Continuing Education Division, State University College, Brockport, New York 14420.

Cast No Shadow. (16 mm, Color, Sound, 27 minutes). Shows wide range of recreation activities for participants with disability at Recreation Center for the Handicapped in San Francisco. Professional Arts, Inc., Box 8484, Universal City, California.

Count Me In. (16 mm, Sound, Color, 17 minutes). Deals with normalization and mainstreaming of the disabled in society, in varied communities and in residential settings; shows leisure programs. Stanfield House, 900 Euclid Street, Santa Monica, California 90403.

Get It Together. (16 mm, Sound, Color, 20 minutes). Story of a young paraplegic who lives as a normal person, finishing college, marrying and beginning a career as a recreational therapist. FMS Productions, 1040 North Las Palmas, Los Angeles, California 90038.

John Baker's Last Race. (16 mm, Sound, Color, 34 minutes). Moving story of a young teacher, a gifted athlete, with a fatal malignancy and his final months. Media Marketing, Brigham Young University, Provo, Utah 84602.

New Concepts in Children's Play Areas. (Filmstrip, 80 frames, Sound, Color, 20 minutes, $33\frac{1}{3}$ rpm record). Shows innovations in playground design to meet children's developmental needs. Associated Film Services, 3419 West Magnolia, Burbank, California 91505.

Paralympics, Israel, 1968. (16 mm, Color, Sound, 14 minutes). Documentary of international Wheelchair Athletic competition. U.S. Wheelchair Sports Fund, 40–24 62nd St., Woodside, N.Y. 11377.

Physical Education for Blind Children. (16 mm, Color, Sound, 20 minutes). Shows visually handicapped school children in varied physical education and recreational sports activities. Charles Buell, 4244 Heather Rd., Long Beach, California 90808.

Recreational Activities for Mentally Retarded Children. (16 mm, Color, Sound, 28 minutes). Comprehensive summer recreational program, including games, crafts, music, swimming, outings and parties, for mentally retarded. National Association for Retarded Children, 420 Lexington Ave., New York, N.Y. 10017.

Recreation and Occupational Therapy. (16 mm, Black and White, Sound, 13 minutes). Adapted activities suited for patients with limited mobility or physical disability. Audio-Visual Media Center, Washington State University, Pullman, Washington 99163.

Recreation for the Handicapped. (16 mm, Color, Sound, 23 minutes). Shows program, over several months, serving varied ages of disabled. Filmed by Stanford University film group. Recreation Center for the Handicapped, Great Highway at Sloat Blvd., San Francisco, California 94132.

Recreation Unlimited. (16 mm, Black and White, Sound, 15 minutes). Swimming, folk dancing, acting and crafts for mentally retarded children. National Association for Retarded Children, 420 Lexington Ave., New York, N.Y. 10017.

The Shape of a Leaf. (16 mm, Black and White, Color, Sound, 26 minutes). Creative approach to arts and crafts instruction with retarded children. Perkins School, Lancaster, Massachusetts 01523.

The Therapeutic Community. (16 mm, Color, Sound, 28 minutes). Milieu therapy approach in hospitalization of geriatric patients. University of Michigan Television Center and Division of Gerontology, Ann Arbor, Michigan.

Therapeutic Camping. (16 mm, Color, Sound, 28 minutes). Shows multidisciplinary approach of workers with emotionally disturbed adolescents in summer camp. Devereux Schools, Santa Barbara, California 93102.

Therapy Through Play. (16 mm, Color, Sound, 17 minutes). Adapted sports for physically disabled children. Human Resources Center, Albertson, N.Y. 11507.

To Paint is to Love Again. (16 mm, Color, Sound, 21 minutes). Art work with retarded children at Exceptional Children's Foundation in Los Angeles. Conrad Films, 6331 Weidlake Drive, Hollywood, California 90028.

To Serve a Purpose. (16 mm, Color, Sound, 15 minutes). Depicts scope of services and populations served in field of therapeutic recreation. Resource Development Specialist, Therapeutic Recreation Curriculum Development Project, Office of Recreation and Park Resources, University of Illinois, Champaign-Urbana, Illinois.

You're It. (16 mm, Color, Sound, 25 minutes). Shows role of recreation in educational program for mentally retarded. MacDonald Training Center, 4424 Tampa Bay Boulevard, Tampa, Florida 33614.

1975 International Special Olympics Games. (16 mm, Color, Sound, 23 minutes). Covers Fourth International Special Olympics held in Michigan, with CBS sports team reporting on mentally retarded athletes competing in eight major sports. Joseph P. Kennedy, Jr. Foundation, 1701 K St., N.W., Suite 205, Washington, D.C. 20006.

Appendix D
List of Organizations*

National Organizations Active in the Recreation Field or with a Special Concern with Disability

Administration on Aging, 330 C Street, S.W., Washington, D.C. 20201

American Art Therapy Association, 6010 Broad Branch Road, N.W., Washington, D.C. 20015

American Association for Leisure and Recreation, 1201 Sixteenth St., N.W., Washington, D.C. 20036

American Association on Mental Deficiency, 5201 Connecticut Ave., N.W., Washington, D.C. 20015

American Association of Retired Persons, 1225 Connecticut Ave., N.W., Washington, D.C. 20036

American Camping Association, Bradford Woods, Martinsville, Indiana 46151

American Cancer Society, 219 E. 42nd St., New York, N.Y. 10017

American Diabetes Association, 18 E. 48th St., New York, N.Y. 10017

American Foundation for the Blind, 15 W. 16th St., New York, N.Y. 10011

American Heart Association, 44 East 23rd St., New York, N.Y. 10010

American National Red Cross, 17th and D Sts., N.W., Washington, D.C. 20000

American Nursing Home Association, 1346 Connecticut Ave., N.W., Washington, D.C. 20006

American Occupational Therapy Association, 251 Park Ave. So., New York, N.Y. 10010

American Physical Therapy Association, 1156 15th St., N.W., Washington, D.C. 20005

American Psychiatric Association, 1700 18th St., N.W., Washington, D.C. 20000

Arthritis and Rheumatism Foundation, 10 Columbus Circle, New York, N.Y. 10019

Athletic Institute, 705 Merchandise Mart, Chicago, Ill., 60654

Bureau of Education for the Handicapped, U.S. Office of Education, 400 Maryland Ave., S.W., Washington, D.C. 20202

Children's Bureau, Office of Child Development, 300 Independence Ave., S.W., Washington, D.C. 20201

Epilepsy Foundation of America, 733 15th St., N.W., Washington, D.C. 20005

International Society for Rehabilitation of the Disabled, 219 E. 44th St., New York, N.Y. 10017

Joseph P. Kennedy, Jr. Foundation, 1411 K St., N.W., Washington, D.C. 20005

Muscular Dystrophy Association of America, 1790 Broadway, New York, N.Y. 10019

National Association for Mental Health, 10 Columbus Circle, New York, N.Y. 10019

National Association for Music Therapy, P.O. Box 610. Lawrence, Kansas 66044

National Association for Retarded Children, 420 Lexington Ave., New York, N.Y. 10017

National Association of the Deaf, 814 Thayer Ave., Silver Spring, Maryland 20910

National Community Education Association, 1017 Avon St., Flint, Michigan 48503

National Council on the Aging, 1828 L Street N.W., Washington, D.C. 20036

---

* This list includes only organizations in the United States. There are a number of comparable organizations in Canada, on the national and provincial levels. The major Canadian organization in the recreation field is the Canadian Parks/Recreation Association, 333 River Rd., Vanier City, Ontario.

National Easter Seal Society for Crippled Children and Adults, 2023 W. Ogden Ave., Chicago, Illinois 60612

National Foundation for Neuromuscular Diseases, 250 W. 57th St., New York, N.Y. 10019

National Institutes of Health, 9000 Rockville Pike, Bethesda, Maryland 20010

National Multiple Sclerosis Society, 257 Park Ave. So., New York, N.Y. 10010

National Paraplegia Foundation, 333 North Michigan Ave., Chicago, Illinois 60601

National Recreation and Park Association (National Therapeutic Recreation Society), 1601 N. Kent St., Arlington, Virginia 22209

National Rehabilitation Association, 1522 K St., N.W., Washington, D.C. 20005

National Tuberculosis and Respiratory Association, 1740 Broadway, New York, N.Y. 10019

President's Committee on Mental Retardation, U.S. Department of Health, Education and Welfare, Washington, D.C. 20201

Rehabilitation Services Administration (Social and Rehabilitation Service), 330 C St., S.W., Washington, D.C. 20201

United Cerebral Palsy Association, 66 E. 34th St., New York, N.Y. 10036

Veterans Administration Central Office, Washington, D.C. 20420

World Leisure and Recreation Association, 345 East 46th St., New York, N.Y. 10017

Other Organizations Serving Specific Groups of Disabled with Sports

American Association for the Deaf, P.O. Box 105, Talladega, Alabama 35160

American Blind Bowling Association, P.O. Box 306, Louisville, Kentucky 40201

American Junior Blind Bowling Association, 4244 Heather Rd., Long Beach, California, 90808

American Wheelchair Bowling Association, Route 2, Box 750, Lutz, Florida 33549

National Amputation Foundation (Golf), 12–45 150th St., Whitestone, N.Y. 11357

National Amputee Skiing Association, 3738 Walnut Ave., Carmichael, California 95608

National Track and Field Committee for the Visually Impaired, 4244 Heather Rd., Long Beach, California 90808

National Wheelchair Basketball Association, Rehabilitation-Education Center, Oak St. and Stadium Dr., University of Illinois, Champaign-Urbana, Illinois 61820

National Wheelchair Athletic Association, 40–24 62nd St., Woodside, N.Y. 11377

Special Olympics, Inc., 1701 K St. N.W., Washington, D.C. 20006

Appendix E
Equipment and
Supply Sources*

This list identifies a number of major manufacturers and distributors of recreation equipment, materials and supplies that may be used directly in community programs, hospitals, special schools and other institutions serving the disabled, or may be adapted to such use.

Boin Arts and Crafts Company, 87 Morris St., Morristown, New Jersey 07960. Wide range of kits, tools and supplies for varied craft activities useful for all ages.

CEDCO Distributors Corporation, 128 Main Street, Hempstead, New York 11550. Useful arts and crafts materials, with projects specially designed for exceptional children and adults, nursing homes and similar settings.

Children's Music Center, 5373 West Pico Blvd., Los Angeles, California 90019. Records, books and instruments for use in programs of music and dance therapy.

Economy Handcrafts, 50–21 69th St., Woodside, New York 11377. Extensive supplies for arts and crafts activities useful for all ages.

Flaghouse, Inc., 18 West 18th St., New York, N.Y. 10010. Distributes full range of athletic, recreational and camping supplies and equipment for schools, colleges, public recreation, institutions and similar agencies.

Game Time, Inc., 6874 Washington Ave., South Eden Prairie, Minnesota 55343. One of the largest manufacturers of playground equipment, such as swings, slides, jungle gyms, and other creative equipment for children's play.

Hoctor Products for Education, Waldwick, New Jersey 07463. Distributes music, instruction, records and related products for varied forms of dance, gymnastics and children's rhythms.

Lansford Publishing Company, P.O. Box 8711, San Jose, California 95155. Manufactures and distributes management aids and audio-visual materials useful in staff development, group dynamics programs and related activities.

Mexico Forge, P.O. Box 565, Reedsville, Pennsylvania 17084. Manufactures heavy-duty recreational equipment, play systems, benches, lockers and related products.

Miracle Recreation Equipment Company, Grinnell, Iowa 50112. Manufactures standard playground equipment, along with creative or theme structures or products, accessories, wood "villages," pools and so on; also provides design service.

J. A. Preston Corporation, 71 Fifth Avenue, New York, N.Y. 10003. Manufactures equipment, games, tests, kits and so forth designed to promote perceptual-motor development for exceptional children and youth.

Theraplay Products (Division of PCA Industries), 2298 Grissom Drive, St. Louis, Missouri 63141. Manufactures rehabilitative play equipment for special populations, such as blind, deaf, mentally retarded and so on. Includes safety-designed playground equipment (slides, beams, bridges, bouncers, etc.), manipulative games and equipment geared for use with wheelchairs.

---

* Most of these companies will send catalogues on request. They and hundreds of other manufacturers and distributors advertise in professional recreation journals and exhibit their products at recreation and park conferences.

U.S. Games, Inc., 1009 Aurora Road, Melbourne, Florida 32935. Designs and manufactures standard recreational sports equipment, along with new and improvised game materials for active groups.

World Wide Games, Box 450, Delaware, Ohio 43015. Manufactures unique group of game materials for folk games from many nations, useful with participants of all ages and abilities.

Bibliography

I.   General References on Recreation, Rehabilitation and Therapeutic Recreation

W. Scott Allan: *Rehabilitation: A Community Challenge.* New York, John Wiley. 1958.

American Alliance for Health, Physical Education and Recreation: *Careers in Activity and Therapy Fields.* Washington, D.C., 1976.

Elliott M. Avedon: *Therapeutic Recreation Service: An Applied Behavioral Science Approach.* Englewood Cliffs, New Jersey, Prentice-Hall, 1974.

Doris L. Berryman, Annette Logan and Dorothy Lander: *Enhancement of Recreation Service to Disabled Children* and *Recommended Standards with Evaluative Criteria for Recreation Services in Residential Institutions.* New York, New York University School of Education and U.S. Children's Bureau, 1971.

George D. Butler: *Introduction to Community Recreation.* New York, McGraw-Hill, 1976.

Reynold Carlson, Theodore Deppe and Janet MacLean: *Recreation in American Life.* Belmont, California, Wadsworth, 1972.

Frederick Chapman: *Recreation Activities for the Handicapped.* New York, Ronald, 1960.

Effie Fairchild and Larry Neal: *Common-Unity in the Community: A Forward-Looking Program of Recreation and Leisure Services for the Handicapped.* Eugene, Oregon, Center for Leisure Studies, 1975.

Virginia Frye and Martha Peters: *Therapeutic Recreation: Its Theory, Philosophy and Practices.* Harrisburg, Pennsylvania, Stackpole, 1972.

Geoffrey Godbey and Stanley Parker: *Leisure Studies and Services: An Overview.* Philadelphia, W. B. Saunders, 1976.

Paul Haun: *Recreation: A Medical Viewpoint* (Elliott M. Avedon, ed.). New York, Teachers College, Columbia, Bureau of Publications, 1965.

Valerie Hunt: *Recreation for the Handicapped.* Englewood Cliffs, New Jersey, Prentice-Hall, 1960.

Jerry D. Kelley (ed.): *Expanding Horizons in Therapeutic Recreation II.* Urbana-Champaign, Illinois, University of Illinois, Office of Recreation and Park Resources, 1974.

Richard Kraus: *Recreation and Leisure in Modern Society.* Santa Monica, California, Goodyear, 1978; *Recreation Today: Program Planning and Leadership.* Santa Monica, Goodyear, 1977; and (with Barbara Bates): *Recreation Leadership and Supervision.* Philadelphia, W. B. Saunders, 1975.

Janet MacLean (ed.): *Therapeutic Recreation in the Community,* Conference Report, Bloomington, Indiana, University of Indiana, 1962.

Susanna Millar: *The Psychology of Play.* Baltimore, Penguin, 1968.

Norman Miller and Duane Robinson: *The Leisure Age.* Belmont, California, Wadsworth, 1963.

James F. Murphy: *Recreation and Leisure Service: A Humanistic Perspective.* Dubuque, Iowa, Wm. C. Brown, 1975.

John A. Nesbitt, Paul D. Brown and James F. Murphy (eds.): *Recreation and Leisure Service for the Disadvantaged.* Philadelphia, Lea and Febiger, 1970.

Gerald S. O'Morrow: *Administration of Activity Therapy.* Springfield, Illinois, Charles C Thomas, 1966; and *Therapeutic Recreation: A Helping Profession.* Reston, Virginia, Reston, 1976.

Robert P. Overs, Elizabeth O'Connor and Barbara DeMarco: *Avocational Activities for the Handicapped: A Handbook for Avocational Counseling.* Springfield, Illinois, Charles C Thomas, 1974.

Janet Pomeroy: *Recreation for the Physically Handicapped.* New York, Macmillan, 1964.

Josephine L. Rathbone and Carol Lucas: *Recreation in Total Rehabilitation.* Springfield, Illinois, Charles C Thomas, 1970.

Frank M. Robinson, Jr.: *Therapeutic Recreation: Ideas and Experiences.* Springfield, Illinois, Charles C Thomas, 1974.

Howard Rusk: *Basic Concepts of Hospital Recreation.* Washington, D.C., American Recreation Society, 1953.

H. Douglas Sessoms, Harold D. Meyer and Charles K. Brightbill: *Leisure Services: The Organized Recreation and Park System.* Englewood Cliffs, New Jersey, Prentice-Hall, 1975.

Thomas M. Shea: *Camping for Special Children.* St. Louis, C. V. Mosby, 1977.

Jay S. Shivers and Hollis Fait: *Therapeutic and Adapted Recreational Services.* Philadelphia, Lea and Febiger, 1975.

Thomas Stein and H. Douglas Sessoms: *Recreation and Special Populations.* Boston, Holbrook, 1977.

Jody Witt, Marilyn Campbell and Peter Witt: *A Manual of Therapeutic Group Activities for Leisure Education.* Ottawa, Canada, Leisurability, 1975.

II. Recreation and the Mentally Retarded or Learning Disabled

Issam B. Amary: *Creative Recreation for the Mentally Retarded.* Springfield, Illinois, Charles C Thomas, 1975.

American Association for Health, Physical Education and Recreation (AAHPER): *Physical Activities for the Mentally Retarded: Ideas for Instruction* and *Guidelines for Programming in Recreation and Physical Education for the Mentally Retarded.* Washington, D.C., 1968.

AAHPER and Sex Information and Education Council of the United States: *A Resource Guide in Sex Education for the Mentally Retarded.* Washington, D.C., 1971.

Elliott M. Avedon: *Recreation and Mental Retardation.* Washington, D.C., Public Health Service, Division of Mental Retardation, U.S. Dept. of H.E.W., 1966.

Elliott M. Avedon and Frances B. Arje: *Socio-Recreative Planning for the Retarded: A Handbook for Sponsoring Groups.* New York, Teachers College, Columbia, Bureau of Publications, 1964.

Norman R. Bernstein (ed.): *Diminished People, Problems and Care of the Mentally Retarded.* Boston, Little, Brown, 1970.

La Donna Bogardus: *Camping with Retarded Persons.* Nashville, Tennessee, Cokesbury, 1970.

Bernice Wells Carlson and David R. Ginglend: *Recreation for Retarded Teenagers and Young Adults.* Nashville, Tennessee, Abingdon, 1968.

Philip Chinn, Clifford J. Drew and Don R. Logan: *Mental Retardation, A Life Cycle Approach.* St. Louis, C. V. Mosby, 1975.

Herbert J. Grossman (ed.): *Manual on Terminology and Classification in Mental Retardation.* Washington, D.C., American Association on Mental Deficiency, 1973.

James H. Humphrey and Dorothy D. Sullivan: *Teaching Slow Learners Through Active Games.* Springfield, Illinois, Charles C Thomas, 1970.

Helen Jo Mitchell, et al.: *The Young Retarded Child at Play: A Guide for Pre-School Play Centers.* Washington, D.C., Department of Recreation, 1969.

William K. Murphy and R. C. Scheerenberger: *Establishing Day Centers for the Mentally Retarded.* Springfield, Illinois, State Division of Mental Retardation Services, 1967.

Larry L. Neal: *Recreation's Role in the Rehabilitation of the Mentally Retarded.* Eugene, Oregon, University of Oregon, 1970.

President's Committee on Mental Retardation: *MR 72: Islands of Excellence.* Washington, D.C., U.S. Government Printing Office, 1973.

G. Lawrence Rarick, A. Alan Dobbins and Geoffrey D. Broadhead: *The Motor Domain and Its Correlates in Educationally Handicapped Children.* Englewood Cliffs, New Jersey, Prentice-Hall, 1976.

III. Recreation and the Aging

Nancy N. Anderson: *Senior Centers: Information from a National Survey.* Minneapolis, American Rehabilitation Foundation, 1969.

Edward Bortz: *Creative Aging.* New York, Macmillan, 1963.

Gertrude Cross: *Program Ideas for Senior Citizens* and *Senior Citizens Travel Manual.* Flint, Michigan, Recreation and Park Board, 1970.

Elaine Cumming and William E. Henry: *Growing Old: The Process of Disengagement.* New York, Basic Books, 1961.

Joan M. Cutter, Edna B. Russell and Elizabeth A. Stetler: *An Activity Center for Senior Citizens.* Washington, D.C., Administration on Aging, U.S. Dept. of H.E.W., 1961.

Wilma Donahue, et al. (eds.): *Free Time—Challenge to Later Maturity.* Ann Arbor, Michigan, University of Michigan Press, 1958.

Paula Gross Gray: *Dramatics for the Elderly: A Guide for Residential Care Settings and Senior Centers.* New York, Teachers College, Columbia, Press, 1974.

Douglas Kimmell: *Adulthood and Aging.* New York, John Wiley, 1974.

Robert Kleemeier: *Aging and Leisure.* New York, Oxford University Press, 1961.

Susan H. Kubie and Gertrude Landau: *Group Work with the Aged.* New York, International Universities Press, 1969.

Carol Lucas: *Recreational Activity Development for the Aging in Hospitals and Nursing Homes.* Springfield, Illinois, Charles C Thomas, 1974.

Toni Merrill: *Activities for the Aged and Infirm, A Handbook for the Untrained Worker.* Springfield, Illinois, Charles C Thomas, 1967.

Dorothy G. Mullen: *Recreation in Nursing Homes.* Arlington, Virginia, National Recreation and Park Association Management Aid, No. 88, 1971.

President's Task Force on Aging: *Toward a Brighter Future for the Elderly.* Washington, D.C., Report of the Task Force, 1970.

Public Health Service: *Activity Supervisor's Guide: A Handbook for Activities Supervisors in Long-Term Nursing Care Facilities.* Washington, D.C., U.S. Dept. of H.E.W., 1969.

Suzanne Reichard, Florine Livson and Paul Peterson: *Aging and Personality.* New York, John Wiley, 1962.

Retirement Roles and Activities. Washington, D.C., Report of White House Conference on Aging, 1971.

Shura Saul: *Aging: An Album of People Growing Old.* New York, John Wiley, 1974.

Bernard Stotsky: *The Nursing Home and the Aged Psychiatric Patient.* New York, Appleton-Century-Crofts, 1970.

Claire Townsend: *Old Age: The Last Segregation.* New York, Grossman, 1971.

Arthur Williams: *Recreation in the Senior Years.* Washington, D.C.: National Recreation Association, 1962.

IV.   Recreation and Physical Disability

Ronald C. Adams, Alfred N. Daniel and Lee Rullman: *Games, Sports and Exercises for the Physically Handicapped.* Philadelphia, Lea and Febiger, 1975.

Daniel D. Arnheim, David Auxter and Walter C. Crowe: *Principles and Methods of Adapted Physical Education.* St. Louis, C. V. Mosby, 1973.

Boy Scouts of America: *Scouting for the Blind, Scouting for the Deaf* and *Scouting for the Physically Handicapped.* North Brunswick, New Jersey, Boy Scouts of America, Health and Safety Service.

Brian Bolton (ed.): *Psychology of Deafness for Rehabilitation Counselors.* Baltimore, University Park Press, 1976.

Charles E. Buell: *Physical Education and Recreation for the Visually Handicapped.* Washington, D.C., A.A.H.P.E.R., 1973.

Bureau of Outdoor Recreation: *Outdoor Recreation Planning for the Handicapped.* Washington, D.C.: Bureau of Outdoor Recreation, Dept. of the Interior, 1967.

Maurice Case: *Recreation for Blind Adults.* Springfield, Illinois, Charles C Thomas, 1966.

Dolores Geddes: *Physical Activities for Individuals with Handicapping Conditions.* St. Louis, C. V. Mosby, 1974.

Sheila Hewett: *The Family and the Handicapped Child: A Study of Cerebral Palsied Children in Their Homes.* Chicago, Aldine, 1970.

Frank H. Krusen, Frederick J. Kottke and Paul M. Ellwood (eds.): *Handbook of Physical Medicine and Rehabilitation.* Philadelphia, W. B. Saunders, 1971.

Louis A. Michaux: *The Physically Handicapped and the Community.* Springfield, Illinois, Charles C Thomas, 1970.

Muscular Dystrophy — The Facts. New York, Muscular Dystrophy Association of America, 1970.

Multiple Sclerosis: The Crippler of Young Adults. New York, Multiple Sclerosis Society, 1968.

National Commission on Architectural Barriers to Rehabilitation of the Handicapped: *Design for All Americans.* Washington, D.C., Rehabilitation Services Administration, U.S. Dept. of H.E.W., 1967.

Sylvia B. O'Brien: *More Than Fun: A Handbook of Recreational Programming for Children and Adults with Cerebral Palsy.* New York, United Cerebral Palsy Association, n.d.

Janet Pomeroy: *Recreation for the Physically Handicapped.* New York, Macmillan, 1964.

Frank L. Porter (ed.): *The Diabetic at Work and Play.* Springfield, Illinois, Charles C Thomas, 1971.

Howard Rusk: *Rehabilitation Medicine: A Textbook on Rehabilitation Medicine.* St. Louis, C. V. Mosby, 1971.

Claudine Sherrill: *Adapted Physical Education and Recreation: A Multidisciplinary Approach.* Dubuque, Iowa, Wm. C. Brown, 1976.

Maryhelen Vannier: *Physical Activities for the Handicapped.* Englewood Cliffs, New Jersey, Prentice-Hall, 1977.

Hilder K. Waldron: *Rehabilitation of the Physically Handicapped Adolescent.* New York, John Day, 1972.

Ruth Hook Wheeler and Agnes M. Hooley: *Physical Education for the Handicapped.* Philadelphia, Lea and Febiger, 1976.

Beatrice Wright: *Physical Disability: A Psychological Approach.* New York, Harper and Row, 1960.

V. Mental Illness and Social Deviance

Ruth Cavan (ed.): *Readings in Juvenile Delinquency.* Philadelphia, Lippincott, 1969.

V. Cumming and E. Cumming: *Ego and Milieu.* New York, Atherton, 1969.

Marshall Edelson: *Sociotherapy and Psychotherapy.* Chicago, University of Chicago Press, 1970.

Joan M. Erikson: *Activity, Recovery, Growth: The Communal Role of Planned Activities.* New York, W. W. Norton, 1976.

Don C. Gibbons: *Delinquent Behavior.* Englewood Cliffs, New Jersey, Prentice-Hall, 1970.

Haim G. Ginot: *Group Psychotherapy with Children: The Theory and Practice of Play-Therapy.* New York, McGraw-Hill, 1961.

William Glasser: *Reality Therapy: A New Approach to Psychiatry.* New York, Harper and Row, 1965.

Julius Hoenig and Marian W. Hamilton: *The Desegregation of the Mentally Ill.* London, Routledge and Paul, 1969.

Malcolm W. Klein: *Street Gangs and Street Workers.* Englewood Cliffs, New Jersey, Prentice-Hall, 1971.

Thomas P. Lowry (ed.): *Camping Therapy: Its Uses in Psychiatry and Rehabilitation.* Springfield, Illinois, Charles C Thomas, 1974.

Jerrold S. Maxmen, Gary J. Tucker and Michael LeBow: *Rational Hospital Psychiatry: The Reactive Environment.* New York, Brunner/Mazel, 1974.

Jack Meislin (ed.): *Rehabilitation Medicine and Psychiatry.* Springfield, Illinois, Charles C Thomas, 1976.

Theodore Millon: *Modern Psychopathology.* Philadelphia, W. B. Saunders, 1969.

B. E. Phillips (ed.): *Recreation for the Mentally Ill.* Washington, D.C., A.A.H.P.E.R. Conference Report, 1958.

Sophia Robison: *Juvenile Delinquency: Its Nature and Control.* New York, Holt, Rinehart and Winston, 1960.

Theodore Rothman (ed.): *Changing Patterns in Psychiatric Care.* New York, Crown, 1970.

Alan B. Tulipan and Saul Feldman (eds.): *Psychiatric Clinics in Transition.* New York, Brunner/Mazel, 1969.

Professional Publications with Articles or Research Related to Therapeutic Recreation

Journal of Leisure Research. Published quarterly by the National Recreation and Park Association, in cooperation with the Bureau of Outdoor Recreation. Address: 1601 North Kent St., Arlington, Va. 22209.

Journal of Physical Education and Recreation (formerly *Journal of Health, Physical Education and Recreation*). Published monthly by the American Alliance for Health, Physical Education and Recreation, except for July and August, with November and December issues combined. Address: 1201 16th St. NW, Washington, D.C. 20036.

Parks and Recreation. Published monthly by the National Recreation and Park Association. Address: 1601 North Kent St., Arlington, Va. 22209.

Recreation Canada. Published monthly by the Canadian Parks/Recreation Association. Address: 333 River Road, Vanier City, Ontario K1L8B9.

Recreation Review. Published Quarterly by Ontario Research Council on Leisure. Address: 400 University Avenue, Toronto, Ontario M7A1H9.

Research Quarterly. Published quarterly by the American Alliance for Health, Physical Education and Recreation. Address: 1201 16th St. NW, Washington, D.C. 20036.

Therapeutic Recreation Journal. Published quarterly by the National Therapeutic Recreation Society. Address: 1601 North Kent St., Arlington, Va. 22209.

Other professional journals related to specific areas of disability are cited throughout the text.

Index